MOVEMENTS FOR HUMAN RIGHTS

How do people work together to advance human rights? Do people form groups to prevent human rights from being enforced? Why? In what ways do circumstances matter to the work of individuals collectively working to shape human rights practices?

Human society is made of individuals within contexts—tectonic plates not of the earth's crust but of groups and individuals who scrape and shift as we bump along, competing for scarce resources and getting along. These movements, large and small, are the products of actions individuals take in communities, within families and legal structures. These individuals are able to live longer, yet continue to remain vulnerable to dangers arising from the environment, substances, struggles for power, and a failure to understand that in most ways we are the same as our neighbors.

Yet it is because we live together in layers of diverse communities that we want our ability to speak to be unhindered by others, use spirituality to help us understand ourselves and others, possess a space and objects that are ours alone, and join with groups that share our values and interests, including circumstances where we do not know who our fellow neighbor is. For this reason sociologists have identified the importance of movements and change in human societies. When we collaborate in groups, individuals can change the contours of their daily lives.

Within this book you will find the building blocks for human rights in our communities. To understand why sometimes we enjoy human rights and other times we experience vulnerability and risk, sociologists seek to understand the individual within her context. Bringing together prominent sociologists to grapple with these questions, *Movements for Human Rights: Locally and Globally*, offers insights into the ways that people move for (and against) human rights.

David L. Brunsma is a Professor of Sociology at Virginia Tech and co-editor of *The Leading Rogue State*.

Keri E. Iyall Smith is Associate Professor of Sociology at Suffolk University and author of *The State and Indigenous Movements*.

Brian K. Gran is Associate Professor of Sociology and Law at Case Western Reserve University whose research focuses on actors and institutions that foster and obstruct human rights advancement. His publications have appeared in *The International Journal of Children's Rights* and in *Child Welfare*.

Movements for Human Rights

Locally and Globally

Edited by

David L. Brunsma
Keri E. Iyall Smith
Brian K. Gran

LONDON AND NEW YORK

First published 2017
by Routledge
711 Third Avenue, New York, NY 10017

and by Routledge
2 Park Square, Milton Park, Abingdon, Oxon, OX14 4RN

Routledge is an imprint of the Taylor & Francis Group, an informa business

© 2017 Taylor & Francis

The right of the editors to be identified as the author of the editorial material, and of the authors for their individual chapters, has been asserted in accordance with sections 77 and 78 of the Copyright, Designs and Patents Act 1988.

All rights reserved. No part of this book may be reprinted or reproduced or utilised in any form or by any electronic, mechanical, or other means, now known or hereafter invented, including photocopying and recording, or in any information storage or retrieval system, without permission in writing from the publishers.

Trademark notice: Product or corporate names may be trademarks or registered trademarks, and are used only for identification and explanation without intent to infringe.

Library of Congress Cataloging in Publication Data
Names: Brunsma, David L., editor.
Title: Movements for human rights : locally and globally / edited by David L. Brunsma, Keri E. Iyall Smith, Brian K. Gran.
Description: 1 Edition. | New York : Routledge, 2016.
Identifiers: LCCN 2016011923| ISBN 9781138698215 (harback) | ISBN 9781138698222 (pbk.) | ISBN 9781315511856 (ebook)
Subjects: LCSH: Social movements. | Collective behavior. | Human rights.
Classification: LCC HM881 .M6726 2016 | DDC 323—dc23
LC record available at https://lccn.loc.gov/2016011923

ISBN: 978-1-138-69821-5 (hbk)
ISBN: 978-1-138-69822-2 (pbk)
ISBN: 978-1-315-51185-6 (ebk)

Typeset in Goudy Old Style
by Keystroke, Station Road, Codsall, Wolverhampton

Contents

Introduction		1
1	Community and Urban Sociology *Kenneth Neubeck*	5
2	Peace, War, and Social Conflict *Nader Saiedi*	16
3	Environment and Technology *Francis O. Adeola and J. Steven Picou*	26
4	Population *Jenniffer M. Santos-Hernández*	36
5	Collective Behavior and Social Movements *Lyndi Hewitt*	42
6	Alcohol, Drugs, and Tobacco *Jennifer Bronson*	51
7	Rationality and Society *Valeska P. Korff, Mimi Zou, Tom Zwart, and Rafael Wittek*	62
8	International Migration *Tanya Golash-Boza*	72
9	Labor and Labor Movements *Héctor L. Delgado*	81
10	Evolution, Biology, and Society *Rosemary L. Hopcroft*	91

Discussion Questions   100
List of Acronyms   103
Bibliography   105
About the Editors   183

INTRODUCTION

How do people work together to advance human rights? Do people form groups to prevent human rights from being enforced? Why? In what ways do circumstances matter to the work of individuals collectively working to shape human rights practices?

Human society is made of individuals within contexts—tectonic plates not of the earth's crust but of groups and individuals who scrape and shift as they bump along, competing for scarce resources and getting along. These movements, large and small, are the products of actions that individuals take in communities, within families and legal structures. Some individuals are able to live longer, yet continue to remain vulnerable to dangers arising from the environment, substances, struggles for power, and a failure to understand that in most ways we are the same as our neighbors. To understand how humans live together, we must ask certain questions. When we answer those questions, we reveal how to identify and distribute the provisions for human rights.

You may spend a lot of time defining your individuality. Via social media, you may post photographs of yourself, your friends, of the meal you just enjoyed from your favorite restaurant, phrases gathered over your day, or share a link to a site that made you laugh, cry, or think. Technology allows us to accomplish these tasks in new and creative ways. Thanks to a wide array of apps that facilitate sharing, new means of taking photographs for achieving just the right angle, and "smart" telephones. Many of these expressions of individualism are missing a crucial piece of a societal puzzle that sociologists want to examine and understand more fully: context.

To comprehend the individual as well as the context in which that individual lives, sociologists employ a "sociological imagination." Among the most prominent American sociologists, C. Wright Mills reminded all of us that to understand a person's biography requires an understanding of the contexts in which a person lives, and to understand those contexts, we must study a person's biography. A sociological imagination enables any individual to recognize, then study how context changes ways an individual sees his or her choices, behaviors, and experiences. Context shapes choices, behaviors, and experiences available to us, and our perception of why certain choices, behaviors, and experiences might be desirable or undesirable. It all comes back to the individual *within* the context.

Context encompasses so many aspects of our lives—the institutions in which we live, the history that shapes us and that we shape, the culture we make and experience, legal structures that guide and constrain our lives. What else does context encompass? The sociologists in this book identify the importance of family, community, courts, laws offering or prohibiting access to drugs, alcohol, and tobacco, international borders, and much more. For them, human rights is always at the center of the analysis. The contexts to which these authors cast their sociological gaze reveal distinctive ways by which we can better understand human rights. These contexts also require us to stretch to observe and study what individuals need in order to be able to experience human rights.

Identification and awareness of context may especially challenge people who live in the United States. From a young age, many people are taught that *the individual* is the key element of U.S. society. People living in the United States learn about the importance of the freedom of individuals to speak, believe in a God (or not), own private property, and gather together. In a country without universal health insurance or universal health care, even the essential feature of private health insurance—*pooling* of resources, vulnerabilities, and crises—ignores the social aspects of these private undertakings. Yet it is because we live together in layers of diverse communities that we want our ability to speak to be unhindered by others, to use spirituality to help us understand ourselves and others, to possess a space and objects that are ours alone, and to join with groups that share our values and interests, including circumstances where we do not know who our fellow neighbor is.

Individuals

People, of course, are the necessary ingredients to social movements. As you read this book, you are participating in the making of society and the making of yourself. To better understand social movements behind human rights, movements *for* change and movements *against* change, we must recognize people as individuals—individuals who possess unique histories, needs, and goals, individuals who change every day. We must try to understand ourselves and others as people who live in varying contexts that shape our decisions, including decisions to live, work, and cooperate together. Individuals take action as biological entities—sharing the vast majority of our biological selves with the over seven billion other biological entities (human beings) on this planet. But, importantly, individuals collectively move as members of groups.

A sociological perspective of human rights offers both opportunities and challenges. The role of individuals takes on new importance when we examine our actions as individuals doing things together within groups, whether formal or informal, whether structured by group norms or by larger, more abstract, but very powerful institutional norms. What all is entailed? Individuals based in powerful institutions must value human rights; they must agree on perceptions of human rights and when those rights are violated. For the International Criminal

Court to hear a case, many individuals must follow rules. For without the actions of individuals, within the International Criminal Court, families, and communities, we all find our human rights are not fully enjoyed.

Movement and Movements

In examining human rights both locally and globally it is essential to consider *movement*. In our fast-paced, ever-changing world, we must attempt to observe movements of objects, people, and ideas. Globalization may lead to movement of objects across the world. Globalization may lead to people moving from rural communities to cities and across national borders. Globalization of objects and people may lead to ideas rapidly moving across cultures. Movement of ideas may lead to sparks in ideas that prompt social movements: social organizations that seek to change society.

We are both fortunate and tested to live in a time of movement and movements. We hope that our time is one of movement away from war and conflict towards peace and compassion. As we struggle to deal with population growth and longevity arising from the successes of public health and widespread sharing in scientific discoveries, we may be on the threshold of new vulnerabilities due to bacteria that resist antibiotics. Just as we confront one demographic struggle, we may be on the threshold of a new demographic transition. Movement of substances around the world, leaving a wide swath of wealth, power, and devastation.

These flows are local and global, within us and encompassing us. We respond to these mobilities in the creation of movements for the protection of the lives of men and women threatened by police, unsafe drinking water, a lack of housing, disastrous resource extraction, and more.

Examining Movement(s) and Human Rights

Representing an exciting moment for sociology to further energize and develop a sociology of human rights (or, more to the point, sociologies of human rights), *Movements for Human Rights: Locally and Globally* brings together leading and emergent scholars who seriously engage in revolutionary questions, resituate their substantive concerns within new terrains, and begin mapping the intellectual and practical contours of a human rights sociology. Each chapter responds to two primary questions: 1) How does a human rights perspective change the questions that sociologists ask, the theoretical perspectives that sociologists utilize, the methods that sociologists use, and the implications of sociological inquiry? and 2) How can the sociological enterprise (its epistemologies, theories, methodologies, results) inform and push forward human rights theory, discourse, and implementation towards a better world for all humanity?

When we began this project, the American Sociological Association sponsored forty-five sections that support its members' interests in substantive, theoretical, methodological, and applied areas (there are now fifty-two, with Human Rights being added just after we started this project, followed by sections on Altruism, Morality, and Social Solidarity; Body and Embodiment; Global and Transnational Sociology; Inequality, Poverty, and Mobility, the Sociology of Development, and Consumers and Consumption). We approached progressive, critical scholars in the hopes they would contribute work to this project that would accomplish several goals. The first objective was to present a brief summary of the state of the area of sociological inquiry and a reckoning of the central concerns and questions that motivate the area. The second objective was to give readers a summary of the key findings in the area as well as the most prominent methods its practitioners use. The third objective is to provide readers with a critical discussion of what the human rights paradigm can learn from the work in their area as well as to describe how the human rights paradigm might resituate the area and its constituent questions, methods, theories, and findings, and, in turn, reorient readers toward a new set of questions, particularly how human rights redefines the research situation and what new questions can and should be asked. Finally, given this, we encouraged the authors to think broadly and critically about doing the work of human rights sociology, a look forward—new questions, new possibilities for both the area/field and human rights realizations.

We asked these authors to pay particular attention to major sites of change in our society, including communities and urban places, peace and social conflict, environment and technology, population, collective behavior and social movements, alcohol, drugs, and tobacco, rationality and society, international migration, labor and labor movements, and evolution and biology. We asked them to take seriously the ideas of human rights for a new, energetic sociology of movement and change. The results, as you will see, are astounding.

Save the Humans!

Within this book you will find the building blocks for human rights in our communities. To understand why sometimes we enjoy human rights and other times we experience vulnerability and risk, sociologists seek to understand the individual within his or her context.

Chapter One

Community and Urban Sociology

Kenneth Neubeck

The contemporary human rights paradigm is quite a recent development, sparked by the signing of the UN Charter and the founding of the United Nations in 1945. UN members quickly reached consensus on a common standard of human rights achievement in the Universal Declaration of Human Rights (UDHR), adopted by the UN General Assembly in 1948. The UDHR, while not a treaty and thus not carrying the force of international law, prompted drafting and adoption of key international human rights treaties and other important human rights instruments (Forsythe 2000; Donnelly 2003). The UDHR's provisions are today reflected in constitutions, laws, and judicial decisions of many nations (Blau and Moncada 2005; Blau and Frezzo 2011). The declaration has also played a role in inspiring social-justice movements around the world.

The contemporary human rights paradigm, crafted largely in response to the horrors and human suffering resulting from World War II, calls for governments at all levels to take forward-looking actions based on a vision of a better world (Lauren 1998). This vision is founded on the belief that there are rights that all people have simply by virtue of being human and that respecting, protecting, and fulfilling these rights is a precondition for individuals to live their lives in freedom and with dignity. The rights involved are political, civil, social, economic, and cultural. They are not only deemed to be inalienable but also, equally importantly, interconnected with and interdependent on one another (Howard 1995).

While sociology, with its nineteenth-century western European origins, is obviously much older than the human rights paradigm, the discipline's adherents and proponents have long maintained that sociologists should study human society and its features to provide knowledge helpful to guiding social change that will improve people's lives. Some European founders of sociological thinking concluded that positive social change would naturally come about and counseled people to accommodate themselves to the prevailing order so as not to disrupt it and thus inhibit social progress. Others, in contrast, argued that social progress would not occur without people actively struggling against injustice and deprivation, and they counseled people to take collective action to bring about change

(Zeitlin 2000). Regardless of differences in how they have thought society could best get there, influential sociological thinkers have shared a belief that sociological knowledge could be used for human betterment.

Unfortunately, human rights advocacy and sociological scholarship have typically been carried out in separate silos. At worst, this has meant that one really has had little to do with the other; at best, there has been a tension between the two that relates to sociologists' tendency to self-identify professionally as scholars as opposed to rights advocates (Frezzo 2011). However, growing interest around the world and within the United States in implementing human rights at the local level, to be discussed later in this chapter, offers possibilities and opportunities for these two silos to merge. As is shown below, both community and urban sociology (CUS) and the human rights paradigm are concerned with serious problems in living that are adversely affecting people's life experiences and life chances. In addition, many of those who are engaged in CUS share human rights advocates' belief that knowledge gained from listening to the voices of those experiencing these problems provides an important basis for crafting solutions. The mutual benefits that can come from collaboration between CUS scholars and human rights advocates is addressed at the end of this chapter.

Community and Urban Sociology as Human Rights Work

Community and urban sociology in the United States has often reflected a reformist orientation. While CUS covers an enormous range of topics, since the early-twentieth-century city-centered scholarship of the Chicago School (Bulmer 1984; Fine 1995), there has been a tradition of sociologists studying "urban problems." In doing so, many CUS scholars have documented instances or effects of what human rights advocates call human rights violations. The rights being violated are fundamental to the framework of human rights set forth in the 1948 UDHR and incorporated into international law through subsequent UN human rights treaties.

The human right to freedom from discrimination is a key component of the human rights framework, as is the right to an adequate living standard. CUS scholarship has documented ways in which racism and poverty impact and severely limit the life chances of many who inhabit cities (Wilson 2009) and has shown ways in which these phenomena contribute to residential segregation and social isolation, and vice versa (Saito 2009). Segregation is both economic (Dreier, Mollenkopf, and Swanstrom 2005) and racial (Hartman and Squires 2009). CUS scholars have shown the negative outcomes of segregation and social exclusion for city dwellers (Peterson and Krivo 2010; Zukin 2011). Among these outcomes are ways in which segregation places structural limitations on people's opportunities to rise out of poverty and overcome social marginalization (Squires and Kubrin 2006).

The human rights framework also embraces the right to education, which is seen as necessary for the full development of the human personality. Access to equal educational opportunities and to quality education are directly affected by economic and racial segregation. Such segregation adds to disadvantages many children already face due to low family incomes and institutional racism embedded in schooling (Neckerman 2010). CUS researchers have found that not only disparities in income but also unacknowledged disparities in wealth distribution directly shape urban children's educational choices, opportunities, and ultimate achievements (Johnson 2006). Income and wealth also impact such basic matters as an urban family's choice of day-care facilities for its preschooler, which in turn has important impacts on the child's development of opportunity networks and social capital (Small 2009).

The rights to work and to just and favorable remuneration are likewise central to the human rights framework. Urban poverty largely reflects high rates of unemployment and underemployment, and many city dwellers are permanently trapped in the low-wage job market (O'Connor, Tilly, and Bobo 2001; Newman 2008). Lack of jobs and low wages have been found to exacerbate struggles of low-income female-headed families (Edin 2005) and contribute to failure of federal and state welfare reforms to remedy the extreme poverty in which many such families exist (Edin, Lein, and Jencks 1997). Many city residents have no choice but to derive income from within their city's underground economy (Venkatesh 2009). Without an adequate living standard, families are incapable of achieving the human right to housing and increasingly are found by CUS scholars to be among the nation's homeless (Wright 2009). Nonetheless, many poverty-stricken people do manage to survive with surprising resilience (Sanchez-Jankowski 2008). This includes immigrants, who in the United States have increasingly been people of color (Kasinitz et al. 2009), subject to their own forms of racialization and mistreatment (Merenstein 2008).

The human rights framework also includes rights to security of person and to equal treatment and protection under the law. While crime has been declining in US cities over the last decade, CUS scholars have found that street crime and threats to personal security remain highly problematic in many urban areas (Parker 2008). Involvement in criminal activity has become equivalent to a lifestyle and a form of fictive employment for some urban residents (Anderson 2000; St. Jean 2007). Policing in US cities of people who are poor and of color is often harsh, harassing, and sometimes accompanied by police brutality (Holmes 2008). CUS scholars have found that new forms of social control are increasingly being added to traditional policing powers, such as the creation of "exclusion zones" that enable police and courts to banish class and color "undesirables" from certain parts of cities (Beckett and Herbert 2009). Despite ongoing economic and racial dynamics that function to keep different population segments apart in urban settings, CUS scholars have also investigated the ubiquity and importance of common spaces where people can and do safely interact with civility across class and race lines (Anderson 2011).

The human rights to health and to medical care are important parts of the human rights framework. While the health of people who lack adequate incomes (and health insurance) is a chronic concern across the United States, cities are often the object of special environmental health concerns. CUS scholars have addressed environmental racism in urban settings and environmental justice movements that have arisen in response to urban environmental hazards to which people who are poor or of color are disproportionately exposed (Bullard 2000). In the wake of natural and environmental disasters in the United States that have destroyed or disrupted the lives of tens of thousands, such as low-income people of color disproportionately killed or displaced in New Orleans by Hurricane Katrina, CUS has examined the importance of place and racial and class politics of disaster response in urban settings (Bullard and Wright 2009).

The human rights framework also includes the right to political participation in order that government will reflect the will of the people rather than privileged special interests. CUS scholars have studied cities' power structures, which provide the local governing context within which all harmful conditions mentioned above occur (Strom and Mollenkopf 2006). Urban power structures have been analyzed by CUS scholars with attention to the role that race often plays in the conduct and outcome of city politics (Pattillo 2007; Saito 2009). Much research has also been directed at the dominant role that the local "growth machine" of bankers, real estate developers, and other private stakeholders often plays in influencing decision-making by city officials (Domhoff 2005; Logan and Molotch 2007). CUS has examined the impact of local grassroots movements by urban residents opposing private-sector dominance on affecting decision-making by local governments (Gendron and Domhoff 2008).

Finally, there has been progressive realization within CUS that many conditions existing within US cities are greatly affected by uneven forces of globalization, forces that affect people's abilities to realize their human rights "at home." Scholars have been examining exemplars of "the global city" to understand their dynamics and trajectories and the implications of these processes for the quality of life of urban inhabitants (Sassen 2001, 2006a). Urban dwellers may feel fallout from globalization but not really understand why or what can be done about it. There has been, however, growing popular protest in various urban locales against growth machine politics-as-usual and local neoliberal taxation and spending policies that are resulting in disinvestment in city services (e.g., public education, public safety, public parks and recreation, income assistance, job training) on which many city dwellers, especially low-income people, heavily rely (Hackworth 2007). CUS scholars are now drawing attention to local-level movements that call for a "right to the city" and demanding popular democratic control over city space and its uses (Brenner, Marcuse, and Mayer 2011).

The Power of Methods Employed by Community and Urban Sociologists

The cumulative power of the body of CUS scholarship on urban problems reviewed above rests in large part on researchers' use of a wide range of sociological research methods. A diverse tool kit of both qualitative and quantitative methods has been used to (1) clarify origins and overall magnitude of selected urban problems, and (2) assess their everyday, on-the-ground, human consequences. Selection of different methods for these two purposes has been the hallmark of CUS for years and is reflected in what are considered some of CUS's most classic works. The widely acclaimed *American Apartheid* (Massey and Denton 1993) demonstrated how discriminatory US housing policies produced urban racial ghettos, providing a model of the use of structural, sociodemographic, and policy analysis for assessing directions in which cities and their populations were heading. In contrast, the classic ethnography *Tally's Corner* (Liebow 2003) illustrated the power of studying the voices of the oppressed to understand devastating sociopsychological effects of poverty affecting people residing in urban racial ghettos, in this case impoverishment driven by male breadwinners' under- and unemployment. Human rights advocates need data that can be derived from such a wide range of methods, insofar as these data provide documentation of injuries stemming from human rights violations; reveal how these injuries are socially, politically, and economically constructed; and suggest what must change to eliminate violations.

In short, just as human rights advocates are concerned with conditions that undermine an individual's dignity and freedom—for example, discrimination, poverty, and powerlessness—so are many scholars engaged in CUS. Indeed, much CUS scholarship can be viewed as a form of human rights work, even if scholars do not realize this or have not framed their work with human rights in mind. I return to this point toward the end of this chapter after providing an overview of emergent worldwide interest in the implementation of international human rights at the local level. The latter is a topic on which CUS scholars and human rights advocates can have a lot to say to one another and on which they can find grounds for fruitful collaboration.

The "Human Rights City" Concept and Local Implementation of Human Rights

Creating Human Rights Cities

The concept of Human Rights Cities was initiated and pioneered by the People's Decade for Human Rights Education (PDHRE), also called the People's Movement for Human Rights Learning, a nonprofit, international organization founded in New York City in 1989 (PDHRE 2011). The following definition captures the essence of the concept (Marks and Modrowski 2008, 39–40):

> Human Rights Cities are community-based initiatives, locally conceived and directed by local groups around the world, which combine participation, empowerment and social change with international solidarity based on agreed principles of human rights education and sustainable development.

PDHRE (2011) has consulted with human rights advocates around the world on ways that human rights learning can best be carried out locally; how advocates can turn city inhabitants' learning about human rights into action; and how mechanisms can be created across the city to embed human rights norms into every aspect of people's daily lives.

The most important initial step that PDHRE advises cities to take is establishment of a democratically functioning Human Rights City steering committee that represents all sectors of the city, not simply municipal government. Voices of all groups in the city are to be at the table, particularly those that historically have been marginalized or excluded from participating in decision-making.

PDHRE (2011) has helped facilitate the creation worldwide of more than seventeen Human Rights Cities that are now either firmly established or in the process of formation. Examples include Rosario, Argentina; Graz, Austria; Nagpur, India; Korogocho, Kenya; Bucuy Municipality, Philippines; Edmonton, Winnipeg, Canada; and Kaohsiung, Taiwan, China.

But not all efforts at local human rights implementation adhere to the Human Rights Cities concept. Cities around the world and in the United States are taking a variety of approaches to local human rights implementation.

COUNCIL OF EUROPE CONGRESS OF LOCAL AND REGIONAL AUTHORITIES

Europe has a strong human rights regime and an advanced legal system for addressing the full range of universal human rights. The pan-European Council of Europe (2011), composed of forty-seven member countries, works to implement European Convention principles and other European and international human rights instruments across Europe.

In 2010, the Council of Europe's Congress of Local and Regional Authorities adopted a resolution calling for local and regional European authorities to implement measures to further promotion and protection of human rights in day-to-day operations of local and regional governments. These measures include establishing indicators or indices of human rights fulfillment, action plans for human rights implementation, city budgeting that is guided by human rights standards, independent complaint mechanisms, human rights training for elected officials and staff, nondiscrimination in accessibility of public services, and accountability and quality control in cases where services are being privatized (Council of Europe Congress 2010a).

In their deliberations, participants in the congress drew lessons from the examples of a number of European cities that have taken steps in this direction. These include Graz and Salzburg, Austria; Paris, France; Nuremberg, Germany; Utrecht, Netherlands; and Malopolska, Poland.

2011 WORLD HUMAN RIGHTS CITIES FORUM, GWANGJU, SOUTH KOREA

The movement to implement human rights locally in Asian nations has lagged behind Europe. In 2011, more than one hundred mayors, city representatives, UN experts, scholars, and members of civic and human rights NGOs gathered in South Korea for the first World Human Rights Cities Forum, hosted by Gwangju Metropolitan City.

Gwangju, the site of nationally influential protests against Japanese occupation and a leader in local pro-democracy uprisings against a succession of Korean dictators, is now drawing upon this historical legacy of human rights advocacy in framing its rationale for becoming a Human Rights City. City authorities have now created a Human Rights Office, begun to draft a charter that will guide local human rights implementation, initiated ways to promote human rights learning throughout the city, and started crafting an initial action plan linked to a human rights index that will help city officials monitor progress and change (Gwangju Metropolitan City 2011).

The 2011 World Human Rights Cities Forum showcased the Human Rights City work occurring in Gwangju and also provided an opportunity for participants to hear about other cities' experiences. Forum participants also collectively adopted the Gwangju Declaration on Human Rights City. In this declaration, participants committed to "making the vision of a human rights city a reality on the ground by implementing international human rights norms and standards" (Gwangju World Human Rights Cities Forum 2011).

US Exceptionalism and "Bringing Human Rights Home" to the Local Level

A Brief Comment on US Exceptionalism

The United States is often characterized as an "outlier" regarding its failure to apply the human rights framework to its own legal system and to problems within its own borders (Schulz 2009). In the face of the general US failure to "bring human rights home" and to respect, protect, and fulfill them domestically, a US human rights movement has arisen and gathered strength over the last decade or so (see, e.g., US Human Rights Network 2011). This movement, eclectic and growing in membership, is aimed at pressuring government at all levels to address major domestic issues through a human rights lens (Hertel and Libal 2011).

The drive in the United States to implement human rights principles and standards locally has become a part of the larger domestic movement to bring the US government into conformity with international human rights norms (Soohoo, Albisa, and Davis 2008). Human rights advocates are coming to see local implementation not only as valuable for its own sake but as a means of influencing the US government to meet its human rights obligations (Finnegan, Saltsman, and White 2010). In the United States, city-level efforts at local implementation have taken a number of forms (US Human Rights Fund 2010; Columbia Law School Human Rights Institute and IAOHRA 2010; Sok and Neubeck, forthcoming). Some examples follow.

Human Rights City Efforts in the United States

In 2008, the Washington, DC, City Council (2008) passed a resolution declaring its intention to be the first Human Rights City in the United States. Since then, human rights advocates in Chapel Hill and Carrboro, North Carolina; Richmond, California; and a few other US municipalities have taken initial steps toward or expressed interest in becoming Human Rights Cities (see, e.g., Chapel Hill and Carrboro Human Rights Center 2011). All have been influenced by the PDHRE model discussed above.

Human rights resolutions are not ordinances and do not carry the force of law. However, they may serve to legitimize local human rights advocates' work as they carry out human rights education and help to mobilize city inhabitants to press for the creation of legal frameworks and structural mechanisms to institutionalize local human rights implementation.

San Francisco: Providing Human Rights Protections for Women

San Francisco was the first US city to implement human rights by passing a local version of an international human rights treaty (Menon 2010). In 1998, the San Francisco Board of Supervisors approved an ordinance modeled on the Convention on the Elimination of All Forms of Discrimination against Women (CEDAW), a key international human rights treaty that the US government has not ratified (WILD for Human Rights 2006).

The 1998 ordinance supports women's rights as human rights. Implementation of the San Francisco CEDAW ordinance has included conduct of gender audits in city departments, development of departmental action plans to remedy unintentional discrimination, and a system for overseeing and monitoring action-plan outcomes. An evaluation report issued on the tenth anniversary of the San Francisco ordinance found that its implementation had prompted many policy changes, from ending unintentional discrimination against women and girls in delivery of city services to providing family-friendly employment practices that have improved women's city government employment opportunities and supported employees' work-life balance (Liebowitz 2008).

The New York City Human Rights Initiative: Still an Aspiration

Human rights advocates in New York City were inspired by implementation of San Francisco's CEDAW ordinance, launching in 2002 a campaign to adopt a similar law (New York City Human Rights Initiative 2011). This proposed Human Rights in Government Operations Audit Law (GOAL) calls for human rights audits, action plans, and systematic monitoring of all city departments. It is aimed at remedying and preventing discrimination in delivery of city services, budgeting decisions, and staffing. GOAL was introduced as a bill for consideration by sympathetic city council members in 2004 and 2008 and again in 2010. New York City mayor Michael Bloomberg and his council allies have thus far successfully blocked the bill from a council vote, using arguments that GOAL is unnecessary and would be an added expense.

THE EUGENE (OREGON) HUMAN RIGHTS CITY PROJECT: A WORK IN PROGRESS

Local human rights implementation in Eugene, Oregon, has been driven by its city council-appointed Human Rights Commission. Since 2007 the commission has explored ways that Eugene city government can implement UDHR standards and principles across all its departments and operations (US Human Rights Fund 2010, 95-96). It has conducted citywide human rights awareness events, organized local social-justice groups and their allies into an informal human rights coalition, used mass media to address the need for local implementation, and held a major human rights community summit to identify Eugene's pressing human rights issues (Eugene Human Rights City Project 2011).

City staff have initiated a five-year Diversity and Equity Strategic Plan (2009- 2014) that calls for Eugene to "integrate Human Rights City concepts into City policies and procedures" (City of Eugene 2011a). City staff are also developing a Triple Bottom Line Tool that can be used to assess impacts of program, policy, and budget decisions. The social-equity component of the tool "places priority upon protecting, respecting, and fulfilling the full range of human rights, including civil, political, economic, social, and cultural rights" (City of Eugene 2011b).

OTHER LOCAL IMPLEMENTATION ACTIVITIES

As interest in local implementation of human rights has grown, US efforts have taken different forms (US Human Rights Fund 2010; Columbia Law School Human Rights Institute and IAOHRA 2010):

1. The Chicago City Council passed a resolution in 2009 supporting alignment of the city's children- and family-support policies with the UN Convention on the Rights of the Child.
2. In 2009, the Berkeley, California, City Council passed an ordinance requiring the city to report on its compliance with international human rights treaties directly to the US State Department.
3. The Los Angeles County Human Relations Commission is using international human rights in advocating for death-penalty abolition in California and in its campaign to address violence against people who are homeless.
4. Approximately fifty cities and twenty counties have passed resolutions in support of the Convention on the Elimination of All Forms of Discrimination against Women.
5. Human rights and human relations commissions in Milwaukee, Wisconsin; Portland, Oregon; and several other US cities have adopted the UDHR as a guiding standard for their human rights activities.

The Benefits of Collaboration between Community and Urban Sociologists and Human Rights Advocates

Community and Urban Sociologists Can Contribute to Local Human Rights Implementation

Much CUS research, if we use research on cities in the United States as a case in point, is actually human rights work. Emerging research findings can easily be translated into or reframed in human right terms and provide a scholarly window to assess the breadth and extent of US human rights violations affecting urban inhabitants. The knowledge and skills of those working in CUS can be mobilized and tailored to assist local human rights advocates in their data gathering, organizing, and local implementation efforts. CUS sociologists can contribute directly to a city's human rights implementation efforts by employing demographic skills to document and analyze the city's history and extent of economic and racial segregation, as well as relevant population characteristics (e.g., disaggregated poverty rates, school attendance and dropout rates, unemployment rates, crime rates, and arrest patterns). CUS sociologists can use ethnographic research skills, interviewing, facilitation of focus groups, listening sessions, and online and questionnaire surveys to help determine city inhabitants' level of human rights education, their human rights concerns, and what they experience to be the institutional and interpersonal sources of their concerns. They can use existing research to inform local institutional analyses and data gathering based on testing by volunteers in order to uncover sources and patterns of discrimination (in municipal services, employment agencies, real estate, and banking) that rise above and beyond the interpersonal level. CUS sociologists can employ knowledge of social-movement research to help human rights advocates develop messaging and organizing strategies that are effective in mobilizing civil society around the goal of local implementation of human rights. CUS sociologists can assist in the development of human rights indicators or other metrics that will help identify and measure progress following local human rights implementation efforts. Finally, CUS sociologists can invite human rights advocates and victims of human rights violations to be speakers in classrooms and at other campus venues in order to extend institutional recognition to local human rights efforts, encourage human rights learning on campus, and inform students about volunteer opportunities in local human rights implementation activities.

Addressing Local Implementation Will Enrich Community and Urban Sociology

The movement to implement international human rights locally offers opportunities for CUS to become not only a contributor but also a beneficiary of collaborating with human rights advocates at initial stages of what is promising to become a worldwide movement. Such collaborations will prove beneficial by providing CUS theorists with local laboratories for exploring conflicts arising between the goals of human rights implementation and the interests of major private-sector stakeholders. These collaborations will give CUS theorists of local power structure opportunities to analyze and assess struggles between proponents of neoliberal urban social policies and human rights advocates. These collaborative opportunities will provide unique data-gathering opportunities for CUS scholars who use their ethnographic skills to gain entrée and establish rapport with and to solicit data from disempowered and marginalized population segments whose voices must be heard and brought to the table throughout the local human rights implementation process. These collaborations will open up opportunities for CUS researchers to test theoretical propositions regarding on-the-ground, urban, grassroots human rights movements as participant observers while playing legitimate roles as interested researchers. They will add to theoretical knowledge of CUS regarding how, why, and under what conditions the human rights framework functions to bring groups together across racial and class lines that have not normally collaborated or that political actors have successfully kept at odds. The collaborations will encourage networking and collaborative sharing of professional research interests among CUS scholars in different cities and countries who are functioning as scholarly allies in support of the international human rights movement. These opportunities will offer new opportunities for community service contributions by CUS scholars, whether they choose to use their methodological and analytical skills as behind-the-scenes consultants or as public sociologists assuming active human rights advocacy roles. Collaborations will show students a new and exciting way to think about the relevance of CUS, the contributions it can make to society, and how the knowledge and skills they are acquiring in their CUS studies can be used to help protect, promote, and fulfill human rights.

Chapter Two

Peace, War, and Social Conflict

Nader Saiedi

A human rights–centered sociology must directly address the questions of war and peace. Indeed, it can be argued that security is a human right and that no lasting peace is conceivable without the realization of justice and human rights. In an age of nuclear weapons and the globalization of violence, no social problem is more pressing than war and no need more urgent than peace. Yet, surprisingly, mainstream sociology has largely overlooked both issues. In a study of American and European main sociological journals, Garnett (1988) found that war is not perceived as an important research topic in sociology. Fortunately, there has been a recent resurgence of interest among a specialized circle of sociologists in the study of violence and war (Collins 2008; Giddens 1985; Joas 2003; Kestnbaum 2009; Malesevic 2010; Mann 1988; Shaw 2000; Skocpol 1979; Tilly 1992).

Many sociologists, including Giddens (1985), Mann (1988), and Joas (2003), have commented on the neglect of the issues of war and peace in classical sociological literature. Three main reasons for this neglect have been proposed: the appearance of a relatively long period of peace in nineteenth-century Europe between 1815 and 1914, the reduction of the concept of society to the category of nation-state, and the optimistic faith in modernity as the age of rationality, progress, and development.

Yet Malesevic (2010, 17–49) proposes that classical sociological theory was dominated by the bellicose tradition. However, after World War II, the revulsion against war brought about a reinvention of the classical tradition and turned it into a peaceful tradition. Malesevic reminds us of authors like Gumplowicz, Ratzen-hofer, Ward, Simmel, Oppenheimer, Rostow, Pareto, and Mosca, who presented a sociological theory centered in war and national conflict.

War and Other Forms of Violence

There is a dialectical relationship between war and other forms of violence. On the one hand, war is a special case of violence whose proper analysis requires understanding the mutual relationships among alternate types of violence. On the other hand, war is a unique form of violence. The emphasis on the mutual interaction of war and other forms of violent conflict is one of the central contributions of sociological literature. Consequently a sociological analysis of war or peace will address questions of justice and structural violence. Thus, for example, religious fanaticism, patriarchy, racism, ideologies of national superiority, poverty, social inequality, and class oppression are linked to militarism, war, and the dehumanization of the enemy.

Such sociological insight is compatible with a positive definition of peace. Negative peace is the absence of war. For Galtung (1996), however, war is the absence of peace. Positive peace refers to an objective form of social relations that foster harmony, mutual growth, communication, and unity among the interacting partners. In such a definition, the absence of coercive conflicts is a necessary, but not a sufficient, condition of peace. Positive peace therefore depends on the existence of social justice and a culture of communication, peace, and human rights. Violence is conceptualized as systematic denial of human needs and human rights. It can be direct or structural, physical or ideal. The idea of positive peace assigns conceptual primacy to peace rather than war. It is in this spirit that Collins (1974) distinguishes between three types of violence as ferociousness or direct coercion against others, callousness or impersonal structural violence, and asceticism or violence directed against one's own self.

At the same time, wars are highly organized forms of social conflict that are qualitatively different from ordinary forms of violence. In his book *Violence*, Collins (2008) discusses ordinary forms of violence to highlight the fact that contrary to the prevalent ideas, human beings abhor violence, try to avoid it, and seek alternative ways to save face without engaging in physical fights. The principal error of various macro theories of violence is that they all assume that violence comes easily to individuals. Collins argues that contrary to a common Hollywood portrayal of violence, ordinary violence rarely occurs, is very short in duration, is not infectious, and is accompanied by intense anxiety rather than a joking attitude. Even literature on war shows that soldiers frequently prefer to escape rather than fight and are intensely afraid and anxious, a fact that explains the prevalence of friendly fire (Picq 2006; Marshall 1947). Such a perspective is completely at odds with a neo-social Darwinist ideology that sees aggression as a biologically induced tendency among young males in order to further the reproduction of their genes (Wilson 1978, 125-130).

Extensive social organization is necessary in order to compel individuals to engage in military conflict and kill other human beings. As Malesevic argues, human beings, left to their own devices, "are generally incapable of violence and unwilling to kill and die." Therefore, it is the "institutional trappings of the networks of organizations and ideological doctrines that make us act more violently" (Maelsevic 2010, 117).

Peace and War in Classical Sociological Theory

War and peace were central questions in the social theories of both Auguste Comte (1970) and Herbert Spencer (1967). Both theorists conceived of social change as evolutionary movements toward progress and characterized the emerging modern society as industrial rather than military. Industrial society is a peaceful society in which military conquest aimed at acquisition of land is replaced with economic and industrial competition. For Comte this is part of his "law of three stages." Spencer defined a military society as a form of society in which the social function of regulation is dominant. Conversely, in an industrial society it is the economic function that becomes predominant.

With the onset of World War I, most of the social theorists sided with their own country. A unique case is Georg Simmel (1990), who identified war as an "absolute situation" in which ordinary and selfish preoccupations of the individuals with an impersonal money economy are replaced with an ultimate life-and-death situation. Thus war liberates moral impulse from the boredom of routine life and makes individuals willing to sacrifice their lives for the good of society. Simmel's (1968) idea is partly rooted in his theory of conflict in which conflict becomes a force of group integration and solidarity.

On the other side, we see Durkheim and Mead, who both take strong positions against Germany. Discussing Heinrich von Treitschke's worship of war and German superiority, Durkheim (1915) writes of a "German mentality" that led to the militaristic politics of that country. Such militarism is an outdated morality that is opposed to an existing "universal conscience and a universal opinion, and it is no more possible to escape the empire of these than to escape that of physical laws, for they are forces which, when they are violated, react against those who offend them" (Durkheim 1915, 44). A similar analysis is found in the writings of Mead, who contrasts German militaristic politics with Allied liberal constitutions. Immanuel Kant's distinction between the realm of appearances and the things in themselves has led to a theory in which reason is capable of legislating only the form, not the content, of the moral act. The determination of practical life is then left in the hands of military elites. Romantic and idealist schools, represented by Fichte, Schelling, and Hegel, connect this abstract individual to the absolute self, demanding obedience to the dictates of the Prussian state. Such a state "could by definition only rest upon force. Militarism became the necessary form of its life" (Mead 2008 [1918], 167). While liberal democratic countries conceptualize the state as a technical means for realizing individual rights, their full realization of democracy requires institutionalization of substantive social rights for the people. Only in a democratic society with a democratic nationalism will the rule of force and militarism be abandoned both within and between national borders (Mead 2008 [1918], 159–174).

Another classic thinker who wrote on war and peace during World War I is Veblen, who applies his theory of pecuniary emulation to the question of international relations. In his analysis of the leisure class, Veblen (1991) argues that consumption has become the main indicator of social honor. Ownership is mainly sought for its role in claiming prestige. It is the emulation of the wealthy and competition for honor that are the main motivators of human behavior. Thus, both wasteful conspicuous consumption and leisure become the mark of success in pecuniary emulation. However, this same process of emulation is the basis of the claims for national honor and patriotism. According to Veblen, patriotism is "a sense of partisan solidarity in respect of prestige," for "the patriotic spirit is a spirit of emulation" (1998, 31-33). No permanent peace is possible without a fundamental transformation of these patriotic habits of thought. Veblen regards the dynastic militarism of imperial Germany and Japan as a feudal vestige based on the subservience of people to ruling individuals. Such a system necessarily seeks imperial expansion and initiates war. Liberal states are based on impersonal loyalty to things rather than individuals, and they avoid initiating wars. However, the other cause of war is the economic interests of the captains of business and finance. The persistent inequality of possession and control in liberal societies may lead to revolution by the poor. In this situation the liberal states may be tempted to initiate war in order to diffuse the revolutionary sentiments of the workers and farmers. The only thing that is common between the rich and the poor is the sense of patriotism.

Another significant classical theorist who made contributions to the study of war is Werner Sombart. Like Weber, Sombart was interested in understanding the causes of modern capitalism and emphasized the centrality of both religious and political/military factors in its development. Sombart (1913) argued that war between the European states was a major factor in the development of capitalism. The development of a standing army and the state's demand for military uniforms, weapons, and naval ships created the first mass demand for economic production, leading to the development of large-scale capitalistic enterprise. Modernity, in other words, is unthinkable without its genesis in war.

No discussion of classical social theorists is complete without referring to the ideas of Marx and Weber. Both are indispensable for any analysis of war or peace. Marxist tradition has always been a main theoretical model for such analysis. On the other hand, most of the recent sociological contributions to the issue of war and violence are inspired by a Weberian model emphasizing the significance of the modern state and the rationalization of coercion and discipline.

Principal Theories of War and Peace

Social-scientific literature seeks social reasons for war and investigates the social conditions that are conducive to peace. Five such theories are discussed below.

Realism

Realism is the dominant theory in the field of international relations, and it is rooted in a Machiavellian and Hobbesian conception of human beings. Waltz (1979) introduced the theory of structural realism, according to which states are the main actors in international relations. However, the main determinant of a state's decision to engage in war or peace is the international political and military structure. This international structure, however, is none other than international anarchy. In other words, the Hobbesian state of nature is the dominant reality at the level of international relations since there is no binding global law or authority in the world. States are left in a situation of self-help. Consequently, each state regards all other states as a potential or actual threat to its security. Thus arms races and militarism are rational strategies for safeguarding national security. States must act in rational and pragmatic ways and must not be bound by either internal politics or moral principles in determining their policies. In this situation there is no chance for permanent peace. War is a normal result of the structure of international relations. For Waltz, however, the primary interest of states is security. Therefore, states seek a balance of power. Discussing the so-called long peace during the Cold War, he argues that this peace was the product of the two structural conditions of bipolarity and nuclear armament. Another realist, Mearsheimer (2001), introduced offensive structural realism. In this model, states are primarily interested in attaining or securing a hegemonic position.

The closest allies of the realist model in sociological literature are the classical bellicose authors, who conceived of social change in terms of a state-centered theory of war and military conflict. Weber partly defends a state-centered concept of realpolitik. His emphasis on the relativity of all values, his rejection of the ethics of ultimate ends, and his support for the ethics of responsibility in the context of political decision-making are various expressions of this position (Weber 1948b). Yet, for Weber and the neo-Weberians, realism is an inadequate theory because the state represents the intersection of the internal and the external (Skocpol 1979). Furthermore, sociological literature conceives of international structure in terms of both political/military and economic characteristics. Realist theory is criticized from many directions. In a sense, all other theories of war and peace are various forms of rejection of realism.

Joseph (1993) calls for a change of paradigm in understanding the idea of security, replacing a war politics of national security with a peace politics of global security. According to Joseph, realism sees the other states as the main threat to security, whereas peace politics emphasizes the common threats to humanity, namely, environmental pollution, global inequality, poverty, violation of human rights, and nuclear disaster. War politics considers the appropriate response as militarism, whereas peace politics finds demilitarization and global cooperation to be the rational strategy. War politics defines peace in negative terms, while peace politics regards it in positive terms.

Democratic Peace Theory

One of the best-known theories in relation to war and peace is a liberal theory according to which democracies rarely, if ever, engage in war with each other. Kant first advanced this doctrine in 1875 in his historic work *Perpetual Peace*. Contrary to realism, democratic peace theory seeks the root cause of war or peace in the internal political structure of societies. Varieties of empirical tests have confirmed the existence of a significant positive correlation between democracy and peace (Oneal and Russet 2001). Two sets of explanations have been offered for this relationship. Institutional explanations emphasize the existence of systematic restraining forces in democracies. The vote of the people matters in democracies, and therefore war is less likely to occur because the people, rather than the rulers, will pay the ultimate price of war. Cultural explanations argue that democracies respect other democracies and therefore are more willing to engage in peaceful resolution of conflicts. The internal habit of democratic resolution of conflicts is said to be extended to the realm of foreign relations. Among classical social theorists, there is considerable sympathy for this idea. Durkheim, Mead, and Veblen all identify the undemocratic culture and politics of Germany and Japan as the cause of World War I. Similarly, Spencer (1967) finds political democracy compatible with peace.

However, a sociological discussion of democratic peace theory may point to a number of modifications. First, it reexamines the concept of democracy and defines it in both formal and substantive ways. Marxists and critical theorists, as well as Durkheim, Mead, and Veblen, emphasize the necessity of social democracy in addition to formal political democracy for the existence of a genuine participatory democracy. Second, as Held (1995) argues, in a globalized world, where the most important decisions are blind outcomes of the anarchy of particularistic decisions made by states and transnational corporations, democratization of nation-states does not furnish a real democracy. Consequently, an adequate theory of democratization must address the issue of arbitrary and particularistic decision-making in the context of international anarchy. Such a perspective emphasizes the need for a further extension of democratic decision-making to the global level. Strengthening institutions such as the United Nations, the World Court, and global civil societies becomes a vital step in attaining peace.

Marxist Theory

The Marxist theory of violence can be discussed in terms of three issues: the relation of capitalism to war or peace, the role of violence in transition from capitalism to communism, and the impact of colonialism on the development of colonized societies. The dominant Marxist views on these issues are usually at odds with Marx's own positions.

Marx did not address the issue of war and peace extensively. He shared the nineteenth century's optimism about the outdated character of interstate wars. In fact, he mostly believed that capitalism benefits from peace. Marx (1956, ch. 6) considered Napoleon's war a product of Napoleon's obsession with fame and glory. As Mann (1987) argues, Marx saw capitalism as a transnational system and therefore regarded it as a cause of peace rather than war. He believed that violence is mostly necessary for revolution but affirmed the possibility of peaceful transition to socialism in the most developed capitalist societies. Furthermore, Marx saw colonization of the non-European societies as mostly beneficial for the development of those stagnant societies, a development that would in turn lead to socialist revolutions (Kara 1968).

In the midst of World War I, Lenin (1939) radically changed Marxist theory of war and peace. He argued that imperialism, or the competition for colonial conquest, necessarily brings Western capitalist states into war with each other. This war would destroy capitalism and lead to the triumph of socialism. Furthermore, violence was the only possible way of attaining socialism (Kara 1968). The main opposition to Lenin's ideas was Kautsky's (1931) defense of a democratic and parliamentary way of achieving socialism. Lenin's predictions proved to be wrong. In the early twenty-first century, we witness peace among Western capitalist states. More recent Marxist theories are divided in two camps: some find capitalism engendering war between the imperialist (North) and dependent (South) countries, while others see it triggering war within and among poor countries (Frank 1991; Bauman 2001).

Marxist theory has inspired many sociological theories of war and peace. A prominent case is C. Wright Mills's (1956) famous thesis of the military-industrial complex, in which the complex unity of military and industrial enterprises creates conditions conducive to war. Another influence can be found in Wallerstein's (1984) theory of the world capitalist system. Through networks of exchange and trade, the world is divided into center, periphery, and semiperiphery. The structure of this system is the main explanation for wars, including hegemonic ones.

Symbolic Interactionism and Social Constructivism

A sociological perspective that has influenced the field of international relations is the theory of social constructivism. The main advocate of this theory in discussions of war and peace is Alexander Wendt, who systematically criticizes the realist perspective. Emphasizing the symbolic and interpretive character of social relations and practices, Wendt (1999) argues that the objective anarchy of international relations by itself does not lead to a system of mutual threat, antagonism, and selfhelp. Rather, it is the interpretation of the behavior that determines whether anarchy leads to a system of cooperation and trust among nations or a system of antagonism and distrust. For example, Canada and the United States are two sovereign states neighboring each other. Yet the relationship is mutually interpreted as one of trust and cooperation. Similarly, the development of a single nuclear missile in North Korea creates security panic in the United States, whereas the existence of a massive nuclear arsenal in England creates no such concern. Consequently, it is how states perceive and interpret identities and interests that determines the prospects of peace and war.

Wendt's theory is influenced by symbolic interactionism. Mead's (1967) emphasis on the social and interactive construction of self, whereby it comes into existence through language and internalization of the generalized other, is compatible with a host of philosophical and sociological theories that have emphasized the significance of language in defining human reality. Unlike utilitarian and rationalist theories that perceive humans as selfish and competitive, the linguistic turn has emphasized the social and cooperative nature of human beings. Being with others is not an external addition to human consciousness. Rather, it is the very constitutive element of human consciousness and self. For Habermas (1979), for example, the very structure of language presupposes acknowledgment of the presence and legitimate claim of the other. Thus, in the very structure of language, the normative legitimacy of arguments and communication is implicit as the regulating principle of social life.

CULTURE-OF-VIOLENCE/-PEACE THEORY

Cultural theories emphasize the causal significance of the culture of violence or peace as the main determinant of war or peace. Mueller (1989) argues that prior to the twentieth century, war was perceived as a natural, moral, and rational phenomenon. However, through World Wars I and II, this culture changed. According to Mueller, the Western world is moving increasingly in the direction of a culture of peace, with the non-Western world lagging behind. But the future is bright since we are moving in this direction.

Such a perspective may be compatible with Durkheim's (1964) view of organic solidarity. For Durkheim, the appropriate culture corresponding to the modern division of labor is a culture of solidarity that recognizes differences in the context of the equal right of all individuals to self-determination. Therefore, Durkheim believes, the individual's right to autonomy and individuality becomes the new sacred of the modern society. However, for Durkheim, organic solidarity is associated with the rise of a global human consciousness, where such right is extended to all human beings (Lukes 1972, 550).

Lasting peace, therefore, requires a critique of various forms of the culture of violence. These include, among others, cultures of patriarchy, racism, social Darwinism, religious fanaticism, and aggressive nationalism. For example, a culture of violence defines identities through the opposition of the self to the other, whereas a culture of peace defines identities through their mutual interdependence. Patriarchy becomes particularly important because a patriarchal system is likely to produce a negative type of male identity, one that is defined in terms of the negation of the female (Reardon 1985). This is due to the absence of fathers from home and the consequent negative definition of the father image as nonmother.

There is an extensive debate on the reciprocal effects of patriarchy and militarism. Authors like Caprioli (2000) have found a positive correlation between patriarchy and war, where the low social, political, and economic status of women leads to a higher likelihood of interstate wars. On the other hand, many anthropologists (Ember and Ember 1994; Goldstein 2001) have argued that it is war and militarism that lead to violent socialization of males.

A culture of violence is accompanied by a culture of othering and estrangement characterized by the dehumanization of others, reducing them to the level of biology, and violence of singular identity (Sen 2006). Concepts of both social justice and human rights are inseparable principles of a culture of peace.

Modernity, War, and the New Wars

As Malesevic (2010, 118-145) notes, a most perplexing characteristic of the twentieth century is the fact that while it was a century of almost universal acceptance of the principles of human rights and peace, it was the bloodiest century in the history of humankind. Modernity represents the increasing integration of the state, the military, technology, and the economy. War requires extensive and massive social organization. Consequently, the history of modernity is a history of such militaristic, technological, and nationalistic integration and mobilization. Sociologists such as Mann (1988), Giddens (1985), and Tilly (1992) have studied the rise of the modern state and nationalist ideologies. Their main inspiration is Weber's concept of the modern state and bureaucratization. War and coercion played a crucial role in the creation of the present system of nationalism. Military competition among the European states led to the military revolution, the rise of the standing army, the emergence of the conscript army, military discipline, and national integration of the populace in war industry. It was partly this bureaucratization of the army that led to the bureaucratization of other aspects of society, shaping the factory in the image of the army.

Weber defined the modern state as having monopolistic control of the means of coercion. In the modern state, industry, technology, and war become increasingly integrated. The machine gun, the train, the telegraph, airplanes, and high-tech/nuclear war have transformed the nature of modern warfare. Equally important has been the rise of nationalistic ideologies, which opened the masses to militarism. Napoleon introduced national mobilization of people, propaganda, and revolutionary zeal to the art of death and militarism, replacing the old army with a conscript citizen army. Nationalism increasingly became the most powerful determinant of identity in the modern world, replacing religion as the center of the mobilization of emotions.

The paradox of the twentieth century can therefore be explained by the interaction of various causes. First, the destructive character of recent military technology has increased the deadly nature of war. Second, the rise of popular nationalism has led to mass participation of citizens with patriotic and ideological zeal in war. Third, the justification of violence by an instrumental ethics has legitimized all kinds of wars in the name of peace and justice. Fourth, the integration of industry and the military has eroded the distinction between civilian and military institutions. In spite of modern agreements to confine war to the military sector and protect civilians from military violence, the twentieth century became the century of total war. Both popular support for war and the integration of industry and the military encouraged the destruction of the industrial and civilian infrastructure of the enemy. World War II was a major expression of this type of war. It eroded the distinction between the soldier and the civilian. The enemy's civilian industry and infrastructure became the legitimate target of military attack.

Yet three developments—the end of modernism, the end of the Cold War, and globalization—have led to some weakening of national sovereignty and nationalistic identification. They have turned some social movements, such as human rights, environment, and peace movements, into global civil societies. As Kaldor (2003) notes, this development represents a hopeful path of peace for the future.

But they also have triggered the rise of new wars and global uncivil societies. According to Kaldor (1999), new wars are qualitatively different from the old wars. The aim of new war is usually extermination or mass expulsion of the other, whereas in the old war the aim was securing geopolitical control. New war is frequently based on identity politics, and therefore the other must be eliminated. The means utilized by old war were a centralized professional military. New war uses gangs of decentralized warlords and criminal groups, even child soldiers, for murder. The basis of finance of old war was the state treasury and taxation, whereas its base in new war is criminal enterprise as well as the financial support of sympathetic people in other parts of the world. New wars are usually associated with failed states unable to have any meaningful control of the means of coercion in their territory. Both the end of the Cold War and globalization of economic competition contribute to state failure.

What emerges from the story of new wars is the insightful removal of the distinction between the war hero and the criminal, corresponding to the elimination of the distinction between military and civilian targets. However, new war is partly a further extension of the modern concept of total war. Critique of nationalism is indeed a critique of this distinction.

A New Sociology

A human rights-centered sociology will define peace in positive ways, emphasize the connection between violence and injustice, assign theoretical primacy to the study of peace rather than war, and question the pervasive and alienating cultural and institutional habits of thought related to identity politics, nationalism, and national security, while promoting a holistic orientation to the study of war and peace. In addition, such a paradigm will question the traditional distinction between facts and values and approach peace studies in the same way that positive science approaches medical studies. In both cases the study of facts is accompanied by a normative commitment to universalism and health. Methodologically, this perspective will embrace not only positivistic but also hermeneutical and critical methods of studying war and peace. The human rights perspective will encourage the discourse of war and peace to overcome disciplinary reifications and to include questions regarding nationalism, national security, and the connection of war to patriarchy, racism, and social inequality—issues that are normally excluded in the dominant literature on international relations. Finally, a human rights paradigm will transcend the nationalistic heritage of nineteenth-century sociology, appropriate the discourse of globalization in all sociological studies, and, consequently, address issues of war and peace as central questions of sociological theory.

Chapter Three

Environment and Technology

Francis O. Adeola and J. Steven Picou

The relationships between technology, environment, and human rights have not been thoroughly addressed by social-science research. Study of the nexus between human rights, environment, and technology is a recent development and does not enjoy the methodological rigor or sophistication and richness of theories and empirical data that characterize more established fields (see Coosmans, Grunfeld, and Kamminga 2010). An important question yet to be resolved is whether technology represents a cure for environmental and human rights ills or, rather, is the major culprit behind or catalyst for these problems. In other words, does technology represent a blessing or a curse for both environmental and human rights protection? A second question facing human rights scholars and activists addresses the extent to which the environment is universally recognized as a component of human rights. Issues of environmental justice are seminal, as the human rights of minority, indigenous, and low-income people are compromised by negative externalities of industrial production and other environmental risks (Bullard 2000, 2005; Bevc et al. 2007; Washington 2010; Wakefield and Baxter 2010; Lerner 2010). These communities are often regarded as "sacrifice zones" for economic and national-security imperatives. Also posing a challenge to human rights scholars is the question of whether access to technologies and protection from adverse effects of technologies is part and parcel of basic human rights demands. These questions remain unsettled and will be addressed in this chapter through an analysis of the relationships between the concepts of technology, environment, and human rights and their historical development.

Are technological impacts universally regarded as positive or negative? While there are quantitative or objective impacts that tend to draw a universal consensus, the qualitative impacts that are socially constructed at the local or regional level may not be universally agreed upon, especially due to cultural differences in risk perception (see Douglas and Wildavsky 1982; Lupton 1999; Slovic 2000; Adeola 2004). We contend that technologies are used to subdue nature as well as to control and dominate other humans. As stated more than thirty-nine years ago by Leon Kass, "What we really mean by 'Man's Power over Nature' is a power exercised by some men over other men, with a knowledge of nature as their instrument"

(1971, 782). Cases involving the use of technology to oppress, subdue, and annihilate technologically challenged people and to commit other types of human rights violations have been documented around the globe, both before and after the original Universal Declaration of Human Rights (UDHR) (Wronka 1998; Ackerly 2008). Using sociological theory regarding technology, the environment, and human rights, it is possible to respond to human rights abuses.

Defining the Environment and Some Reasons for Concern

The concept of the natural environment encompasses conditions and factors in the surroundings of an organism or group of organisms, including living and nonliving components, as well as the complex of sociocultural conditions associated with individuals, groups, communities, and populations of various species (Cunningham and Cunningham 2008). A distinction is often made between the natural and built environments within which various populations, communities, and organisms live and interact. The built environment consists of physical structures within communities, in cities and towns where people live, work, go to school, play, and conduct daily activities. From architectural designs to city- and town-planning features, industrial structures, extensive street and road networks, and technical infrastructure, the role of technology in the design and maintenance of the built environment is undeniable in modern societies. The natural environment has relatively less human modification, as found in rural areas, the undisturbed wilderness, and ecosystems. However, with technological encroachment, the undisturbed ecosystems around the globe are vanishing at an alarming rate (Brown 2009; Chew 2001). In fact, as pointed out by a number of scholars, human civilization seems to face imminent risk as a result of our application of technology to resource exploitation and subsequent degradation of the environment (Beck 1996, 1999, 2007b). Our growing population and voracious appetite for resources are both directly linked to global environmental problems and resource depletion (see DeSouza, Williams, and Meyerson 2003; Brown 2009).

The decline of the natural environment and the proliferation of emerging risks to the human community are occurring at an alarming rate (Beck 2007b; Barry and Woods 2009). A single generation is witnessing the rapid disappearance of thousands of animal and plant species, the destruction of habitats, and declining air and water quality (De Souza, Williams, and Meyerson 2003; Brown 2009; Gardner and Prugh 2008). Erratic and unusual weather patterns with catastrophic outcomes are becoming common (Adikari and Yoshitani 2009; International Federation of Red Cross and Red Crescent Societies 2004). Resource-induced conflicts and human rights violations are occurring in many regions of the world (World Resources Institute's Earth Trends 2008). Fossil-fuel reserves have been depleted, which is one reason for venturing into fragile ecosystems to extract fossil fuels through the application of remote sensing devices and other sophisticated technologies to find oil deposits in delicate geological zones (World Resources Institute's Earth Trends 2008). The Gulf Coast is just one among many cases where multinational oil corporations have destroyed the environment and violated human rights—including causing deaths, health diminution, violence, deprivation of livelihoods, and insecurity—in order to extract oil and gas (see Adeola 2000a, 2001, 2009; Barry and Woods 2009; Freudenburg and Gramling 2010; Maas 2009; Okonta and Douglas 2001; Sachs 1996). The aggressive use of modern technological systems has resulted in serious human rights violations and the wanton destruction of sensitive environmental resources.

Technology: The Bright and Dark Sides

Technology has been defined in numerous ways by different authors (Volti 1995; Weinstein 2010; Gould 2009; Headrick 2010). The term "technology" was originally coined by Harvard professor Jacob Bigelow (1831) in his book *Elements of Technology*, first published in 1829, in which he describes technology as systematic knowledge, tools, implements, techniques, and machines employed in the production and distribution of goods and services in society. According to Volti (1995, 6), technology is a system based on the application of knowledge, manifested in physical objects and organizational forms, for the attainment of specific objectives. Technologies are created and used to accomplish otherwise impossible tasks or to perform tasks more efficiently—that is, more cheaply, quickly, and easily, with less drudgery. For Gould (2009, 97), technology is simply a series of entanglements with social systems and ecosystems, close and far, obvious and hidden. In other words, there is a social dimension to technology that shapes the division of labor, how tasks are structured, how technologies are used, and how goals are attained. The concept of technology refers to those aspects of material culture used in the manipulation and exploitation of the biophysical environment for the purpose of meeting the material needs of people in society. As such, technology is a critical part of modern society and has helped to advance improved quality of life for untold millions around the globe.

Technology is involved in the process of social interaction, as well as in the process of human interaction with the biophysical environment. Headrick (2010, 3) defines technology as all the ways in which humans harness the materials and energy in the environment for their own ends, beyond what they can do with their own bodies. Weinstein (2010) refers to technology as a stock of knowhow developed or borrowed by a population to extend its members' abilities to transcend natural and biological limits. He describes technology as a uniquely human possession that has provided Homo sapiens with a powerful advantage over all other species on the planet, resulting in some species being driven to extinction, as well as threatening human survival (Weinstein 2010, 194). Humans are different from all other species given their intelligence and ability to acquire and transmit knowledge and to apply this knowledge to create tools and techniques.

Along these lines, Volti (1995, 4) has noted that without the human capacity to invent and use a great variety of technologies, humankind would never have been able to establish itself in virtually every part of the globe and exploit every ecosystem on the planet. Volti (1995, 4) further contends that our dependence on technology is as old as the species, and any evils that have accompanied the application of a particular technology are not enough to indict technology as being unnatural. He states that our past, present, and future are inextricably linked to our capacity to shape our existence through the invention and application of implements and techniques that enable us to transcend our own limited physical endowment. The history of technology has been described as the history of human society's increasing adaptability. This pattern of adaptation identifies human prowess and the increasing ability of the species to manipulate nature—from Stone Age primitive axes to nuclear bombs, from small dugout canoes to supertankers, from simple horticulture and gardening to genetic engineering and the creation of genetically modified crops (Headrick 2010). Yet, following patterns of social stratification, modern technologies are not evenly distributed throughout society; it is always advantageous to own technology, especially in nonegalitarian societies. Technological systems are often concentrated in the hands of those who can afford them.

Technology has both positive and negative exponential impacts on the biophysical environment and across different dimensions of society (see Mesthene 2000). On the positive side, technological advances have led to increased life expectancy, less infant mortality, increased food production, economic growth, better standards of living, improved communication and transportation systems, and accelerated rates of diffusion of sociocultural elements, including technological innovations (Mesthene 2000; Khalili-Borna 2007; Haugen 2008). Globalization, the rapid or accelerated flow of capital, information, and cultural elements around the world, is driven by technological innovation (Haynes 2008). Technology represents the engine of sociocultural transformation (Nolan and Lenski 2011; Takacs-Santa 2004) and is a key element for enhancing progress and prosperity. Technology holds the solutions to most, if not all, of our social problems, including the liberation of individuals from tyranny (Mesthene 2000). Essentially, technology has shaped civilizations and defined societal progress, from major medical breakthroughs to space missions, the production of arrays of materials goods and services, and the innovation and diffusion of ideas across the globe.

The globalization of technology is a transformative force with the potential to improve human rights monitoring and protection around the globe. For example, Lauren (2008) indicates that revolutionary changes in transportation and communication systems played a pivotal role in bringing human rights abuses in one region of the world to the attention of people and governments in other areas. Human rights abusers are increasingly finding it difficult to hide or deny information about their oppressive and inhumane actions. Global awareness of human suffering rose sharply during the nineteenth century with advances in transportation and communication systems, the mass media, transistor radios, telegraphy, photography, and the invention of relatively inexpensive postage stamps. These initial advances have continued at an accelerated pace.

Now, as a product of the electronic and Internet revolution of the twentieth and twenty-first centuries and the powerful forces of globalization, there are abundant technological devices readily available to monitor the breach of international human rights norms even in the most remote regions of the world. Both Apocada (2007) and Lauren (2008, 97) have compiled lists of technological accoutrements available for use to safeguard human rights, including handheld portable electronic devices such as cellular phones, iPods, and MP3 players equipped with digital cameras and text-messaging options, as well as video cameras, fax machines, laptop computers, the Internet, scanners, YouTube, and television cable networks. The most repressive regimes around the world are increasingly finding it difficult to stop the diffusion of information through the use of these tools. Nonetheless, public protests in Egypt in 2011 resulted in the government's obliteration of Facebook, Twitter, BlackBerry Messenger, and the Internet as operative resources; it appears that astute hackers and sympathizers within Egypt's borders thwarted the government's action. Although communications technologies are liberating in one sense, they can be controlled by repressive governments (Hendawi 2011). How much control a government can exert is open to debate, especially in the wake of WikiLeaks and unsuccessful attempts by many Arab countries facing revolutionary changes. It is also important to understand that a large proportion of the world population is still excluded from the benefits of science and technology. According to Human Rights Watch (2010, 7-8), many societies remain closed to international human rights scrutiny. Some governments are so repressive that no domestic human rights organization or movement can exist openly. Visits or penetrations by international human rights monitors are typically discouraged by these governments, such as in Burma (Myanmar), Eritrea, Iran, North Korea, Somalia, and Turkmenistan.

Technologies can be used to commit human rights atrocities. As noted by Volti (1995, 16), it has become a cliché that a particular technology can be used for either good or evil purposes: while a construction team employs dynamite to build a road, a terrorist uses it to blow up an airplane, automobile, or people. Transportation and communication technologies propelling globalization are the same tools of choice for trafficking women and children across international borders for prostitution and child slavery, as well as for drug trafficking. Computer and communication technologies are also resources for spreading political misinformation and propaganda or jamming information-transmission channels (Apocada 2007; Lauren 2008; Hendawi 2011). Many terrorist groups use computers, the Internet, and handheld portable electronic devices to plan and achieve their violent objectives. The basic rights to life and a safe and healthy environment are imperiled by the invention and production of weapons of mass destruction, such as nuclear, chemical, and biological weapons, that can be misused by terrorist groups or irrational leaders of rogue states.

About thirty-two years ago, David Orr indicated that a society becomes vulnerable to catastrophe the moment it becomes dependent upon complex, energy- and capital-intensive "high" technologies that radically extend control over nature and at the same time increase the potential for catastrophic side effects and social dysfunction. For instance, the development of automobiles, chemical pesticides, nuclear energy, supersonic transports, supertankers, recombinant

DNA, and so on suggests a large number of potential disasters due to latent effects that often manifest as surprises when accidents occur. The earthquake-tsunami-triggered nuclear-meltdown potential at the Fukushima Daiichi nuclear power plant in Japan is a recent example of complex technological surprise (Clayton 2011). Risk in contemporary modern societies is viewed as a function of high technology, which is primarily a product of the growth and diffusion of technologies that took place after 1945 (Orr 1979, 43).

Among other negative impacts of technologies on society are the rising numbers of casualties associated with a variety of catastrophic events triggered or exacerbated by technology. For example, technological disasters, wars, crimes, terrorism, health problems, global pollution, environmental injustice, and threats of global climate change all reflect human rights abuse (Adeola 2001). Historically, science and technology have been implicated in several atrocities involving the blatant violation of human rights—including their application as instruments of mass repression, torture, genocide, ethnic cleansing, and slavery both before and after the UDHR (Toney et al. 2010; Evans 2007). Technology has been employed in cases of infanticide in many parts of Asia, including India, Pakistan, and China. There are also cases of eugenics, the Tuskegee experiment, the poisoning of Vietnam residents with Agent Orange, and the strategic deployment of weapons of mass destruction (Khalili-Borna 2008; Toney et al. 2010). The detonation of atomic bombs over Hiroshima and Nagasaki in Japan provides further examples of massive loss of life and environmental destruction spanning several generations (Erikson 1994). Unfortunately, the jury is still out in terms of whether the benefits of technology outweigh the costs. It is important to note that humanity is a part of nature and is systematically involved with nature's continuity and evolution. Nonetheless, science and technology have the untoward potential to cause the elimination of humankind through misapplication (Szell 1994).

Human Rights: The Importance of Environment and Technology

In both first- and second-generation rights, environmental rights and rights to technology were not clearly addressed. This is not surprising given the anthropocentric nature of the human rights movement and UDHR. Also, it is important to note that even though a number of scholars raised alarms about environmental pollution and the problems associated with pesticide use as far back as the 1960s, especially with the 1962 publication of *Silent Spring* by Rachel Carson, environmental rights did not emerge as a primary concern both in the United States and within the United Nations until the late 1960s and the 1970s (Carson 1962; Johansen 2003). A number of memorable events, such as the passage of the National Environmental Policy Act, the establishment of the Environmental Protection Agency, the celebration of the first Earth Day, the Santa Barbara oil spill, the energy crisis, the Three Mile Island disaster, and other disturbing environmental-contamination episodes in the 1970s, sparked vigorous modern environmental movements within the United States and global outrage about environmental problems (Carson 1962; Giddens 1999; Hernan 2010; Johansen 2003; Perrow 1999). The issue of illegal waste movements from the Global North to the Global South has also gained international attention (Clapp 2001; Pellow 2007). These modern environmental risks are often invisible, transgenerational, transnational, and uninsurable and pose the ultimate threat to human rights and human security (Beck 1996, 1999; Giddens 1999).

The Declaration of the United Nations Conference on the Human Environment held in Stockholm is often regarded as the first international attempt to address pressing environmental problems. Representatives of 113 countries attended the conference, and as contentious as environmental issues were at the time, they all agreed to twenty-six principles that direct governments to cooperate in protecting and improving the natural environment. Shortly after the Stockholm conference, several environmental catastrophes occurred both in the United States and other parts of the world, raising social consciousness about threats to environmental sustainability and the latent dysfunctions of modern complex technologies. Among these, the dioxin contamination of Seveso in Italy in 1976; the toxic waste contamination at Love Canal, New York; the Three Mile Island nuclear reactor accident; the deadly contamination of a neighborhood in Woburn, Massachusetts; the mass killings of thousands of people by poisonous gas released at the Union Carbide Corporation factory in Bhopal, India; the mega nuclear reactor meltdown at Chernobyl, Ukraine, in 1986; and the massive *Exxon Valdez* oil spill in Prince William Sound, Alaska, provided growing evidence of the problem of technological failure and environmental destruction (Erikson 1994; Picou, Gill, and Cohen 1997). In addition, a plethora of alarming cases of toxic contamination across the United States, especially in lower-income, minority communities, provide evidence of the risks that threaten human rights to life, a safe and healthy environment, and psychosocial well-being (see Adeola 2011; Hernan 2010; Marshall and Picou 2008; Gill and Picou 1998). Clearly, most of these cases depict the dark side of technology for humans and all other organisms in the environment. Citizens, sociologists, and environmental activists have increasingly addressed patterns of environmental injustice and how these events expose issues related to human rights, technology, and the environment (Bullard 2000, 2005). Sociologists have also played a key role in the environmental health movement, addressing the manifest and latent outcomes of technologies and their psychosocial impacts (see Perrow 1999, 2008; Erikson 1994; Gill and Picou 1998). They are increasingly involved in applied research offering policy guidelines and choices to public administrators.

Social vulnerability to changes in the environment and environmental hazards is a direct function of technology and social relations. The history of global inequality makes some groups more vulnerable to environmental hazards than others. Despite the existence of the UN instruments, as well as other local, national, and regional structures establishing human rights, some groups experience a disproportionate share of negative environmental externalities imposed by technology and industrial activities. As emphasized in the environmental-justice literature, disadvantaged groups—including racial and ethnic minorities, indigenous peoples, people of color, and the poor all over the world—are more vulnerable to environmental hazards than other groups (Bullard 2000, 2005). For people who live with disadvantages, the rights to healthy habitats, clean natural resources, including air and water, and occupational safety are considered expendable for the sake of economic gain, national security, and national energy imperatives (Johnston 1995). Many communities of color are regarded and treated as "paths of least resistance" for absorbing the deleterious consequences of industrial pollution. These communities exist within and contiguous to sources of toxic emissions that threaten health and social wellbeing (Adeola 1994; Johnston 1995; Bullard 2000, 2005; Agyeman 2005). These increased risks also characterize third-world countries where hazardous wastes from affluent societies of the Global North are overtly or covertly dumped, showing a global pattern of environmental injustice (Adeola 2000a; Pellow 2007; Clapp 2001). To mitigate this pattern of environmental injustice against the people as well as against the biophysical environment, the World People's Conference on Climate Change and the Rights of Mother Earth convened in April 2010 in Bolivia and developed a draft Universal Declaration of the Rights of Mother Earth.

Does every human being have a right to the positive benefits of environment and technology? A consideration of global and local structured social inequality suggests that unequal command of technology results in exposure to deadly environmental hazards regardless of existing human rights. The rights to a clean environment and positive applications of technology are often considered as part of the third-generation rights recently recognized within the United Nations (Johnston 1995; Glazebrook 2009; Ruppel 2009). This category of human rights has become controversial because addressing this issue is contingent upon both the positive and negative duties of the state, individuals, and organizations (Wronka 1998; Ishay 2004a; Boersema 2011). As mentioned, among these third-generation rights are the rights to development, to peace, to a healthy environment, to the benefits of science and technology, and to intergenerational equity. As mentioned by Ruppel (2009), the right to a clean environment requires healthy human habitats that are free of pollutants, toxins, or hazards that pose threats to human health. The right to a healthy environment therefore requires the commitment of states (1) to refrain from directly or indirectly interfering with the enjoyment of the right to a healthy environment; (2) to guard against third parties, such as corporations, interfering with the right to a healthy and productive environment; and (3) to adopt all necessary measures to achieve the full realization of the right to a safe and healthy environment (Ruppel 2009).

The principal instruments asserting the third- and fourth-generation category of rights are the African Charter on Human and People's Rights of 1981 and the Declaration of the Rights of Indigenous Peoples of 2007 (Battersby and Siracusa 2009). Indigenous rights are considered under the purview of conventions addressing biodiversity and intellectual property. Even though genetic research delivers medical benefits, it is also argued that biotechnologies have allowed food and drug companies to distill and manipulate the genetic structure of plants known to indigenous communities for their medicinal qualities. Such genetically modified crops pose threats to indigenous cultures and traditional biophysical environments.

While most of the first-and second-generation rights have been ratified by many states and codified within international laws, the third- and emerging fourth-generation rights remain controversial. This was apparent at the 1992 Earth Summit convened in Rio de Janeiro, Brazil, where concerns for economic development among the less developed countries were pitted against the protection of the biophysical environment advocated by most affluent nations of the Global North. Instead of focusing on an ecocentric approach to addressing environmental rights for people, emphasis was shifted to the goal of sustainable development. Nevertheless, the Earth Summit gave impetus to a Framework Convention on Climate Change, which addresses the problem of global warming. The World Summit on Sustainable Development held in Johannesburg, South Africa, in 2002 focused on sustainable development as reflected in the Johannesburg Declaration (UN 2002). These developing trends in human rights advances clearly reveal the emerging role of environmental concern for protecting the health and well-being of citizens throughout the world.

Conclusion

The future of human rights in the twenty-first century poses many challenges and opportunities for humankind. In particular, issues directly related to the biophysical environment and technological advances will increasingly become a permanent source of controversy and a potential platform for advances in the human rights arena. Human rights scholars need to address the fact that technological systems are far from perfect, and the lesson from Hurricane Katrina's destruction of New Orleans is that even natural catastrophes can be technologically engineered (Freudenburg, Gramling, and Laska 2009). The failure of technology is a "normal" event, and as technological systems become increasingly complex, humankind faces "surprises" and "worst-case scenarios" that have the potential to obliterate the scientific advances of the last century (see Perrow 1999, 2008; Clarke 2006). This increasing inventory of risk permeates the social fabric and is embedded throughout the global biophysical environment (Beck 2007b). As such, technological advances and failures, coupled with environmental degradation, become inextricably linked to our consciousness of issues for advancing human rights. These advances can be fostered by declarations of global organizations, such as the United Nations, by international agreements, and also by raising individual consciousness through educational empowerment, or individualization (Beck 1996).

From a social-policy standpoint, Hayward (2005) suggests the usefulness of embedding environmental rights within national constitutions, which would serve a broader purpose than simply providing for the protection of the environment by legal actions. A potential effect of environmental human rights would be mandating several procedural rights, including the right to know, to be informed of any proposed developments in one's locality, to information about environmental-impact and technological-impact assessments, to information about toxic releases into the environment, and to freedom of assembly to facilitate protests against locally undesirable land uses, such as creation of brown fields and erection of noxious facilities, as well as extensive rights to self-determination, encompassing the right to participate in decision-making forums. As noted by Barry and Woods (2009, 324), the legal recognition of these rights would enhance the democratic efficacy of environmental decision-making processes, thereby facilitating environmental justice while at the same time promoting an ethic of custodianship of the biophysical environment. The mandatory precautionary principle (the notion that we should strive to prevent harm to human health and the environment even in the face of scientific uncertainty about risks) has also been advanced in the literature and within the United Nations as an important mechanism for ensuring environmental justice, human rights, and protection of the integrity of nature. In fact, the precautionary principle has become a key component of EU environmental policy and is included in Principle 15 of the Rio Declaration. The extent to which all the declarations have been implemented remains subject to debate. Several NGOs, such as Human Rights Watch, Amnesty International, and Earth Justice, among others, are monitoring and reporting human-environmental rights situations across nations.

The relationship between the biophysical environment, technology, and human rights is complex and critical for understanding the human condition in the twenty-first century. While human rights encompass the right to life, a clean environment, liberty, and security, guaranteed access to environmental amenities and protection against environmental harms for present and future generations remain elusive. Although the application of technology as a liberating force for enhancing quality of life and economic development is a laudable and important goal, alternative outcomes that ensure the protection of ecological integrity, human rights, and sustainable development need to be addressed. The irresponsible application of modern technologies has resulted in massive contamination of the natural environment, loss of life, and the destruction of human communities. Coinciding with this "dark side" of technology are numerous examples of the worldwide violation of human rights emphasized in this chapter. Sociological research should become more actively engaged in understanding the dynamic linkage between technology, environment, populations, level of affluence, political regime characteristics, and human rights around the globe in an attempt to positively influence social change in the twenty-first century. Hopefully this chapter will be a source of encouragement for future inquiry.

Chapter Four

Population

Jenniffer M. Santos-Hernández

In 1993 Bryan Turner explored and proposed the creation of a theory of human rights within the discipline of sociology. Over the last two decades, several sociologists have focused on understanding the value of moving beyond the limited engagement of our discipline in normative debates (Waters 1996; Hafner-Burton and Tsutsui 2005; Blau and Frezzo 2011). In the summer of 2005, Michael Burawoy, in his presidential address to the American Sociological Association, called for a public sociology and stressed our responsibility to focus on understanding and preventing the devastation of society. He highlighted the widespread appeal of human rights as a framework to ensure human dignity and stand against human atrocities.

This chapter discusses some opportunities for the human rights paradigm for cross-disciplinary collaborations between demographers and sociologists interested in population studies and human rights. It is important to highlight that studies in population have greatly contributed to securing and extending human rights. Research in demography is at the heart of human rights discussions. For example, the Population Division of the United Nations Department of Economic and Social Affairs is one of the main international organizations collecting, monitoring, analyzing, and distributing global population data. The data collected by the Population Division is used by all dependencies in the UN system to create policies and to monitor their implementation. Externally, the data offered by the UN Population Division presents information that governments can use to explore demographic trends in other countries.

The Growth of World Population and Population Studies

Sometime during the last quarter of 2011, the world's population reached 7 billion. The growth is not because people are having more children. In contrast with common belief, people are in fact having fewer children. Fertility, or the average number of children per woman, has steadily declined in the last fifty years. What has happened is that after the second half of the nineteenth century, the world was transformed dramatically through several processes of change, including secularization, industrialization, increased access to education, and improvements in sanitation and health services, among others. People are now living longer, and their children are less likely to die of communicable or preventable diseases. As a result of all these changes, the world's population has grown faster than ever before. What is interesting about these changes is the fact that they occurred as part of a larger and longer process of social change that demographers have named the "demographic transition" (Caldwell 2006).

Improvements in transportation and communication systems have also transformed societies. The world is now connected in ways that seemed unimaginable a century ago, facilitating the flows of people and objects and leading to the emergence of not only a network society (Castells 2000), but also a world economy (Goldfrank 2000). The challenge is that the relationship among countries is not equal; rather, it has led to the emergence of a global division of labor or social structure that renders some countries and their citizens as subordinates to the market demands of others (Wallerstein 1974). With all the changes mentioned, human rights emerged as a universal set of rules for interactions among all humans (Donnelly 2003).

Sociology as a discipline emerged to study the social changes that in many ways have facilitated the demographic-transition process and the development of states that are now increasingly part of this global society. Current debates in our discipline discuss the need to extend beyond the boundaries of states and allow for the development of a "connected sociology" that emerges from the bottom up and integrates challenging perspectives in order to reconstruct our understanding of society and the sociological endeavor.

While not all demographers are sociologists and not all sociologists are demographers, the two fields have long been related. Demography has truly evolved as a multidisciplinary area of inquiry, attracting researchers who study how changes in a wide variety of phenomena affect people and how they react to those effects. For instance, demographers are interested in questions such as, How many children are born? To what families are children being born? In what types of housing arrangements do those families live? What are the characteristics of their neighborhoods? What resources are accessible to them? How do people move? How many people die? What is their cause of death? Where are all these events and processes happening? To answer such questions, the field of demography has increasingly relied on statistical methods that allow us to standardize and systematize data-collection procedures (Hinde 1998). In addition, the development of information-system technologies has also improved the study of population by reducing the uncertainty of the data collected and increasingly making the data available in formats that are easier to use and understand.

Demographers have also focused on refining demographic theories. The field of demography has long been criticized for the lack of depth of its associated theories (Crimmins 1993). Micklin and Poston (2005) argue that despite their disagreement with such a view, evaluating and clarifying demographic theories remains a challenge. They argue that the challenge is not necessarily due to the complexity of those theories but stems from the diversity of demographic theories used in population studies. The collaboration of sociologists and demographers is promising because it affords an opportunity to extend critical approaches within demography and reflect on the characteristics and patterns observed in a group (Horton 1999). For example, instead of assuming progress by relying on proxy variables that seek to measure progress toward the attainment of specific human rights, a contextualized approach that captures how the global order affects the rights of citizens in different societies would be more effective in advancing the promise of human rights. The importance of such cross-disciplinary collaboration lies in the opportunity to really understand the situation of people in a particular social context instead of simply assuming that progress is being made because of a reduction in the prevalence of a characteristic or indicator.

Population Studies and Human Rights

The collection of information about the population in a political jurisdiction dates back to the beginning of civilization. Population data are used by governments for a wide variety of reasons, including taxation, military recruitment, development of military strategies, provision of public services, allocation of government funds, and assessment of the effects of policies implemented. Population data collected by states around the world has functioned as a mechanism to facilitate governance.

In an ideal situation, population data would always be used to ensure the welfare of individuals. However, the social categories used to group individuals are not socially neutral. On several occasions, information about a population has also been used to target vulnerable groups (Seltzer and Anderson 2002). In other cases, marginalized groups have been systematically excluded from data-collection efforts (Anderson and Fienberg 2001). Table 4.1 provides an overview of crimes against humanity and the populations affected.

At the same time, realization of the human rights of some and enhancements in their standard of living have sometimes come at the cost of the human freedoms of marginalized groups. These changes are, to a great extent, a result of population policies. Some population policies have transformed societies through programs that facilitate institutional arrangements that treat everyone equally and with dignity. Those population policies allow men and women to plan their futures and their families and to make decisions with a clear understanding of their consequences. Other population policies have failed to respect the rights of men and women. Some of them have focused on neo-Malthusian or eugenics beliefs and have targeted specific groups, resulting in some of the most atrocious crimes against humanity (Levine and Bashford 2010), as Table 4.1 shows. Some of those appalling policies have led to social movements or to civil and/or military conflicts.

For example, modern family-planning methods have facilitated a reduction in fertility, the emergence of smaller families, the integration of women into the

Table 4.1 Selected crimes against humanity

Country	System
South Africa: apartheid	Apartheid was a racial-segregation system in place in South Africa until the mid-1990s. The system maintained four categories—black, colored, Indian, and white—and prevented them from interacting with each other through physical separation and prohibition of intermarriage. Institutional power was held by whites, and other groups were denied the right to participate in politics (Ozler 2007).
Germany: Holocaust	During World War II, approximately 6 million Jews were killed by the Nazi government (Longerich 2010; Bauman 1988).
Guatemala: genocide	During the 1980s, more than two hundred thousand people were killed by the military in more than six hundred Mayan villages (Higonnet 2009).
Rwanda: genocide	More than five hundred thousand were killed in a conflict against the Tutsi ethnic minority in the 1990s. About a third of the Tutsi population was killed (Barnett 2003).
Bosnia: genocide	More than one hundred thousand Bosnians and Croatians were killed in the 1990s by military forces (Ching 2009).
Darfur, Sudan: genocide	State-led genocide in Darfur has resulted in more than 400,000 people killed and 2.5 million displaced (Suleiman 2011).

labor market, and the alleviation of poverty. Nevertheless, for many women in Puerto Rico, Haiti, and other countries, the potential side effects of the use of contraceptives, such as permanent sterilization, were not well understood when these methods were adopted (Salvo, Powers, and Cooney 1992; López 1993; Briggs 1998). In fact, birth-control programs implemented in many countries throughout the world were built around neo-Malthusian and eugenic-supremacy beliefs (López 2008). Researchers have long documented that women often accepted undergoing sterilization procedures offered by government social workers at no cost because they believed the procedures were reversible. The main idea behind such policies was that poverty was caused by overpopulation. As such, in order to reduce poverty and promote economic development, population-control policies were perceived as necessary to reduce reproduction among those on the lower rungs of society. Similarly, in the United States many people of color and those considered inferior because of physical or mental limitations were sterilized in the first half of the twentieth century. While these family-planning initiatives can allow people to make their own childbearing choices, when family-planning methods are mandatory or target specific groups, or when all potential consequences are not understood, they fail to recognize the rights of those who adopt them.

Population Growth, Adaptation to Climate Change, and Human Rights

Research in population will continue to be vital for the advancement of human rights. Moreover, assisting in the realization of human rights will depend on the methods we use and how well they capture the experiences of those we group into larger categories. Society now confronts the most crucial challenge of all times: climate change (Giddens 2009). Modernization has brought great advances but also has accelerated the degradation of our environment. Climate change is already affecting the lives of people around the world (Stringer et al. 2009).

Moreover, although fertility continues to decline, the world's population will continue expanding for the upcoming decades, with the fastest growth taking place in the poorest nations (Campbell-Lendrum and Lusti-Narasimhan 2009). Why? Because more people live in less advanced societies that are at an earlier stage of the demographic-transition process. The challenge is to develop a way of living that can sustain the current population, adapt to an increasingly changing climate, and account for the needs of the population that is being added to our planet.

While we often take for granted the food we eat and the water we drink, in some areas of the world drought-driven famines have profound social and political impacts. In other areas of the world (e.g., the Horn of Africa), famines have been caused or triggered not by droughts but by faulty governments, civil conflicts, and war (Wisner et al. 2004; Sen 1981). In many areas of countries such as China, Pakistan, Somalia, Sudan, and Iraq, people are increasingly affected by food and water scarcity, living in poverty, and oppression by authoritarian political regimes. Therefore, the challenge of climate change calls upon sociologists to examine the dialectical relationship between society and environment (Grundmann and Stehr 2010).

Sociology and Population Studies for the Future of Human Rights

The transformation of social life and the enhancement of infrastructure to facilitate the exchange of goods and resources have created a new global community that extends beyond the boundaries of states. With the transformation of societies, human rights emerged to provide guidance regarding social interactions. Population research has been crucial in the advancement of human rights by providing much-needed information to support the development of policy that addresses the needs of those whose rights are being denied or postponed. Drawing on the strengths of population and sociological research affords an opportunity to critically examine the past, understand the challenges of the present, and in doing so prevent the future devastation of society.

The development of effective population policy in the twenty-first century is essential to confront the challenges of a changing climate. Sociology can greatly contribute to addressing the fissures of current social arrangements and can help reduce the pressures that human activities place on the environment. Climate change challenges not only our current social arrangements but our capacity to ensure the realization of human rights for others. Population studies and sociology can greatly contribute to understanding how the current world order affects the capacity of different groups and societies to secure the human rights of their members. Moreover, population studies and sociology can greatly contribute to the process of identifying challenges and opportunities for securing the human rights of citizens as we also adapt to the challenges posed by a changing climate.

Chapter Five

Collective Behavior and Social Movements

Lyndi Hewitt

Richard Flacks has characterized the study of social movements as an examination of "the conditions under which human beings become capable of wanting freedom and acting freely" (2005, 4). Thought about in this way, social movement research goes to the very heart of human rights, linking intellectual and political endeavors for actors in the academy and in the field. In collaboration with interlocutors from political science, sociologists of collective behavior and social movements (CBSM) have long striven to illuminate the multilayered action of social movement participants in their efforts to achieve social change. Taking up questions around the emergence, trajectories, and outcomes of collective action, movement scholars offer theoretical and empirical insights of considerable relevance to human rights.

Scholars of social movements have addressed human rights to the extent that the political actors they study are (1) engaging human rights frameworks in their struggles, (2) documenting human rights abuses as a form of advocacy, (3) contesting and reshaping political and public understandings of human rights, and (4) fighting to secure the rights of oppressed groups. Not surprisingly, then, the literatures examining transnational resistance to neoliberalism and struggles for the rights of women are particularly active sites for such work; I focus on these literatures here. Surveys, case studies, qualitative interviewing, document analysis, comparative historical approaches, field research, and more have been used to address questions where human rights and movements intersect. And while it is not uncommon for scholars to be deeply engaged with the movements they study, there is ample room for more explicit adoption of participatory and human rights approaches to movement research.

This chapter briefly reviews key threads, questions, and recent developments in the social movements literature and, further, argues that conceptual and empirical work on social movements offers important insights into understanding human rights. Social movement scholars are well positioned to facilitate the advancement of human rights activism but must work diligently to develop praxis-oriented research agendas in order to maximize their impact.

History and Key Questions of CBSM Scholarship

Scholars generally agree that social movements are defined by (relatively) sustained and organized efforts on the part of collectivities engaging in at least some non-institutionalized tactics and seeking to achieve or resist social change. Prior to the 1960s and 1970s, dominant understandings of collective action focused heavily on the role of grievances and depicted movement participants as largely irrational actors. The field then shifted and expanded substantially as the US civil rights, women's, student, and antiwar movements illustrated the shortcomings of existing explanations of collective action. Researchers, many of whom were activists themselves, studied these agitations and ultimately rejected psychologically driven approaches to explaining mobilization in favor of more structural perspectives that took into account factors such as resources, organizations, networks, and political context. Leading scholars, including Charles Tilly, William Gamson, Doug McAdam, and Sidney Tarrow, demonstrated the influence of these structural factors across a range of mobilization efforts and carved out ambitious research agendas for the field of movement studies.

Researchers have consistently investigated influences on the emergence, trajectories, and outcomes of collective action at local, national, and increasingly transnational levels. Key questions have included, Why do people protest? How do contextual conditions support or hinder collective action? How do movements influence cultural attitudes and policy change? What differentiates a successful from an unsuccessful movement? In their efforts to describe and analyze these multiple sites of collective action, movement scholars have highlighted the importance of resources, political and cultural contexts, and also the agency of movement actors. The resource mobilization perspective (Jenkins 1983; McCarthy and Zald 1977) emphasized the importance of organizational resources in catalyzing movement action. Early conversations about resources yielded useful concepts, such as social movement organization, social movement industry, and social movement sector, that facilitated systematic empirical study. Generally speaking, research in this tradition demonstrates that higher levels of resources are beneficial for mobilization efforts (Cress and Snow 1996; Zald 1992), with the importance of different types of resources (e.g., material, human, social) varying according to the nature and phase of the movement. Scholars have also explored the consequences of resource accumulation and professionalization, concluding that the effects on movement trajectories are mixed (Piven and Cloward 1977; Staggenborg 1988).

The notion of political opportunities (Kitschelt 1986; Meyer 2004) further transformed the field of social movement study, illuminating the role of factors such as elite allies and the openness of political systems in facilitating or preventing protest. Political opportunity is the crucial ingredient in what became known as the political process model of collective action (Kriesi 2004; McAdam 1982), which remains a dominant perspective. The political process model synthesized existing insights in the field and prioritized the influence of political opportunities and threats, or lack thereof, in understanding movement development. Shifting opportunities over time and across locales have helped explain why collective action emerges and/or succeeds in some situations but not in others. Even while the political process perspective was arguably at its height, though, scholars worried about the overextension of key concepts (Gamson and Meyer 1996). While numerous studies attempted to measure and assess the impact of contextual conditions, they often utilized different indicators. At the same time, studies exploring the cultural and emotional aspects of movements were on the rise.

Although resource mobilization and political process models contributed a great deal to understandings of collective action, scant attention was paid to the ways that culture, ideology, and meaning construction came to bear on the emergence and development of social movements. The "cultural turn" in social movement theory brought with it more careful attention to the role of framing, emotions, and collective identity in building and sustaining movements. This gradual shift in the study of social movements over the past twenty-five years has been well documented by social science researchers (Benford and Snow 2000; Gamson 1992; Goodwin and Jasper 2004; Johnston and Klandermans 1995; McAdam 1994), and the explosion of research on collective action frames and framing processes is the most prominent example of this phenomenon (Johnston and Noakes 2005). The considerable influence of collective action frames in movement emergence, development, and outcomes is now widely recognized (Cress and Snow 2000; Gamson 1992; McCammon et al. 2007; Zuo and Benford 1995). Scholars of social movements have come to understand framing processes as the means by which movement actors translate grievances into action, as a major impetus for participation in protest, and as a vehicle for creating and sustaining collective identity (McAdam, McCarthy, and Zald 1996; Benford and Snow 2000; Snow 2004). This symbolic, or "signifying," work is an important tool not only for recruiting participants during the early life of a movement but also for maintaining membership and morale and communicating with other targets, such as the media, the state, and movement opponents, in order to achieve both political and cultural outcomes (Cress and Snow 2000; McAdam, McCarthy, and Zald 1996; McCammon 2001).

Some of the research in this cultural vein fundamentally challenged structural approaches (e.g., Jasper 1997), but other culturally focused research developed in tandem with structurally centered explanations of collective action rather than seeking to overhaul them. However, the dominance of political process approaches to the study of social movements has been increasingly criticized in recent years by scholars calling for more nuanced, dynamic approaches that make central the agency and strategic choices of movement actors (Goodwin and Jasper 2004; Jasper 2004). While scholars continue to debate the relative importance of contextual conditions and agency in determining movement trajectories and outcomes, other criticisms have also been raised about the relationships between researchers and activists. Cox and Fominaya argue that

> Contemporary social movement studies as it now exists, institutionalized as an increasingly canonized body of knowledge within North American and West European academia, has become increasingly distant from any

relationship to movements other than the descriptive and analytic—despite the fact that a number of its most significant authors started from positions sympathetic to social movements, if not actually within them. (2009, 6)

A lack of strong, equitable connections between researchers and the movements they study poses a particular obstacle to the political usefulness of social movement theory as a whole. I explore this issue in greater detail in a later section but turn first to a brief review of CBSM scholarship examining human rights activism.

Human Rights Movements: Findings from the CBSM Field

Although rights claims are invoked in local, national, and transnational struggles, a substantial portion of social movement theory has been generated through examinations of US-based movements, which tend to use human rights frameworks less frequently than others. But explosive growth in human rights activism, much of it outside the United States, over the past two decades has encouraged movement scholars to turn their attention to various dynamics of transnational human rights organizing (Bandy and Smith 2005; Bob 2005, 2009; Della Porta et al. 2006; Ferree and Tripp 2006; Keck and Sikkink 1998; Risse, Ropp, and Sikkink 1999; Smith, Pagnucco, and López 1998; Tarrow 2005). The rise of transnational advocacy networks (TANs) has been an especially influential topic of study in the field. Keck and Sikkink write, "What is novel in these networks is the ability of nontraditional international actors to mobilize information strategically to help create new issues and categories and to persuade, pressure, and gain leverage over much more powerful organizations and governments" (1998, 2). On human rights issues, in particular, TANs have been successful in transforming global norms through the use of information politics, symbolic politics, leverage politics, and accountability politics.

While some refer to a "human rights movement," one is hard-pressed to discern where the human rights movement ends and the global justice movement begins. In a political era characterized by global network relationships, overlapping issues, and a commonly shared diagnosis of neoliberalism, many movements consider themselves part of a broader human rights movement. Many transnational organizations have also moved away from single-issue foci toward multi-issue agendas that encompass and even emphasize economic rights (Smith 2004). This is made possible in part by the inclusive, indivisible notion of human rights that has gained steam since the early 1990s. Feminist activists in particular have pushed for inclusive and interdependent notions of human rights that go beyond civil and political rights to account for economic, social, and cultural rights violations, as well as those that occur in the private sphere (Ackerly 2008; Ackerly and D'Costa 2005; Bunch 1990).

The language of human rights has long been embraced by the United Nations, as evidenced by numerous key documents, such as the Universal Declaration of

Human Rights, the Convention on the Rights of the Child, the Vienna Declaration, the Beijing Platform for Action, and the Millennium Development Goals. Thanks in large part to the efforts of activists, many governments have joined the United Nations in its promotion of a human rights framework, helping these discourses gain greater traction transnationally. Human rights ideas have thus become part of the "dominant symbolic repertoire" (Woehrle, Coy, and Maney 2008), which has enabled not only transnational but also local movements working on a range of issues (e.g., violence, environment, labor, peace, sexuality) to harness and adapt the human rights discourse to further their goals (Ackerly and D'Costa 2005; Levitt and Merry 2009).

The global justice movement represents one of the most active and fruitful areas of scholarship addressing human rights and social movements (Blau and Karides 2008; Cox and Nilsen 2007; Della Porta et al. 2006; Juris 2008; Smith 2008; Smith et al. 2008). Local, regional, national, and transnational movement organizations have articulated a shared set of grievances identifying ubiquitous neoliberal values and policies as the common target (Blau and Karides 2008; Naples and Desai 2002; Tazreiter 2010). Many of these organizations have also adopted master frames of human rights and democracy as alternatives to the existing neoliberal order. In 2001, the World Social Forum (WSF) emerged under the banner "Another World Is Possible" as a site for shared resistance to neoliberalism. The WSF and the ongoing social forum process more generally have spawned a proliferation of new research among scholars in many disciplines and parts of the world.

Jackie Smith, along with multiple colleagues, has been at the forefront of documenting the emergence and trajectories of transnational organizations and of the global justice movement (Bandy and Smith 2005; Smith 2008; Smith and Johnston 2002). Smith (2008) provides one of the most comprehensive examinations to date of the global justice movement. Her analysis illuminates the complex relationships between rival networks of neoliberal actors (e.g., corporations, the commercial media, the International Monetary Fund) and the activist globalizers from below who seek to prioritize democracy and human rights over profit.

The global women's movement may be the single best contemporary illustration of activists working for the advancement of human rights while simultaneously transforming understandings of them (Antrobus 2004; Ferree and Tripp 2006; Friedman 2003; Keck and Sikkink 1998; Naples and Desai 2002; Moghadam 2005; Peters and Wolper 1995). Feminists and women's rights activists have continuously pushed for a human rights perspective that transcends multiple issues and identities. Utilizing opportunities such as the UN conferences of the early 1990s and the social forums since 2001, women's and feminist activists built alliances with other movements and insisted that no rights are secure unless all rights are secure. They rejected a silo model of human rights and encouraged other movements to do the same, with considerable success.

While the scholarship mentioned above represents a growing and dynamic body of work, the intersection of social movements and human rights is, on the whole, surprisingly understudied. In a somewhat rare endeavor that explicitly examines the relationship between social movements and human rights, political scientist Neil Stammers (1999, 2009) makes a compelling, historically informed case that social movements have always been key players in shaping social values. Drawing on the work of Melucci (1989), Stammers (1999, 987–988) emphasizes the dual instrumental and expressive dimensions of social movements, arguing that the role movement actors play in constructing and reconstructing human rights is no less important than their role in actually securing those rights. Moreover, Stammers reminds us that expansive human rights claims that move beyond civil and political rights to encompass economic and social rights are not new but rather emerged in the context of eighteenth-century workers' struggles. Finally, he considers the relatively recent movements against corporate-led globalization to hold tremendous potential for advancing human rights.

Methods in CBSM Scholarship

Methods of data collection and analysis in social movement scholarship run the gamut. CBSM researchers have used participant observation and in-depth interviews with activists, protest-event analysis, case studies, discourse and frame analysis, comparative historical designs, statistical analysis of survey data, and mathematical simulations to investigate the dynamics of collective action (Klandermans and Staggenborg 2002). The Yearbook of International Organizations has been a popular source of data for scholars using quantitative methods to study human rights and other transnational movement organizations (Smith, Pagnucco, and López 1998). Recently, Internet technology has enabled scholars to examine movement identity and framing more systematically through information available on organizational websites (Ferree and Pudrovska 2006; Hewitt 2009). Network analysis has also been used to map connections among different organizations and sectors affiliated with the broader global justice movement (Chase-Dunn et al. 2007).

The methodological diversity in the study of social movements is widely viewed as a great strength. In their edited volume *Methods of Social Movement Research*, Klandermans and Staggenborg (2002) note that movement scholars have always been quick to assess and revise theoretical developments through rigorous empirical study, and the use of and respect for multiple methodological approaches has been a driving force behind the tremendous growth and advancement in the field.

The Utility of Social Movement Thinking for the Human Rights Paradigm

Because social movements play such a critical role in constructing human rights and achieving them, researchers in the CBSM field have much to offer. Flacks argues that social movement research is "essential for those engaged in social struggle, helping to provide them with the theoretical and practical knowledge needed for effective action" (2005, 4). Perhaps most importantly, movement researchers can help document the theoretical insights of activists and bring them to bear on public thinking and conversations about human rights. That movements generate theory is widely recognized but not sufficiently discussed in academic circles. CBSM scholars can and should capture this theorizing, with proper attribution and respect. Baxi (2002) has argued that social movements of oppressed peoples have long been the unrecognized intellectual engines of human rights thinking. Feminist political theorist Brooke Ackerly (2008) highlights the important contributions of women's human rights activists in developing a theory of human rights that is universal without being universalizing.

The idea of universal human rights is often pitted against cultural relativism, but feminist activists have repeatedly insisted that cultural sensitivity and respect for human rights can coexist. Transnational women's movements have been especially successful at building human rights coalitions and infusing human rights language into international institutions (Desai 2002; Friedman 2003; Moghadam 2005; Ferree and Tripp 2006; Joachim 2003). Perhaps more than any other movement, they have been forced to confront tensions between universalist and relativist approaches to human rights and have modeled ways of building solidarities across differences of class, race, culture, religion, and sexuality (Desai 2005). The theoretical lessons emerging from women's human rights struggles and documented by movement scholars continue to be influential in critiquing and shaping the human rights paradigm.

In addition to illuminating the theoretical insights of activists, movement scholars can also document the challenges and successes of activists, making visible patterns of strategic efficacy for human rights movements. Organizations working for human rights face a multitude of obstacles and threats. Most are eager to learn from the strategies and experiences of other organizations, but some have limited opportunity to interact. This is particularly true for under-resourced groups that do not have regular access to Internet communication. CBSM scholars may be able to increase the strategic capacity of social movement organizations by synthesizing and sharing insights based on their research.

The social movements literature helps us remain attentive to the multiple stakeholders constituting the landscape of rights struggles and to the varying organizational, political, and cultural contexts in which they do their work. Researchers are thus well situated to integrate the theoretical and strategic lessons of multiple movements. From a more aerial view, they can identify potential allies and facilitate connections. Furthermore, they may be able to assist movement actors in making their cases to donors and grant makers, a vitally important task in this era of shrinking funding for many social-change efforts.

In short, social movement theory and research can be useful to human rights activism. While the potential exists, utility has been limited thus far and will continue to be limited without heightened attention to relevance. The onus is on scholars to demonstrate the added value of academic research to movement actors working for human rights advancement.

CBSM Scholarship Informed by a Human Rights Paradigm

A human rights lens would surely compel us to ask different research questions, but more importantly it would lead us to develop our questions and methods differently, often in collaboration with movement actors. If we believe in human dignity for all, and if we attend to activists' theorizing around the indivisibility of human rights, what are our responsibilities as scholars? Considering this question and its implications may require both an epistemological and a methodological shift. Where do our questions come from? How do we study them? How do we develop and use concepts? Where and how do we disseminate our work?

I want to suggest that CBSM scholarship is a natural site in the academy for supporting human rights struggles; however, taking seriously a human rights approach to CBSM scholarship makes the calls for movement-relevant scholarship all the more urgent (Flacks 2004, 2005; Bevington and Dixon 2005). While CBSM scholars engaging in praxis-oriented research have been grappling with these issues for some time (e.g., Croteau, Hoynes, and Ryan 2005), they have not been at the forefront of the field. Recent developments are promising, though, and indicate that movement scholars may be returning in earnest to their more grounded beginnings. At the recent CBSM workshop held just before the 2011 American Sociological Association meetings in Las Vegas, producing useable knowledge was a key organizing theme. In the opening plenary of that workshop, Maney (2011) argued for movement-based research that entails collective critical inquiry, sustained relationships with activists, and respect for multiple forms of knowledge. He asserted that movement-based research is equally rigorous as, if not more so than, traditional approaches and presented clear examples from collaborative projects, several of which dealt directly with protecting human rights. While Maney's model implies study of and with contemporary movements, much as Bevington and Dixon's (2005) framework calls for "direct engagement," scholars investigating historical movements can also elucidate movement-relevant knowledge. McCammon et al.'s (2008, 2012) work on strategic adaptation among advocates for US women's jury rights in the twentieth century reveals how specific strategic practices on the part of movement organizations influence the pace of outcome achievement. Given that a key goal of any movement is to achieve one or more favorable outcomes, and in the case of human rights movements to ensure that all people can exercise the full range of human rights, strategic insights may be particularly important.

Doing movement research from a human rights perspective also requires us to think more carefully about dissemination. In order for knowledge to be accessible to all stakeholders for consumption and critique, movement scholars need to think outside the boundaries of traditional academic publishing. As I have argued elsewhere (Hewitt 2008), we should share our work at earlier stages, solicit feedback from activists, and create more spaces for open dialogue. Human rights activists have demonstrated effective, democratic models of sharing knowledge for years, and scholars could learn from their examples. *Interface: A Journal for and about Social Movements*, a peer-reviewed periodical that published its first issue in

2009, is devoted explicitly to promoting dialogue between movement researchers and practitioners.

The Road Ahead

Cassie Schwerner writes, "If movement scholars wish to continue theorizing about social movements in the manner in which we have done for the past forty years, that is clearly a personal choice. These scholars, however, must recognize that their work is not being used by activists who need their insights the most" (2005, 171). Most CBSM scholars have an interest in producing useable knowledge, which means that some reflection is in order. As CBSM scholars set future agendas, they would do well to attend carefully to the intellectual, political, and moral dimensions of movement studies and to make the methodological adjustments required to do so. Specifically, CBSM scholars should deepen their commitment to ethical relationships with movement actors and make a more concerted effort to include actors not only in data collection but also in other research stages such as question formation and data analysis.

The most critical questions in the years to come will likely focus on movement strategy and outcomes. And if recent events are any indication, CBSM researchers will have no shortage of new research questions and empirical material to engage. In the wake of the Arab Spring and Occupy movements, questions about repressive states, police aggression, and Internet communication have moved front and center. Protesters have forcefully articulated the inextricability of political, civil, economic, and social rights and demanded the public's and the media's attention. Furthermore, scholars have only just begun to examine the newly significant role of e-mail campaigns and social media in facilitating information exchange and propelling protest (Earl and Kimport 2011). In this era of rapid technological and political change, movement scholars have their work cut out for them.

Chapter Six

Alcohol, Drugs, and Tobacco

Jennifer Bronson

Through time and space, alcohol, drugs, and tobacco have been, and continue to be, a feature of social and cultural life. Today, substance use is less likely to have ceremonial or ritual purposes and more likely to manifest through a complex intersection of social fragmentation, poverty, alienation, anomie, and urbanization inherent in modern life (UNODC 1997). Historical shifts have also occurred in the realms of drug control and regulation, with the dominant players in this changing construction of drugs coming from a place of privilege. Global economic, political, and social forces create and perpetuate human rights violations at the individual and community levels around the world. The United States is a key player in the current state of alcohol-, drug-, and tobacco-related issues, both as the highest consumer of illicit drugs in the world and as a leader in shaping international drug policy regarding legal sanctions (Oppenheimer 1991).

Whether legal or illegal, drugs are inherently shaped by social context. By locating alcohol, drugs, and tobacco within their sociocultural context, sociology provides an important foundation for understanding patterns of use, media and advertising influences, and social-control mechanisms. Despite invaluable contributions made by sociologists to drug-related research, it is not a principal topic within the discipline (Blum 1984). In addition, a definition of sociological alcohol, drug, and tobacco research does not exist (Bucholz and Robins 1989), which results in the absence of a coherent position within the discipline (Zajdow 2005). The complex, multifaceted nature of drugs, alcohol, and tobacco necessitates transversal research; therefore, fields such as public health, medicine, psychology, economics, criminology and criminal justice, anthropology, international studies, and policy studies crosscut research and analysis of drugs, alcohol, and tobacco (Bucholz and Robins 1989; Husak 2003; Peretti-Watel 2003).

In order to unite the different disciplines and address drug-related problems worldwide, we should place human rights at the center of a discussion on alcohol, drugs, and tobacco. A human rights perspective provides an organizing set of principles to guide, direct, and maintain the universal freedoms of individuals that instill equality, as well as accomplishes public health and public security aims. Human rights documents, such as the Universal Declaration of Human Rights, outline the broad responsibilities of the state to respect, protect, and fulfill the complete range of interdependent, inalienable, and indivisible rights belonging to all persons (UNODC 2010). Yet many states fail to extend these concepts to drug-related matters. A human rights lens enables us to examine macro-level violations created through the transnational production and consumption of drugs, as well as to preserve not only the rights of substance users and those convicted of criminal offenses, but also individuals' abilities to seek appropriate treatment with dignity.

Historical Shifts: Defining and Regulating Drugs

Variations exist between sociocultural groups and nations with regard to their attitudes toward and the acceptability of drug use and production. Neilson and Bamyeh note that, historically, most drugs were governed by some sort of social-control mechanisms geared "towards aims that served, protected or enhanced the customary order" (2009, 4). For example, tobacco was most often used by Native American cultures for religious purposes (Courtwright 2001), and in Morocco only elderly members of society could smoke hashish (Neilson and Bamyeh 2009). These mechanisms serve to proscribe social norms surrounding drug substances, which separates them from today's rigid sanctions and arbitrary prohibition policies.

The rise of capitalism contributed to the development of the plantation-based slave economy in the Americas (Moulier Boutang 1998) and helped define the acceptability of some "drugs" over others. Plantations based on production of sugar cane for rum, tobacco, and coffee beans dominated the economies of the Caribbean and the American South for centuries and shaped other economies as well, while perpetrating one of the largest cases of human rights violations in world history. In addition, capitalism was a central factor in the determination of the legality and acceptability of particular drugs. Those labeled licit were substances "more compatible with the emergent capitalist order" (Courtwright 2001, 59). Stimulants such as tobacco and coffee became subsumed by capitalism because they were easy to grow, transport, and distribute (Courtwright 2001). The production and sale of tobacco, alcohol, and coffee generated vast profits for capitalists while offering escapism and relief for the laboring masses.

During the early twentieth century, a coalition of political, religious, moral, and medical forces united to ban alcohol in the United States. This was accompanied by an overall reframing of "illicit drugs" that was codified into law (Husak 2003). Political power and money were the largest influences in dichotomizing drugs into legal or illicit designations, and Courtwright (2001) posits that the use of tobacco and alcohol by elites is likely the reason for selective prohibition. This selective regulation does not correspond to the degree to which actual harm is inflicted by a particular substance (Husak 2003; Courtwright 2001). For example, tobacco and alcohol are the first and third most common causes, respectively, of preventable death in the United States (CDC 2011). This contrasts starkly with the zero deaths attributed to marijuana use, which is illegal.

QUESTIONS SOCIOLOGISTS ASK AND WHAT THEY FIND

WHO USES ILLEGAL DRUGS? PATTERNS OF USE

Research on patterns of tobacco, alcohol, and illicit drug use based on any number of organizing variables dominates sociological literature. While by no means constituting a comprehensive list of the breadth and scope of the research, past and present studies examine alcohol, drug, and tobacco use and the following: age (Peretti-Watel 2003; Filmore 1987a), sex (Peretti-Watel 2003; Wilsnack and Cheloha 1987; Filmore 1987b; Sobell et al. 1986; Hoffmann 2006), type of school (Peretti-Watel 2003; Hoffmann 2006), religiosity (Wallace et al. 2007; Shields et al. 2007; Gillum 2005), race and ethnicity (Kitano 1988; Caetano 1984b; Weibgel-Orlando 1989; Herd 1988), degree of assimilation (Caetano 1987), and self-esteem (Peretti-Watel 2003). The role of the media and advertising (Kohn and Smart 1984; Sobell et al. 1986; Atkin et al. 1983; Strickland 1983; Lindsay 2009), as well as the social construction of space for purposes of engaging in drug-related activities, is also discussed in the literature.

Of particular interest to a human rights perspective on alcohol, drugs, and tobacco are discriminations related to one's race or ethnicity. According to some sociologists, the significance of race in the United States influences cultural and political processes, resulting in the definition of certain drugs and behaviors in racialized terms (Brubaker, Lovemen, and Stamatov 2004; Hall et al. 1978). Although blacks have lower rates of alcohol and drug consumption, they suffer from stiffer social consequences than their white counterparts due to the erroneous belief that blacks are the primary users and sellers of illicit drugs. This belief is evident in a 1986 federal law that created sentencing disparities for possession of crack cocaine and powdered cocaine, with the former used more by blacks. Under this law possession of five grams of crack cocaine warranted a five-year sentence, whereas an offender would have to be holding five hundred grams of powdered cocaine to receive the same punishment (Duster 1997; Tonry 1995). This law was overturned in 2010, but a sentencing disparity of eighteen to one still remains (ACLU 2010).

A discussion of racial injustice in the United States is incomplete without a class analysis. Research shows that harmful drug use is disproportionately concentrated in poor communities of color (Beckett et al. 2005), stemming from systemic social and economic inequality (Baumer 1994; Currie 1994; Duster 1997; Hagan 1994). High rates of addiction are often correlated with a lack of opportunities, high unemployment or underemployment, low-paying jobs, overwork, stress, and poor health (Beckett et al. 2005).

Defining Abuse and Addiction: Is a Medical Model Correct?

An area of debate in sociological research on alcohol, drugs, and tobacco concerns whether substance addiction is a medical disorder or a behavioral or moral problem. This is an important question, and one unresolved by the field, because whether addiction is viewed as a disease or a failure of personal character is reflected in society's responses to alcoholism. Sociologists Conrad and Schneider theorize that deviance, such as drug and alcohol addiction, has become medicalized and argue that "medicalization of deviance changes the social response to such behavior to one of treatment rather than punishment" (1992, 28). Thus, a medical model of deviance demands a corresponding medical intervention by trained professionals to treat or cure the illness (Conrad and Schneider 1992). Others are weary of applying a medical model to addiction. These critics believe that although a moral-defect approach is significantly flawed, a medical approach is too limiting to represent the full spectrum of addiction experiences and consequences (Valliant 1983; Leigh and Gerrish 1986). As patterns of experimentation, use, and addiction vary across social and economic classes, with the greatest consequences disproportionally experienced by the poor and people of color, a disease model cannot explain these variations or rationalize the prohibition of some drugs over others (Husak 2003).

Common Tools and Methods

Sociology has a rich history of qualitative studies of drug and alcohol users. Examples include studies of cannabis users (Becker 1963), Alcoholics Anonymous (Denzin 1997), homeless heroin and crack addicts (Bourgois and Schonberg 2009), and teenage drug users (Dixon and Maher 2002). These participant observation and ethnographic studies connect seemingly insignificant elements of life to larger social processes (Zajdow and Lindsay 2010), provide insight into people's motives for substance use, and uncover the learned behaviors related to drug use (Hughes 2003).

There is a preference toward quantitative data in sociology. In quantitative studies on alcohol, drugs, and tobacco topics, sociologists often utilize cross-disciplinary instruments and surveys (Bucholz and Robins 1989). For example, the Federal Bureau of Investigation's Uniform Crime Reports compile police-department incident reports with data on race, crime of arrest, and drug involved in drug arrests (Beckett et al. 2005). Quantitative research on alcohol, drugs, and tobacco is not without its problems, regardless of an abundance of available statistical instruments and survey data (Peretti-Watel 2003). Statistical data simply do not provide a full picture of a person's experiences, motives, and feelings surrounding drug use. It also removes the individual from the larger sociocultural context of drugs and the transnational drug circuit. Additionally, this type of data may be flawed, as social desirability can bias the accuracy of self-reported usage (Gillum 2005), or indicators may not be correctly operationalized.

A mixed-method approach may be best suited to understanding the individual, local, national, and international dimensions of drug-related social problems and human rights violations.

Filling in the Gaps with a Human Rights Paradigm

Although sociology has contributed to research on drugs, it offers few answers (Bucholz and Robins 1989) and remains underdeveloped (Bucholz and Robins 1989; Zajdow 2005). Sociology could better address macro-level dynamics such as the role of economic forces in shaping transnational alcohol, drug, and tobacco demand and production patterns, the effects of drug trafficking on citizens and communities, and the influence of the capitalist political-economic system on drug-related policies. Despite applicable globalization and commodities theories, such as Wallerstein's (1983) world-systems theory, sociologists seem hesitant to analyze alcohol, drugs, and tobacco and the individual user in the context of an interconnected global market. A discussion of drugs should not omit "the larger and connected realms of cross-border politics, economics, and culture" (Neilson and Bamyeh 2009, 5).

A human rights perspective can enhance the sociological literature by connecting patterns of individual-level actions to global forces and help to evaluate the impact of alcohol, drugs, and tobacco on human dignity, freedoms, and equality. This framework highlights the flaws in the dominant legal-sanctions model that perpetuates human rights abuses and excludes those persons most in need of treatment and rehabilitation (UNODC 2010). Additionally, given the well-documented connection between poverty and increased participation in all levels of drug-related activities, it is likely that rising economic inequality will increase the current global drug cycle (Neilson and Bamyeh 2009). The United Nations General Assembly states that the world drug problem is best addressed in principles of universal human rights and fundamental freedoms (UNODC 2010).

Human Rights Violations: Unjust Due Process, Sentencing, and Legal Enforcement

According to the United Nations Office on Drugs and Crime (UNODC), effective drug control cannot exist without fair criminal justice and successful crime prevention. While formal sanctions and policies concerning drug-related activities can easily be instituted in a manner that is not damaging to human rights, often they are not. Nations vary in the severity of punishments for drug-related activity as well as in the number and types of crimes deemed illegal. From a human rights perspective, the most extreme and unacceptable is the utilization of the death penalty for drug-related offenses, as practiced by China (UNODC 2010). In other countries, such as the United States, human rights violations can manifest through the creation, implementation, and enforcement of racially biased or classist laws (HRW 2000).

The United States has been a leader in advocating and promulgating rigid legal sanctions for a host of minor and substantial drug-related offenses. Since President Richard Nixon first declared the "war on drugs" in the 1970s, drug-related human rights violations have increased domestically and internationally. The strict legislation and enhanced law enforcement that followed led to an astronomical number of people arrested and convicted for drug-related offenses. This spike in incarceration is widely documented as affecting African Americans disproportionately (McWhorter 2011; HRW 2000; SAMHSA 2010). A 2000 report by Human Rights Watch estimated that blacks comprised 62.7 percent and whites 36.7 percent of all drug offenders in prison, despite the fact that five times more whites use drugs than blacks (HRW 2000). According to a recent Bureau of Justice Statistics report, the arrest rate in 2009 for African Americans was three times that of whites for drug possession and four times that of whites for drug sale or manufacture (Snyder 2011). Human dignity cannot be delinked from the principle of nondiscrimination, and current US efforts are clearly biased against nonwhites. To be effective, criminal-justice processes must ensure that law-enforcement activities are evidence based and not carried out solely on the grounds of racial or class bias (UNODC 2010).

Less widely known is that the "war on drugs" produced a "war" on the rights to education, social security, and housing. Policies enacted in the 1990s resulted in the denial of high school education or college opportunities to tens of thousands of American students (Blumenson and Nilsen 2002). Due to federal zero-tolerance policies for drugs, 80 percent of students charged with drug or alcohol infractions were suspended or expelled from school in 2001 (CASA 2001), with African Americans being the most likely to be expelled or suspended. In 1998, black students comprised 17 percent of the American public-school student body but accounted for 33 percent of zero-tolerance suspensions or expulsions (CASA 2001). Poor or low-income students are doubly penalized in that they cannot afford private school.

Further representing an attack on the right to education is the US Drug-Free Student Loan Act of 1998, which can deny federal college loans and grants to students convicted of a misdemeanor or felony controlled-substances offense (Blumenson and Nilsen 2002; GAO 2005). It is estimated that during the 2003–2004 academic year alone, this act resulted in the disqualification of about forty-one thousand applicants for postsecondary education loans and grants (GAO 2005).

As regards rights to social security and an adequate standard of living, dignity, and affordable housing, under the Personal Responsibility and Work Opportunity Reconciliation Act of 1996, offenders convicted of a felony drug offense can be denied receipt of Temporary Assistance to Needy Families (TANF) and food stamps. Federal law mandates a lifetime ban on receiving these benefits, unless the stricture is modified by state law. In 2005, eighteen states had fully implemented the TANF ban (GAO 2005). It has been estimated that approximately 5 percent of public-housing applicants are disqualified because of a drug-related offense (GAO 2005).

The US Government Accountability Office report titled *Denial of Federal Benefits* explicitly states that these policies only affect those drug offenders who would otherwise meet the eligibility requirements for federal benefits, representing clear discrimination against poor and low-income individuals. In some cases, drug offenders can be exempt from these bans in federal service if they undergo rehabilitation or treatment services. However, this provision is biased against low-income persons—the very group most in need of student loans and college opportunities—who may not be able to afford the cost of treatment, transportation costs, or the lost wages from attending classes (Blumenson and Nilsen 2002).

Human Rights Violations: International Implications of US Policy

While the United States is the largest consumer of illicit drugs, the vast majority of drug production occurs in other countries. Therefore, US drug policy extends around the world to reduce and contain the supply of drugs entering the country. Targeted governments, particularly those in the Andean region of South America, argue that military-like policies are misdirected, and efforts should focus on the social and economic structural roots of the problem. Furthermore, while widespread impoverishment and the need to make an income spur many to become involved in drug production and trafficking, these activities exist largely to satisfy the large American market (Youngers and Rosin 2005).

An example of human rights violations produced through US drug-control strategies can be observed in Colombia. Because 90 percent of the cocaine in the United States originates in that country, aerial fumigation of coca fields emerged as a central strategy in the early 1980s and intensified under Plan Colombia. It is estimated that between 2000 and 2003, fumigation efforts destroyed coca on 380,000 hectares, or approximately 8 percent of Colombia's arable land (Lemus, Stanton, and Walsh 2005). Fumigation not only destroyed the environment but ruined the only economic option for peasants who grew coca. Between 2001 and 2003, more than seventy-five thousand Columbians were displaced due to crop fumigation, food scarcity, and, according to reports, painful skin, respiratory, and other ailments (Lemus, Stanton, and Walsh 2005).

A latent effect of efforts to reduce cocaine production and trafficking in Colombia has been the rise of Mexican drug cartels to take their place. The Department of Justice (2010) estimates that Mexican drug cartels directly control illegal drug markets in at least 230 American cities. Violence in Mexico has sharply escalated, largely due to the increase in drug-production and -trafficking activities. Since 2006, more than thirty-five thousand people have been killed in drug-related violence in Mexico (*Los Angeles Times* 2011). This does not include the countless others who have been kidnapped or tortured. Much of this violence initially took place between rival drug cartels, but now it is not unusual for civilians, police officials, activists, and family members of cartel members also to fall victim.

As a last example, the United States' labeling of drug traffickers as terrorists and cartels as terrorist organizations violates rules of war and human rights.

This policy effectively renders nonmilitary persons objects for "justified" military intervention, despite international rhetoric condemning this position (Gallahue 2010). Although monies from drug production and distribution can and do benefit insurgent movements, this is not an activity that costs civilians their protected status and invalidates their placement on a "kill list." Drug trafficking is not synonymous with combat, and therefore such acts cannot be equated with direct military or combat participation (US 111th Cong. 2009). Yet, in 2009, the US Pentagon announced that fifty Afghan drug traffickers were now listed as people "to be killed or captured" (US 111th Cong. 2009).

Human Rights Violations Related to Developing Nations and Market Exploitation

The exploitation of land, labor, and people inherent in capitalism continues to shape alcohol, drug, and tobacco markets. The United States is a driving force behind consumer culture, including sale of alcohol and tobacco. These industries increasingly target developing nations as new markets. As such, we are seeing a global rise in alcohol and tobacco use, along with its individual and social consequences (Sengupta 2003). However, we fail to see a corresponding increase in the export of either accessible, affordable, and dignified treatment options for individuals who become addicted or just legislation related to illicit drugs. Perhaps this is because treatment is underemphasized in America, with approximately 10 percent of those who need treatment actually receiving it (SAMHSA 2010).

As the antismoking campaign gained momentum in the United States, multinational tobacco companies turned to undeveloped markets in impoverished countries. Although persons of consenting age are permitted to smoke cigarettes, the issue here is whether individuals in these nations are sufficiently aware of smoking's health consequences. Not only did marketing efforts entice people to smoke, but pro-tobacco policies extended to agriculture as well. To encourage peasant farmers in these nations to grow tobacco, tobacco corporations, the World Bank, and the UN Food and Agriculture Organization offered loans, extension advice, pesticides, and tobacco seeds (Motley 1987; Muller 1983). One estimate places the value of World Bank loans for tobacco production at $1 billion and rising (Nichter and Cartwright 1991). In most cases, this assistance has eroded traditional economies and endangered the production of food crops in lieu of tobacco's higher profits (Nichter and Cartwright 1991).

The word "drug" signifies both a substance that is illegal and prohibited by formal regulations and a substance to cure illness (Neilson and Bamyeh 2009). Economic forces shape pharmaceutical distribution as well. Pharmaceutical companies generate profit by controlling drug patents and monopolizing knowledge. Research, development, and marketing efforts are not solely driven by illness and disease patterns; rather, they are influenced by the profit motive and who can pay for treatment. Today, pharmaceutical research and development is skewed toward drugs for diseases most prevalent in developed countries, such as cancer, or "lifestyle" drugs, such as Viagra. Research estimates that only 4 percent of pharmaceutical research money goes toward developing new drugs for diseases, such as cholera, prevalent in developing countries. This means that only 10 percent of the $56 billion spent annually on medical research is for ailments that affect 90 percent of the world's population (Sengupta 2003).

The Right to Use Alcohol, Drugs, and Tobacco and to Seek Treatment

The rights of the individual to use alcohol, drugs, or tobacco and to seek accessible, appropriate, and dignified treatment are also important. A caveat is that these rights are compromised when personal agency and informed choice are removed or when crimes are committed due to drug use (UNODC 2010). This is not to say that human rights principles support a general "right to abuse drugs" (UNODC 2010); rather, this position reminds us that personal responsibilities are interrelated with freedoms and rights. For example, the rights of smokers and nonsmokers are debated as smoking in public spaces is banned through national or local legislation around the world. At the center of this issue is informed consent as to the well-documented health risks associated with smoking. One on side, antismoking advocates point to the dangers of secondhand smoke and the inability of nonsmokers, children, and fetuses to give informed consent to smoking (Bailey 2004). However, smokers, tobacco corporations, and pro-tobacco lobbyists insist that adult smokers have the right to smoke and to incur associated risks so long as an "informed consumer risk" policy is in place (Viscusi 1998).

Drug dependency is recognized by virtually all international bodies and national organizations as a medical condition or disorder. From a human rights perspective, the right to health applies equally to drug dependency as it does to any other health condition. Through criminalization efforts to curb drug use, dependent drug users, particularly injecting drug users, suffer not only from the condition itself but also from a lack of effective programs, such as clean-needle and -syringe exchanges, and dignified psychosocial and pharmacological treatment (UNODC 2010; Elliott et al. 2005). These and similar socially responsible programs are fully compatible with international drug-control conventions (UNODC 2010), yet we continue to see a scarcity of such services nationally and globally. Intravenous drug users with HIV/AIDS are particularly vulnerable to human rights infringements (Wodak 1998; Elliot et al. 2005; Oppenheimer 1991), as criminal sanctions against drug use contribute to a lack of services and treatment options for this population. At the other end of the spectrum is the issue of forced or coerced substance-abuse treatment or drug testing. Nonconsensual treatment or testing endangers the right to health, to freedom from inhuman or degrading treatment, and to liberty and security of person, as well as the right not to be subjected to arbitrary or unlawful interference with privacy (UNODC 2010).

Employing a Human Rights Approach to Alcohol, Drugs, and Tobacco

As noted by the UN High Commissioner for Human Rights, drug laws frequently overemphasize criminalization and punishment while underemphasizing treatment and respect for human rights (UNODC 2010). Law-enforcement approaches toward drug policy are costly, ineffective, and often counterproductive to policy aims, yet law enforcement remains the major response toward illicit drugs in the United States and the international community. This trend is especially evident in the United States, where 82 percent of the 1.6 million arrests in 2009 were for drug possession alone (DOJ 2010). Despite high incarceration rates for drug possession, the threat of prison has not deterred Americans from using illicit drugs, which more than 47 percent of persons over the age of twelve admit to having done (SAMHSA 2010). The default position of the criminal-justice system is to punish substance users simply for using or being addicted to an illegal substance (Husak 2003).

As stricter drug possessions laws have not deterred drug use in America and are enacted across color lines, sociologists should reframe their research, applying a harm-reduction approach rather than a criminal-justice approach. In recent years, international and intergovernmental drug-policy reforms have attempted to incorporate protections of human rights for drug users through harm-reduction programs (Elliot et al. 2005). These programs differ from criminal-justice approaches because they work to decrease substance use and abuse in a dignified and just manner, rather than penalizing users and addicts. Informed consent, legalization, and decreased regulation of marijuana and other illicit drugs also fall under harm reduction. Many harm-reduction programs in the United Kingdom, Switzerland, and the Netherlands show evidence of positive outcomes and the protection of human rights.

We must revise legislation on substance addiction and abuse treatment based on current knowledge and human rights awareness. By curbing the demand for illegal drugs, we curb production, trafficking, and deadly violence. This entails the understanding that problems related to drugs and alcohol go beyond dependent individuals. Substance abuse cannot be examined or treated in a vacuum; therefore, prevention efforts should aim to improve human lives and communities, including by providing access to health care, education, and gainful employment (WHO 2001). As views toward addiction and substance abuse vary cross-culturally, the World Health Organization advises treatment programs to consider political feasibility, the capacity of a country or community to treat individuals, public acceptability, and the likelihood of impact (2001).

Lastly, we should invest in people and communities to eliminate poverty, provide fiscal opportunities within the mainstream of socioculturally acceptable limits, promote education, and give people the resources they need to make informed and rational choices to engage in drug-related activities of any sort. The United States can play a role by ending its "war on drugs" and fostering more equitable partnerships with drug-producing and -trafficking nations. To do this effectively, it should shape drug-control policy based on the sociocultural context within which drug production and circulation occur, and local needs and views. If this shift were to occur, poverty elimination and democratic development would become the centerpiece of the US drug policy in Latin America and the Caribbean (Youngers 2005).

Human rights violations related to alcohol, drugs, and tobacco occur on a continuum, but they all prevent individuals from realizing a dignified life in some manner. Drug-related problems are best analyzed within appropriate sociocultural frameworks. Sociology provides direction and methods to examine many of these problems, and its emphasis on the individual can clarify the different variations in drug-related activities across social groups. Further, sociology has shed light on the social inequalities created by unjust drug policies and the effects these laws have on individuals and their communities. This information on patterns of drug use and abuse complements human rights principles. A synthesis of sociology and human rights theory can locate these patterns in a globally situated analysis of the international drug circuit to better pinpoint areas for social change.

Chapter Seven

Rationality and Society

Valeska P. Korff, Mimi Zou, Tom Zwart, and Rafael Wittek

One of the key objectives of the international human rights movement is to institutionalize adherence to human rights principles in societies around the world. Institutionalization refers to a situation in which a set of rules is considered as legitimate, widely accepted, and "infused with value" (Selznick 1957, 17). The key argument we seek to elaborate in this chapter is that rational-choice theory and its core methodological principle, structural individualism, offers a valuable contribution to the human rights paradigm in general and to explaining variations in the institutionalization of human rights in particular. Structural individualism posits that all social phenomena on the macro and meso levels—like the institutionalization of human rights—need to be explained by referring, or descending, to the micro level of individual decisions and behavior. Hence, when explaining the structural conditions under which human rights become institutionalized in a society, we need to understand the decision-making and behavior of the involved actors.

While challenging the macro-level focus of human rights discourse, this proposition in fact is linked to a seminal development in legal conception: the emergence of the field of international criminal law. International criminal law and international human rights law are interlinked in many ways (De Than and Shorts 2003), whereby the former can basically be regarded as an individual-centered subcategory of the latter. Presupposing the responsibility of individual offenders for human rights violations, international criminal law departs from the main focus of international law on obligations of states. With the implementation of the Rome Statute and the establishment of the International Criminal Court (ICC), the individual has taken center stage in the area of international human rights. As we will elaborate, rational-choice theory provides a framework to accommodate the role of actors relevant in this context: offenders, prosecutors, and judges. By specifying the factors that shape these actors' decisions and behaviors, it allows us to systematize the inquiry into the conditions influencing the protection and promotion of human rights on the state or macro level.

Key Assumptions and Concepts of Rational-Choice Theory

The theoretical tradition generally referred to as rational-choice theory incorporates a multiplicity of theoretical and methodological approaches (for accessible introductions, see, e.g., Elster [1989, 2007] and Little [1991, ch. 3]; for a more comprehensive treatment in sociology and philosophy, see, respectively, Coleman [1990] and Mele and Rawling [2004]). These share the key conviction that all social phenomena need to be explained as the outcomes of individual actions that can in some way be construed as rational (Goldthorpe 2007). Rationality refers to goal-directed behavior: individuals try to realize their preferences by selecting the best action alternative, taking into consideration the opportunities and constraints of the situation in which the decision takes place. This set of core assumptions underlies all rational-choice approaches and allows for theory building and formal modeling. While the respective interpretations of these core assumptions vary substantially between rational-choice approaches, all of them share the conviction that rationality, preferences, and individualism are crucial categories needed to explain human behavior and societal development.

Rationality assumptions refer to the extent to which an individual's decisions meet a set of internal consistency conditions (Bhattacharyya, Pattanaik, and Xu 2011). Individual rationality is shaped by an actor's perception of existing decision alternatives. This perception is in turn influenced by an actor's beliefs and the available information allowing for the evaluation of decision alternatives and their probable outcomes. Rational action is always based on the available information and beliefs, which together generate means-end frames (Simon 1957).

Preference assumptions refer to the extent to which individual decision-makers are selfish egoists striving to maximize material gain. Preference assumptions within the rational-choice paradigm range from "self-seeking with guile" to "linked-utility" assumptions in which individuals derive utility from solidarity acts toward others, without direct personal and material benefit for themselves.

Individualism is a methodological principle holding that any societal phenomena at the macro level can only be explained in a satisfactory way if the preferences, constraints, and behaviors of the involved individuals have been explicated. Thus, while the theoretical primacy (that is, the phenomenon to be explained) is situated at the macro level, the analytical primacy (that is, the social mechanisms leading to the behavior of individual actors) is located at the micro level of individual choices. While all rational-choice theory approaches uphold some individualism assumption, these can differ in the degree to which macro- and meso-level conditions, such as institutions or social structures, are incorporated into the explanation. Most sociological perspectives consider individual decision-makers as embedded in social contexts and influenced by institutions in their preferences and rationality (Udehn 2001). Consequently, a sociological rational-choice explanation needs to specify three steps: first, a macro-micro step, or *situational mechanism*, explicating how the social situation at the macro level affects the preferences and constraints of individual actors; second, a micro-micro step, or *action-generating mechanism*, specifying intra-individual decision-making processes

Figure 7.1 Mechanisms linking macro-level phenomena and micro-level behavior

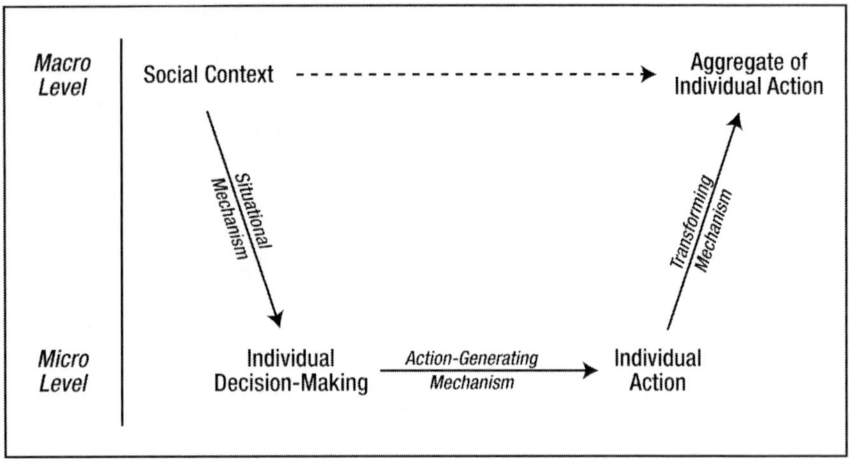

```
Macro    Social Context  - - - - - - - - - - - - - ->  Aggregate of
Level                                                   Individual Action
              \                                      ↑
               \ Situational                        / Transforming
                \ Mechanism                        /  Mechanism
                 ↓                                /
Micro         Individual      Action-Generating   Individual
Level        Decision-Making    Mechanism     →    Action
```

and the resulting action; and third, a micro-macro step, or transformation mechanism, to explain the aggregation of individual action on the macro level (Hedström and Swedberg 1998). The relation between macro-level factors, individual perception and behavior, and macro-level outcomes is illustrated in Figure 7.1.

Flexibility in the interpretation of core assumptions makes rational-choice theory a broad and highly diverse theoretical paradigm integrating such distinct approaches as neoclassical economics and social-rationality conceptualizations (Lindenberg 2006a, 2006b; Macy and Flache 1995). Variation, however, is not limited to theoretical reasoning. In terms of empirical application, rational-choice models have been used to examine systematically a broad variety of social phenomena pertaining to basically all areas of human behavior and interaction. These studies make use of all methods commonly applied in the social sciences, including quantitative survey studies, psychological experiments, qualitative interviews, text analyses, ethnographic observations, and computer-assisted simulations. Irrespective of the chosen method, the focus of all rational-choice research is on individual behavior as the primary explanans of macro-level phenomena. Applying a rational-choice perspective to the study of the institutionalization of human rights accordingly implies a departure from the macro-level perspective common in this field and a new focus on the role of the diverse actors involved in the process.

INTERNATIONAL CRIMINAL LAW

International criminal law is a distinct body of law that comprises both principles of public international law—which human rights law has become part of (Brownlie 2008)—and criminal law. Its relatively recent development over the past fifty years reflects a departure from the "traditional" focus of international law, which only recognized rights and obligations of states and tended to ignore the individual as a subject of law. As an extension of criminal law at the national level, international criminal law regulates and punishes the conduct of individuals rather than states. Many of the crimes now defined by international law are also considered violations of the human rights of individuals (Ratner, Abrams, and Bischoff 2009).

International criminal law encompasses substantive aspects of international law that deal with defining and punishing international crimes and mechanisms and procedures used by states to facilitate international cooperation in investigating and enforcing national criminal law (Brown 2011). The sources of international criminal law are those of international law, which are usually considered to be treaty law, customary international law (a body of peremptory rules of international law, known as *jus cogens*, "the compelling law," from which states may not derogate), and general principles of law recognized by the world's major national legal systems (see Statute of the International Court of Justice, Article 38). It is not always straightforward to determine what constitutes a crime under international law. International treaties rarely explicitly declare something to be an international crime. Broadly speaking, crimes that have risen to the level of international *jus cogens* include aggression, genocide, crimes against humanity, and war crimes (Cassese et al. 2011).

The first international criminal tribunals were set up after World War II, when the Nuremberg and Tokyo International Military Tribunals tried key "war criminals" of the Axis powers for crimes against peace, crimes against humanity, and traditional war crimes. These trials marked the beginning of jurisprudence regarding individual criminal responsibility under international law. The next important step in the process was taken with the setting up of two ad hoc tribunals for the prosecution of crimes committed, respectively, in the former Yugoslavia (ICTY) in 1993 and in Rwanda (ICTR) in 1994. These tribunals represent major progress toward the institution of a kind of permanent jurisdiction (hybrid domestic-international tribunals have been established in Sierra Leone [2000], East Timor [2000], Kosovo [2000], Cambodia [2003], Bosnia [2005], and Lebanon [2007]). A permanent international criminal tribunal was finally established in 2002, when the Rome Statute of the ICC entered into force.

There is growing attention to the relationship between international criminal law and human rights law (Ratner, Abrams, and Bischoff 2009; De Than and Shorts 2003). Some recently adopted provisions of international criminal law appear to be influenced by human rights rules and standards of protection. For example, the Rome Statute refers to concepts such as "personal dignity," prohibition of "humiliating and degrading treatment," "judicial guarantees," and prohibition of group-/collective-based "persecution," discrimination, and apartheid. These concepts have all been established in the main UN instruments for the protection of the rights of the individual.

As a result of the establishment of numerous ad hoc and hybrid tribunals, as well as the permanent ICC, the individual has taken center stage in the area of international human rights.

A Rational-Choice Perspective on the Commitment, Prosecution, and Judgment of International Crimes

The recognition of individual responsibility in the prosecution of human rights violations under international criminal law calls for a better understanding of the motives and behavioral alternatives of the involved actors—offenders as well as prosecutors and judges. Rational-choice theory provides a heuristic suitable for such venture.

As previously described, the basic assumption underlying all rational-choice approaches is the notion that individuals act rationally in pursuit of their goals. Following the fundamental convictions of rational-choice theory, this rationality (that is, the actual decision-making process) is influenced by three factors: the actor's perception of decision alternatives, the preferences of the actor in the sense of the goals strategically pursued, and the constraints and opportunities faced by the actor, which determine behavioral alternatives. Examining the realization of these three dimensions forms the basis for understanding individual rational action. It allows tracing the reasoning that underlies observed behavior. Accordingly, these three dimensions form the core of the rational-choice research framework, which we propose in this chapter. The three dimensions not only directly shape the decision-making process but are also interrelated. Constraints and opportunities in the institutional and social environments influence the perceptions as well as the preferences of an actor. The available information and beliefs about opportunities and constraints shape an actor's evaluation of decision alternatives, which in turn influences preferences. Thus, an analysis of individual rationality implies the consideration of the available information and beliefs, of goals and preferences, and of opportunity/constraint structures simultaneously and in relation to each other.

Explaining Violations of International Criminal Law

Understanding the prevalence of structural human rights violations requires examining the conditions under which individuals violate international criminal law. Accordingly, as a first step we turn our attention to the offenders to inquire about the factors influencing their decisions to act in violation of international criminal law. Applying the above-outlined research framework, we assume that international crimes are a product of rational decision-making, influenced by the perpetrator's goals, perception of decision alternatives, and constraints and opportunities faced.

The case of the strategic use of violence against civilians by the Ugandan Allied Democratic Forces, including killing, looting, and forcible recruitment, constitutes a suitable example to explore this relation. Fundamentally, violence against civilians in civil wars appears irrational as it jeopardizes the loyalty of the very citizens for which both insurgents and incumbents compete. In the case of the Allied Democratic Forces, repeated attacks on villages and refugee camps indeed showed no substantial benefits in a military sense. Hovil and Werker (2005) argue that the violence was a rational tactic that served to maintain the support of external financiers, which included state sponsors such as Zaire and Sudan, as well as radical Islamist groups like al-Qaeda, which had a shared interest in destabilizing the Ugandan government. In a situation of asymmetric information between the insurgents and their financiers, where the latter were, due to being distanced from the actual events, not in a position to judge the reality of the battle, the highly visible atrocities and excessive violence were a credible signal through which the rebels could demonstrate their true commitment to the rebellion. Looking at the three analytical dimensions outlined above, the underlying reasoning becomes comprehensible. A main goal of the Allied Democratic Forces was to secure its survival as an organization. Strong dependence on the resources provided by external financiers posed a major constraint. At the same time, the threat of sanctions for violence against civilians was very limited. Finally, in terms of perception, the asymmetric information structure between Allied Democratic Forces and financiers led the Allied Democratic Forces to consider excessive campaigns against civilians as a necessary signal of commitment to the financier. Under these conditions, the apparently irrational and ineffective strategy of violence against civilians appears in a different light and can be understood as a result of a rational effort to maintain financier support.

Explaining Prosecution Decisions

The second aspect to consider is the prosecution of international crimes. The powers of the prosecutor who acts before the ICC are mainly discretionary. Although the Rome Statute offers some criteria, they are vague enough not to fetter the prosecutor. Accordingly, critical inquiries are needed to understand how the prosecutor's beliefs and goals and the constraint/opportunity structure influence the decision to bring a case before an international tribunal.

The Republic of Uganda submitted the first case to the ICC, which related to the atrocities committed by the Lord's Resistance Army (LRA), a violent rebel group, in the northern part of the country. There are strong indications that President Yoweri Museveni made the referral for strategic reasons (Nouwen and Werner 2010; Branch 2007): unable to beat the LRA, he saw "outsourcing" the fight to the ICC as a viable option. Involvement in an ICC case would delegitimize the LRA, which would diminish its support by external suppliers. Interestingly, the prosecutor accepted the referral in the proposed form. In a statement he declared that even though both sides may have engaged in crimes, those committed by the regular army were not of "sufficient gravity"—which is one of the admissibility criteria in the Rome Statute—while those committed by the LRA were. This meant that only atrocities by the LRA were actually brought before the ICC.

Taking into account the constraint and opportunity structure faced by the prosecutor, this startling decision becomes comprehensible. As a fully equipped court without any live cases, the ICC had increasingly come under criticism. The fundamental goal of the prosecutor under these conditions was the legitimization of the ICC. Prosecuting the LRA, while granting immunity to the regular army, generated a case urgently needed to establish the legitimacy and relevance of the ICC. The prosecutor went to even further lengths to secure this case, thereby effectively limiting his power to discontinue a case and substantially fettering his discretion. While apparently irrational, this approach likely constitutes a structural strategy of depoliticizing through legalizing (Ferguson 1994). Portraying the Office of the Prosecutor as a neutral, expert body that is unwilling to engage in political negotiations, the prosecutor justifies his actions by presenting them as dictated by law and by downplaying the political dimension.

Explaining Tribunal Decisions

The final rationality to examine is that of the court, or, more specifically, the decision-making that informs the ruling of judges. In order to examine the factors influencing such decisions, we draw on Epstein and Knight's (1998) work on the strategic behavior of judges.

This perspective considers judges and courts as strategic actors who make rational decisions in pursuit of a variety of goals. The implementation of his or her own policy preferences may be the goal of the judge, but there are other potential aims as well, such as the desire to reach "principled" decisions based on impartial doctrines, the strengthening of the institutional legitimacy of the court, and using a career on the court as a stepping stone for political office. In addition, the strategic model assumes that judges carefully calculate the consequences of their choices. It postulates that judges are strategic actors who realize that their ability to achieve their goals depends on a consideration not only of the preferences of others, such as their colleagues on the bench, the political branches, and the public at large, but of the choices they expect others to make. Judges will also take into consideration the institutional context within which they act, for instance, the concept of stare decisis, which can constrain them from acting on their individual policy preferences. Epstein and Knight's (1998) assumptions concerning the factors influencing judges' rulings correspond closely to our previously outlined research framework. A judge's ruling is shaped by his or her goals as well as by his or her general perception of decision alternatives and potential outcomes, given existing constraints and opportunities.

While the ICC has yet to hand down a judgment, in its dealings with prospective cases, strategic behavior can be observed. The above-mentioned example of the LRA case again illustrates this. The ICC's Pre-Trial Chamber, much like the prosecutor and likely for similar reasons, did its best to secure the first case. When it became known that national proceedings were being initiated that might trump the ICC's jurisdiction under the concept of complementarity, it made clear, on its own initiative, that the ICC and not Uganda determines whether a case is admissible (Nouwen and Werner 2010, 17).

Previously, however, the Trial Chamber has twice decided to discontinue proceedings against a defendant because the prosecutor, in its view, did not play by the rules. On the first occasion, Trial Chamber judges suspended the trial against Lubanga, a Congolese militia leader accused of recruiting and deploying child soldiers, because the prosecutor was unwilling to disclose information that might exonerate the defendant. On the second occasion, Trial Chamber judges found that the prosecutor had ignored their order to reveal the identity of an intermediary who had been assisting witnesses. Several possible explanations for the judges' position have been put forward. It has been argued that the Trial Chamber judges showed their commitment to a fair trial to enhance the ICC's legitimacy (Anoushirvani 2010). An alternative view is that the judges were eager to slap the prosecutor on the wrist for ignoring due-process requirements to achieve results (Verrijn 2008). In each instance there was a risk that Lubanga would walk free as a result of these actions, which would have been a very serious consequence. However, in both cases the prosecutor was saved by the Appeals Chamber. In the second case, while agreeing with the Trial Chamber judges that the prosecutor had violated the rules, judges of the Appeals Chamber emphasized that there were less drastic means to correct that behavior, compared to letting Lubanga walk away, such as imposing sanctions on the prosecutor. The Appeals Chamber judges felt that the Trial Chamber judges should have considered imposing disciplinary sanctions on the prosecutor as an alternative in this case. It looks as though the Appeals Chamber was eager to caution and reprimand the prosecutor—perhaps to display the fair-trial image—while being unwilling to let the trial collapse.

In their acceptance or rejection of cases, the different chambers of the ICC obviously pursue a variety of goals: sanctioning perceived misbehavior of the prosecutor, establishing legitimacy, and demonstrating authority. Their actions thereby are influenced by each other, as well as by the general political environment. Thus, the judges certainly do not decide in an apolitical and mechanical way; on the contrary, they appear to navigate complex constraint and opportunity structures in their pursuit of diverse and partly even contradictory goals.

The (De)institutionalization of Human Rights

Rational-choice theory contends that macro-level phenomena are aggregate outcomes of micro-level action. Thus, the institutionalization of a human rights regime depends on the behavior of individual actors, which in turn is guided by their rational pursuit of goals. Individual actors' rationality, hence their behavior, is influenced by three factors: their perception of decision alternatives based on the available information and their general beliefs, their distinct preferences and goals, and the constraints and opportunities they face.

These fundamental assumptions are of crucial relevance to understanding the institutionalization of human rights on the macro level. Following them we can deduce that the institutionalization of human rights in a society requires that individual actors act in accordance with the related legal and normative principles. As actors are rational and goal-oriented, acting in accordance with human rights has to be the most advantageous and beneficial action alternative for the individual. Finally, as the evaluation of decision alternatives fundamentally depends on an actor's beliefs, the information available to him or her, and the constraints and opportunities faced, these factors can be considered determinants for the successful institutionalization of a human rights regime.

More specifically, in order to make it rational for individual actors to act in accordance with and in support of human rights, several conditions need to be fulfilled: First, individuals need to be well educated about human rights and the consequences of violating them. Second, these consequences or sanctions—both formal and informal—need to be substantial and to outweigh the potential benefits of defection. Third, opportunities need to favor behavior that respects human rights. Fourth, resources need to be available to allow for the provision of information about human rights and for the implementation of sanctions—positive and negative. Under such conditions, human rights adherence is the most sensible option, which in the aggregate enables the institutionalization of human rights. Responsibility for establishing and implementing the necessary conditions lies with the state and its agencies. The ideologies represented and the sanctions enforced by a government have fundamental effects on the behavior of its subjects.

Genocides, as the structural and systematic destruction of a people by a state bureaucracy, constitute the most horrifying expressions of just how intensive such influence can be (Horowitz 1980). Cases such as Nazi Germany, the former Yugoslavia, and Rwanda exemplify the potentially devastating capacity of states to reframe their subjects' perceptions (e.g., Sekulic, Massey, and Hodson 2006; Prunier 1997; Brubaker 1996). The systematic dehumanization of certain social groups, together with the creation of opportunities for members of the majority to benefit from the exertion of violence, creates a frame in which systematic violations of human rights become a rational means of goal pursuit. This certainly paints a bleak picture, yet at the same time creates a ray of hope. If governments can succeed in making rational individuals commit heinous acts that require the repression of fundamental feelings of empathy and pity, they are also able to make it reasonable for individuals to respect each other's dignity and act in accordance with the principles of human rights.

Human rights are not just an abstract ideal transcending social reality, but also can become integrated as guiding principles of rational human action. The "receptor approach" developed at the Netherlands Institute of Human Rights constitutes an original and auspicious perspective on how such integration could be implemented (Zou and Zwart 2011). Following Moore (1978) in conceptualizing behavior as influenced by a diversity of institutions—informal norms and values as well as the formal legal framework—this approach contends that human rights need to be aligned to the local context in order to be successfully implemented. Such alignment is facilitated by identifying local institutions that match certain human rights and can serve as "receptors" through which the respective principles can be introduced (Zou and Zwart 2011). Preventing dissonance between the formal legal structure and local institutions, the receptor approach provides a strategy to make human rights an influential factor in individual decision-making.

Learning from a Human Rights Paradigm

Rational-choice theory is a general theory of action. As any such theory, its core assumptions (e.g., concerning human nature) are subject to constant refinement, and it has to face empirical findings that do not match its theoretical predictions. Human rights issues are one of the many substantive domains in which the theory can be applied. Their empirical investigation may shed light on a classical puzzle of rational-choice theory: the explanation for cooperation and collective action where actors incur considerable costs without expecting immediate benefits (Scott 2000). The historical and social process of the development and dissemination of the human rights paradigm constitutes a powerful example. Looking at the implementation of human rights in a nation's legislation requires understanding why a government is willing to invest in an effort that effectively restricts its power without necessarily involving immediate benefits. Which considerations and motivations, or, more specifically, which rationalities, underlie such behavior? Or, as human rights scholar David Moore summarizes it, "Rational choice theory has not provided a comprehensive explanation of why a nation would find it in its self-interest to conform to human rights norms when it is not compelled to do so by domestic influences and is not coerced" (2003, 880). Inspired by this problem, Moore develops a signaling model of states' human rights compliance, building on assumptions of strategic rationality as formulated in game theory. More generally, empirical research on the institutionalization of human rights regimes and on the conditions of compliance with or violation of human rights principles may provide invaluable case material to inform recent rational-choice scholarship on altruistic or costly punishment in particular (Fehr and Gächter 2002) and the link between decision theory and morality in general (Dreier 2004).

The establishment of a human rights regime requires the realization of actors' perceptions of decision alternatives, goals and preferences, and opportunities and constraints in a way that makes acting in accordance with human rights principles the most advantageous, hence rational, action alternative. It is the responsibility of governments to implement such conditions. A culturally sensitive approach that aligns general human rights principles and local institutions presumably constitutes the most viable strategy to achieve this objective, thus making human rights the rational choice.

Chapter Eight

INTERNATIONAL MIGRATION

Tanya Golash-Boza

A human rights perspective presumes the fundamental dignity of all people, regardless of national origin, and recognizes that people are members of families and communities (Blau and Moncada 2005, 29). A consideration of the human rights impact of international migration requires the recognition that people have rights not just as citizens of a particular nation-state but as human beings. A human rights analysis necessitates a consideration of how immigration policies affect all people—not solely or primarily citizens of particular countries.

Taking a human rights perspective, we are compelled to see migrants not simply as workers but as husbands, fathers, brothers, wives, mothers, sisters, and community members. As human beings, migrants have the right to be with their families and to be full members of the communities in which they live. These family and community rights are enshrined in the Universal Declaration of Human Rights (UDHR), as well as other declarations. Not only is the importance of these rights internationally recognized, but their realization is fundamental to creating a better society for all. Although the UDHR is not a legally binding doctrine in the United States, it can serve as a moral compass for those of us who believe that all human beings deserve rights and dignity, regardless of national origin.

When we center the human rights paradigm in international-migration scholarship, we change our focus from the costs and benefits of international migration for sending and receiving countries and begin to consider the global, human impact of international migration and immigration control. Centering the human rights paradigm in the field of international migration would fundamentally change how sociologists approach the study of international migration.

THE SOCIOLOGY OF INTERNATIONAL MIGRATION

International-migration scholars are concerned with the movement of people across borders. Sociologists who study international migration ask how many people migrate, who migrates, why people migrate, what happens to them once they arrive in the host country, and how migration affects sending communities.

How Many International Migrants Are There?

To understand how many international migrants there are in the world and in a given country, international-migration scholars develop models. These models measure migration flows, estimate how many immigrants are legally and illegally present in a given country, and consider the extent to which migration is temporary or permanent. Quantifying international migration allows for an analysis of how migration flows change over time and in response to structural forces and changes. Gaining an understanding of the scope of international migration lays the groundwork for other sociological explorations of this phenomenon.

How Many Migrants Are There Around the World?

According to the United Nations, there were 214 million international migrants worldwide—3 percent of the world's population—in 2010. International migration has been on the rise over the past few decades: there were 155 million international migrants in 1990 and 178 million at the turn of the twenty-first century. About half of all migrants are women. The gender balance has been constant since at least 1990 (UN 2008).

How Many Migrants Are There in the United States?

About a fifth of all international migrants—43 million people—can be found in the United States. International migrants account for 13 percent of the US population (UN 2008). About 10 million of these migrants are undocumented; 85 percent of undocumented migrants in the United States come from just ten countries: Mexico (6.65 million), El Salvador (530,000), Guatemala (480,000), Honduras (320,000), Philippines (270,000), India (200,000), Korea (200,000), Ecuador (170,000), Brazil (150,000), and China (120,000) (Rytina, Hoefer, and Baker 2010). Although many undocumented migrants come from Asia, Asian migrants are rarely deported from the United States: 95 percent of the 393,289 people deported from the United States in 2009 were from just ten countries, all in Latin America (Department of Homeland Security 2010, "Immigration Enforcement Actions: 2009").

Why Do People Emigrate?

Most people in the world never leave their home country. Why, then, do some decide to venture out across international borders? International-migration scholars answer these questions by considering how the agency of individual migrants intersects with the structural constraints and possibilities of migration.

A major area of scholarship is the development of theories to explain international migration. Some contend that migration is linked to relations between countries. These scholars argue that foreign direct investment, trade, labor recruitment, and military interventions influence migration flows (Sassen 1989; Golash-Boza 2011). These analyses explain why most migrants to the United States come from just a few countries. Others point to the importance of migrant networks to explain why migration is highly localized—people leave one village in Mexico or Thailand and move to the same neighborhood in San Francisco, California, or Winston-Salem, North Carolina (Rumbaut 1994; Massey, Durand, and Malone 2002). Although one set of factors may lead to migration, once migration flows have begun, new circumstances develop that lead to the perpetuation of these flows (Massey, Durand, and Malone 2002).

International-migration scholars explain that people migrate due to a combination of individual and structural factors. They point out that Emma Lazarus's poem engraved on the Statue of Liberty, which describes immigrants as poor, huddled masses, is inaccurate: the people who migrate to the United States are not the most destitute in the world. In 2009, more than 1 million people became legal permanent residents of the United States. Only 6,718 of them came from the five poorest countries in the world. Nearly half (3,165) of the migrants from the five poorest countries hailed from Afghanistan, a country in the midst of a US military occupation. Niger, the poorest country in the world, only sent 183 legal permanent residents to the United States in 2009 (UN Human Development Reports 2010; Department of Homeland Security 2009).

Documented and undocumented migrants do not come to the United States simply because they are poor, according to international-migration scholars. They come because of strong ties to the United States. Labor recruitment, military interventions, and foreign direct investment create and sustain migration flows (Sassen 1989; Golash-Boza 2011). Countries with long histories of labor migration, such as Mexico and the Philippines, continue to send migrants to the United States because these histories have created strong ties between the countries. In addition, family-reunification policies in the United States encourage further migration by giving preference to those with family members living in the country. This process is known as cumulative causation: migration begets more migration (Massey, Durand, and Malone 2002; Massey 1988).

Military intervention can lead to migration due to the ties it creates as well as the turmoil that ensues. Migration flows develop due to amorous relationships between US soldiers and locals and the emergence of close ties between people in the United States and the country at hand, such as, for example, when Filipinos were recruited to join the US Navy (Rumbaut 1994). The United States has been involved militarily with nearly all the countries that send migrants to the United States (Golash-Boza 2011). In some cases, military interventions create outflows of refugees because of the violence of military operations.

Scholars who look specifically at refugee flows analyze the reasons people find themselves forced to leave their countries of birth. The concept of the refugee was developed in the aftermath of World War I to describe the situation of Armenians fleeing Turkey and Russians fleeing the revolution there (Petersen 1978). Over the past century, the numbers of refugees have increased, and refugees come from dozens of countries. The United Nations High Commissioner for Refugees (2010) estimated that there were more than 15 million refugees in need of resettlement in 2010.

Foreign direct investment creates migration flows through its inevitable effects on the local economy and the integration of the country into the global economy. In an analysis of twenty-five developing countries, Sanderson and Kentor found that "the stock of foreign direct investment has a long-term positive effect on emigration" (2008, 529). These factors have led to both legal and illegal migration to the United States.

What Happens to Migrants?

Another major area of study for international-migration scholars involves an analysis of what happens to voluntary labor migrants and refugees upon reaching their destinations. These scholars consider both how immigrants incorporate into the host society and the extent to which they maintain ties to the home country. Scholars whose primary framework involves an analysis of assimilation measure the extent to which migrants maintain their culture and language, their incorporation into the labor market, and residential patterns (see Alba and Nee 1997; Gans 1997; Gordon 1964; Portes and Rumbaut 2001). Those whose primary mode of analysis revolves around transnational ties consider the extent to which migrants maintain ties to their home country through travel, international communications, and links to conationals in the host country (see Goldring 1998; Guarnizo, Portes, and Haller 2003; Guarnizo and Smith 1998; Mahler 1998; Popkin 1999).

Migrants Assimilate

There are two kinds of international migrants: sojourners and settlers. Sojourners are those who travel to a new country for a fixed period to work, visit, or study and plan to return to their country of origin. Settlers are those who intend to stay. Sociologists often explore the incorporation processes for settlers. The dominant paradigm in sociology is assimilation: the process by which an immigrant settler and future generations of immigrants become part of the host country. The concept of assimilation has been criticized insofar as it seems to imply that immigrants have no option but to become part of a monolithic culture; in reality, the host culture often changes with the arrival of immigrants, and immigrants vary greatly in the ways that they become part of the host society. Scholars such as Richard Alba and Victor Nee (1997) defend the concept of assimilation by pointing out that immigrants can assimilate in many ways: the descendants of the Irish may become part of the Euro-American mainstream, whereas the descendants of Caribbean black immigrants may become part of the African American community.

Migrants Maintain Transnational Ties

Although many international migrants seek to remain in their host countries, they are often inclined to maintain ties with their home countries. Sociologists refer to the cross-border interactions of international migrants as transnational ties. The concept of transnationalism derives from the works of anthropologists Linda Basch, Nina Glick Schiller, and Cristina Szanton Blanc (1994), who argue that contemporary cross-border connections are qualitatively and quantitatively different from those in previous eras in that the relations are more intimate and persistent than ever before.

Recent work in sociology questions both how assimilation works and the extent to which migrants maintain transnational ties. Luis Guarnizo, Alejandro Portes, and William Haller (2003) point out that the maintenance of contacts across borders is perhaps as old as international migration itself, and they contend that only a small subset of international migrants actually engages in cross-border activities on a consistent basis. Remarkably, they also find that transnationalism and assimilation are not at odds: migrants' lengths of stay in the United States do not reduce the likelihood of their maintaining contact with their home countries.

WHAT ARE THE CONSEQUENCES OF INTERNATIONAL MIGRATION?

Sociologists join economists and other scholars in exploring the cultural, social, and economic impact of international migration on sending and receiving locales (Borjas 2004). Understanding the economic impact allows social scientists to inform policy-makers. Discussions of the cultural and social impact of international migration permit scholars to help communities plan for the future of their changing locales. In terms of sending communities, two primary areas of concern revolve around the "brain drain" and the extent to which migration helps or hinders economic and social development in poor countries (Meyer 2001). Concerns over the exodus of highly trained professionals have been present for migrant-sending nations at least since the 1960s (Petersen 1978). The debate over whether migration helps or hinders development is far from settled. Hein De Hass (2010) posits that the contention over the benefits of emigration and remittances arises from the fact that each community and country presents a unique situation. In some cases, remittances help local development; in other cases, emigration upsets local economies and unsettles whole communities.

Sociologists also explore the extent to which migrants help or hinder the economy, the effects of immigration on crime, and how immigrants transform the cities and towns in which they live (Ghosh 1992; Lipton 1980; Lisborg 1993; Rumbaut and Ewing 2007; Taylor 1999). Although many people in the United States associate undocumented migration with crime, Rubén Rumbaut and Walter Ewing (2007) demonstrate with convincing data that immigrants in the United States have lower crime and incarceration rates than their native-born counterparts. They further contend that the flow of immigrants into the United States in recent years is one reason that crime rates in the United States have declined. Their study provides one example of how immigration can change receiving communities in profound ways.

What Tools Do Sociologists Use to Study Migration?

Sociologists use a variety of methodological tools to study migration. Those who wish to gain an in-depth understanding of the local-level effects of international migration and to comprehend the decision-making processes of migrants use ethnography and in-depth interviews (Levitt 2001). Scholars who are interested in large-scale trends of international migration draw from census data and surveys (Guarnizo, Portes, and Haller 2003; Rumbaut and Portes 2001). Demographers paint broad pictures of flows around the world (Durand et al. 1996). Those scholars interested in media and popular-cultural representations draw from textual and content analyses (Diaz-McConnell 2011), and comparative historical sociologists often use archival data in addition to other sources (Brubaker 1990). Sociologists also use mixed methods: one of the most innovative techniques developed by Douglas Massey and his colleagues specifically for the study of international migration is the ethnosurvey, which combines qualitative and quantitative data in a single data-gathering and -analysis strategy (Massey and Zenteno 2000).

What Can the Human Rights Paradigm Learn from the Study of International Migration?

Work in the field of international migration renders it evident that migrants do not live in a vacuum and that connections between countries are intimate and persistent. Human rights scholars who ponder the ethical and philosophical bases of immigration controls can learn from migration scholars that (1) people emigrate from one community to another because of specific ties between their communities, (2) emigration affects sending communities because of the transnational ties it creates and the social and economic remittances migrants send, (3) sojourners often become settlers because of restrictive immigration controls, and (4) the impacts of immigrants on communities in the receiving countries are often profound and frequently positive. The findings from the work of international-migration scholars have important implications for any consideration of the right to mobility.

The work of international migration scholars on the incorporation patterns of migrants also has important bearings for consideration of the cultural rights of migrants. Human rights researchers who ask what protections should hold for migrants' rights to their cultural beliefs and customs can learn from international-migration researchers about the ways in which holding on to cultural beliefs can inhibit as well as enhance migrants' success. Human rights scholars can learn from this field that states' efforts at inclusion can have wide-ranging effects on migrants as well as the communities in which they live.

What Happens When We Center the Human Rights Paradigm in International-Migration Research?

International-migration scholars most often ask why people migrate and what happens to them once they do. This work often takes national borders as givens—people cross or do not cross these borders for a variety of reasons.

A human rights paradigm pushes us to ask a whole new set of questions. What fundamental human dignities are people deprived of in their choice to migrate? What human rights violations do they experience upon arriving in their host countries? What special arrangements need to be made for refugees and asylees? How does the international community deal with migrants deprived of a nationality and who have no country to which they can return? To what extent does international migration allow people to realize their full potential? How are transnational ties necessary to ensure the human rights of migrants and their families? How would ideas of assimilation change were human rights to be considered? And how could we create a world in which people's right not to migrate would be realized?

Whereas international-migration scholars tend to focus on the citizenship rights of individuals, the human rights paradigm allows us to focus on the fundamental rights all people share—not as members of particular nation-states but by virtue of their status as human beings.

Debates in the field of international migration frequently revolve around the economic and cultural costs and benefits of immigration. A human rights analysis compels us to calculate the human costs and benefits. Putting human rights first means asking a different set of questions. For example, some critics who argue that undocumented migration has a negative economic impact include the costs of education for US-citizen children of undocumented migrants in their analyses. A human rights analysis would see education as a fundamental human right and children as deserving of special protections. Others argue that undocumented migrants bring down wages. For example, George Borjas (2004) contends that low-skilled immigrants are only beneficial to their employers, whereas they lower the wages of their native low-skilled counterparts. A human rights analysis would insist that all workers deserve a living wage. Economist Barry Chiswick (1988) points out that low-skilled foreign workers can be economically beneficial, so long as they do not bring their nonworking family members with them to the United States. A human rights analysis considers family unity to be an inalienable right.

Where Do We Go from Here?

Human beings—no matter their national origin—possess fundamental human dignity. The task for researchers is to figure out ways to make it clear that people's rights should depend not on their national origin but on their status as human beings. How can we convince the public and governing bodies that recognizing human rights should take precedence in all decisions? How can we develop scholarship that demonstrates that the rights to mobility, to be with one's family, to shelter, and to a clean environment are all fundamental human rights that should be recognized? How can we render it clear that rather than, Why are they here? the question is, How can we create a world in which the decision to migrate (or not) is a choice and not a survival tactic?

As sociologists, we have a wealth of information and data that can demonstrate the importance of the right to mobility in a globalizing world. We would do well to use that data to bolster human rights claims. A prime example is that sociologists have extensive evidence of how emigration changes sending communities. Human rights scholars who debate the moral bases of the right to mobility benefit when they are able to take into account not only the ways that emigration can be economically beneficial to an individual, but also the extent to which it can change the nature of the community he or she leaves behind.

In human rights scholarship, debate continues around what a right to mobility would look like. For instance, does the right to mobility require open borders and the free movement of people? Does it imply that all people deserve the economic capital requisite for international travel? Or does it shift the burden of proof to states, saying that they must admit noncitizens unless they can provide a valid reason to deny them entry? The right to mobility is undertheorized and underdeveloped both in sociology and in human rights scholarship more generally.

The right to mobility does not form part of current human rights documents. In the human rights tradition, the right to leave one's country is recognized. However, the right to enter another country does not form part of existing human rights conventions and treaties. This leads many critics to argue that the right to mobility is a serious omission in human rights treaties. The right to emigrate is effectively useless if there is no country to which one can migrate (Pécoud and de Guchteneire 2006). Joseph Nevins (2003) adds to this discussion the fact that, in a globalizing world rampant with economic inequality, the human rights to free choice of employment and to an adequate standard of living enshrined in the UDHR are difficult to achieve without the ability to leave one's country of origin.

If human beings had the right to mobility, then states would have to provide compelling reasons to deny individuals the right to enter their territories. One possibility would be to shift the burden of proof, such that states would be required to provide reasons a person should not enter as opposed to the current situation, where it is up to individuals to prove that they deserve to enter another country. This would be one way of incorporating the right to mobility into human rights doctrine. Can we imagine human rights doctrines holding that states shall, except when compelling reasons of national security otherwise require, allow noncitizens to enter their territories? What does the right to mobility mean? What would it actually look like? Crucially, does the right to mobility require open borders?

These questions remain unanswered for human rights scholars (Pécoud and de Guchteneire 2006; Bauböck 2009). There certainly are many immigration scholars who argue for open borders, including, for example, Nandita Sharma, Kevin Johnson, Jonathan Moses, Jane Guskin, and David Wilson. As Guskin and Wilson (2007) point out, open borders would save us billions of dollars in immigration law enforcement, increase tax revenues since all workers would pay payroll taxes, raise wages and improve working conditions since we would no longer have a disenfranchised workforce, and eliminate criminal activity associated with undocumented migration, such as identity theft and human trafficking.

It is now time for human rights scholars to take on these questions and to begin a conversation within the United Nations that explores the extent to which a right to mobility could be incorporated into human rights doctrine.

Chapter Nine

Labor and Labor Movements

Héctor L. Delgado

The human rights and labor rights movements share the fundamental goal of improving human beings' quality of life. While the labor movement is more focused on ensuring that workers can feed themselves and their families, work in a safe environment, and have a voice in the workplace, the ability of workers to secure these rights has consequences far beyond the workplace and typically requires the right to associate freely, a fundamental human right found in several human rights instruments. It is difficult to imagine an aspect of workers' lives with farther-reaching consequences than their ability to secure food and lodging for themselves and their families. In fact, fulfillment of many human rights depends, in some measure at least, on individuals' ability to do just that. Yet, as Leary observes in her seminal article on labor rights as human rights, "the human rights movement and the labor movement run on tracks that are sometimes parallel and rarely meet" (1996, 22). Since Leary's observation in 1996, however, the tracks have started to converge and on occasion cross.

A good bellwether of human rights status, Leary (1996, 22) observes, is workers' rights. But human rights activists have not paid nearly the same attention to economic and social rights as they have to civil and political rights abuses, such as genocide, torture, murder by death squads, and arbitrary arrests and imprisonment (Gross and Compa 2009; Leary 1996; Craven 1995). The tendency has been to view workers' rights, principally if not purely, as economic disputes between workers and their bosses. The following statement by the United Nations Committee on Economic, Social, and Cultural Rights in 1993, however, suggests that some human rights activists recognize the need to pay more attention to labor rights: "Despite the rhetoric, violations of civil and political rights continue to be treated as though they were far more serious, and more patently intolerable, than massive and direct denials of economic, social, and cultural rights" (quoted in Steiner, Alston, and Goodman 2008, 264).

Labor activists and scholars, in turn, have rarely employed a human rights perspective or analysis. But this appears to be changing. In 2005, the AFL-CIO issued a brief stating that freedom of association is a human right that employers too often deny workers, created a "Voice at Work" campaign that referred to the right to organize for a better life as a "basic human right," and held more than one hundred demonstrations and took out full-page ads in newspapers throughout the country in support of workers' human rights, enlisting the signatures of eleven Nobel Prize winners, including the Dalai Lama and Archbishop Desmond Tutu.

The National Employment Law Project (NELP) was created to protect immigrant workers' rights. NELP has filed numerous complaints with international agencies on behalf of immigrant workers in the United States. In concert with Mexican colleagues, NELP sought and received a favorable opinion from the Inter-American Court regarding mistreatment of undocumented workers in the United States. The AFL-CIO filed a complaint with the International Labour Organization's (ILO) Committee on Freedom of Association in response to the US Supreme Court's *Hoffman Plastic Compounds, Inc. v. NLRB* (2002) decision denying undocumented workers back-pay remedies in the event of an unfair labor practice by the employer (Gross 2009).

Observing that sociology should contribute more to scholarly discussions of human rights, the University of Warwick's Sociology of Human Rights website posted a list of question areas sociologists can help find answers to: "historical questions about the emergence of human rights; conceptual questions concerning the relation of human rights to other forms of rights, including civil, political and social rights; normative questions concerning the right of all human beings to have rights; and critical questions concerning the legitimacy of human rights." The first two areas are especially relevant to sociologists of labor and labor movements. Why did it take so long for the labor and human rights movements to collaborate, if not merge, and how can the human rights movement's emphasis on civil, political, and individual rights be reconciled with the labor movement's emphasis on economic, social, and collective rights? Despite labor activists' and scholars' significant movement toward a human rights paradigm, there is still a long road ahead, and it is not one without hazards.

Research on Labor and the Labor Movement

Sociologists are indeed assigning greater importance to human rights, as evidenced by new human rights sections of the American Sociological Association and the International Sociological Association and new publications such as this edited volume and Blau and Frezzo's *Sociology and Human Rights: A Bill of Rights for the Twentieth-First Century*. For the first half of the twentieth century, the study of labor and the labor movement was dominated by the Wisconsin School and economists and labor historians Richard Ely (1886), Selig Perlman (1922, 1928), and John Commons (Commons et al. 1910-1911, 1918-1935). The Wisconsin School played an important role in the creation of industrial relations as a field of serious scholarship and helped to pave the road for US business unionism, but it began to diminish in importance in academic circles after World War II as new scholars introduced new perspectives and approaches (Devinatz 2003). Among these new scholars were David Brody (1960, 1965, 1979), Irving Bernstein (1960b,

1970), and Herbert Gutman (1961, 1962, 1976). They and a new crop of labor historians were inspired by work of British historians E. P. Thompson (1963) and Eric Hobsbawm (1964) to write a "new labor history" from workers' perspectives.

Scholarly interest in labor has not waned since the 1970s; rather, it has flourished, as Kimeldorf and Stepan-Norris (1992) note in a review of historical and sociological studies of the US labor movement. This research has been driven by several key questions, beginning with the notion of exceptionalism in terms of why the US labor movement has failed to develop a socialist philosophy or program (see Laslett 1970; Laslett and Lipset 1974; Mink 1986; Zolberg 1986; Wilentz 1984; Foner 1984) and issues such as employers' sustained assault on unionization and workers' rights (see Klare 1978; Casebeer 1989; Cornfield 1989; Quadagno 1988; Goldfield 1989; McCammon 1990; Wallace, Rubin, and Smith 1988). A second set of questions, Kimeldorf and Stepan-Norris (1992) observe, focuses on workplace dynamics in the industrial sector, which includes research on one of the most important questions for labor scholars: What explains the rapid decline in union membership over the past fifty years? Some scholars have identified as culprits the migration of production from high-union-density regions to regions less friendly to unions and the decline in blue-collar jobs. Other scholars attribute blame to organized labor's failure to invest more resources into organizing and employers' resistance to unionization (see Bluestone and Harrison 1982; Bernstein 1960a; Goldfield 1987; Freeman and Medoff 1984; Lipset 1960; Fantasia 1988; Griffin, Wallace, and Rubin 1986). Measures employers adopt to resist unionization, both legal and illegal, deserve sociological analyses that focus on what a human rights regime deems to be the universal human right to form organizations.

Other studies have focused on the labor movement's organizational history, especially major events in that history that helped to shape the movement. Here, as Kimeldorf and Stepan-Norris (1992) observe, recent sociological work makes an important contribution by linking unionization efforts to larger processes, essential in any discussion of labor rights as human rights (for a review of this literature, see Brody 1979; Kimeldorf 1991). Another important body of research has drawn on concepts of social-movement research. This social-movements approach is especially relevant to a discussion of labor rights as human rights as well. "Thinking of organized labor as a social movement . . . has been a needed corrective—emphasizing contingency and contestation—to earlier sociological analysis, which focused on trade unions as organizations and workers as individuals with varying political attitudes (or on the individual correlates of their political behavior)" (Kimeldorf and Stepan-Norris 1992, 509; see also Griffin, Wallace, and Rubin 1986; Voss 1992; Moody 1997).

Rights Discourse

If the labor movement succeeds in casting labor issues as human rights, it may benefit from a rights language, or discourse, that has existed in the United States from its inception and especially since the civil rights movement. Sociology is unrivaled in its scholarship on the black civil, women's, gay/lesbian, and other rights movements. "In no other large country is rights consciousness of greater potency, in the law, in culture, in foreign policy, in the subtleties of daily life and language" (Lichtenstein 2003, 64). But some of these studies reveal that the labor movement was slow to support the civil rights struggles of the 1950s. The mainstream labor movement, which had fought doggedly for higher wages and better working conditions for white workers for more than a century, was much less dogged about the rights of black workers. In fact, for much of its history, organized labor closed its doors to native workers of color and immigrants. Slowly, however, the mainstream labor movement began supporting important civil rights legislation, such as the Civil Rights Act of 1964 and the Voting Rights Act of 1965.

Reluctant to organize immigrant workers initially, unions began to organize them principally out of necessity. Eventually the AFL-CIO leadership officially endorsed the organization of immigrant workers, including the undocumented, when in 2000 its executive council adopted a pro-immigrant resolution in favor of a new amnesty program for undocumented immigrants and repeal of the employer-sanctions provision of the Immigration Reform and Control Act of 1986. By defending the rights of black and immigrant workers, the AFL-CIO put itself in a better position to invoke a rights discourse and to regain trust lost abroad due to the activities of several foreign arms, including the federation's principal Latin American arm, the government-funded and CIA-connected American Institute for Free Labor Development (Sims 1992; Cantor and Schor 1987).

Why Unions Matter

In many respects, the demands of the black civil rights movement were fundamentally the same as labor's, as the Reverend Martin Luther King Jr. proclaimed at the AFL-CIO's Fourth Constitutional Convention in December 1961: "Our needs are identical with labor's needs: Decent wages, fair working conditions, livable housing, old-age security, health and welfare measures, conditions in which families can grow, have education for their children, and respect in the community" (1986). Unions have played an indispensable role in securing these things for workers. In an Economic Policy Institute (EPI) briefing paper, Mishel and Walters (2003) noted that unionized workers' wages were 20 percent higher than those of their nonunion counterparts, and unionized workers were more likely to have paid leave, health insurance provided by their employer, and a pension plan. It is worth noting as well that the labor movement played an integral role in the enactment of laws and regulations protecting all workers, including the Social Security, Occupational Safety and Health, and Family Medical Leave acts, measures addressing fundamental human rights. Furthermore, unions have secured for workers, especially for their members, recognition that workers are not simply commodities but human beings with rights, including the right to be treated with dignity and respect (see Freeman and Medoff 1984; Yates 2009). The erosion of union membership and power over the past fifty years, then, should alarm human rights activists as much as it does their organized labor counterparts.

Since Dr. King's proclamation in 1961, union membership has declined precipitously. In 2010, 6.9 percent of nonagricultural, private-sector workers enjoyed union representation, down from 37 percent in 1960. Unionization among public-sector workers is much higher at 36.2 percent but is in danger of falling if Republican governors and legislators are successful in their bids to weaken public-sector unions (Bureau of Labor Statistics 2011). At the same time, the income and wealth gaps in the United States have widened appreciably. For example, in 2009 the top 1 percent of the US population averaged nearly $14 million in wealth, while the lowest quintile, on average, owed more than their assets' value. The top 1 percent of the population owned 35.6 percent of all net worth, while the bottom 90 percent owned only 25 percent of all net worth (Allegretto 2011). Between 1949 and 1979, the richest 10 percent of the country received 33 percent of the growth in income, but between 2000 and 2007, it received all the growth (EPI 2011). While organized labor's interest in a human rights regime is opening up new research avenues and is likely to lead to more international and interdisciplinary labor scholarship, sociologists can argue for expansion of human rights or, at minimum, prevail on the human rights community to assign far greater importance to economic, social, and cultural rights.

To claim the human and labor rights movements historically have run on parallel tracks is not to say that human rights bodies have not promoted rights of relevance to workers. Founded in 1919 following the end of World War I, the International Labour Organization (ILO) focuses on social justice as a means of promoting peace. Its Convention 98, adopted in 1949, recognizes workers' right to organize and bargain collectively, free from employer interference. Other conventions supporting workers' rights can be found in the Universal Declaration of Human Rights (UDHR), the International Covenant on Civil and Political Rights, and the International Covenant on Economic, Social, and Cultural Rights (ICESCR). The rights in these declarations or covenants include freedom of association, such as the right to join trade unions and bargain collectively; the rights to be paid equally for comparable work, to protection from discrimination in employment, and to be safe in the workplace; and child labor prohibitions. UDHR Article 23 includes rights "to just and favourable conditions of work," to "remuneration ensuring for [oneself] and [one's] family an existence worthy of human dignity," and "to join trade unions for the protection of [one's] interests." Existence of these rights creates space for the labor movement to promote workers' rights.

Human Rights and Labor Rights Discourses

Organized labor may gain by adopting discourse and strategies that have proved effective for the human rights movement, especially given labor's waning membership, power, and popularity. In fact, according to a 2010 PEW Research survey, only 41 percent of people polled had a favorable opinion of unions, down

19 percent from 2007. While 61 percent agreed that unions were necessary to protect working people, an equal percentage agreed that unions had too much power—up from 52 percent in 1999 (PEW 2010). Clearly, unions have a lot of heavy lifting to do on the public-relations front, but labor might lighten its load if it adopts a human rights approach and if the human rights movement serves increasingly as an advocate for labor rights (Kolben 2010, 461). But this approach is likely to have an empowering psychological impact on union members as well (Gross and Compa 2009, 8).

While the marriage of human and labor rights seems obvious, not everyone agrees; at the very least, there are those who believe labor should proceed with caution. As Kolben observes,

> While strategic deployment of human rights discourse might appear to be advantageous in the short run, the fundamental differences between this discourse and that of labor rights may inhibit the long-term effectiveness of this approach.... The strategies, politics, culture, and ideologies that inform much of the U.S. human rights establishment are quite at odds with those of the labor rights movement, and a serious human rights turn risks weakening commitment to the economic justice and workplace democracy principles that have long underpinned labor rights thought and practice. (2010, 452)

Kolben is not alone. In the *Harvard Law School Human Rights Journal*, Kennedy (2002) recommends a more pragmatic attitude toward human rights due to the fact that they do not address a central issue for labor: redistribution. Another area of concern for Kennedy (2002) is whether human rights might minimize the focus on collective responsibility, a salient difference between labor and human rights, also noted by Kolben. "While human rights concern individuals and, arguably, achieve outcomes such as better working conditions, labor rights are more collectively oriented, and worker mobilization and negotiations processes take precedence" (Kolben 2010, 452). In a similar vein, labor historian David Brody (2001) expressed his own misgivings in a critique of Human Rights Watch's (HRW) 2000 report on labor rights in the United States.

Brody observed that in promoting stronger free speech for workers and not less for employers, the report failed to apprehend what the 1934 Wagner Act's authors understood: that employer speech is more powerful and "inherently" coercive. Employers did understand and worked successfully to restore such speech. In 1947, the Taft-Hartley Act gave employers relatively free rein to use measures to prevent unionization, including mandatory captive-audience meetings with workers and plant-closure threats if workers voted for union representation. Taft-Hartley weakened workers' position dramatically. Recent attempts to enact the Employee Free Choice Act, an antidote to Taft-Hartley, have not gained much traction. US workers are on their own in a legal system that favors their employers. Brody's concern is that "human rights analysis" might deflect workers from this reality and the "hard thinking" required "to negotiate a way through, or around" it (2001, 604). In addition, proponents of a labor rights as human rights perspective face some human rights advocates who treat workers' claims as goals, not rights.

Rights versus Goals

"Human rights" typically refers to civil and political rights, with an individual rights emphasis. Economic and social rights take a back seat to these rights and are seen by some, if not many, human rights activists principally as desirable goals rather than as rights in the same sense as, for example, the right not to be tortured. Do individuals, for example, have a right to a subsistence wage and basic health care? Do collectivities have rights comparable to individual rights? International human rights documents, despite their emphasis on civil, political, and individual rights, do contain provisions that reflect a concern for rights deemed economic or social, and even collective, with the freedom of association being the most notable. Instead of adding economic and social rights to their list of human rights, the United Nations drafted the International Covenant on Economic, Social, and Cultural Rights, adopted by the General Assembly in 1966, to address them.

The covenant recognizes, in accordance with the UDHR, people's right to self-determination and to pursue "economic, social and cultural development" (Article 1, 1). In Article 7, parties to the covenant agree to recognize everyone's right to enjoy fair and favorable work conditions. Article 8 (a) recognizes the right of "everyone" to form and join trade unions. The United Nations is more equivocal about these rights than it is about civic and political rights. The same article states that no restrictions can be placed on these rights, "other than those prescribed by law and which are necessary in a democratic society in the interests of national security or public order or for the protection of the rights and freedoms of others." The right to strike must conform to national laws in which a union operates. The most ominous provision in the article for organized labor, at least in the United States, says, "This article shall not prevent the imposition of lawful restrictions on the exercise of these rights by members of the armed forces or of the police or of the administration of the State."

The covenant does refer to the 1948 ILO convention, especially its granting of freedom of association and the right to organize, stating that nothing in the covenant authorizes legislative bodies to pass laws that would "prejudice" guarantees that the ILO convention provides. But while the ILO convention provides important guarantees for workers, an Article 2 provision makes very clear that economic, social, and cultural rights enumerated in the ICESCR convention lack the urgency of civic and political rights. In effect, economic and social "rights" are characterized more as goals than as rights. The fact that limitations to these rights can only be exercised to promote "the general welfare in a democratic society" is of little consolation in a country in which a growing majority believes that unions benefit their members but harm society.

Historically, for a claim to constitute a right, it had to satisfy several conditions. According to Beetham, "It must be fundamental and universal; it must in principle be definable in justiciable form; it should be clear who has the duty to uphold or implement the right; and the responsible agency should possess the capacity to fulfill its obligation" (1995, 41–42). Arguably, the rights specified in the ICESCR covenant do not satisfy these conditions. This is not only an intellectual but a political explanation for why economic and social claims do not (and should not) rise to the level of rights, since these types of claims, as Kennedy notes (2002), typically require a redistribution of power and wealth down, which economic and political elites are reluctant to embrace. But another factor works against a program to guarantee basic economic and social rights: market forces have eroded governments' capacities to determine their economic destinies. "The structures of power and interest and the forces at work in the international economy and within developing countries themselves," Beetham observes, "pull remorselessly in the opposite direction to a basic rights agenda" (1995, 56–57).

Freedom of association and collective bargaining, abolition of forced labor, elimination of child labor, and freedom from discrimination, according to Kolben, differ from other labor rights because they "do not necessarily require a given level of economic advancement and arguably do not impact comparative advantage" (2010, 454). Organized labor's focus is on the first freedom, but Kolben notes a more expansive view among some scholars. These include a number of "social" rights, such as the right to "full and productive employment," as found in the ICESCR and labor-related social rights contained in the UDHR. Other scholars disagree. Social rights, they argue, depend on economic context, in effect converting a right into a goal and thereby diluting its moral authority. Goals, however, Nickel (2010) avers, can approximate rights if formulated correctly.

Goals gain currency when you are able to assign responsibility, identify beneficiaries, provide reasons for their importance, and assign a level of urgency. International agencies must monitor goals. One advantage of treating rights as goals is that they do not then appear ridiculous in those instances in which a country simply does not have the resources to realize them. "Goals are inherently ability-calibrated" (Nickel 2010). While it is easy to see why someone would characterize a goal as a poor substitute for a right, the goal would still have more power and a greater sense of urgency if it were endorsed internationally and by human rights organizations. The countries that ratified the ICESCR, Nickel points out, agreed to "take steps, individually and through international assistance and co-operation to the maximum of [their] available resources, with a view to achieving progressively the full realization of the rights recognized in the present Covenant" (2010). In a move reminiscent of US affirmative action, and drawing on sociological literature on institutional discrimination, international bodies could conceivably require a plan and timetable and apply sanctions to governments not making good-faith efforts to realize goals.

Internationalizing Labor Rights

While the US decline in union membership and power in the past forty years has been especially pronounced, it is a worldwide phenomenon. Globalization has blurred the employer-employee relationship. "Whereas employees used to work for an identifiable common employer, today they occupy an uncertain location on a global production and distribution chain" (Lichtenstein 2003, 61). In this environment unions are challenged to organize workers and protect their rights. To the degree that unions are principally focused on workers' rights in their own countries, and to the degree that union federations are simply another arm of the government, as they are in some countries, the task is a daunting one. It is difficult to imagine, however, completing the task without a universal standard of labor rights or goals and a labor movement that is not boxed in by national borders. Capital certainly is not.

The human rights movement, international in makeup and scope, can serve both as a model for an international labor movement and as a vehicle for workers' rights advocates. The human rights movement has not experienced the same decline as the labor movement and, in fact, can claim to be stronger today than it was forty years ago. HRW, for example, saw its budget increase from $200,000 in 1979 to $20 million by 2001 (Lichtenstein 2003, 63). Consequently, in its attempts to survive, let alone retrieve lost members and power, US organized labor may not have a choice but to cast labor issues as human rights issues and to align itself when and where it can with the human rights movement, labor movements in other countries, and other progressive US movements and organizations. The task is facilitated by the fact that many human rights documents contain provisions that speak to workers' rights. In the process, organized labor will position itself to persuade international human rights groups to broaden their human rights definitions and to rethink the mutually exclusive distinction made between civil and political rights on the one hand and economic and social rights on the other.

While establishing a set of workers' rights recognized by the international community is essential, enforcement is problematic. Government inspectors, Lichtenstein (2003) notes, are incapable, adding that only an organization representing workers has the resources and expertise to ensure protection of workers' rights, just as the NAACP and other organizations have worked to protect the rights of and advocate for African Americans. A second problem noted by Lichtenstein is that settlement of disputes is taken out of the hands of those most directly affected and placed instead in the hands of government bureaucrats if workers do not have their own representative organizations. Third, workers end up having less control over the work environment because they cannot confront capital directly. Finally, the rights revolution has done little to create a climate conducive to a strong labor movement or to scale back capital's power in determining economic conditions under which workers labor.

Lichtenstein and others are not saying that a vigorous human rights movement is not important to labor. He applauds the ILO's and other international bodies' conventions and the work of organizations such as Amnesty International and Human Rights Watch. The enforcement of civil and human rights in the workplace and of any right that impacts an individual's ability to make a living and to provide for a family is essential. But "without a bold and society-shaping political and social program, human rights can devolve into something approximating libertarian individualism" (Lichtenstein 2003, 71). Trade unions, especially an international trade union movement, can be the vehicles for this "society-shaping political and social program." Whether they can be that and still pitch economic concerns in human rights terms is less certain and certainly a question that sociologists should attempt to answer. It seems clear that doing so will require an expansive view of human rights, expressed succinctly by Beetham: "The idea of economic and social rights as human rights expresses the moral intuition that, in a world rich in resources and the accumulation of human knowledge, everyone ought to be guaranteed the basic means for sustaining life, and that those denied these are victims of a fundamental injustice" (1995, 44).

The culprits, as the human rights movement suggests, are individual states, but the lion's share of the blame is perhaps best placed on corporations—extraordinarily powerful entities that not only are not reined in easily by states but can in fact dictate to states. The United Nations is not a formidable adversary either for these behemoths. At the national level, a resurgent labor movement is one of the few counterweights to this kind of power. Ultimately, a unified and powerful international trade union movement is needed to check the power of these multinational corporations. Without it and a strong international human rights movement, human and labor rights are not likely to flourish. The human rights and labor movements may not need to run on the same track. Parallel tracks that at various junctions converge may not only be sufficient but in fact may be preferable to allow each movement the freedom it needs to secure fundamental rights for everyone, including workers. Their respective goals, however, must at least be compatible, if not the same.

Chapter Ten

Evolution, Biology, and Society

Rosemary L. Hopcroft

The Evolution, Biology and Society Section of the American Sociological Association was established in 2004 to facilitate the integration of biology into what was at the time, and still is, a highly biophobic discipline. Much of this biophobia stems from early work attempting to incorporate biology into sociology in such a way as to reinforce the prejudices of the researcher and justify existing social inequalities between classes, races, and sexes (see Gould 1981 for a review of this work). Yet current biosocial sociologists distance themselves from the faulty methods and reasoning of this early work. Rather than exacerbating existing social inequalities and reinforcing prejudices, I argue in this chapter that integration of biology into sociology can help to further the most humane goals of sociologists, in particular a concern for human rights. The biological unity of humankind and the universality of human nature underline the notion "that all men are created equal," an assumption that is the basis of most declarations of human rights. The biosocial view argues strongly against biologically based divisions between groups, but it does not deny that socially created divisions between groups exist. I argue that dissemination of information about the biological unity of the human group, coupled with understandings of the biological underpinnings of many social phenomena, can contribute to the breaking down of social divisions.

Scholars from a variety of areas were involved in the creation of the Evolution, Biology and Society Section, which is reflected in the wide range of topics it currently encompasses. Topics range from micro- to macrosociological, with the unifying feature being an acknowledgment of the role of biology in human social life. Researchers in the area use a variety of sociological methodologies as well as research results from a wide array of disciplines, including anthropology, history, primatology, paleoanthropology, biology, psychology, and neurology. The questions asked pertain to actors from individuals to whole societies and are relevant to all social institutions and structures.

The field focuses on how the universal, evolved human biology interacts with particular social environments to produce and respond simultaneously to social institutions and structures. In what follows I review the major strands of research within the evolution, biology, and society field (emotions and social behavior, neurosociology, evolution and social behavior, genes and social behavior, hormones and social behavior, and evolutionary macrosociology) and describe some of the major methods and findings within each. I also discuss what the human rights paradigm can learn from the work in this area and, conversely, what the field can learn from the human rights paradigm.

Emotions and Social Behavior

The first major strand of research within the area is microsociological in orientation in that it begins with individual emotions. The primary question for these researchers is, How are our social, symbolic, and emotional selves grounded in our shared, evolved human biology? Turner (2007) and others (Turner and Maryanski 2008; Turner and Stets 2006; Massey 2004) have focused on the implications of evolution for human emotions and the role of emotions in both social solidarity and social change. Their work is based on information from primatology, behavioral ecology, and paleoanthropology.

Turner and Maryanski (2008) trace the evolution of the human species from the early primates, through the last common ancestor of all apes, to the emergence of modern humans. They suggest that for hominoid societies to exist on the open savannah after leaving the relative shelter and safety of the forest, there was likely selection for stronger ties between individuals. They suggest that selection pressures leading to heightened individual emotions, first selected as a means to control noise levels in new, more dangerous environments, were the basis on which social solidarity could build. They show how the areas of the human brain (particularly the amygdala) that control emotions are much larger in humans than in other, less social apes. They draw on contemporary research showing the importance of emotions for human bonding, social interaction, and human reasoning. They further suggest that selection pressures for stronger ties produced the nuclear family and the hunting-and-gathering band. In another work, Turner and Maryanski (2005) argue that the development of incest taboos helped to consolidate human solidarity. Turner and Maryanski (2005, 2008) thus draw a picture of the evolved human that emerged some 150,000 years ago and has changed little since: an individualistic hominid, linked by emotional ties to group members but resistant to domination by other hominids. They note that this is the human nature that cultures have built on but not eradicated.

Other scholars within this group examine how social relations and situations in turn influence human emotions (Stets and Asencio 2008; TenHouten 2005). For example, TenHouten (2005) shows how experiences with four elementary social relations, described as market pricing, authority ranking, communal sharing, and equality matching, are linked to eight basic emotions (acceptance, disgust, happiness, sadness, anger, fear, anticipation, and surprise). Robinson, Rogalin, and Smith-Lovin (2004) discuss how the experience of in-group interactions (e.g., having high or low status) influences emotional and physiological states. Much of the research shows that occupying a low-status position is more stressful than occupying a high-status position. Massey (2004) argues that long-term exposure to stress and violence produces a high allostatic load in African Americans, and this has a variety of deleterious health and cognitive outcomes (see also Davis and Were 2008).

This research reveals the nature of humans as emotional beings with a fundamental social focus, and the human rights paradigm can benefit from a consideration of the social and emotional, as well as the economic, needs of individuals. Researchers in the area can contribute to human rights goals by examining how human emotions and social solidarity can be used both to support and to violate human rights goals.

Neurosociology

The second primary area of research in the section may be referred to as neurosociology. Franks (2010) and others (Franks and Smith 2009; Smith 2004; Hammond 2004) have been interested in work in neuroscience as it relates to emotions and other aspects of cognition. They examine the neurological basis of emotions, unconscious behavior, the role of mirror neurons in imitation and empathy, and how the social self is based on brain processes. This draws on findings in neurological research using fMRI and PET scans to examine how different parts of the brain are involved in social behaviors and emotions.

Findings include the importance of normal social interactions for the development of the individual brain and the development of the self. Another finding is the fact that the individual is not conscious of the large majority of what the brain does, perhaps as much as 80 percent. Last, contrary to many beliefs, emotion is the basis of rational decision-making. For people to make sensible decisions, the available choices must have an emotional valence. When that emotional valence is missing, for whatever reason, the person cannot make rational decisions.

Franks (2010) notes that research on mirror neurons supports the work of the Chicago pragmatists. Mirror neurons are neurons in the brain that mimic the neurons of others. So when a person falls and feels pain neurons in his or her brain fire, the same neurons in the brain of a person witnessing the event also fire. This means that, to a certain extent, the witness actually feels the faller's pain. As a result, mirror neurons are importantly involved in empathy. They are also involved in helping individuals to see how others see them, and this is an important component of the development of self-identity and self-esteem. This is the mechanism for what Charles Horton Cooley referred to as the "looking-glass self," although Cooley, of course, was not aware of the neural basis of the phenomenon he described (Franks 2010). Other neurosociologists show how additional social processes are based on the existing neurology of the human brain. For example, Hammond (2004) shows how social experiences such as religious experience piggyback on neurological circuits evolved for different purposes.

The area of neurosociology once again shows the importance of a normal social life for individual well-being. The human rights paradigm can shape work in this area through a renewed focus on the implications of our neurology for the functioning of small groups—for example, group solidarity, status processes, and conflict—and their consequences for human rights. Methodologically, more work with groups from outside Western cultures would be helpful.

Evolution and Social Behavior

This next area of research takes the opposite stance to the microsociological research discussed above—that is, evolved human universals are assumed to shape culture and aggregate social behavior in all societies, and the question is how they do so. The focus is thus on aggregate trends across human societies. Research has been done primarily in six areas: family processes and fertility, sex differences, religion, crime, ethnic behavior, and sociological theory. Each of these areas is discussed below. Methods used include standard statistical methods such as survey methods and analysis of existing data, experimental methods, as well as more qualitative methods such as field research and comparative historical sociology.

Pioneering work in the area of the family using the evolutionary perspective was done by van den Berghe (1979). He notes the centrality of kin processes in all societies, as well as commonalities in mate choice and parenting across societies. For example, in all human societies women marry men who are older than they are, on average, although the age gap varies across cultures. In all human societies women perform the majority of childcare, whether for their own children or the children of others (Brewster and Rindfuss 2000, 272). In the United States, Biblarz and Raftery (1999) found the counterintuitive finding that single mothers are better at sponsoring the educational and occupational attainment of their children than reconstituted families, and they note this is consistent with evolutionary theory that posits greater investment by women than men in their children, on average. In terms of measured investment, adopted children receive more investment than biological children, but this is because adoptive parents have higher socioeconomic status than other parents (Hamilton, Cheng, and Powell 2007). Adjusting for parental income, adoptive parents invest at the same rate as biological parents. There have been tests of the Trivers-Willard hypothesis of biased investment in sons and daughters by family income in the United States, with mixed results both supportive of Trivers-Willard (Hopcroft 2005) and not supportive (Freese and Powell 1999). Work focusing on male fertility finds that for men, and not women, personal earnings are positively associated with number of biological children in the United States, Sweden, and the United Kingdom (Hopcroft 2005; Fieder and Huber 2007; Nettle and Pollet 2008)

Researchers also note a variety of sex differences they suggest have an evolved basis. A comprehensive survey of sex differences was published by Ellis et al. (2008). Rossi (1984) noted sex differences in parenting behavior in the United States. Other researchers have examined the sex difference in depression (Hopcroft and Bradley 2007); some have examined the implications of sex differences for gender inequality (Huber 2007; Ellis 2001; Hopcroft 2009).

Sanderson (2008) has argued for an evolutionary perspective on religion. He argues that during the human evolutionary period religiosity was an adaptive trait—that is, it helped individuals survive and reproduce—and this has ensured a universal predisposition toward religious sentiments. Miller and Stark (2002) have suggested that the sex difference in religiosity may be innate and hence evolved, although others prefer socialization arguments (e.g., Collett and Lizardo 2009).

Regarding crime, Ellis (2004; see also Savage and Vila 2003) notes that universally young men are more involved in crime than any other group. Ellis argues that there are evolutionary reasons to explain this. Crime may be seen as a risky way of attaining status and resources. In the evolutionary environment, there was likely selection for traits promoting status-striving behavior in males. This encourages males to use a variety of methods to attain status—even risky methods if others are not available. Ethnic behavior such as altruism to fellow ethnic group members is another universal human phenomenon, examined by van den Berghe (1981), who argues that ethnic behavior may be seen as an extension of kin selection to the wider ethnic group (see also Whitmeyer 1997).

The implications of evolutionary theory for sociological theory have been evaluated by a number of authors. Blute (2006, 2010) examines the possibility of using models from evolutionary biology to model cultural evolution. Kiser and Welser (2010) have made a similar argument for comparative historical sociology. Sanderson (2001, 2007; see also Horne 2004) has argued that materialist theories need help from evolutionary theories particularly to explain many nonrational behaviors. Hopcroft (2008) has suggested that evolutionary theory can help create a unifying paradigm for sociology, as many of the pro-social behaviors of interest to sociologists (within the family, for example) are likely based on evolved predispositions.

Much work remains to be done on the entire range of human social behaviors—family, race and ethnicity, stratification, fertility, and gender. Family is of particular interest to the human rights paradigm, as the Universal Declaration of Human Rights singles out special protection for the family as follows: "The family is the natural and fundamental group unit of society and is entitled to protection by society." Understanding human universals in the family and how they contribute to individual well-being will further both this subfield and the human rights paradigm.

Genes and Social Behavior

The next area is primarily focused on individual variation and is the focus of significant current research. The central question in this area is, How do human genetic potentials interact with specific social contexts to produce social behavior? This is macrosociology because the researchers generally use statistical methods to find patterns in large data sets. Much of this research relies on DNA data collection along with typical survey data on attitudes and behaviors. One of the major data sets is the National Longitudinal Study of Adolescent Health (Add Health), collected by researchers at the University of North Carolina, Chapel Hill.

Using these data, criminologist Kevin Beaver (2008; Vaughn et al. 2009) and Guang Guo, Michael Roettger, and Tianji Cai have examined the interaction between genes and environment in criminal and delinquent behavior. Using a variety of data sets, researchers have examined the interaction of genes and environment in substance dependence (Button et al. 2009), smoking (Boardman, Blalock, and Pampel 2010), and drinking (Pescosolido et al. 2008; Guo et al. 2009). A variety of studies also examine the interaction of genes and social contexts in physical and mental health (Adkins, Wang, and Elder 2008; Kendler, Jaffee, and Romer 2010). Other researchers have examined the relative effects of genes on educational attainment (Shanahan, Bauldry, and Freeman 2008), happiness (Schnittker 2008), age at first intercourse (Guo and Tong 2006), number of sexual partners (Guo, Tong, and Cai 2008), and fertility behavior (Kohler, Rodgers, and Christensen 1999, 2002).

One general finding that emerges from a number of these studies is that genetic influence on behavior is stronger during affluent periods when individuals (presumably) have more choice. This has been capitalized on by Nielsen (2006), who suggests that the degree to which individuals achieve genetic potential can reflect the opportunities present in their societies (see also Adkins and Vaisey 2009). Although this generally rises with affluence, there is variation in such opportunities across developed societies.

One limitation of this area, as Perrin and Hedwig (2007) have argued, is that it focuses too much on individuals and too little on social contexts. This is in part because most of the early research in the area was produced by nonsociologists, who are less aware of social contexts and their roles in shaping behavior. Sociologists engaging in this work are less likely to make this mistake (Shanahan et al. 2010). A human rights approach should maintain the focus on the importance of context and keep in mind that individual variability exists within overarching universals. After all, human beings share the vast majority of their genes, and genetic variants are only a tiny fraction of the entire human genome.

Hormones and Social Behavior

Other researchers examine the effects of various hormones on individual behavior. The central question in this area is, What is the role of hormones in human social behavior? Some of this research shows the direct relationship between hormones and social behavior. For example, Mazur (2004; Mazur and Booth 1998) has shown that the hormone testosterone fluctuates with social position: winning competitions causes a rise in testosterone; conversely losing in competitions causes a fall in testosterone. These effects of winning and losing even extend to people who watch sports. During the 1994 World Cup in which Brazil beat Italy, the Brazilian fans who watched the match on TV saw a rise in testosterone after the game, whereas the Italian fans who watched the match saw a decline (Dabbs and Dabbs 2000). Udry (2000) examined how different in utero exposure to testosterone was associated with women's gendered behavior thirty years later.

Other researchers note there is a complex interaction between hormones and social context. Updegraff, Booth, and Thayer (2006) show that testosterone's effects are dependent on social context: when boys had close relationships with their mothers and sisters, testosterone was positively associated with peer involvement and competence; the reverse held when they did not have close relationships with their mothers and sisters. Booth, Johnson, and Granger (2005) likewise found that the effects of husbands' testosterone levels on marital quality depended on whether the husbands perceived high levels of role overload.

Much of this research has focused on easily measured biochemicals such as testosterone and cortisol (e.g., Booth, Granger, and Shirtcliff 2008), and much of it has focused on the effects in males. Much less research has focused on females. A human rights perspective necessitates that more attention be given to women. Future work should examine the range of socially related biochemicals and their interactions with social contexts, as well as examine both women and men. Another area of study promoted by human rights approaches is the effect of human-made biochemicals (such as antibiotics and steroids routinely given to farm animals, biochemical residuals in the water supply, etc.) in the environment and their effects on human health.

Evolutionary Macrosociology

The last area is a macrosociological one that examines large-scale societal change and the evolution of human societies. The primary question for these researchers is, What are the constraints placed by human nature on social arrangements and social change at the macro-level? The primary method is comparative-historical.

Gerhard Lenski (1966, 2005), the pioneering scholar in this area, was the first to note the importance of subsistence technology in shaping social arrangements and the degree of social stratification. Lenski's conclusion that a society's subsistence technology (hunting and gathering, horticulture, plow agriculture, or industrialization) predicts its population (size), social organization, and ideology is well known and much used. The association of complexity of subsistence technology with complexity in occupational and political structures is also well known. Lenski's (1966) finding that social inequality increases with increased complexity of subsistence technology until we reach industrial societies has also been widely recognized (Nielsen 2004). Others note the implications of subsistence technology for gender stratification. While the amount of gender stratification in society most often tracks the degree of stratification in general, Blumberg (2004) suggests that the most important factor influencing gender stratification in a society is women's relative control of key economic resources. Women are more likely to have a higher status in societies where they contribute to the society's main productive activities, but women's work does not enhance gender equality unless it also results in control of significant economic resources.

Lenski and Nolan (2005) hypothesized that societies that were previously agrarian do better in terms of various measures of development than societies that were previously horticultural. The hypothesis is strongly supported empirically. Lenski's theory also has implications for the failures of Marxist societies, which in Lenski's view stemmed from the failure of Marxism to fully understand human nature. Marxist societies ended with a concentration of power at the top, resulting in communist societies more closely resembling monarchies and oligarchies in agrarian societies. This form of government is also associated with many human rights abuses, both in the Soviet case and the current Chinese market-oriented communist regime.

Unlike Lenski, who focuses on internal characteristics of societies for explaining societal evolution, other authors link the process of societal evolution to the society's place in the modern world-system and adopt a world-systems theoretical perspective (e.g., Chase-Dunn 2005). Hall and Fenelon (2009) have looked at the distinctiveness of indigenous movements and how they have responded to recent policy reforms and globalization. Findings from this research highlight the importance of the influence of global and historical forces on indigenous movements.

One of the primary limitations of this research is that most studies are qualitative—few scholars employ quantitative methodologies. This is partly because good-quality, comparable quantitative data are not available for many historical societies. A human rights focus also necessitates more quantitative comparative research, as abuses of human rights are often most effectively documented with quantitative evidence.

Implications of the Evolution, Biology, and Society Area for the Human Rights Paradigm

All these subtopics within the evolution, biology, and society area stress the interaction of human biology with social contexts in explaining social phenomena. Unlike earlier attempts to incorporate biology into sociology, however, this research mitigates against biological divisions between human groups, as it stresses the fundamental biological unity of humankind. Most of the great variation in social behavior exists because of differing social, cultural, and economic contexts of peoples around the world. Only a small amount of this variation in social behavior exists because of individual differences in biological makeup, although genetically based individual variation does exist and can be consequential for individual behavior. Whether it is or not, once again, depends on the social, cultural, and economic context.

This research demonstrates the importance for all humans of experiencing a socially rich life, as well as the deleterious effects of social and economic deprivation and stress. Research in this area also shows how some social, cultural, and economic contexts are better at enabling individuals to live normal lives, achieve their potential as individuals, and avoid violence, hunger, and stress. Generally, more affluent societies are better at this, although there is variation among developed societies.

These findings have a variety of implications for the human rights paradigm. First, it is important that the paradigm acknowledge the role that this research suggests economic development and the acquisition of affluence play in promoting individual well-being and the achievement of individual potential. At the same time, development that forces people to sever social ties or that does not promote meritocracy is unlikely to further human well-being. One-size-fits-all development policies should be avoided in favor of policies that offer maximum flexibility to all individuals.

The evolution, biology, and society area can also benefit from a consideration of the human rights paradigm. For example, researchers in the area should give more explicit attention to the implications for human rights and well-being and to policy recommendations. Furthermore, researchers should be careful to state that findings apply to the average person and not each individual, and policy-makers should ensure that policies based on findings of this research allow for individual variation.

DISCUSSION QUESTIONS

Chapter 1: Community and Urban Sociology

1. What is globalization? How do the forces of globalization affect cities in ways that make it difficult for community members (whether urban, rural, or suburban) to realize their human rights?
2. Are human rights, as studied by community and urban sociologists, reformist or radical? In what ways? What is the difference?
3. What are the key human rights concerns facing our urban areas in the United States? How are these similar to or different from those facing urban dwellers in other countries? China? The U.K.? Japan?
4. What is a "human rights city"?
5. If you were to create movement in your own hometown to ensure human rights of your neighbors (known and unknown), what would that process look like?

Chapter 2: Peace, War, and Social Conflict

1. Why do you think war, as well as peace, is not considered an important topic in sociology? How does taking a human rights perspective change how we see war and peace?
2. What are the four principle theories of war and peace? How do human rights figure (or not figure) into each?
3. Why does the author point to the end of modernism, the end of the Cold War, and the rise of globalization? How have these global sociopolitical changes affected the shape of both war and peace?
4. Is it important to transcend the nationalistic heritage of sociology? Why? Is there such a thing as a "sociology without borders"?

Chapter 3: Environment and Technology

1. From a human rights perspective, do the benefits of technology outweigh the costs? Explain your response.
2. What might the aggressive use of modern technology for human rights look like?

3. How does thinking with a human rights lens change our reaction to environmental catastrophes? Think about both human-made disasters and natural disasters.
4. How can we better prepare for the inevitable failure of technologies?
5. Does every human being have a right to the positive benefits of environment or technology? How can we protect this right?

Chapter 4: Population

1. How can population data be used to advance human rights?
2. How can demographers contribute to efforts to prevent genocide?
3. What is an example of a social movement that arose from a population policy?
4. Should we expect a demographic transition process to shape human rights advancement?
5. In what ways can human rights prevent human-made disasters?

Chapter 5: Collective Behavior and Social Movements

1. Have you ever participated in "collective behavior" and/or "social movements"? What was your experience like?
2. What are Transnational Advocacy Networks? How do they function?
3. Why does the author claim that "the global women's movement may be the single best contemporary illustration of activists working for the advancement of human rights while simultaneously transforming understandings of them"?
4. Can cultural sensitivity and respect for human rights coexist?

Chapter 6: Alcohol, Drugs, and Tobacco

1. There is a lack of science behind determining the legality and illegality of drugs. Given this fact, how might we better respond to drug use in our society?
2. Should drug dependency be treated or punished in communities and in courts? Why?
3. What would be the effects of the legalization of drugs and alcohol (lowering the drinking age)? Think about the effects in our local communities and on international drug growth, manufacture, and trade.
4. Why are cigarettes, a known carcinogen, still manufactured and sold? Why do we still support the growth of tobacco with World Bank loans?

Chapter 7: Rationality and Society

1. According to rational-choice theory, how might we make adherence to human rights a more likely outcome?

2. Is it always rational to promote and protect human rights? Why or why not?
3. According to rational-choice theorists, you have behaved in a way that you see as benefiting you. How have these decisions perhaps threatened or protected human rights?
4. This chapter applies rational-choice theory to the workings of the ICC. What about other institutions or nongovernmental organizations? How do you think individuals in these organizations work to protect both their individual best interests and human rights more broadly?

Chapter 8: International Migration

1. Is migration a human right?
2. According to the chapter, what are the variety of reasons individuals and families migrate internationally? Are these reasons linked to human rights issues?
3. What are the potential human rights consequences of migration?
4. What new questions does a human rights approach to international migration encourage us to ask?

Chapter 9: Labor and Labor Movements

1. What types of human rights are needed to advance labor rights?
2. In what ways can human rights shape the work of organized labor?
3. What strategies taken by labor movements could be useful to advancing human rights?
4. When we think of the human rights of labor, what "goals are inherently ability-calibrated?"

Chapter 10: Evolution, Biology, and Society

1. In what ways may human rights be useful to the functioning of small groups?
2. Chicken or egg? Will human rights become part of evolved human universals, or vice versa? How?
3. How does the human right to scientific progress shape scientific studies of biochemicals?
4. In what ways can a human rights approach help an expert recommend a policy that suits the needs of individuals, rather than a one-size-fits-all policy?

List of Acronyms

AFL-CIO	American Federation of Labor and Congress of Industrial Organizations
ANT	actor network theory
ASA	American Sociological Association
CA	conversation analysis
CBSM	collective behavior and social movements
CEDAW	Convention on the Elimination of All Forms of Discrimination against Women
CUS	community and urban sociology
DOMA	Defense of Marriage Act
EM	ethnomethodology
EPI	Economic Policy Institute
FGC	female genital cutting
fMRI	functional magnetic resonance imaging
HRW	Human Rights Watch
ICANN	Internet Corporation for Assigned Names and Numbers
ICC	International Criminal Court
ICCPR	International Covenant on Civil and Political Rights
ICESCR	International Covenant on Economic, Social, and Cultural Rights
ICJ	International Court of Justice
ICT	information and communication technology
ICTY	International Criminal Tribunal for the Former Yugoslavia
ILO	International Labour Organization
IMF	International Monetary Fund
INGO	international nongovernmental organization
IRAF	International Association for Religious Freedom
IRLA	International Religious Liberty Association
LGBT	lesbian, gay, bisexual, and transgender
LIS	Luxembourg Income Study
MCA	membership categorization analysis
MSM	men who have sex with men
NAACP	National Association for the Advancement of Colored People
NAFTA	North American Free Trade Agreement
NELP	National Employment Law Project
NGO	nongovernmental organization

NHSL	National Health and Social Life
NIA	National Institute on Aging
NICHD	National Institute of Child Health and Human Development
NSF	National Science Foundation
OECD	Organization for Economic Cooperation and Development
PDHRE	People's Decade for Human Rights Education
PET	positron emission tomography
PISA	Programme for International Student Assessment
SA	sequential analysis
SALC	sociology of age and the life course
SKAT	science, knowledge, and technology
SSP	social structure and personality
STD	sexually transmitted disease
STI	sexually transmitted infection
STS	science and technology studies
SWS	Sociologists for Women in Society
TAN	transnational advocacy network
TANF	Temporary Aid to Needy Families
TINA	there is no alternative
TVA	Tennessee Valley Authority
UDHR	Universal Declaration of Human Rights
UN	United Nations
UNCRC	United Nations Convention on the Rights of the Child
UNESCO	United Nations Educational, Scientific, and Cultural Organization
UNICEF	United Nations International Children's Emergency Fund
WHO	World Health Organization
WSF	World Social Forum
WTO	World Trade Organization
WWII	World War II

BIBLIOGRAPHY

A., E. 1950a. "Grace Abbot and Hull House 1908-1921. Part 1." *Social Service Review* 24: 374-394.
———. 1950b. "Grace Abbot and Hull House 1908-1921. Part 2." *Social Service Review* 24: 493-518.
Abbot, Andrew. 1988. *The System of Professions: An Essay on the Division of Expert Labor.* Chicago: University of Chicago Press.
———. 2001. "Self-Similar Social Structures." In *Chaos of Disciplines,* 157-196. Chicago: University of Chicago Press.
Abolafia, Mitchell. 2001. *Making Markets: Opportunism and Restraint on Wall Street.* Cambridge, MA: Harvard University Press.
Abraham, David. 2009. "Doing Justice on Two Fronts: The Liberal Dilemma in Immigration." *Ethnic and Racial Studies* 33, no. 6: 968-985.
Abraham, John. 2010. "Pharmaceuticalization of Society in Context: Theoretical, Empirical and Health Dimensions." *Sociology* 44, no. 4: 603-622.
Abramovitz, Mimi. 1998. "Social Work and Social Reform: An Arena of Struggle." *Social Work* 43: 512-526.
Achenbaum, Andrew W. 1978. *Old Age in the New Land: The American Experience since 1790.* Baltimore: Johns Hopkins University Press.
———. 2009. "A Metahistorical Perspective on Theories of Aging." In *Handbook of Theories of Aging,* edited by V. L. Bengston, D. Gans, N. M. Putney, and M. Silverstein. 2nd ed. New York: Springer Publishing.
Acker, Joan. 2006. "Inequality Regimes: Gender, Class and Race in Organizations." *Gender and Society* 20: 441-464.
Ackerly, B. A. 2008. *Universal Human Rights in a World of Difference.* New York: Cambridge University Press.
Ackerly, Brooke A., and Bina D'Costa. 2005. "Transnational Feminism: Political Strategies and Theoretical Resources." Working paper, Australian National University Department of International Relations.
Adam, Barry D. 1998. "Theorizing Homophobia." *Sexualities* 1: 387-404.
Adam, Barry D., Dan Willem Duyvendak, and André Krouwel. 1999. *The Global Emergence of Gay and Lesbian Politics: National Imprints of a Worldwide Movement.* Philadelphia: Temple University Press.
Adams, Carol. 1990. *The Sexual Politics of Meat.* New York: Continuum Press.
Adams, Guy, and Danny Balfour. 1998. *Unmasking Administrative Evil.* Thousand Oaks, CA: Sage.
———. 2004. "Human Rights, the Moral Vacuum of Modern Organizations, and Administrative Evil." In *Human Rights and the Moral Responsibilities of Corporate and Public Sector Organizations,* edited by Tom Campbell and Seamus Miller, 205-221. New York: Kluwer Academic Publishers.
Adams, Vincanne. 1998. "Suffering the Winds of Lhasa: Politicized Bodies, Human Rights, Cultural Difference, and Humanism in Tibet." *Medical Anthropology Quarterly* 12: 74-102.
———. 2010. "Against Global Health? Arbitrating Science, Non-Science, and Nonsense through Health." In *Against Health: How Health Became the New Morality,* edited by Jonathan M. Metzl and Anna Kirkland, 40-58. New York: New York University Press.
Adas, Michael. 2006. *Dominance by Design: Technological Imperatives and America's Civilizing Mission.* Cambridge, MA: Harvard University Press.
Addams, Jane. 1999. *Twenty Years at Hull House.* New York: Signet Classics.
Adelson, Joseph. 2001. "Sex among the Americans." In *Speaking of Sexuality: Interdisciplinary Readings,* edited by J. Kenneth Davidson Sr. and Nelwyn B. Moore, 57-63. Los Angeles: Roxbury Publishing.
Adeola, F. O. 1994. "Environmental Hazards, Health, and Racial Inequity in Hazardous Waste Distribution." *Environment and Behavior* 26: 99-126.
———. 2000a. "Cross-National Environmental Injustice and Human Rights Issues: A Review of Evidence in the Developing World." *American Behavioral Scientist* 43: 686-706.
———. 2000b. "Endangered Community, Enduring People: Toxic Contamination, Health and Adaptive Responses in a Local Context." *Environment and Behavior* 32: 209-249.
———. 2001. "Environmental Injustice and Human Rights Abuse: The States, MNCs, and Repression of Minority Groups in the World System." *Human Ecology Review* 8: 39-59.

———. 2004. "Environmentalism and Risk Perception: Empirical Analysis of Black and White Differentials and Convergence." *Society and Natural Resources* 17: 911-939.
———. 2009. "From Colonialism to Internal Colonialism and Crude Socioenvironmental Injustice: Anatomy of Violent Conflicts in the Niger Delta of Nigeria." In *Environmental Justice in the New Millennium: Global Perspectives on Race, Ethnicity, and Human Rights*, edited by F. C. Steady, 135-163. New York: Palgrave Macmillan.
———. 2011. *Hazardous Wastes, Industrial Disasters, and Environmental Health Risk: Local and Global Environmental Struggles*. New York: Palgrave Macmillan.
Adikari, Y., and J. Yoshitani. 2009. *Global Trends in Water-Related Disasters: An Insight for Policymakers*. Paris: UNESCO.
Adkins, Daniel E., and Stephen Vaisey. 2009. "Toward a Unified Stratification Theory: Structure, Genome, and Status across Human Societies." *Sociological Theory* 27: 99-121.
Adkins, Daniel E., Victor Wang, and Glen H. Elder Jr. 2008. "Stress Processes and Trajectories of Depressive Symptoms in Early Life: Gendered Development." *Advances in Life Course Research* 13: 107-136.
Adkins, W. 2003. "The Social Construction of Disability: A Theoretical Perspective." Paper presented at the annual meeting for the American Sociological Association, Atlanta, Georgia, 1-31.
Adler, Patricia A., and Peter Adler. 2011. *The Tender Cut: Inside the Hidden World of Self-Injury*. New York: New York University Press.
Adorno, T. 2003. "Education after Auschwitz." In *Can One Live after Auschwitz? A Philosophical Reader*, edited by R. Tiedemann, 19-33. Stanford, CA: Stanford University Press.
AFL-CIO. 2005. "The Silent War: The Assault on Workers' Freedom to Choose a Union and Bargain Collectively in the United States." Issue Brief. AFL-CIO. September. http://www.aflcio.org/joinaunion/how/upload/vatw_issuebrief.pdf.
Agyeman, J. 2005. *Sustainable Communities and the Challenge of Environmental Justice*. New York: New York University Press.
Ajrouch, Kristine J. 2007. "Global Contexts and the Veil: Muslim Integration in the United States and France." *Sociology of Religion* 68: 321-325.
Alba, R., and V. Nee. 1997. "Rethinking Assimilation Theory for a New Era of Immigration." *International Migration Review* 31: 826-874.
Albritton, Robert B. 2005. "Thailand in 2004: The 'Crisis in the South.'" *Asian Survey* 45: 166-173.
Aldrich, Howard E. 1999. *Organizations Evolving*. London: Sage.
Alexander, D. 2006. "Globalization of Disaster: Trends, Problems and Dilemmas." *Journal of International Affairs* 59: 1-22.
Alexander, Jeffrey. 2006. *The Civil Sphere*. New York: Oxford University Press.
———. 2010. "Power, Politics, and the Civil Sphere." In *Handbook of Politics: State and Society in Global Perspective*, edited by K. T. Leicht and J. C. Jenkins, 111-126. Heidelberg and New York: Springer Science and Business Media.
Alexander, Jeffrey C. 2004. "On the Social Construction of Moral Universals: The 'Holocaust' from War Crime to Trauma Drama." In *Cultural Trauma and Collective Identity*, edited by J. C. Alexander et al., 196-263. Berkeley: University of California Press.
Alexander, Jeffrey C., Ron Eyerman, Bernard Giesen, Neil J. Smelser, and Piotr Sztompka. 2004. *Cultural Trauma and Collective Identity*. Berkeley: University of California Press.
Alexander, M. Jacqui, and Chandra Talpade Mohanty. 1997. "Introduction." In *Feminist Genealogies, Colonial Legacies, Democratic Future*, edited by M. Jacqui Alexander and Chandra Talpade Mohanty, xiii-xlii. New York: Routledge.
Allegretto, Sylvia A. 2011. "The State of Working America's Wealth, 2011: Through Volatility and Turmoil, the Gap Widens." Economic Policy Institute, State of Working America. http://www.epi.org/page/-/BriefingPaper292.pdf?nocdn=1 (accessed March 23, 2011).
Allen, Beverly. 1996. *Rape Warfare: The Hidden Genocide in Bosnia-Herzegovina and Croatia*. Minneapolis: University of Minnesota Press.
Allman, Paula. 2001. *Critical Education against Global Capitalism: Karl Marx and Revolutionary Critical Education*. Westport, CT: Bergin and Garvey.
———. 2007. *On Marx: An Introduction to the Revolutionary Intellect of Karl Marx*. Rotterdam: Sense Publishers.
Allport, G. W. 1954. *The Nature of Prejudice*. Reading, MA: Addison-Wesley.
Altbach, Philip G., and Patti Peterson. 1971. "Before Berkeley: Historical Perspectives on American Student Activism." *Annals of the American Academy of Political and Social Science* 395: 1-14.
Altenbaugh, Richard J. 1990. *Education for Struggle: The American Labor Colleges of the 1920s and 1930s*. Philadelphia: Temple University Press.
Alvarez-Jimenez, Alberto. 2009. "The WTO Appellate Body's Decision-Making Process." *Journal of International Economics Law* 12, no. 2: 289-331.

Alvesson, Mats, and Hugh Willmott, eds. 1992. *Critical Management Studies.* London: Sage.
———. 2003. *Studying Management Critically.* London: Sage Publications.
Alwin, Duane F., Scott M. Hofer, and Ryan J. McCammon. 2006. "Modeling the Effects of Time: Integrating Demographic and Developmental Perspectives." In *Handbook of Aging and the Social Sciences,* edited by R. H. Binstock and L. K. George, 20–41. 6th ed. Amsterdam: Elsevier.
American Civil Liberties Union (ACLU). 2010. "President Obama Signs Bill Reducing Sentencing Disparities." ACLU. http://www.aclu.org/drug-law-reform/president-obama-signs-bill-reducing-cocaine-sentencing-disparity (accessed October 18, 2011).
American Sociological Association (ASA). 2011. "Animals and Society Section." ASA. www2.asanet.org/sectionanimals (accessed March 1, 2011).
Amirthalingam, Kumaraligam. 2005. "Women's Rights, International Norms, and Domestic Violence: Asian Perspectives." *Human Rights Quarterly* 27: 683–708.
Amnesty International. 2010. *Amnesty International Report 2010.* London: Amnesty International British Section.
An Na'im, Abdullahi Ahmed. 1992. "Toward a Cross-Cultural Approach to Defining International Standards of Human Rights: The Meaning of Cruel, Inhuman or Degrading Treatment or Punishment." In *Human Rights in Cross-Cultural Perspectives,* edited by Abdullahi Ahmed An-Na'im, 19–43. Philadelphia: University of Pennsylvania Press.
———. 2001. "Human Rights." In *The Blackwell Companion to Sociology,* edited by Judith Blau, 86–99. Malden, MA: Blackwell.
Ancheta, Angelo N. 1998. "Race, Rights, and the Asian American Experience." *Journal of Asian American Studies* 1: 293–297.
Anderson, Benedict. 2006 [1983]. *Imagined Communities: Reflections on the Origin and Spread of Nationalism.* London: Verso, New Left Books.
Anderson, Elijah. 1994. *Code of the Street.* New York: W. W. Norton.
———. 2000. *Code of the Street: Decency, Violence, and the Moral Life of the Inner City.* New York: W. W. Norton.
———. 2011. *The Cosmopolitan Canopy: Race and Civility in Everyday Life.* New York: W. W. Norton.
Anderson, Leon, and David A. Snow. 2001. "Inequality and the Self: Exploring Connections from an Interactionist Perspective." *Symbolic Interaction* 24: 395–406.
Anderson, Margo, and Stephen Fienberg. 2001. *Who Counts: The Politics of Census-Taking in Contemporary America.* New York: Russell Sage Foundation.
Andersson, Matthew A., and Colleen S. Conley. 2008. "Expecting to Heal through Self-Expression: A Perceived Control Theory of Writing and Health." *Health Psychology Review* 2: 138–162.
Anghie, Antony. 1970. "On the Measurement of Inequality." *Journal of Economic Theory* 2: 244–263.
———. 2005. *Imperialism, Sovereignty and the Making of International Law.* Cambridge, UK: Cambridge University Press.
Annette, John. 2005. "Character, Civic Renewal and Service Learning for Democratic Citizenship in Higher Education." *British Journal of Educational Studies* 53: 326–340.
Anoushirvani, S. 2010. "The Future of the International Criminal Court: The Long Road to Legitimacy Begins with the Trial of Thomas Lubanga Dyilo." *Pace International Law Review* 22: 213–239.
Antrobus, Peggy. 2004. *The Global Women's Movement: Origins, Issues, and Strategies.* London: Zed Books.
Apocada, C. 2007. "The Whole World Could Be Watching." *Journal of Human Rights* 6: 147–164.
Archibugi, Daniele. 2008. *The Global Commonwealth of Citizens.* Princeton, NJ: Princeton University Press.
Arena, Jay. 2010. "The Contested Terrains of Public Sociology: Theoretical and Practical Lessons from the Movement to Defend Public Housing in Pre- and Post-Katrina New Orleans." *Societies without Borders* 5: 103–125.
Aries, Philippe. 1962. *Centuries of Childhood.* New York: Vintage.
Arington, Michele. 1991. "English Only Laws and Direct Legislation: The Battle in the States over Language Minority Rights." *Journal of Law and Politics* 7: 325–352.
Armstrong, Susan J., and Richard G. Botzler, eds. 2008. *The Animal Ethics Reader.* 2nd ed. London and New York: Routledge.
Aronowitz, Stanley. 1988. *Science as Power: Discourse and Ideology in Modern Society.* Minneapolis: University of Minnesota Press.
Arum, Richard. 2011. *Academically Adrift: Limited Learning on College Campuses.* Chicago: University of Chicago Press.
Arzberger, Peter, Peter Schroeder, Anne Beaulieu, Geof Bowker, Kathleen Casey, Leif Laaksonen, David Moorman, Paul Uhlir, and Paul Wouters. 2004. "An International Framework to Promote Access to Data." *Science* 303, no. 5665: 1777–1778.
Asch, A. 2001. "Disability, Bioethics, and Human Rights." In *Handbook of Disability Studies,* edited by G. L. Albrecht, K. D. Seelman, and M. Bury, 297–326. Thousand Oaks, CA: Sage.

Asencio, Marysol. 2009. *Latina/o Sexualities: Probing Powers, Passions, Practices, and Policies.* New Brunswick, NJ: Rutgers University Press.
Ashar, Sameer. 2003. "Immigration Enforcement and Subordination: The Consequences of Racial Profiling after September 11." *Immigration and National Law Review* 23: 545–560.
Atkin, C. K., K. Neuendorf, and S. McDermott. 1983. "The Role of Alcohol Advertising in Excessive and Hazardous Drinking." *Journal of Drug Education* 13: 313–325.
Atkinson, A. B. 1970. "On the Measurement of Inequality." *Journal of Economic Theory* 2: 244–263.
Atkinson, Anthony B. 1975. *The Economics of Inequality.* London: Oxford.
Atterton, Peter, and Matthew Calarco, eds. 2004. *Animal Philosophy: Ethics and Identity.* New York: Continuum.
Aylward, Carol A. 2010. "Intersectionality: Crossing the Theoretical and Praxis Divide." *Journal of Critical Race Inquiry* 1: 1–48.
Baars, Jan, Dale Dannefer, Chris Philipson, and Alan Walker. 2006. *Aging, Globalization, and Inequality: The New Critical Gerontology.* Amityville, NY: Baywood Publishing Company.
Babugura, Agnes A. 2008. "Vulnerability of Children and Youth in Drought Disasters: A Case Study of Botswana." *Children, Youth, and Environments* 18, no. 1: 126–157.
Baca, Maxine Zinn, and Bonnie Thornton Dill. 1994. "Difference and Domination." In *Women of Color in U.S. Society.* Philadelphia: Temple University Press.
———. 1996. "Theorizing Difference from Multiracial Feminism." *Feminist Studies* 22: 321–331.
Baden, Sally, and Anne Marie Goetz. 1997. "Who Needs [Sex] When You Can Have [Gender]? Conflicting Discourses on Gender at Beijing." In *Women, International Development, and Politics,* edited by Kathleen Staudt, 37–58. Philadelphia: Temple University Press.
Bagemihl, Bruce. 2000. *Biological Exuberance: Animal Homosexuality and Natural Diversity.* New York: St. Martin's Press.
Bailey, Christopher. 2004. "'Informed Choice' to 'Social Hygiene': Government Control of Smoking in the US." *Journal of American Studies* 38, no. 1: 41–65.
Baker, Carrie N. 2007. *The Women's Movement against Sexual Harassment.* New York: Cambridge University Press.
Bakker, J. I. (Hans). 1993. *Toward a Just Civilization: Gandhi.* Toronto: Canadian Scholars' Press.
———. 2010a. "Theory, Role of." In *Encyclopedia of Case Study Research,* edited by Albert J. Mills, Gabrielle Durepos, and Elden Wiebe, 930–932. Los Angeles, CA: Sage.
———. 2010b. "Deference versus Democracy in Traditional and Modern Bureaucracy: A Refinement of Max Weber's Ideal Type Model." In *Society, History and the Global Condition of Humanity,* edited by Zaheer Baber and Joseph M. Bryant, 105–128. Lanham, MD: Lexington Publishers.
Bales, Kevin, and Ron Soodalter. 2009. *The Slave Next Door: Human Trafficking and Slavery in America Today.* Berkeley: University of California Press.
Baltrušaitytė, G. 2010. "Psychiatry and the Mental Patient: An Uneasy Relationship." *Culture and Society* 1. http://culturesociety.vdu.lt/wp-content/uploads/2010/11/G.-Baltrusaityte-Psychiatry-and-the-Mental-Patient-An-Uneasy-Relationship1.pdf (accessed January 22, 2012).
Bandy, Joe, and Jackie Smith. 2005. *Coalitions across Borders: Transnational Protest and the Neoliberal Order.* Lanham, MD: Rowman & Littlefield.
Barak, Gregg, ed. 1991. *Crimes by the Capitalist State: An Introduction to State Criminality.* Albany: State University of New York Press.
Barbalet, J. M. 1995. "Symposium: Human Rights and the Sociological Project (a Social Emotions Theory of Basic Rights)." *Australian and New Zealand Journal of Sociology* 31: 36–42.
Barbotte, E., F. Guillemin, and N. Chau. 2002. "Prevalence of Impairments, Disabilities, Handicaps and Quality of Life in the General Population: A Review of Recent Literature." *Bulletin of the World Health Organization* 79: 1047–1055.
Barham P. 1992. *Closing the Asylum.* London: Penguin Books.
Barnes, C. 1996. "Theories of Disability and the Origins of the Oppression of Disabled People." In *Disability and Society: Emerging Issues and Insights,* edited by L. Barton, 43–60. London: Longman.
Barnes, C., and G. Mercer. 2010. *Exploring Disability.* 2nd ed. Cambridge, UK: Polity Press.
Barnett, H. G. 1948. "On Science and Human Rights." *American Anthropologist* 50, no. 2: 352–355.
Baron, James N. 1984. "Organizational Perspectives on Stratification." *Annual Review of Sociology* 10: 37–69.
Barry, John, and K. Woods. 2009. "The Environment." In *Human Rights: Politics and Practice,* edited by M. Goodhart, 316–333. London: Oxford University Press.
Basch, Linda, Nina Glick Schiller, and Cristina Szanton Blanc. 1994. *Nations Unbound: Transnational Projects, Postcolonial Predicaments, and Deterritorialized Nation-States.* Routledge: London.
Bashford, Alison, and Phillipa Levine, eds. 2010. *The Oxford Handbook of the History of Eugenics.* Oxford: Oxford University Press.

Bass, Gary J. 2000. *Stay the Hand of Vengeance: The Politics of War Crimes Tribunals.* Princeton, NJ: Princeton University Press.
Basu, Amrita, ed. 2010. *Women's Movements in the Global Era: The Power of Local Feminisms.* Boulder, CO: Westview Press.
Batliwala, S. 2007. "Taking the Power Out of Empowerment—an Experiential Account." *Development in Practice* 17: 557-565.
Battersby, P., and J. M. Siracusa. 2009. *Globalization and Human Security.* Lanham, MD: Rowman & Littlefield.
Battle, Juan. 2009. *Black Sexualities: Probing Powers, Passions, Practices, and Policies.* New Brunswick, NJ: Rutgers University Press.
Bauböck, Rainer. 2009. "Global Justice, Freedom of Movement, and Democratic Citizenship." *European Journal of Sociology* 50: 1-31.
Bauman, Zygmunt. 1989. *Modernity and the Holocaust.* Ithaca, NY: New York University Press.
———. 2001. "Wars of the Globalization Era." *European Journal of Social Theory* 4: 11-28.
Baumer, Eric. 1994. "Poverty, Crack and Crime: A Cross-City Analysis." *Journal of Research in Crime and Delinquency* 31: 311-327.
Baumol, William J. 2002. *The Free-Market Innovation Machine: Analyzing the Growth Miracle of Capitalism.* Princeton, NJ: Princeton University Press.
Baxi, Upendra. 2002. *The Future of Human Rights.* New Delhi: Oxford University Press.
Baxter, David. 1989. "Marx, Lukes and Human Rights." *Social Theory and Practice* 15, no. 3: 355-373.
Bearman, Peter S., and Hannah Bruckner. 2001. "Promising the Future: Virginity Pledges and First Intercourse." *American Journal of Sociology* 106: 859-912.
Beating, J. 1993. "Technological Impacts on Human Rights: Models of Development, Science and Technology, and Human Rights." In *The Impact of Technology on Human Rights: Global Case Studies,* edited by C. G. Weeramantry. Tokyo, Japan: United Nations Press. http://unu.edu/unupress/unubooks/uu08ie/uu08ie00.htm (accessed November 12, 2010).
Beaver, Kevin M. 2008. "Nonshared Environmental Influences on Adolescent Delinquent Involvement and Adult Criminal Behavior." *Criminology* 46, no. 2: 341-369.
Beck, Ulrich. 1996. "Risk Society and the Provident State." In *Risk, Environment, and Modernity,* edited by S. Lash, B. Szerszynski, and B. Wynne, 27-43. Thousand Oaks, CA: Sage.
———. 1999. *World Risk Society.* Malden, MA: Polity Press.
———. 2007a. *Cosmopolitan Europe.* Cambridge, UK: Polity Press.
———. 2007b. *World at Risk.* Malden, MA: Polity Press.
Beck, Ulrich, and Natan Sznaider. 2006. "Unpacking Cosmopolitanism for the Social Sciences." *British Journal of Sociology* 57, no. 1: 1-23.
Becker, Anne E. 1994. "Nurturing and Negligence: Working on Others' Bodies in Fiji." In *Embodiment and Experience: The Existential Ground of Culture and Self,* edited by Thomas J. Csordas, 100-115. Cambridge, UK: Cambridge University Press.
Becker, Howard S. 1963. *Outsiders: Studies in the Sociology of Deviance.* New York: The Free Press.
———. 1967. "Whose Side Are We On?" *Social Problems* 14: 239-247.
———. 1982. *Art Worlds.* Berkeley: University of California Press.
Beckett, Katherine, and Steve Herbert. 2009. *Banished: The New Social Control in Urban America.* New York: Oxford University Press.
Beckett, Katherine, Kris Nyrop, Lori Pfingst, and Melissa Bowen. 2005. "Drug Use, Drug Possession Arrests, and the Question of Race: Lessons from Seattle." *Social Problems* 52, no. 3: 419-441.
Beckoff, Marc. 2002. *Minding Animals: Awareness, Emotions, and Heart.* New York: Oxford.
Beetham, David. 1995. "What Future for Economic and Social Rights?" *Political Studies* 43: 41-60.
Behar, Ruth. 1997. *The Vulnerable Observer: Anthropology that Breaks Your Heart.* Boston: Beacon Press.
Bell, Daniel. 1978 [1976]. *The Cultural Contradictions of Capitalism.* New York: Basic Books, Harper.
———. 2000. *East Meets West: Human Rights and Democracy in East Asia.* Princeton, NJ: Princeton University Press.
Bell, L. A. 1997. "Theoretical Foundations for Social Justice Education." In *Teaching for Diversity and Social Justice: A Sourcebook,* edited by M. Adams, L. A. Bell, and P. Griffin, 3-15. New York: Routledge.
Beneke, Timothy. 1983. *Men on Rape: What They Have to Say about Sexual Violence.* New York: St. Martin's Press.
Benford, Robert D., and David A. Snow. 2000. "Framing Processes and Social Movements." *Annual Review of Sociology* 26: 611-639.
Bengston, Vern L., Daphna Gans, Norella M. Putney, and Merril Silverstein, eds. 2009a. *Handbook of Theories of Aging.* 2nd ed. New York: Springer Publishing.
———. 2009b. "Theories about Age and Aging." In *Handbook of Theories of Aging,* edited by Vern L. Bengston, Daphna Gans, Norella M. Putney, and Merril Silverstein, 3-24. 2nd ed. New York: Springer Publishing.

Benhabib, Seyla, and Judith Resnick. 2009. "Introduction: Citizenship and Migration Theory Engendered." In *Migrations and Mobilities: Citizenship, Borders, and Gender*, edited by Seyla Benhabib and Judith Resnik, 1-46. New York: New York University Press.

Bennett, Angela. 2006. *The Geneva Convention*. Charleston, SC: History Press.

Bennett, Michael, and Juan Battle. 2001. "'We Can See Them, but We Can't Hear Them': LGBT Members of African American Families." In *Queer Families, Queer Politics: Challenging Culture and the State*, edited by Mary Bernstein and Renate Reimann, 53-67. New York: Columbia University Press.

Benoit, Cecelia, Dena Carroll, and Munaza Chaudhry. 2003. "In Search of a Healing Place: Aboriginal Women in Vancouver's Downtown Eastside." *Social Science and Medicine* 56: 821-833.

Benson, J. Kenneth. 1975. "The Interorganizational Network as a Political Economy." *Administrative Science Quarterly* 20: 229-249.

———. 1977. "Innovation and Crisis in Organizational Analysis." *Sociological Quarterly* 18: 3-16.

———. 1982. "A Framework for Policy Analysis." In *Interorganizational Coordination: Theory, Research, and Implementation*, edited by David L. Rogers and David A. Whetten, 137-176. Ames: Iowa State University Press.

———. 1983. "Paradigm and Praxis in Organizational Analysis." In *Research on Organizational Behavior*, edited by Barry Staw and L. L. Cummings, 33-56. Annual Series 5. Greenwich, CT: JAI Press.

Beresford, P., and A. Wilson. 2002. "Genes Spell Danger: Mental Health Service Users/Survivors, Bioethics and Control." *Disability and Society* 17: 541-553.

Berger, Joseph, Bernard P. Cohen, and Morris Zelditch Jr. 1966. "Status Characteristics and Expectation States." In *Sociological Theories in Progress*, edited by Joseph Berger, Morris Zelditch Jr., and Bo Anderson, 1:29-46. Boston: Houghton Mifflin.

Berger, Peter, and Thomas Luckmann. 1966. *The Social Construction of Reality*. Garden City, NY: Anchor.

Berkovitch, Nitza. 1999. *From Motherhood to Citizenship: Women's Rights and International Organizations*. Baltimore: Johns Hopkins University Press.

Berlant, Lauren, and Michael Warner. 1998. "Sex in Public." *Critical Inquiry* 24: 547-566.

Bernard, L. L. 1945. "The Teaching of Sociology in the United States in the Last Fifty Years." *American Journal of Sociology* 50: 534-548.

Bernerjee, D. 2008. "Environmental Rights." In *The Leading Rogue State: The U.S. and Human Rights*, edited by Judith Blau et al., 163-172. Boulder, CO: Paradigm Publishers.

Bernstein, Basil. 1970. "Education Cannot Compensate for Society." *New Society* 387: 344-347.

———. 1977. *Class, Codes, and Control*. Vol. 3: *Towards a Theory of Educational Transmissions*. London: Routledge and Kegan Paul.

———. 1990. *Class, Codes, and Control*. Vol. 4: *The Structuring of Pedagogic Discourse*. London: Routledge.

———. 1996. *Pedagogy, Symbolic Control, and Identity: Theory, Research, Critique*. London: Taylor and Francis.

Bernstein, Irving. 1960a. *The Lean Years: A History of the American Worker, 1920-1933*. Boston: Houghton Mifflin.

———. 1960b. "Union Growth and Structural Cycles." In *Labor and Trade Unionism*, edited by W. Galenson and S. M. Lipset, 73-89. New York: Wiley.

———. 1970. *The Turbulent Years: A History of the American Worker, 1933-1941*. Boston: Houghton Mifflin.

Bernstein, Mary. 2004. "Paths to Homophobia." *Sexuality Research and Social Policy* 1: 41-55.

———. 2005. "Identity Politics." *Annual Review of Sociology* 31: 47-74.

Bernstein, Mary, and Constance Kostelac. 2002. "Lavender and Blue: Attitudes about Homosexuality and Behavior toward Lesbians and Gay Men among Police Officers." *Journal of Contemporary Criminal Justice* 18: 302-328.

Bernstein, Mary, Constance Kostelac, and Emily Gaarder. 2003. "Understanding 'Heterosexism': Applying Theories of Racial Prejudice to Homophobia Using Data from a Southwestern Police Department." *Race, Gender and Class* 10: 54-74.

Bernstein, Mary, and Renate Reimann, eds. 2001. *Queer Families, Queer Politics: Challenging Culture and the State*. New York: Columbia University Press.

Berry, J. G., and W. H. Jones. 1991. "Situational and Dispositional Components of Reaction towards Persons with Disabilities." *Journal of Social Psychology* 131: 673-684.

Berry, Jason. 1992. *Lead Us Not into Temptation: Catholic Priests and the Sexual Abuse of Children*. New York: Doubleday.

Bertman, Martin. 2004. "The Theoretical Instability and Practical Progress of Human Rights." *International Journal of Human Rights* 8, no. 1: 89-99.

Best, Joel. 2007. *Social Problems*. New York: W. W. Norton and Company.

Best, Steve, and Anthony J. Nocella II. 2004. *Terrorists or Freedom Fighters? Reflections on the Liberation of Animals*. New York: Lantern Books.

Bevc, Christine, Brent K. Marshall, and J. Stephen Picou. 2007. "Environmental Justice and Toxic Exposure: Toward a Spatial Model of Physical Health and Psychological Well-Being." *Social Science Research* 37: 48-67.
Bevington, Douglas, and Chris Dixon. 2005. "Movement-Relevant Theory: Rethinking Social Movement Scholarship and Activism." *Social Movement Studies* 4, no. 3: 185-208.
Beyer, Peter. 2001. *Religion in the Process of Globalization*. Würzburg, Germany: Ergon.
——. 2006. *Religions in Global Society*. London and New York: Routledge.
Beyrer, Chris. 1998. "Burma and Cambodia: Human Rights, Social Disruption, and the Spread of HIV/AIDS." *Health and Human Rights* 2: 84-97.
Bhabha, Homi K. 2004. *RC Series Bundle: The Location of Culture*. 2nd ed. London: Routledge.
Bhattacharji, Preeti. 2009. *Uighurs and China's Xinjiang Region*. Washington, DC: Council on Foreign Relations. http://www.cfr.org/china/uighurs-chinas-xinjiang-region/p16870 (accessed September 30, 2011).
Bhattacharyya, A., P. K. Pattanaik, and Y. Xu. 2011. "Choice, Internal Consistency and Rationality." *Economics and Philosophy* 27, no. 2 (July): 123-149.
Biblarz, Timothy J., and Adrian E. Raftery. 1999. "Family Structure, Educational Attainment, and Socioeconomic Success: Rethinking the 'Pathology of Matriarchy.'" *American Journal of Sociology* 105: 321-365.
Bierne, Piers. 2009. *Confronting Animal Abuse: Law, Criminology, and Human-Animal Relationships*. Lanham, MD: Rowman & Littlefield.
Bigelow, J. 1831. *Elements of Technology*. Boston: Hilliard, Gray, Little and Wilkins.
Bilder, Richard B. 2006. "The Role of Apology in International Law and Diplomacy." *Virginia Journal of International Law* 46: 433-473.
Billson, Janet Mancini. 2008. "Focus Groups in the Context of International Development: In Pursuit of the Millennium Development Goals." In *International Clinical Sociology*, edited by Jan Marie Fritz, 188-207. New York: Springer.
Bilton, C. 2007. *Management and Creativity: From Creative Industries to Creative Management*. Malden, MA: Blackwell.
Binion, Gayle. 1995. "Human Rights: A Feminist Perspective." *Human Rights Quarterly* 17: 509-526.
Binstock, Robert H. 2007. "The Doomsters Are Wrong: What's Needed Are Policies Aimed at Several Generations." *AARP Bulletin* 48, no. 3: 33.
Binstock, Robert H., Linda K. George, Stephen J. Cutler, Jon Hendricks, and James H. Schultz. 2006. *Handbook of Aging and the Social Sciences*. Amsterdam: Elsevier.
——. 2011. *Handbook of Aging and the Social Sciences*. Amsterdam: Elsevier.
Binstock, Robert H., and Stephen G. Post. 1991. *Too Old for Health Care? Controversies in Medicine, Law, Economics, and Ethics*. 6th ed. Baltimore: Johns Hopkins University Press.
Bird, Chloe E., Peter Conrad, and Allen M. Fremont. 2000. "Medical Sociology at the Millennium." In *Handbook of Medical Sociology*, edited by Chloe E. Bird, Peter Conrad, and Allen M. Fremont, 1-10. 5th ed. Upper Saddle River, NJ: Prentice Hall.
Birren, J. E., ed. 1959. *Handbook of Aging and the Individual: Psychological and Biological Aspects*. Chicago: University of Chicago Press.
Black, Donald. 1972. "The Boundaries of Legal Sociology." *Yale Law Journal* 81, no. 6: 1086-1100.
——. 1976. *The Behavior of the Law*. New York: Academic Press.
Black, R. S., and L. Pretes. 2007. "Victims and Victors: Representation of Physical Disability on the Silver Screen." *Research and Practice for Persons with Severe Disabilities* 32: 66-83.
Black, Timothy. 2010. *When a Heart Turns Rock Solid: The Lives of Three Puerto Rican Brothers on and off the Streets*. New York: Vintage.
Blair, T., and M. Minkler. 2009. "Participatory Action Research with Older Adults: Key Principles in Practice." *Gerontologist* 49: 651-662.
Blau, J., and A. Moncada. 2005. *Human Rights: Beyond the Liberal Vision*. Lanham, MD: Rowman & Littlefield.
——. 2006. *Justice in the United States: Human Rights and the U.S. Constitution*. London: Rowman & Littlefield.
——. 2007a. "It Ought to Be a Crime: Criminalizing Human Rights Violations." *Sociological Forum* 22: 364-371.
——. 2007b. "Sociologizing Human Rights: Reply to John Hagan and Ron Levi." *Sociological Forum* 22: 381-384.
——. 2009. *Human Rights: A Primer*. Boulder, CO: Paradigm Publishers.
Blau, Judith. 2005. "Don't Blink Now: It's the Transition to the Second World System." *Contemporary Sociology* 34, no. 1: 7-9.
——. 2006. "Why Should Human Rights Be Important to Sociologists?" *Sociologists without Borders*. http://www.sociologistswithoutborders.org/president.html (accessed September 5, 2012).

———. 2010. Personal communication with J. M. Fritz. December 24.
———. 2011. "Human Rights Cities: The Transformation of Communities, or Simply Treading Water?" In *Essentials of Community Intervention*, edited by J. M. Fritz and J. Rheaume, draft chapter. The Netherlands: Springer.
Blau, Judith, David Brunsma, Alberto Moncada, and Catherine Zimmer, eds. 2008. *The Leading Rogue State*. Boulder, CO: Paradigm Publishers.
Blau, Judith, and Mark Frezzo, eds. 2011. *Sociology and Human Rights: A Bill of Rights for the Twenty-First Century*. Newbury Park, CA: Pine Forge Press.
Blau, Judith, and Marina Karides. 2008. *The World and US Social Forums: Another World Is Possible and Necessary*. Leiden: Brill Publishers.
Blau, Judith, and Keri Iyall Smith. 2006. *Public Sociologies Reader*. Lanham, MD: Rowman & Littlefield.
Blau, P. M. 1974. "Presidential Address: Parameters of Social Structure." *American Sociological Review* 39: 615-635.
Blau, Peter M., and Richard Schoenherr. 1971. *The Structure of Organizations*. New York: Basic Books.
Blauner, Robert. 1964. *Alienation and Freedom: The Factory Worker and His Industry*. Chicago: University of Chicago Press.
Bloom, Samuel. W. 2000. "The Institutionalization of Medical Sociology in the United States, 1920-1980." In *Handbook of Medical Sociology*, edited by Chloe E. Bird, Peter Conrad, and Allen M. Fremont, 11-31. 5th ed. Upper Saddle River, NJ: Prentice Hall.
Bluestone, Barry, and Bennett Harrison. 1982. *The Deindustrialization of America: Plant Closings, Community Abandonment, and the Dismantling of Basic Industry*. New York: Basic Books.
Blum, T. 1984. "Problem Drinking or Problem Thinking? Patterns of Abuse in Sociological Research." *Journal of Drug Issues* 14: 655-665.
Blumberg, Rae Lesser. 2004. "Extending Lenski's Schema to Hold Up Both Halves of the Sky—a Theory-Guided Way of Conceptualizing Agrarian Societies that Illuminates a Puzzle about Gender Stratification." *Sociological Theory* 22: 278-291.
Blumenson, Eric, and Eva S. Neilsen. 2002. "How to Construct an Underclass, or How the War on Drugs Became a War on Education." NELLCO Legal Scholarship Repository. http://lsr.nellco.org/suffolk_fp/1 (accessed September 2011).
Blute, Marion. 2006. "Gene-Culture Coevolutionary Games." *Social Forces* 85: 145-149.
———. 2010. *Darwinian Sociocultural Evolution: Evolutionary Solutions to Dilemmas in Cultural and Social Theory*. Cambridge, UK: Cambridge University Press.
Boardman, Jason D., Casely L. Blalock, and Fred C. Pampel. 2010. "Trends in the Genetic Influences on Smoking." *Journal of Health and Social Behavior* 51: 108-123.
Bob, Clifford, ed. 2005. *The Marketing of Rebellion: Insurgents, Media, and International Activism*. Cambridge, UK: Cambridge University Press.
———. 2009. *The International Struggle for New Human Rights*. Philadelphia: University of Pennsylvania Press.
Boersema, D. 2011. *Philosophy of Human Rights: Theory and Practice*. Boulder, CO: Westview Press.
Bogason, Peter. 2006. "The Democratic Prospects of Network Governance." *American Review of Public Administration* 36, no. 1: 3-18.
Bogle, Kathleen. 2008. *Hooking Up: Sex, Dating, and Relationships on Campus*. New York: New York University Press.
Boli, John, and George M. Thomas. 1997. "World Culture and the World Polity: A Century of International Non-Governmental Organization." *American Sociological Review* 62, no. 2: 171-190.
———. 1999. *Constructing World Culture: International Nongovernmental Organizations since 1875*. Stanford, CA: Stanford University Press.
Bond, Johanna E. 2003. "International Intersectionality: Theoretical and Pragmatic Exploration of Women's International Human Rights Violations." *Emory Law Journal* 52: 71-187.
Bonilla-Silva, Eduardo. 2003. *Racism without Racists: Color-Blind Racism and the Persistence of Racial Inequality in the United States*. Lanham, MD: Rowman & Littlefield Publishers.
———. 2008. "'Look, a Negro': Reflections on the Human Rights Approach to Racial Inequality." In *Globalization and America*, edited by A. J. Hattery, D. G. Embrick, and E. Smith, 9-22. Lanham, MD: Rowman & Littlefield Publishers.
Bonilla-Silva, Eduardo, and Sarah Mayorga. 2009. "Si Me Permiter Hablar: Limitations of the Human Rights Tradition to Address Racial Inequality." *Societies without Borders* 4: 366-382.
Bonnell, Victoria E. 1980. "The Uses of Theory, Concepts and Comparison in Historical Scholarship." *Comparative Study of Society and History* 22: 156-173.
Bonnin, Debbie. 1995. "Road to Beijing." *Agenda* 27: 74-77.
Bookchin, Murray. 1982. *The Ecology of Freedom: The Emergence and Dissolution of Hierarchy*. Palo Alto, CA: Cheshire Books.

Booth, Alan, Douglas A. Granger, and Elizabeth A. Shirtcliff. 2008. "Gender- and Age-Related Differences in the Association between Social Relationship Quality and Trait Levels of Salivary Cortisol." *Journal of Research on Adolescence* 18: 239-260.

Booth, Aland, D. Johnson, and Douglas Granger. 2005. "Testosterone, Marital Quality, and Role Overload." *Journal of Marriage and the Family* 67: 483-498.

Border Network for Human Rights (BNHR). 2003. *Two–US/Mexico Border Reports.* BNHR. http://www.bnhr.org/reports/u-s-mexico-border-reports-2000-2005 (accessed July 17, 2012).

Bordo, Susan. 2004. *Unbearable Weight: Feminism, Western Culture, and the Body.* Berkeley: University of California Press.

Borjas, George. 2004. "Increasing the Supply of Labor through Immigration: Measuring the Impact on Native-Born Workers." Center for Immigration Studies. http://www.cis.org/LaborSupply-Immigration EffectsNatives (accessed July 17, 2012).

Bottomore, T. B. 1963. *Karl Marx: Early Writings.* New York: McGraw-Hill.

Bottomore, Tom. 1985. *Theories of Modern Capitalism.* London: Allen & Unwin.

Bouilloud, J.-P. 2010. Personal communication with J. M. Fritz. December 13 and 15.

Bourdieu, Pierre. 1973. "Cultural Reproduction and Social Reproduction." In *Knowledge, Education, and Cultural Change,* edited by Richard Brown, 71-112. London: Tavistock.

——. 1977. *Outline of a Theory of Practice.* Cambridge, UK: Cambridge University Press.

——. 1984. *Distinction: A Social Critique of the Judgment of Taste.* Translated by Richard Nice. London: Routledge and Kegan Paul.

——. 1998. *Acts of Resistance: Against the Tyranny of the Market.* Translated by Richard Nice. New York: The New Press.

Bourdieu, Pierre, and Loic J. D. Wacquant. 1992. *An Invitation to Reflexive Sociology.* Chicago: University of Chicago Press.

Bourgois, Philippe. 1990. "Confronting the Ethics of Ethnography: Lessons from Fieldwork in Central America." In *Ethnographic Fieldwork: An Anthropological Reader,* edited by Antonius C. G. M. Robben and Jeffery A. Sluka. Malden, MA: Blackwell Publishing.

Bourgois, Philippe, and Jeff Schonberg. 2009. *Righteous Dopefiend.* Berkeley: University of California Press.

Bowles, Samuel, and Herbert Gintis. 1976. *Schooling in Capitalist America: Educational Reform and the Contradictions of Economic Life.* London: Routledge and Kegan Paul.

——. 1986. *Democracy and Capitalism: Property, Community, and the Contradictions of Modern Social Thought.* New York: Basic Books.

Boyer, Ernst. 1997. *Scholarship Reconsidered: Priorities of the Professorate.* San Francisco: Jossey-Bass.

Boyle, Elizabeth Heger. 2002. *Female Genital Cutting: Cultural Conflict in the Global Community.* Baltimore: Johns Hopkins University Press.

——. 2007. "Processes of Legislative Globalization." In *Encyclopedia of Law and Society: American and Global Perspectives,* edited by David Scott Clark, 661-665. Thousand Oaks, CA: Sage Publications.

——. 2009. "The Cost of Rights or the Right Cost? The Impact of Global Economic and Human Rights Policies on Child Well-Being since 1989." NSF Grant, Law and Social Science Program.

Boyle, Elizabeth Heger, and Amelia Corl. 2010. "Law and Culture in a Global Context: The Practice of Female Genital Cutting." *Annual Review of Law and Social Science* 6: 195-215.

Brabant, Sarah Callaway. 2008. "Clinical Sociology and Bereavement." In *International Clinical Sociology,* edited by Jan Marie Fritz, 97-114. New York: Springer.

Brabeck, Kalina, and Qingwen Xu. 2010. "The Impact of Detention and Deportation on Latino Immigrant Children and Families: A Quantitative Exploration." *Hispanic Journal of Behavioral Sciences* 32: 341-361.

Brackett, Jeffrey R. 1907. "Contribution to Symposium on How Should Sociology Be Taught—As a College or University Course?" *American Journal of Sociology* 12: 602-603.

Bradshaw, W., D. Roseborough, and M. Armour. 2006. "Recovery from Severe Mental Illness: The Lived Experience of the Initial Phase of Treatment." *International Journal of Psychosocial Rehabilitation* 10: 123-131.

Branch, A. 2007. "Uganda's Civil War and the Politics of ICC Intervention." *Ethics and International Affairs* 21: 179-198.

Branningan, Augustine, and Kelly H. Hardwick. 2003. "Genocide and General Theory." In *Control Theories of Crime and Delinquency,* edited by Chester L. Britt and R. Michael, 109-131. New Brunswick, NJ: Transaction.

Brass, Martin. 2011. *Labour Regime Change in the Twenty-First Century.* Leiden, The Netherlands: Brill.

Braverman, Harry. 1974. *Labor and Monopoly Capital.* New York: Monthly Review Press.

Brenkert, George G. 1986. "Marx and Human Rights." *Journal of the History of Philosophy* 24, no. 1: 55-77.

Brenner, Neil, Peter Marcuse, and Margit Mayer, eds. 2012. *Cities for People, Not for Profit: Critical Urban Theory and the Right to the City*. New York: Routledge.
Brewer, Marilynn. 1997. "The Social Psychology of Intergroup Relations: Can Research Inform Practice?" *Journal of Social Issues* 53: 197–211.
Brewer, Rose. 1993. "Theorizing Race, Class and Gender: The New Scholarship of Black Feminist Intellectuals and Black Women's Labor." In *Theorizing Black Feminisms: The Visionary Pragmatism of Black Women*, edited by Stanlie M. James and Abena P. A. Busia, 13–30. New York: Routledge.
Brewington, David V. 2005. "Late to the Party: Organizing Religious Human Rights." Paper presented at the annual meeting of the American Sociological Association, Philadelphia, Pennsylvania.
———. 2011. "International Associations at the Nexus of Globalization, Religion, and Human Rights." PhD diss., Emory University, Atlanta.
Brewster, Karin L., and Ronald R. Rindfuss. 1990. "Homophobia and Homosociality: An Analysis of Boundary Maintenance." *Sociological Quarterly* 31: 423–439.
———. 2000. "Fertility and Women's Employment in Industrialized Nations." *Annual Review of Sociology* 26: 271–296.
Brice, Arthur. 2010. "Mexico Asks for Probe into Teen's Shooting Death by U.S. Border Agent." CNN News. June 10. http://articles.cnn.com/2010-06-08/us/texas.border.patrol.shooting_1_ciudad-juarez-fbi-agent?_s=PM:US (accessed March 23, 2011).
Briggs, Laura. 1998. "Discourses of 'Forced Sterilization' in Puerto Rico: The Problem with the Speaking Subaltern." *Differences* 10, no. 2: 30–66.
Brinkmann, Svend. 2010. "Human Vulnerabilities: Toward a Theory of Rights for Qualitative Researchers." In *Qualitative Inquiry and Human Rights*, edited by Norman Denzin and Michael Giardina, 82–99. Walnut Creek, CA: Left Coast Press.
Britton, Dana M. 2003. *At Work in the Iron Cage: The Prison as Gendered Organization*. New York: New York University Press.
Brod, H. 1987. *The Making of Masculinities: The New Men's Studies*. Boston, MA: Allen and Unwin.
Brody, David. 1960. *Steelworkers in America: The Nonunion Era*. Cambridge, MA: Harvard University Press.
———. 1965. *Labor in Crisis: The Steel Strike of 1919*. Philadelphia: Lippincott.
———. 1979. "The Old Labor History and the New: In Search of an American Working Class." *Labor History* 20: 111–126.
———. 2001. "Labour Rights as Human Rights: A Reality Check." *British Journal of Industrial Relations* 39: 601–605.
Broido, E. M. 2000. "The Development of Social Justice Allies during College: A Phenomenological Investigation." *Journal of College Student Development* 41: 3–17.
Bronshtein, I. N., and K. A. Semendyayev. 1985. *Handbook of Mathematics*. English translation edited by K. A. Hirsch. Leipzig edition. Based on the original 1945 Russian edition and the 1957 translation into German. New York: Van Nostrand Reinhold.
Brown, B. S. 2011. *Research Handbook on International Criminal Law*. Northampton, MA: Edward Elgar Publishing.
Brown, Lester R. 2009. *Plan B 4.0: Mobilizing to Save Civilization*. New York: W. W. Norton.
Brown, Phil. 2000. "Popular Epidemiology and Toxic Waste Contamination: Lay and Professional Ways of Knowing." In *Perspectives in Medical Sociology*, edited by Phil Brown, 157–181. Prospect Heights, IL: Waveland Press.
Brown, Phil, and Edwin J. Mikkelsen. 1990. *No Safe Place: Toxic Waste, Leukemia, and Community Action*. Berkeley: University of California Press.
Brown, Roger, and Andrew Gilman. 1960. "The Pronouns of Power and Solidarity." In *Style in Language*, edited by Thomas A. Sebeok, 253–276. Cambridge, MA: MIT Press.
Brown, Stephen. 2003. "The Problem with Marx on Rights." *Journal of Human Rights* 2, no. 4: 517–522.
Brown, Tony N., Sherrill L. Sellers, Kendrick T. Brown, and James S. Jackson. 1999. "Race, Ethnicity, and Culture in the Sociology of Mental Health." In *Handbook of the Sociology of Mental Health*, edited by Carol S. Aneshensel and J. C. Phelan, 167–182. New York: Springer.
Brown, Wendy. 1995. *States of Injury*. Princeton, NJ: Princeton University Press.
Browning, Christopher R. 1998. *Ordinary Men: Police Battalion 101 and the Final Solution in Poland*. 2nd ed. New York: HarperCollins.
Brownlie, I. 2008. *Principles of Public International Law*. 7th ed. Oxford: Oxford University Press.
Brubaker, R. 1996. *Nationalism Reframed: Nationhood and the National Question in the New Europe*. Cambridge, UK: Cambridge University Press.
Brubaker, Rogers, Mara Lovemen, and Peter Stamatov. 2004. "Ethnicity as Cognition." *Theory and Society* 33: 31–64.

Brubaker, William Rogers. 1990. "Immigration, Citizenship, and the Nation-State in France and Germany: A Comparative Historical Analysis." *International Sociology* 5, no. 4: 379–407.

Brückner, H., and K. U. Mayer. 2005. "De-Standardization of the Life Course: What It Might Mean? And if It Means Anything, whether It Actually Took Place." In *The Structure of the Life Course: Standardized? Individualized? Differentiated?*, edited by R. Macmillan, 27–54. Advances in Life Course Research 9. Amsterdam: JAI Elsevier.

Brunnhölzl, Karl. 2007. "'Introduction' to Nagarjuna." In *In Praise of Dharmadhātu*, edited and translated by Karl Brunnhölzl, 21–55. Ithaca, NY: Snow Lion Publications.

Brunsson, Nils. 1985. *The Irrational Organization*. New York: John Wiley.

Brush, Lisa D. 2002. *Gender and Governance*. Lanham, MD: AltaMira Press.

Bryant, Rachel, and Robin Shura. 2010. "A Life Course of Human Rights? The 'Rising Sun' of Medical Decision-Making over the Life Course." Paper presented at the annual meeting of the American Sociological Association, Atlanta, Georgia, August 16, 2010.

Bucholz, Kathleen, and Lee Robins. 1989. "Sociological Research on Alcohol Use, Problems, and Policy." *Annual Review of Sociology* 15: 163–186.

Bullard, R. D. 1993. *Confronting Environmental Racism: Voices from the Grassroots*. Cambridge, MA: South End Press.

———. 2000. *Dumping in Dixie: Race, Class, and Environmental Quality*. Boulder, CO: Westview Press.

———. 2005. *The Quest for Environmental Justice: Human Rights and the Politics of Pollution*. San Francisco: Sierra Club Books.

Bullard, Robert D., and Beverly Wright, eds. 2009. *Race, Place, and Environmental Justice after Hurricane Katrina*. Boulder, CO: Westview Press.

Bulmer, Martin. 1984. *The Chicago School of Sociology: Institutionalization, Diversity, and the Rise of Sociological Research*. Chicago: University of Chicago Press.

Bumpass, L., and J. Sweet. 1989. *Children's Experience in Single-Parent Families: Implications of Cohabitation and Marital Transitions*. Madison: University of Wisconsin, Center for Demography and Ecology.

Bunch, Charlotte. 1990. "Women's Rights as Human Rights: Toward a Re-Vision of Human Rights." *Human Rights Quarterly* 12: 486–498.

Bunch, Charlotte, and Susana Fried. 1996. "Beijing '95: Moving Women's Human Rights from Margin to Center." *Signs* 22: 200–204.

Bunch, Charlotte, and Niamh Reilly. 1994. *Demanding Accountability: The Global Campaign and Vienna Tribunal for Women's Human Rights*. Rutgers, NJ: Center for Women's Global Leadership and the United Nations Development Fund for Women.

Burawoy, Michael. 1983. "Between the Labor Process and the State: The Changing Face of Factory Regimes under Advanced Capitalism." *American Sociological Review* 48: 587–605.

———. 2004. "Public Sociologies: Contradictions, Dilemmas and Possibilities." *Social Forces* 82, no. 4: 1603–1618.

———. 2005. "For Public Sociology." *American Sociological Review* 70: 4–28.

———. 2006. "A Public Sociology for Human Rights." Introduction to *Public Sociologies Reader*, edited by Judith Blau and Keri Iyall Smith, 1–18. Lanham, MD: Rowman & Littlefield.

———. 2007. "Evaluating 'No Child Left Behind.'" *The Nation*. http://www.thenation.com/doc/20070521/darling-hammond (accessed May 19, 2009).

Burawoy, Michael, and Janos Lukács. 1992. *The Radiant Past: Ideology and Reality in Hungary's Road to Capitalism*. Chicago: University of Chicago Press.

Burchardt, T. 2004. "Capabilities and Disability: The Capabilities Framework and the Social Model of Disability." *Disability and Society* 19: 735–751.

Bureau of Labor Statistics. 2011. "Union Members Summary." Bureau of Labor Statistics, U.S. Department of Labor. http://www.bls.gov/news.release/union2.nr0.htm (accessed January 21, 2011).

Burgers, Jan Herman. 1992. "The Road to San Francisco: The Revival of the Human Rights Idea in the Twentieth Century." *Human Rights Quarterly* 14: 447–477.

Burke, Mary C. 2010. "Transforming Gender: Medicine, Body Politics, and the Transgender Rights Movement." PhD diss., University of Connecticut, Storrs.

Burke, Roland. 2010. *Decolonization and the Evolution of International Human Rights*. Philadelphia: University of Pennsylvania Press.

Burkett, Elinor, and Frank Bruni. 1993. *A Gospel of Shame: Children, Sexual Abuse and the Catholic Church*. New York: Viking.

Burris, Beverly H. 1993. *Technocracy at Work*. Albany: State University of New York Press.

Burton, Linda. 1990. "Teenage Childbearing as an Alternative Life-Course Strategy in Mulit-Generational Black Families." *Human Nature* 1: 58–81.

Burton, Linda, Eduardo Bonilla-Silva, Victor Ray, Rose Buckelew, and Elizabeth H. Freeman. 2010. "Critical Race Theories, Colorism, and the Decade's Research on Families of Color." *Journal of Marriage and Family* 72: 440-459.

Busfield, J. 1996. *Men, Women and Madness: Understanding Gender and Mental Disorder*. London: Macmillan Press.

Bush, Melanie, and Deborah Little. 2009. "Teaching towards Praxis and Political Engagement." In *Engaging Social Justice: Critical Studies of 21st Century Social Transformation*, edited by David Fasenfest, 9-36. Leiden, the Netherlands: Brill.

Bush, Roderick. 2000. *We Are Not What We Seem: Black Nationalism and Class Struggle in the American Century*. New York: New York University Press.

——. 2009. *The End of White World Supremacy: Black Internationalism and the Problem of the Color Line*. Philadelphia: Temple University Press.

Bustamante, Jorge A. 1972. "The Wetback as Deviant: An Application of Labeling Theory." *American Journal of Sociology* 77: 706-718.

Butin, Daniel. 2010. *Service-Learning in Theory and Practice: The Future of Engagement in Higher Education*. New York: Palgrave.

Butler, Judith. 1990. *Gender Trouble: Feminism and the Subversion of Identity*. New York: Routledge.

——. 1993. *Bodies that Matter: On the Discursive Limits of "Sex."* New York: Routledge.

Butler, R. 2002 [1972]. *Why Survive? Being Old in America*. Baltimore: Johns Hopkins.

Button, Graham, ed. 1993. *Technology in Working Order: Studies of Work, Interaction and Technology*. London: Routledge.

Button, Graham, Jeff Coulter, John R. E. Lee, and Wes Sharrock. 1995. *Computers, Minds and Conduct*. Cambridge, UK: Polity Press.

Button, Tanya M. M., Michael C. Stallings, Soo Hyun Rhee, Robin P. Corley, Jason D. Boardman, and John K. Hewitt. 2009. "Perceived Peer Delinquency and the Genetic Predisposition for Substance Dependence Vulnerability." *Drug and Alcohol Dependence* 100: 1-8.

Buvinic, Mayra. 1998. "Women in Poverty: A New Global Underclass." Women in Politics. http://www.onlinewomeninpolitics.org/beijing12/womeninpoverty.pdf (accessed April 11, 2011).

Bynum, Thomas. 2009. "'We Must March Forward!': Juanita Jackson and the Origins of the NAACP Youth Movement." *Journal of African American History* 94: 487-508.

Caetano, R. 1984. "Self-Reported Intoxication among Hispanics in Northern California." *Journal of Studies of Alcohol and Alcoholism* 45: 349-354.

——. 1987. "Acculturation and Attitudes towards Appropriate Drinking among US Hispanics." *Alcohol and Alcoholism* 22: 427-433.

Cagatay, Nilufur. 2001. *Trade, Gender, and Poverty*. New York: United Nations Development Program.

Cahill, Sean. 2009. "The Disproportionate Impact of Antigay Family Policies on Black and Latino Same-Sex Couple Households." *Journal of African American Studies* 13: 219-250.

Caldwell, John C. 2006. *Demographic Transition Theory*. Dordrecht, The Netherlands: Springer.

Calhoun, Craig, ed. 2007. *Sociology in America: A History*. Chicago: University of Chicago Press.

California Legislature. Senate. 1943. *The Report of Joint Fact-Finding Committee on Un-American Activities in California*. Internet Archive. http://www.archive.org/details/reportofjointfac00calirich (accessed December 21, 2011).

Callahan, D. 1987. *Setting Limits: Medical Goals in an Aging Society*. New York: Simon and Schuster.

Callon, Michel. 1986. "Some Elements of a Sociology of Translation: Domestication of Scallops and the Fisherman of St. Brieuc Bay." In *Power, Action, and Belief: A New Sociology of Knowledge?*, edited by J. Law, 196-223. London: Routledge.

Callon, Michel, Pierre Lascoumes, and Yannick Barthe. 2009. *Acting in an Uncertain World: An Essay on Technical Democracy*. Translated by Graham Burchell. Cambridge, MA: MIT Press.

Callon, Michel, and Jean-Pierre Vignolle. 1975. "Breaking Down the Organization: Local Conflicts and Societal Systems of Action." *Social Science Information* 16, no. 2: 147-167.

Campbell, John. 2011. "Neoliberalism in Crisis: Regulatory Roots of the U.S. Financial Meltdown." In *Markets on Trial: The Economic Sociology of the U.S. Financial Crisis*, edited by Michael Lounsbury and Paul M. Hirsch, 65-102. Research in the Sociology of Organizations 30A. London: Emerald Group Publishing.

Campbell-Lendrum, Diarmid, and Majula Lusti-Narasimhan. 2009. "Taking the Heat out of the Population and Climate Change." World Health Organization. http://www.who.int/bulletin/volumes/87/11/09-072652/en/index.html (accessed August 21, 2012).

Cancian, Francesca M., and Steven L. Gordon. 1988. "Changing Emotion Norms in Marriage: Love and Anger in U.S. Women's Magazines since 1900." *Gender and Society* 2: 308-342.

Cantor, Daniel, and Juliet Schor. 1987. *Tunnel Vision: Labor, the World Economy, and Central America*. Boston: South End Press.

Caprioli, Mary. 2001. "Gendered Conflict." *Journal of Peace Research* 37, no. 1: 51–68.
Carlton-Ford, Steve. 2010. "Major Armed Conflicts, Militarization, and Life Chances: A Pooled Time Series Analysis." *Armed Forces and Society* 36: 864–889.
Carpenter, M. 2000. "'It's a Small World': Mental Health Policy under Welfare Capitalism since 1945." *Sociology of Health and Illness* 22: 602–620.
Carson, Rachel. 1962. *Silent Spring.* Boston: Houghton and Mifflin Press.
Casebeer, Kenneth M. 1989. "Drafting Wagner's Act: Leon Keyserling and the Pre-Committee Drafts of the Labor Disputes Act and the National Labor Relations Act." *Industrial Relations Law Journal* 11: 73–131.
Cassese, Antonio A., Guido G. Acquaviva, Mary D. Fan, and Alex A. Whiting. 2011. *International Criminal Law: Cases and Commentary.* Oxford: Oxford University Press.
Castel, R. 1988. *The Regulation of Madness: The Origins of Incarceration in France.* Oxford: Blackwell.
Castells, Manuel. 2000. *The Information Age: Economy, Society and Culture.* Vol. 1: *The Rise of the Network Society.* 2nd ed. Cambridge, UK: Cambridge University Press.
Cavanagh, Shannon E. 2007. "The Social Construction of Romantic Relationships in Adolescence: Examining the Role of Peer Networks, Gender, and Race." *Sociological Inquiry* 77: 572–600.
Centeno, Miguel Angel, and Joseph N. Cohen. 2010. *Global Capitalism: A Sociological Perspective.* Cambridge, MA: Polity.
Centers for Disease Control (CDC). 2011. "Tobacco Use: Targeting the Nation's Leading Killer." CDC. http://www.cdc.gov/chronicdisease/resources/publications/AAG/osh.htm (accessed January 1, 2011).
Cerna, Christina M. 1995. "East Asian Approaches to Human Rights: Proceedings of the Annual Meeting." *American Society of International Law* 89: 152–157.
Cerulo, Karen A. 2007. "The Forum Mailbag." *Sociological Forum* 22: 555–565.
Césaire, Aimé. 2001. *Discourse on Colonialism.* New York: Monthly Review Press.
Chabbott, Collette. 1999. "Development INGOs." In *Constructing World Culture: International Nongovernmental Organizations since 1875*, edited by J. Boli and G. M. Thomas. Stanford, CA: Stanford University Press.
Chambliss, William J. 1964. "A Sociological Analysis of the Law of Vagrancy." *Social Problems* 12, no. 1: 67–77.
———. 1989. "State Organized Crime." *Criminology* 27: 183–208.
Chandler, Alfred D., Jr. 1962. *Strategy and Structure: Chapters in the History of the American Industrial Enterprise.* Cambridge, MA: MIT Press.
———. 1977. *The Visible Hand. The Managerial Revolution in American Business.* Cambridge, MA: Harvard University Press.
Chapel Hill and Carrboro Human Rights Center. 2011. http://www.humanrightscities.org (accessed May 24, 2011).
Chapkis, Wendy. 2000. "Power and Control in the Commercial Sex Trade." In *Sex for Sale: Prostitution, Pornography, and the Sex Industry*, edited by Ronald Weitzer, 181–202. New York: Routledge.
Charlton, Sue Ellen, Jana Everett, and Kathleen Staudt. 1989. *Women, the State, and Development.* Albany: State University of New York Press.
Chase-Dunn, Christopher. 2005. "Social Evolution and the Future of World Society." *Journal of World-Systems Research* 11: 171–192.
Chase-Dunn, Christopher, Robert A. Hanneman, Richard Niemeyer, Christine Petit, and Ellen Reese. 2007. "The Contours of Solidarity and Division among Global Movements." *International Journal of Peace Studies* 12, no. 2: 1–16.
Chaves, Mark. 1994. "Secularization as Declining Religious Authority." *Social Forces* 72: 749–774.
Chavez, Leo R. 2008. *The Latino Threat: Constructing Immigrants, Citizens, and the Nation.* Stanford, CA: Stanford University Press.
Cheng, Shu-Ju Ada, and Lester R. Kurtz. 1998. "Third World Voices Redefining Peace." *Peace Review* 10 (March): 5–12. Available at http://works.bepress.com/lester_kurtz/7 (accessed January 20, 2012).
Cherlin, Andrew. 2008. "Public Display: The Picture-Perfect American Family? These Days, It Doesn't Exist." *Washington Post.* September 7, B1.
Chew, Sing. 1997. "For Nature: Deep Greening World Systems Analysis of the 21st Century." *Journal of World-Systems Research* 3, no. 3: 381–402.
———. 2001. *World Ecological Degradation: Accumulation, Urbanization, and Deforestation: 3000 BC–AD 2000.* New York: Altamira Press.
Child, J. 1972. "Organization Structure, Environment, and Performance: The Role of Strategic Choice." *Sociology* 6: 1–22.
Chiquiar, Daniel, and Gordon H. Hanson. 2005. "International Migration, Self-Selection, and the Distribution of Wages: Evidence from Mexico and the United States." *Journal of Political Economy* 113: 239–281.

Chirayath, Heidi T. 2007. "Difficult, Dysfunctional, and Drug-Dependent: Structure and Agency in Physician Perceptions of Indigent Patients." *Social Theory and Health* 5, no. 1: 30-52.
Chiswick, Barry, and Michael Wenz. 2005. "The Linguistic and Economic Adjustment of Soviet Jewish Immigrants in the United States, 1980 to 2000." IZA DP No. 1726. Institute for the Study of Labor. ftp://repec.iza.org/RePEc/Discussionpaper/dp1238.pdf (accessed July 17, 2012).
Chiswick, Barry R. 1988. "Illegal Immigration and Immigration Control." *Journal of Economic Perspectives* 2, no. 3 (summer): 101-115.
Chomsky, Noam, and Edward S. Herman. 1979. *The Political Economy of Human Rights: The Washington Connection and Third World Fascism.* Boston: South End Press.
Chomsky, Noam, Ralph Nader, Immanuel Wallerstein, Richard C. Lewontin, and Richard Ohmann. 1998. *The Cold War and the University: Toward an Intellectual History of the Postwar Years.* New York: The New Press.
Chow, Esther Ngan-ling. 1996. "Making Waves, Moving Mountains: Reflections on Beijing '95 and Beyond." *Signs* 22: 185-192.
Christakis, Nicholas A., and James H. Fowler. 2009. *Connected: The Surprising Power of Social Networks and How They Shape Our Lives.* New York: Simon and Schuster.
Chudacoff, H. 1989. *How Old Are You? Age Consciousness in America.* Princeton, NJ: Princeton University Press.
Ciganda, Daniel, Alain Gagnon, and Eric Tenkorang. 2010. "Child and Young Adult Headed Households in the Context of the AIDS Epidemic in Zimbabwe, 1988-2006." PSC Discussion Papers Series 24, no. 4: 1-17.
City of Eugene. 2011a. "Equity and Human Rights." City of Eugene. http://www.eugene-or.gov/diversity (accessed May 26, 2011).
———. 2011b. "Sustainable Eugene." City of Eugene. http://www.eugene-or.gov/sustainability (accessed May 26, 2011).
Clanton, Gordon. 1989. "Jealousy in American Culture, 1945-1975: Reflections from Popular Culture." In *The Sociology of Emotions: Original Essays and Research Papers*, edited by D. D. Franks and E. D. McCarthy, 179-193. Greenwich, CT: JAI Press.
Clapham, Andrew. 2007. *Human Rights: A Very Short Introduction.* New York: Oxford University Press.
Clapp, J. 2001. *Toxic Exports: The Transfer of Hazardous Wastes from Rich to Poor Countries.* Ithaca, NY: Cornell University Press.
Clark, Adele E., Laura Mamo, Jennifer R. Fishman, Janet Shim, and Jennifer Fosket. 2003. "Biomedicalization: Technoscientific Transformations of Health, Illness and U.S. Biomedicine." *American Sociological Review* 68, no. 2: 161-194.
Clark, Candace. 1990. "Emotions and Micropolitics in Everyday Life: Some Patterns and Paradoxes of 'Place.'" In *Research Agendas in the Sociology of Emotions*, edited by T. D. Kemper, 305-333. Albany: State University of New York Press.
Clark, Cindy Dell. 2010. *A Younger Voice: Doing Child-Centered Qualitative Research.* New York: Oxford University Press.
Clark-Ibáñez, Marisol. 2007. "Inner-City Children in Sharper Focus: Sociology of Childhood and Photo-Elicitation Interviews." In *Visual Research Methods: Image, Society, and Representation*, edited by Gregory C. Stanczak, 167-196. Thousand Oaks, CA: Sage Publications.
Clarke, Lee. 2006. *Worst Cases: Terror and Catastrophe in the Popular Imagination.* Chicago: University of Chicago Press.Clawson, Dan. 1980. *Bureaucracy and the Labor Process.* New York: Monthly Review Press.
———. 2003. *The Next Upsurge: Labor and the New Social Movements.* Ithaca, NY: ILR Press.
Clayton, Mark. 2011. "Fukushima Meltdown Could Be Template for Nuclear Terrorism, Study Says." *Christian Science Monitor.* June 7.
Clegg, Stewart. 1989. *Frameworks of Power.* London: Sage.
———. 1990. *Modern Organization: Organization Studies in the Postmodern World.* London: Sage.
Clegg, Stewart, and Winton Higgins. 1987. "Against the Current: Organizational Sociology and Socialism." *Organization Studies* 8: 201-221.
Cohany, Sharon, and Emy Sok. 2007. *Trends in Labor Force Participation of Married Mothers of Infants.* Washington, DC: Bureau of Labor Statistics.
Cohen, Beth. 2007. *Case Closed: Holocaust Survivors in Postwar America.* New Brunswick, NJ: Rutgers University Press.
Cohen, Carl. 1986. "The Case for the Use of Animals in Biomedical Research." *New England Journal of Medicine* 315: 865-870.
Cohen, Cathy. 1999. *The Boundaries of Blackness: AIDS and the Breakdown of Black Politics.* Chicago: University of Chicago Press.
Cohen, Stanley. 2001. *States of Denial: Knowing about Atrocities and Suffering.* Cambridge, UK: Polity Press.

Cohn, Marjorie. 2001. "The World Trade Organization: Elevating Property Interests above Human Rights." *Georgia Journal of International and Comparative Law* 29: 427-440.
Cole, W. M. 2005. "Sovereignty Relinquished? Explaining Commitment to the International Human Rights Covenants, 1966-1999." *American Sociological Review* 70: 472-495.
Coleman, James. 1964. *Introduction to Mathematical Sociology.* New York: The Free Press.
———. 1990. *Foundations of Social Theory.* Cambridge, MA: Belknap Press.
———. 2006. *The Criminal Elite.* New York: Worth Publishers.
Coleman, Matthew. 2007. "Immigration Geopolitics beyond the Mexico-U.S. Border." *Antipode* 39: 54-76.
Colker, R. 2005. *The Disability Pendulum the First Decade of the Americans with Disabilities Act.* New York: New York University Press.
Collett, Jessica L., and Omar Lizardo. 2009. "A Power-Control Theory of Gender and Religiosity." *Journal for the Scientific Study of Religion* 48: 213-231.
Collins, Patricia Hill. 1990. *Black Feminist Thought: Knowledge, Consciousness, and the Politics of Empowerment.* New York: Routledge, Chapman and Hall.
———. 1993. "Toward a New Vision: Race, Class, and Gender as Categories of Analysis and Connection." *Race, Sex and Class* 1: 25-45.
———. 1994. "Shifting the Center: Race, Class, and Feminist Theorizing about Motherhood." In *Representations of Motherhood,* edited by Donna Basin and Margaret Honey, 56-74. New Haven, CT: Yale University Press.
———. 2005. *Black Sexual Politics.* New York: Routledge.
Collins, Randall. 1974. "Three Faces of Cruelty: Towards a Comparative Sociology of Violence." *Theory and Society* 1, no. 4 (winter): 415-440.
———. 1975. *Conflict Sociology: Toward an Explanatory Science.* New York: Academic Press.
———. 1990. "Stratification, Emotional Energy, and the Transient Emotions." In *Research Agendas in the Sociology of Emotions,* edited by T. D. Kemper, 27-57. Albany: State University of New York Press.
———. 1998. *The Sociology of Philosophies: A Global Theory of Intellectual Change.* Cambridge, MA: Belknap Press.
———. 2008. *Violence.* Princeton, NJ: Princeton University Press.
Coltraine, Scott, and Michelle Adams. 2008. *Gender and Families.* Lanham, MD: AltaMira Press.
Columbia Law School Human Rights Institute and International Association of Official Human Rights Agencies (IAOHRA). 2010. *State and Local Human Rights Agencies: Recommendations for Advancing Opportunity and Equality through an International Human Rights Framework.* New York: Columbia Law School Human Rights Institute and IAOHRA.
Comin, Diego, and Bart Hobijn. 2004. "Cross-Country Technology Adoption: Making the Theories Face the Facts." *Journal of Monetary Economics* 51: 39-83.
Committee on Science, Engineering, and Public Policy (COSEPUP). 1995. *On Being a Scientist: Responsible Conduct in Research.* Washington, DC: National Academy Press.
Committee on the Elimination of Racial Discrimination. 2000. "General Recommendation 25, Gender Related Dimensions of Racial Discrimination." University of Minnesota, Human Rights Library. http:// www1.umn.edu/humanrts/gencomm/genrexxv.htm (accessed September 6, 2012).
Commons, John, Ulrich Bonnell Phillips, Eugene Allen Gilmore, and John B. Andrews, eds. 1910-1911. *A Documentary History of American Industrial Society.* 11 vols. Cleveland, OH: Arthur Clark Company.
———. 1918-1935. *History of Labor in the United States.* 4 vols. New York: Macmillan.
Compa, Lance. 2000. *Unfair Advantage: Workers' Freedom of Association in the United States under International Human Rights Standards.* Ithaca, NY: ILR Press.
Comte, Auguste. 1970. *Introduction to Positive Philosophy.* Indianapolis: Bobbs Merrill.
Conley, Dalton, Kate W. Strully, and Neil G. Bennett. 2003. *The Starting Gate: Birth Weight and Life Chances.* Berkeley: University of California Press.
Connell, Raeyn. 1987. *Gender and Power: Society, the Person, and Sexual Politics.* Stanford, CA: Stanford University Press.
———. 1995. "Symposium: Human Rights and the Sociological Project (Sociology and Human Rights)." *Australian and New Zealand Journal of Sociology* 31: 25-29.
———. 2005. *Masculinities.* Berkeley: University of California Press.
Conrad, Peter. 2000. "Medicalization, Genetics and Human Problems." In *Handbook of Medical Sociology,* edited by Chloe E. Bird, Peter Conrad, and Allen M. Fremont, 322-333. 5th ed. Upper Saddle River, NJ: Prentice Hall.
———. 2007. *Medicalization of Society: On the Transformation of Human Conditions into Treatable Disorders.* Baltimore: Johns Hopkins University Press.
Conrad, Peter, and Joseph Schneider. 1992. *Deviance and Medicalization: From Badness to Sickness.* Philadelphia: Temple University Press.
Cook, Daniel T., and John Wall, eds. 2011. *Children and Armed Conflict.* Hampshire, UK: Palgrave Macmillan.

Cook, J. A., and E. R. Wright. 1995. "Medical Sociology and the Study of Severe Mental Illness: Reflections on Past Accomplishments and Directions for Future Research." *Journal of Health and Social Behaviour* 35: 95–114.
Cooley, Charles Horton. 1964 [1902]. *Human Nature and the Social Order.* New York: Schocken Books.
Cooney, Mark. 1997. "From Warre to Tyranny: Lethal Conflict and the State." *American Sociological Review* 62: 316–338.
Coontz, S. 1992. *The Way We Never Were: American Families and the Nostalgia Trap.* New York: Basic Books.
———. 1997. *The Way We Really Are: Coming to Terms with America's Changing Families.* New York: Basic Books.
Coosmans, F., F. Grunfeld, and M. T. Kamminga. 2010. "Methods of Human Rights Research: A Primer." *Human Rights Quarterly* 32: 179–186.
Cornfield, Daniel B. 1989. *Becoming a Mighty Voice: Conflict and Change in the United Furniture Workers of America.* New York: Russell Sage.
Corrêa, S., and V. Muntarbhorn. 2007. "The Yogyakarta Principles on the Application of International Human Rights Law in Relation to Sexual Orientation and Gender Identity." The Yogyakarta Principles. http://www.yogyakartaprinciples.org/principles_en.htm (accessed July 21, 2010).
Corsaro, William A. 2005. *The Sociology of Childhood.* Newbury Park, CA: Pine Forge Press.
Corsaro, William A., and Laura Fingerson. 2003. "Development and Socialization in Childhood." In *Handbook of Social Psychology*, edited by John Delamater, 125–156. New York: Kluwer.
Cotterrell, Roger. 2007. "Sociology of Law." In *Encyclopedia of Law and Society: American and Global Perspectives*, edited by David Scott Clark, 1413–1419. Thousand Oaks, CA: Sage Publications.
Coulter, Jeff. 1979. *The Social Construction of Mind: Studies in Ethnomethodology and Linguistic Philosophy.* Totowa, NJ: Rowman & Littlefield.
———. 1982. "Remarks on the Conceptualization of Social Structure." *Philosophy of the Social Sciences* 12: 33–46.
———. 1989. *Mind in Action.* Atlantic Highlands, NJ: Humanities Press International.
Coulter, Jeff, and Wes Sharrock. 2007. *Brain, Mind, and Human Behaviour in Contemporary Cognitive Science: Critical Assessments of the Philosophy of Psychology.* Lewiston, NY: Edwin Mellen.
Council of Europe. 2011. http://www.coe.int (accessed May 24, 2011).
Council of Europe Congress of Local and Regional Authorities. 2010. "The Role of Local and Regional Authorities in the Implementation of Human Rights." Draft Resolution, Congress of Local and Regional Authorities, 18th Session, Strasbourg, France, March 1.
Courant, Richard. 1937 [1934]. *Differential and Integral Calculus.* Translated by E. J. McShane. 2 vols. New York: Wiley.
Courtwright, David. 2001. *Forces of Habit: Drugs and the Making of the Modern World.* Cambridge, MA: Harvard University Press.
Cousins, S. 1989. "Culture and Selfhood in Japan and the U.S." *Journal of Personality and Social Psychology* 56: 124–131.
Cox, Laurence, and Cristina Flesher Fominaya. 2009. "Movement Knowledge: What Do We Know, How Do We Create Knowledge and What Do We Do with It?" *Interface: A Journal for and about Social Movements* 1, no. 1: 1–20.
Cox, Laurence, and Alf Gunvald Nilsen. 2007. "Social Movements Research and the 'Movement of Movements': Studying Resistance to Neoliberal Globalisation." *Sociology Compass* 1, no. 2: 424–442.
Cox, Oliver Cromwell. 1948. *Caste, Class, and Race: A Study in Social Dynamics.* New York: Monthly Review Press.
Crane, Diana. 2005. "Democracy and Globalization in the Global Economy." In *The Blackwell Companion to the Sociology of Culture*, edited by Mark D. Jacobs and Nancy Weiss Hanrahan. 412–427. Malden, MA: Blackwell.
Craven, Matthew C. R. 1995. *The International Covenant on Economic, Social, and Cultural Rights: A Perspective on Its Development.* Oxford: Oxford University Press.
Crenshaw, Kimberlé. 1991. "Mapping the Margins: Intersectionality, Identity Politics, and Violence against Women of Color." *Stanford Law Review* 43: 1241–1299.
Cress, Daniel M., and David A. Snow. 1996. "Mobilization at the Margins: Resources, Benefactors, and the Viability of Homeless Social Movement Organizations." *American Sociological Review* 61: 1089–1109.
———. 2000. "The Outcomes of Homeless Mobilization: The Influence of Organization, Disruption, Political Mediation, and Framing." *American Journal of Sociology* 105: 1063–1104.
Crimmins, Eileen M. 1993. "Demography: The Past 30 Years, the Present, and the Future." *Demography* 30, no. 4: 571–594.
Crocker, Jennifer. 2002. "Contingencies of Self-Worth: Implications for Self-Regulation and Psychological Vulnerability." *Self and Identity* 1: 143–149.

Croissant, Jennifer, and Sal Restivo. 1995. "Technoscience or Tyrannoscience Rex: Science and Progressive Thought." In *Ecologies of Knowledge*, edited by Susan Leigh Star, 39-87. Albany: State University of New York Press.
Crompton, Tom, and Tim Kasser. 2009. *Meeting Environmental Challenges: The Role of Human Identity*. Devon, UK: Green Books (World Wildlife Fund).
Crooms, Lisa. 1997. "Indivisible Rights and Intersectional Identities or 'What Do Women's Rights Have to Do with the Race Convention?'" *Howard Law Journal* 40: 620-640.
Crosnoe, Robert. 2011. *Fitting In, Standing Out: Navigating the Social Challenges of High School to Get an Education*. New York: Cambridge University Press.
Crosnoe, Robert, and Glen H. Elder Jr. 2004. "From Childhood to the Later Years: Pathways of Human Development." *Research on Aging* 26, no. 6: 623-654.
Croteau, David, William Hoynes, and Charlotte Ryan. 2005. *Rhyming Hope and History: Activists, Academics, and Social Movement Scholarship*. Minneapolis: University of Minnesota Press.
Cummins, E. E. 1936. "Workers' Education in the United States." *Social Forces* 14: 597-605.
Cunningham, W. P., and M. A. Cunningham. 2008. *Principles of Environmental Science: Inquiry and Applications*. New York: McGraw-Hill.
Currah, Paisley, Richard M. Juang, and Shannon Price Minter. 2006. *Transgender Rights*. Minneapolis: University of Minnesota Press.
Currie, Elliot. 1994. *Reckoning: Drugs, the Cities, and the American Future*. New York: Hill and Wang.
Cutler, J. Elbert. 1907. "Contribution to Symposium on How Should Sociology Be Taught as a College or University Course." *American Journal of Sociology* 12: 604-606.
Cyert, Richard, and James March. 1963. *A Behavioral Theory of the Firm*. 2nd ed. Malden, MA: Wiley-Blackwell.
Czarniawska, Barbara. 1997. *Narrating the Organization: Dramas of Institutional Identity*. Chicago: University of Chicago Press.
D'Cunha, J. 2005. "Claim and Celebrate Women Migrants' Human Rights through CEDAW: The Case of Women Migrant Workers, a UNIFEM Briefing Paper." United Nations Entity for Gender Equality and the Empowerment of Women. http://www.unwomen-eseasia.org/projects/migrant/mig_pub.htm (accessed July 17, 2012).
Dabbs, J. M., Jr., and M. G. Dabbs. 2000. *Heroes, Rogues, and Lovers: Testosterone and Behavior*. New York: McGraw-Hill.
Dagum, Camilo. 1983. "Income Inequality Measures." In *Encyclopedia of Statistical Sciences*, edited by Samuel Kotz, Norman L. Johnson, and Campbell B. Read, 4:34-40. New York: Wiley.
Dahrendorf, Ralf. 1958. "Out of Utopia: Toward a Reorientation of Sociological Analysis." *American Journal of Sociology* 64, no. 2: 115-127.
Dalai Lama and Paul Eckman. 2008. *Emotional Awareness: Overcoming the Obstacles to Psychological Balance and Compassion*. Foreword by Daniel Goleman. New York: Times Books, Henry Holt and Co.
Dallaire, Bernadette, Michael McCubbin, Paul Morin, and David Cohen. 2000. "Civil Commitment Due to Mental Illness and Dangerousness: The Union of Law and Psychiatry within a Treatment-Control System." *Sociology of Health and Illness* 22: 679-699.
Daniels, Roger. 2004. *Guarding the Golden Door: American Immigration Policy and Immigrants since 1882*. New York: Hill and Wang.
Dannefer, Dale. 1984. "Adult Development and Social Theory: A Paradigmatic Reappraisal." *American Sociological Review* 49: 1.
———. 2010. "Age, the Life Course, and the Sociological Imagination: Prospects for Theory." In *Handbook of Aging and the Social Sciences*, edited by R. Binstock and L. George, 3-16. New York: Academic.
Dannefer, Dale, and P. Uhlenberg. 1999. "Paths of the Life Course: A Typology." In *Handbook of Theories of Aging*, edited by V. Bengtson and K. W. Schaie, 306-327. New York: Springer.
Dannefer, Dale, and Chris Phillipson, eds. 2010. *International Handbook of Social Gerontology*. London: Sage.
Dannefer, Dale, and Robin Shura. 2007. "The Second Demographic Transition, Aging Families, and the Aging of the Institutionalized Life Course." In *Social Structures: Demographic Changes and the Well-Being of Older Persons*, edited by K. Warner Schaie and Peter Uhlenberg, 212-229. New York: Springer.
———. 2009. "Experience, Social Structure and Later Life: Meaning and Old Age in an Aging Society." In *International Handbook of Population Aging*, edited by P. Uhlenberg, 747-755. Dordrecht, the Netherlands: Springer.
Danto, Arthur C. 1967. "Philosophy of Science, Problems of." In *Encyclopedia of Philosophy*, edited by Paul Edwards, 6:296-300. New York: Macmillan.
Davidson, Alastair. 2010. "History, Human Rights and the Left." *Thesis Eleven* 100: 106-116.
Davis, Gerald F., Doug McAdam, W. Richard Scott, and Mayer N. Zald, eds. 2005. *Social Movements and Organization Theory*. Cambridge, UK: Cambridge University Press.

Davis, Jeff, and Daniel Were. 2008. "A Longitudinal Study of the Effects of Uncertainty on Reproductive Behaviors." *Human Nature* 19: 426-452.
Davis, Kingsley, and Wilbert E. Moore. 1945. "Some Principles of Stratification." *American Sociological Review* 10: 242-249.
De Genova, Nicholas. 2005. "In Re: Rodriguez." In *The Oxford Encyclopedia of Latinos and Latinas in the United States*, edited by S. Oboler and D. J. González, 2:380-382. New York: Oxford University Press.
De Haas, H. 2010. "Migration and Development: A Theoretical Perspective." *International Migration Review* 44: 227-264.
De Souza, Roger-Mark, J. S. Williams, and F. A. B. Meyerson. 2003. "Critical Links: Population, Health, and Environment." *Population Bulletin* 58: 1-43.
De Than, C., and E. Shorts. 2003. *International Criminal Law and Human Rights*. London: Sweet and Maxwell.
Deci, Edward L., and Richard M. Ryan. 2000. "The 'What' and 'Why' of Goal Pursuits: Human Needs and the Self-Determination of Behavior." *Psychological Inquiry* 11: 227-268.
Deegan, Mary Jo. 1988. *Jane Addams and the Men of the Chicago School, 1892-1918*. New Brunswick, NJ: Transaction Publishers.
——. 2002. *Race, Hull House, and the University of Chicago: A New Conscience against Ancient Evils*. Westport, CT: Praeger.
Deflem, Mathieu. 2008. *Sociology of Law: Visions of a Scholarly Tradition*. Cambridge, UK: Cambridge University Press.
Deflem, Mathieu, and Stephen Chicoine. 2011. "The Sociological Discourse on Human Rights: Lessons from the Sociology of Human Rights." *Development and Society* 40, no. 1 (June): 101-115.
Delanty, Gerard. 2009. *The Cosmopolitan Imagination*. New York: Cambridge University Press.
Della Porta, Donatella, Massimillano Andretta, Lorenzo Mosca, and Herbert Reiter. 2006. *Globalization from Below: Transnational Activists and Protest Networks*. Minneapolis: University of Minnesota Press.
DeMartino, George. 2010. "On Marxism, Institutionalism, and the Problem of Labor Exploitation." *Rethinking Marxism* 22, no. 4: 524-530.
Denning, Michael. 1998. *The Cultural Front: The Laboring of American Culture in the Twentieth Century*. New York: Verso Books.
Denzin, Norman. 1997. *Interpretative Ethnography: Ethnographic Practices for the 21st Century*. Thousand Oaks, CA: Sage.
——. 2010. *The Qualitative Manifesto: A Call to Arms*. Walnut Creek, CA: Left Coast Press.
Denzin, Norman, and Michael D. Giardina. 2010. *Qualitative Inquiry and Human Rights*. Walnut Creek, CA: Left Coast Press.
Department of Homeland Security (DHS). 2009. "Immigration Statistics." DHS. http://www.dhs.gov/files/ statistics/immigration.shtm (accessed January 31, 2011).
——. 2010. "Immigration Enforcement Actions: 2009." DHS. http://www.dhs.gov/xlibrary/assets/statistics/publications/enforcement_ar_2009.pdf (accessed October 12, 2010).
Department of Justice. 2010. "Crime in the United States, 2009." Federal Bureau of Investigation. http://www2.fbi.gov/ucr/cius2009/arrests/index.html (accessed January 1, 2011).
Derrida, Jacques. 1978. *Writing and Difference*. London: Routledge and Kegan Paul.
——. 2004. "The Animal that I Am." In *Animal Philosophy: Essential Readings in Continental Thought*, edited by Peter Allerton and Matthew Calarco: 113-128. New York: Continuum.
Desai, Manisha. 2002. "Transnational Solidarity: Women's Agency, Structural Adjustment, and Globalization." In *Women's Activism and Globalization: Linking Local Struggles and Transnational Politics*, edited by N. Naples and M. Desai, 15-33. New York: Routledge.
——. 2005. "Transnationalism: The Face of Feminist Politics Post-Beijing." *International Social Science Journal* 57: 319-330.
DeSouza, Roger-Mark, John S. Williams, and Frederick A. B. Meyerson. 2003. *Critical Links: Population, Health, and the Environment*. Population Resource Bureau. http://www.prb.org/Publications/PopulationBulletins/2003/CriticalLinksPopulationHealthandtheEnvironmentPDF340KB.aspx.
——. 2006. "From Autonomies to Solidarities: Transnational Feminist Practices." In *Handbook of Gender and Women's Studies*, edited by Kathy Davis, Mary Evans, and Judith Lorber, 459-470. Thousand Oaks, CA: Sage Publications.
DeVault, Marjorie. 2007. "Knowledge from the Field." In *Sociology in America: A History*, edited by Craig Calhoun, 155-182. Chicago: University of Chicago Press.
Devinatz, Victor G. 2003. "U.S. Labor and Industrial Relations Historiography: A Review Essay." In *Work in America: An Encyclopedia of History, Policy and Society*, edited by Carl E. Van Horn and Herbert A. Schaffner, xxvii-xxxviii. Santa Barbara, CA: ABC-CLIO.

Devine, Patricia G. 1989. "Stereotypes and Prejudice: Their Automatic and Controlled Components." *Journal of Personality and Social Psychology* 56: 5-18.
Dewey, J. 1922. *Human Nature and Conduct.* New York: Holt.
———. 1980 [1934]. *Art as Experience.* Reprint. New York: Perigree.
———. 1985. *The Later Works, 1925-1953.* Vol. 6. Carbondale: Southern Illinois University Press.
Dhamoon, Rita. 2010. *Identity/Difference Politics: How Difference Is Produced, and Why It Matters.* Vancouver: University of British Columbia.
Diamond, Lisa. 2006. "Careful What You Ask For: Reconsidering Feminist Epistemology and Autobiographical Narrative in Research on Sexual Identity Development." *Signs* 31: 471-491.
Diaz-McConnell, Eileen. 2011. "An 'Incredible Number of Latinos and Asians': Media Representations of Racial and Ethnic Population Change in Atlanta, Georgia." In "Latino/as and the Media," special issue, *Latino Studies* 9, no. 2/3: 177-197.
Dill, Bonnie Thornton. 1983. "Race, Class, and Gender: Prospects for an All-Inclusive Sisterhood." *Feminist Studies* 9: 131-150.
Dillon, Michele. 2005. "Sexuality and Religion: Negotiating Identity Differences." In *The Blackwell Companion to the Sociology of Culture*, edited Mark D. Jacobs and Nancy Weiss Hanrahan, 220-233. Malden, MA: Blackwell.
DiMaggio, Paul, and Walter W. Powell. 1983. "The Iron Cage Revisited: Institutional Isomorphism and Collective Rationality in Organizational Fields." *American Sociological Review* 48: 147-160.
DiMauro, Diane. 1995. *Sexuality Research in the United States: An Assessment of the Social and Behavioral Sciences.* New York: Social Sciences Research Council.
DiPrete, Thomas, and Gregory M. Eirich. 2006. "Cumulative Advantage as a Mechanism for Inequality: A Review of Theoretical and Empirical Developments." *Annual Review of Sociology* 32: 271-297.
Dixit, Raman. 2010. "Naxalite Movement in India: The State's Response." *Journal of Defense Studies* 4, no. 2: http://www.idsa.in/jds/4_2_2010_NaxaliteMovementinIndia_rdixit (accessed July 17, 2012).
Dixon, D., and L. Maher. 2002. "Anh Hai: Policing, Culture, and Social Exclusion in a Street Heroin Market." *Policing and Society* 12, no. 2: 93-110.
Dobbin, Frank. 1994. *Forging Industrial Policy: The United States, Britain, and France in the Railway Age.* Cambridge, UK: Cambridge University Press.
———. 2005. "Comparative and Historical Perspectives in Economic Sociology." In *The Handbook of Economic Sociology*, edited by Neil Smelser and Richard Swedberg, 26-48. 2nd ed. Princeton, NJ: Princeton University Press and Russell Sage Foundation.
Dolgon, Corey, and Chris Baker. 2010. *Social Problems: A Service Learning Approach.* Thousand Oaks, CA: Sage Publications.
Dolgon, Corey, and Mary Chayko. 2010. *Pioneers of Public Sociology: 30 Years of Humanity and Society.* New York: Sloan Publishing.
Dolgon, Corey, Mavis Morton, Tim Maher, and James Pennell. 2012. "Civic Engagement and Public Sociology: Two 'Movements' in Search of a Mission." *Journal of Applied Social Science* 6, no. 1: 5-30.
Domhoff, G. William. 2005. "Power at the Local Level: Growth Coalition Theory." University of Santa Cruz Sociology Department. http://sociology.ucsc.edu/whorulesamerica/local/growth_coalition_theory.html (accessed May 29, 2011).
Donaldson, L. 1987. "Strategy and Structural Adjustment to Regain Fit and Performance: In Defence of Contingency Theory." *Journal of Management Studies* 24, no. 1: 1-24.
Donnelly, Jack. 1982. "Human Rights and Human Dignity: An Analytic Critique of Non-Western Conceptions of Human Rights." *American Political Science Review* 76, no. 2: 303-316.
———. 1985. *The Concept of Human Rights.* London: St. Martin's Press.
———. 2003. *Universal Human Rights in Theory and Practice.* 2nd ed. Ithaca, NY: Cornell University Press.
———. 2006. *International Human Rights.* Boulder, CO: Westview Press.
———. 2007. "The Relative Universality of Human Rights." *Human Rights Quarterly* 28: 281-306.
Donoho, Douglas Lee. 1990-1991. "Relativism versus Universalism in Human Rights: The Search for Meaningful Standards." *Stanford Journal of International Law* 27: 345-391.
Donovan, Josephine, and Carol Adams, eds. 1995. *Animals and Women: Feminist Theoretical Explorations.* Durham, NC: Duke University Press.
———, eds. 2007. *The Feminist Care Tradition in Animal Ethics.* New York: Columbia University Press.
Douglas, Karen Manges, and Rogelio Sáenz. 2010. "The Making of 'Americans': Old Boundaries, New Realities." In *Teaching and Studying the Americas: Cultural Influences from Colonialism to the Present*, edited by A. B. Pinn, C. F. Levander, and M. O. Emerson, 139-156. New York: Palgrave Macmillan.
Douglas, M., and A. Wildavsky. 1982. *Risk and Culture: An Essay on the Selection of Technological and Environmental Dangers.* Berkeley: University of California Press.
Dowd, Jacquelyn Hall. 1993. *Revolt against Chivalry.* New York: Columbia University Press.

Dowse, L. 2001. "Contesting Practices, Challenging Codes: Self Advocacy, Disability Politics and the Social Model." *Disability and Society* 16: 123-141.
Doyal, Lesley. 1995. *What Makes Women Sick: Gender and the Political Economy of Health.* London: Macmillan.
———. 2001. "Sex, Gender, and Health: The Need for a New Approach." *British Medical Journal* (November 3): 323-331.
Dreby, Joanna. 2010. *Divided by Borders.* Berkeley: University of California Press.
Dreier, J. 2004. "Decision Theory and Morality." In *The Oxford Handbook of Rationality,* edited by A. Mele and P. Rawling, 156-181. Oxford: Oxford University Press.
Dreier, Peter, John Mollenkopf, and Todd Swanstrom. 2005. *Place Matters: Metropolitics for the Twenty-First Century.* 2nd ed. Lawrence: University Press of Kansas.
Drew, Paul, and John Heritage, eds. 2006. *Conversation Analysis.* 4 vols. London: Sage.
Drori, Gili, John Meyer, Francisco Ramirez, and Evan Schofer. 2003. *Science in the Modern World Polity: Institutionalization and Globalization.* Palo Alto, CA: Stanford University Press.
Drucker, Peter. 2000. *Different Rainbows.* London: Gay Men's Press.
DuBois, W. E. B. 1983. *Dusk of Dawn: An Essay toward an Autobiography of a Race Concept.* Piscataway, NJ: Transaction Publishers.
———. 2010 [1899]. *The Philadelphia Negro.* New York: Cosimo Classics.
Dudley-Marling, C. 2004. "The Social Construction of Learning Disabilities." *Journal of Learning Disabilities* 37: 482-489.
Dumas, Alex, and Bryan S. Turner. 2007. "The Life-Extension Project: A Sociological Critique." *Health Sociology Review* 16: 5-17.
Dunaway, Wilma A., ed. 2003. *Emerging Issues in the 21st Century World-System.* Vol. 2: *New Theoretical Directions for the 21st Century World System.* Westport, CT: Praeger Publishers.
Duncan-Andrade, Jeffrey, and Ernest Morrell. 2008. *The Art of Critical Pedagogy: Possibilities for Moving from Theory to Practice in Urban Schools.* New York: Peter Lang.
Dunn, Timothy J. 2001. "Border Militarization via Drug and Immigration Enforcement: Human Rights Implications." *Social Justice* 28: 7-30.
———. 2009. *Blockading the Border and Human Rights: The El Paso Operation that Remade Immigration Enforcement.* Austin: University of Texas Press.
Dunn, Timothy J., Ana Maria Aragones, and George Shivers. 2005. "Recent Mexican Migration in the Rural Delmarva Peninsula: Human Rights versus Citizenship Rights in a Local Context." In *New Destinations: Mexican Immigration in the United States,* edited by V. Zúñiga and R. Hernández-León, 155-183. New York: Russell Sage.
Durand, Jorge, William Kandel, Emilio A. Parrado, and Douglas S. Massey. 1996. "International Migration and Development in Mexican Communities." *Demography* 33: 249-264.
Durkheim, Émile. 1915. *L'Allemagne au-desus de tout: la mentalite allemande et la guerre.* Paris: A. Colin.
———. 1951a. *The Division of Labor in Society.* New York: The Free Press.
———. 1951b [1933]. *Suicide.* New York: The Free Press.
———. 1956. *Education and Sociology.* New York: The Free Press.
———. 1962. *Moral Education.* New York: The Free Press.
———. 1964 [1893]. *The Division of Labour in Society.* Translated by George Simpson. New York: The Free Press.
———. 1977. *The Evolution of Educational Thought.* Translated by Peter Collins. London: Routledge and Kegan Paul.
———. 1982. *The Rules of the Sociological Method,* edited by Steven Lukes. New York: The Free Press.
———. 1995. *Elementary Forms of Religious Life.* New York: The Free Press.
Duster, Troy. 1997. "Pattern, Purpose and Race in the Drug War." In *Crack in America: Demon Drugs and Social Justice,* edited by Craig Reinarman and Harry Levine, 260-287. Berkeley: University of California Press.
———. 2003. *Backdoor to Eugenics.* New York: Routledge.
———. 2005. "Race and Reification in Science." *Science* 307: 1050-1051.
Earl, Jennifer, and Katrina Kimport. 2011. *Digitally Enabled Social Change: Activism in the Internet Age.* Cambridge, MA: MIT Press.
Eaton, W. W. 1980. "A Formal Theory of Selection for Schizophrenia." *American Journal of Sociology* 86: 149-158.
Eckel, Jan. 2009. "Utopie der Moral, Kalkül der Macht: Menschenrechte in der globalen Politiknach 1945." *Archiv für Sozialgeschichte* 49: 437-484.
Economic Policy Institute (EPI). 2011. "Income Inequality: It Wasn't Always This Way." EPI. http://www.epi.org/economic_snapshots/entry/income_inequality_it_wasnt_always_this_way (accessed February 9, 2011).
Economist, The. 2006. "Asia: A Specter Haunting India: India's Naxalites." *The Economist* 380, no. 8491: 52.

Edelman, Lauren B. 2004. "Rivers of Law and Contested Terrain: A Law and Society Approach to Economic Rationality." *Law and Society Review* 38, no. 2: 181-198.
Edin, Kathryn, and Maria Kefalas. 2005. *Promises I Can Keep: Why Poor Women Put Motherhood before Marriage.* Berkeley: University of California Press.
Edin, Kathryn, Laura Lein, and Christopher Jencks. 1997. *Making Ends Meet: How Single Mothers Survive Welfare and Low-Wage Work.* New York: Russell Sage Foundation.
Edwards, Bob, and John D. McCarthy. 1992. "Social Movement Schools." *Sociological Forum* 7: 541-550.
Edwards, C., S. Staniszweska, and N. Crichton. 2004. "Investigation of the Ways in Which Patients' Reports of Their Satisfaction with Healthcare Are Constructed." *Sociology of Health and Illness* 26: 159-183.
Edwards, K. E. 2006. "Aspiring Social Justice Ally Identity Development: A Conceptual Model." *NASPA Journal* 43: 39-60.
Edwards, Richard. 1979. *Contested Terrain: The Transformation of the Workplace in the Twentieth Century.* New York: Basic Books.
Egan, Patrick J., and Kenneth Sherrill. 2009. *California's Proposition 8: What Happened, and What Does the Future Hold?* San Francisco: Evelyn and Walter Haas Jr. Fund and the National Gay and Lesbian Task Force Policy Institute.
Ehrenfeld, David. 2002. "The Cow Tipping Point." *Harper's* 305: 13-20.
Eisenstein, Hester. 1983. *Contemporary Feminist Thought.* Boston: G. K. Hall.
Elder, Glen H., Jr. 1999 [1974]. *Children of the Great Depression: Social Change in Life Experience.* 25th anniv. ed. Boulder, CO: Westview Press.
Elder, Glen H., Jr., Elizabeth Colerick Clipp, J. Scott Brown, Leslie R. Martin, and Howard S. Friedman. 2009. "The Life-Long Mortality Risks of World War II Experiences." *Research on Aging* 30, no. 4: 391-412.
Elias, Norbert. 1978. *The Civilizing Process.* New York: Urizen.
Elliott, Michael. 2007. "Human Rights and the Triumph of the Individual in World Culture." *Cultural Sociology* 1: 343-363.
———. 2008. "A Cult of the Individual for a Global Society: The Development and Worldwide Expansion of Human Rights Ideology." PhD diss., Emory University, Atlanta.
Elliott, Richard, Joanne Csete, Evan Wood, and Thomas Kerr. 2005. "Harm Reduction, HIV/AIDS, and the Human Rights Challenge to Global Drug Control Policy." *Health and Human Rights* 8, no. 2: 104-138.
Ellis, Lee. 2001. "The Biosocial Female Choice Theory of Social Stratification." *Social Biology* 48: 298-320.
———. 2004. "Sex, Status, and Criminality: A Theoretical Nexus." *Social Biology* 51: 144-165.
Ellis, Lee, Scott Hershberber, Evelyn Field, and Scott Wersinger. 2008. *Sex Differences: Summarizing More Than a Century of Scientific Research.* London: Psychology Press.
Ellwood, Charles A. 1907. "How Should Sociology Be Taught as a College or University Subject?" *American Journal of Sociology* 12: 588-606.
Elster, J. 1989. *Nuts and Bolts for the Social Sciences.* Cambridge, UK: Cambridge University Press.
———. 1992. *Local Justice: How Institutions Allocate Scarce Goods and Necessary Burdens.* New York: Russell Sage Foundation.
———. 2007. *Explaining Social Behavior: More Nuts and Bolts for the Social Sciences.* Cambridge, UK: Cambridge University Press.
Ely, Richard T. 1886. *The Labor Movement in America.* New York: Thomas Y. Crowell.
Ember, Carol R., and Melvin Ember. 1994. "War, Socialization, and Impersonal Violence: A Cross Cultural Study." *Journal of Conflict Resolution* 38: 620-646.
Emerson, Rupert. 1975. "The Fate of Human Rights in the Third World." *World Politics* 27: 201-226.
End Corporal Punishment. http://www.endcorporalpunishment.org.
Engels, Friedrich. 1847. "The Principles of Communism." Marxists Internet Archive. http://www.marxists .org/archive/marx/works/1847/11/prin-com.htm (accessed July 17, 2012).
England, Paula. 2005. "Gender Inequality in Labor Markets: The Role of Motherhood and Segregation." *Social Politics* 12: 264-288.
Engles, Eric. 2008. "Human Rights According to Marxism." *Guild Practitioner* 65, no. 249: 249-256.
Enloe, Cynthia. 1990. *Bananas, Beaches, and Bases: Making Feminist Sense of International Politics.* Berkeley: University of California Press.
———. 2000. *Maneuvers: The International Politics of Militarizing Women's Lives.* Berkeley: University of California Press.
———. 2007. *Globalization and Militarism: Feminists Make the Link.* Boulder, CO: Rowman & Littlefield.
Epstein, L., and J. Knight. 1998. *The Choices Justices Make.* Washington, DC: Congressional Quarterly.
Epstein, Steven. 1998. *Impure Science: AIDS, Activism, and the Politics of Knowledge.* Berkeley: University of California Press.

Ericksen, Julia A., with Sally A. Steffen. 2001. *Kiss and Tell: Surveying Sex in the Twentieth Century.* Cambridge, MA: Harvard University Press.
Erikson, Kai. 1994. *A New Species of Trouble: Explorations in Disaster, Trauma and Community.* New York: W. W. Norton.
Ermann, M. David, and Richard J. Lundman, eds. 2002. *Corporate and Governmental Deviance: Problems of Organizational Behavior in Contemporary Society.* New York: Oxford University Press.
Ervin-Tripp, Susan. 1972. "On Sociolinguistic Rules: Alternation and Co-Occurrence." In *Directions in Sociolinguistics: The Ethnography of Communication,* edited by John J. Gumperz and Dell Hymes, 213-250. New York: Holt, Rinehart and Winston.
Eschbach, Karl, J. Hagan, N. Rodriguez, R. Hernandez-Leon, and S. Bailey. 1999. "Death at the Border." *International Migration Review* 33: 430-454.
Escober, Arturo. 2006. "Difference and Conflict in the Struggle over Natural Resources: A Political Ecology Framework." *Development* 49: 6-13.
Esping-Andersen, G. 1994. "Welfare States and the Economy." In *The Handbook of Economic Sociology,* edited by N. J. Smelser and R. Swedberg, 711-732. Princeton, NJ: Princeton University Press.
Esping-Andersen, Gøsta. 1999. *Social Foundations of Postindustrial Economies.* Oxford and New York: Oxford University Press.
Esposito, John L., and John O. Voll. 2001. "Islam and Democracy." *Humanities* 22 (November/December). http://www.neh.gov/news/humanities/2001-11/islam.html (accessed January 20, 2012).
Estes, C. L., S. Goldberg, S. Shostack, K. Linkins, and R. Beard. 2006. "Implications of Welfare Reform for the Elderly: A Case Study of Provider, Advocate, and Consumer Perspectives." *Journal of Aging and Social Policy* 19, no. 1: 41-63.
Etzioni, Amatai. 1961. *A Comparative Analysis of Complex Organizations.* Glencoe, IL: Free Press.
———. 1988. *The Moral Dimension: Toward a New Economics.* New York: The Free Press.
———. 2009. "Minorities and the National Ethos." *Politics* 29, no. 2 (June): 100-110.
Etzkowitz, Henry. 2003. "Innovation in Innovation: The Triple Helix of University-Industry-Government Relations." *Social Science Information* 42, no. 3: 293-338.
Eugene Human Rights City Project. 2011. http://www.humanrightscity.com (accessed May 26, 2011).
Eurobarometer. 2010. "Mental Health. Part One: Report." Special Eurobarometer 345/Eurobarometer 73.2. http://ec.europa.eu/health/mental_health/docs/ebs_345_en.pdf (accessed April 20, 2011).
Evans, Derek G. 2007. "Human Rights: Four Generations of Practice and Development." In *Educating for Human Rights and Global Citizenship,* edited by A. Abdi and L. Shultz, 1-12. Albany: State University of New York Press.
Evans, N. J., J. L. Assadi, and T. K. Herriott. 2005. "Encouraging the Development of Disability Allies." *New Directions for Student Services* 110: 67-79.
Evans, Tony. 2001a. "If Democracy, Then Human Rights?" *Third World Quarterly* 22: 623-642.
———. 2001b. *The Politics of Human Rights.* London: Pluto Press.
Ewen, Lynda Ann. 1991. "Coming Home: A Sociological Journey." In *Radical Sociologists and the Movement: Experiences, Lessons, and Legacies,* edited by Martin Oppenheimer, Martin J. Murray, and Rhonda F. Levine, 140-157. Philadelphia: Temple University Press.
Facio, Alda, and Martha I. Morgan. 2009. "Morgan Symposium on the Gender of Constitutional and Human Rights Law: Equity or Equality for Women? Understanding CEDAW's Equality Principles." *Alabama Law Review* 60: 1133.
Fakhoury, W., and S. Priebe. 2002. "The Process of Deinstitutionalization: An International Overview." *Current Opinion in Psychiatry* 15: 187-192.
Fals-Borda, Orlando. 1988. *Knowledge and People's Power.* New Delhi: Indian Social Institute.
Fanon, Frantz. 2005. *The Wretched of the Earth.* New York: Grove Press.
———. 2008. *Black Skin, White Masks.* Revised. New York: Grove Press.
Fantasia, Rick. 1988. *Cultures of Solidarity: Consciousness, Action, and Contemporary American Workers.* Berkeley: University of California Press.
Fararo, Thomas J. 1973. *Mathematical Sociology: An Introduction to Fundamentals.* New York: Wiley.
———. 1989. *The Meaning of General Theoretical Sociology: Tradition and Formalization.* Cambridge, UK: Cambridge University Press.
Farmer, Paul. 2003. *Pathologies of Power: Health, Human Rights, and the New War on the Poor.* Berkeley: University of California Press.
———. 2010. *Partner to the Poor: A Paul Farmer Reader.* Berkeley: University of California Press.
———. 2011. *Haiti after the Earthquake.* New York: Public Affairs.
Farnall, O., and K. A. Smith. 1999. "Reactions to People with Disabilities: Personal Contact versus Viewing of Specific Media Portrayal." *Journalism and Mass Communication Quarterly* 76: 659-672.

Farr, Thomas F., Richard W. Garnett IV, T. Jeremy Gunn, and William L. Saunders. 2009. "Religious Liberties: The International Religious Freedom Act." *Houston Journal of International Law* 31: 469-514.

Fasenfest, David. 2009. *Engaging Social Justice: Critical Studies of 21st Century Social Transformation.* Leiden, the Netherlands: Brill.

Faugeron, C., and M. Kokoreff. 1999. "Les practiques sociales des drogues: elements por una mise en perspective des recherché en France." *Societes Contemporaines* 36: 5-17.

Fausto-Sterling, Anne. 2000a. "The Five Sexes Revisited." *Sciences* 40: 18-23.

———. 2000b. *Sexing the Body: Gender Politics and the Construction of Sexuality.* New York: Basic Books.

Feagin, Joe R. 2006. *Systemic Racism: A Theory of Oppression.* New York: Routledge.

———. 2010. *The White Racial Frame: Centuries of Racial Framing and Counter-Framing.* New York: Routledge.

Feagin, Joe R., and Hernan Vera. 2008. *Liberation Sociology.* 2nd ed. Boulder, CO: Paradigm Publishers.

Feher, Ferenc, Agnes Heller, and Gyorgy Markus. 1986. *Dictatorship over Needs: An Analysis of Soviet Societies.* Oxford: Basil Blackwell.

Fehr, E., and S. Gächter. 2002. "Altruistic Punishment in Humans." *Nature* 415: 137-140.

Fein, Helen. 1979. *Accounting for Genocide.* Chicago: University of Chicago Press.

Fenster, T., ed. 1999. *Gender, Planning and Human Rights.* London and New York: Routledge.

Ferguson, J. 1994. *The Anti-Politics Machine: Development, Depoliticization, and Bureaucratic Power in Lesotho.* Minneapolis: University of Minnesota Press.

Ferguson, Kathy E. 1991. "Interpretation and Genealogy in Feminism." *Signs: Journal of Women in Culture and Society* 16: 322-339.

Ferraris, Maurizio. 1996 [1988]. *History of Hermeneutics.* Translated by Luca Somigli. Atlantic Highlands, NJ: Humanities Press International.

Ferree, Myra Marx, and Tetyana Pudrovska. 2006. "Transnational Feminist NGOs on the Web: Networks and Identities in the Global North and South." In *Global Feminism: Transnational Women's Activism, Organizing, and Human Rights,* edited by Myra Marx Ferree and Aili Mari Tripp, 247-274. New York: New York University Press.

Ferree, Myra Marx, and Aili Mari Tripp. 2006. *Global Feminism: Transnational Women's Activism, Organizing, and Human Rights.* New York: New York University Press.

Fieder, M., and S. Huber. 2007. "The Effects of Sex and Childlessness on the Association between Status and Reproductive Output in Modern Society." *Evolution and Human Behavior* 28: 392-398.

Field, Les W. 1994. "Review: Who Are the Indians? Reconceptualizing Indigenous Identity, Resistance, and the Role of Social Science in Latin America." *Latin American Research Review* 29: 237-248.

Fields, Belden. 2010. "Human Rights Theory, Criteria, Boundaries, and Complexities." In *Qualitative Inquiry and Human Rights,* edited by Norman Denzin and Michael Giardina, 66-81. Walnut Creek, CA: Left Coast Press.

Fillmore, K. M. 1987a. "Prevalence, Incidence and Chronicity of Drinking Patterns and Problems among Men as a Function of Age: A Longitudinal and Cohort Analysis." *British Journal of Addiction* 82: 77-83.

———. 1987b. "Women's Drinking across the Adult Life Course as Compared to Men's: A Longitudinal and Cohort Analysis." *British Journal of Addiction* 82: 801-811.

Fine, Gary Alan. 1993. "The Sad Demise, Mysterious Disappearance, and Glorious Triumph of Symbolic Interactionism." *Annual Review of Sociology* 19: 61-87.

———. 1995. *A Second Chicago School: The Development of a Postwar American Sociology.* Chicago: University of Chicago Press.

Fink, Leon. 2003. *The Mayan of Morganton.* Chapel Hill: University of North Carolina Press.

Finnegan, Amy, Adam R. Saltsman, and Shelley K. White. 2010. "Negotiating Politics and Culture: The Utility of Human Rights for Activist Organizing in the United States." *Journal of Human Rights Practice* 2, no. 3: 307-333.

Finnemore, Martha. 1999. "Rules of War and Wars of Rules: The International Red Cross and the Restraint of State Violence." In *Constructing World Culture: International Nongovernmental Organizations since 1875,* edited by J. Boli and G. M. Thomas, 149-168. Stanford, CA: Stanford University Press.

Firebaugh, Glenn. 1999. "Empirics of World Income Inequality." *American Journal of Sociology* 104: 1597-1630.

Firth, Roderick. 1952. "Ethical Absolutism and the Ideal Observer." *Philosophy and Phenomenological Research* 12: 317-345.

Fish, Stanley. 2008. *Save the World on Your Own Time.* New York: Oxford University Press.

Fitzgerald, Amy, Linda Kalof, and Thomas Dietz. 2009. "Slaughterhouses and Increased Crime Rates: An Empirical Analysis of Spillover from 'The Jungle' into the Surrounding Community." *Organization and Environment* 22: 158-184.

Fitzgerald, John. 2010. "Images of the Desire for Drugs." *Health Sociology Review* 19, no. 2: 205-217.
Fix, Michael, and Wendy Zimmermann. 2001. "All under One Roof: Mixed-Status Families in an Era of Reform." *International Migration Review* 35: 397-419.
Flacks, Richard. 2004. "Knowledge for What? Thoughts on the State of Social Movement Studies." In *Rethinking Social Movements: Structure, Culture, Emotion*, edited by J. Goodwin and J. Jasper, 135-155. Lanham, MD: Rowman & Littlefield.
———. 2005. "The Question of Relevance in Social Movement Studies." In *Rhyming Hope and History: Activists, Academics, and Social Movement Scholarship*, edited by David Croteau, William Hoynes, and Charlotte Ryan, 3-19. Minneapolis: University of Minnesota Press.
Fleischer, D. A., and F. Zames. 2001. *The Disability Rights Movement: From Charity to Confrontation*. Philadelphia: Temple University Press.
Fligstein, Neil. 2001. *The Architecture of Markets: An Economic Sociology of Twentieth Century Capitalist Societies*. Princeton, NJ, and Oxford, UK: Princeton University Press.
Fligstein, Neil, and Adam Goldstein. 2010. "The Anatomy of the Mortgage Securitization Crisis." In *Markets on Trial: The Economic Sociology of the U.S. Financial Crisis*, edited by Michael Lounsbury and Paul M. Hirsch, 20-70. Research in the Sociology of Organizations 30A. London: Emerald Group Publishing.
Flippen, Chenoa Anne. 2004. "Unequal Returns to Housing Investments? A Study of Real Housing Appreciation among Black, White, and Hispanic Households." *Social Forces* 82: 1523-1551.
Florini, Ann, Nihon Kokusai, Koryu Senta, and Carnegie Endowment for International Peace. 2000. *The Third Force: The Rise of Transnational Civil Society*. Tokyo: Japan Center for International Exchange, Washington Carnegie Endowment for International Peace, and Brookings Institution Press.
Fone, Byrne. 2000. *Homophobia: A History*. New York: Metropolitan Books.
Foner, A. 1974. "Age Stratification and Age Conflict in Political Life." *American Sociological Review* 39, no. 2: 187-196.
Foner, Eric. 1984. "Why Is There No Socialism in the United States?" *History Workshop Journal* 17: 57-80.
Forbes, Catherine, Merran Evans, Nicholas Hastings, and Brian Peacock. 2011. *Statistical Distributions*. 4th ed. New York: Wiley.
Fore, Matthew L. 2002. "Shall Weigh Your God and You: Assessing the Imperialistic Implications of the International Religious Freedom Act in Muslim Countries." *Duke Law Journal* 52: 423-453.
Forman, Tyrone A., and Amanda E. Lewis. 2006. "Racial Apathy and Hurricane Katrina: The Social Anatomy of Prejudice in the Post-Civil Rights Era." *Du Bois Review: Social Science Research on Race* 3: 175-202.
Forsythe, David. 2000. *Human Rights in International Relations*. New York: Cambridge University Press.
———. 2007. *The Humanitarians*. New York: Cambridge.
Fortman, Bas de Gaay. 2011. *Political Economy of Human Rights: Rights, Realities and Realization*. London: Routledge.
Foster-Fishman, Pennie, Tiffany Jimenez, Maria Valenti, and Tasha Kelley. 2007. "Building the Next Generation of Leaders in the Disabilities Movement." *Disability and Society* 22: 341-356.
Foucault, Michel. 1978. *The History of Sexuality: An Introduction*. Vol. 1. New York: Vintage Books.
———. 1980. *Power/Knowledge*, edited by Colin Gordon, translated by Colin Gordon, Leo Marshall, John Mephan, and Kate Soper. New York: Pantheon Books.
———. 1995 [1971]. *Madness and Civilization: A History of Insanity in the Age of Reason*. London: Tavistock.
Fox, Mary Frank. 1995. "From the President." *SWS Network News*, 2.
———. 2008. "Institutional Transformation and the Advancement of Women Faculty: The Case of Academic Science and Engineering." In *Higher Education: Handbook of Theory and Research*, edited by John C. Smart, 23: 73-103. New York: Springer.
———. 2010. "Women and Men Faculty in Academic Science and Engineering: Social-Organizational Indicators and Implications." *American Behavioral Scientist* 53, no. 7: 997-1012.
Francis, David, and Stephen Hester. 2004. *An Invitation to Ethnomethodology: Language, Society and Social Interaction*. London: Sage.
Franck, Thomas M. 2001. "Are Human Rights Universal?" *Foreign Affairs* 80: 191-204.
Frank, A. W. 1988. "Garfinkel's Deconstruction of Parsons's Plenum." *Discourse Analysis Research Group Newsletter* 4, no. 1: 5-8.
Frank, Andre G. 1991. *Third World War: A Political Economy of the Gulf War and New World Order*. Róbinson Rojas Archive. http://www.rrojasdatabank.info/agfrank/gulf_war.html (accessed July 17, 2012).
Frankenberg, Ruth. 1993. *White Women, Race Matters: The Social Construction of Whiteness*. London: Taylor and Francis.
Frankl, Viktor E. 1984 [1959]. *Man's Search for Meaning*. New York: Simon and Schuster.
Franklin, James C. 2008. "Shame on You: The Impact of Human Rights Criticism on Political Repression in Latin America." *International Studies Quarterly* 52: 187-211.

Franks, David. 2010. *Neurosociology: The Nexus between Neuroscience and Social Psychology*. New York: Springer.
Franks, David, and Thomas Smith. 2009. "A Neurosociological Perspective on Emotions. A Review Article by David Franks and Thomas Smith: *Mind, Brain and Society: Toward a Neurosociology of Emotion*." *Sociologie* 5: 244–256.
Fraser, Nancy. 1992. "Rethinking the Public Sphere: A Contribution to the Critique of Actually Existing Democracy." In *Habermas and the Public Sphere*, edited by Craig Calhoun, 109–142. Cambridge, MA: MIT Press.
———. 2009. *Scales of Justice: Reimagining Political Space in a Globalizing World*. New York: Columbia University Press.
Fraser, Nancy, and Axel Honneth. 2003. *Redistribution or Recognition: A Political-Philosophical Exchange*. Translated by Joel Golb, James Ingram, and Christiane Wilke. London: Verso.
Freedman, M. 2007. *Prime Time: How Baby Boomers Will Revolutionize Retirement and Transform America*. Cambridge, MA: Perseus Books.
Freeman, M. 2002. *Human Rights: An Interdisciplinary Approach*. Malden, MA: Blackwell Publishers.
Freeman, Marsha. 1999. "International Institutions and Gendered Justice." *Journal of International Affairs* 52: 513–533.
Freeman, Michael, ed. 2006. *Law and Sociology*. Oxford: Oxford University Press.
Freeman, R. B., and James L. Medoff. 1984. *What Do Unions Do?* New York: Basic Books.
Freese, Jeremy, and Brian Powell. 1999. "Sociobiology, Status, and Parental Investment in Sons and Daughters: Testing the Trivers-Willard Hypothesis." *American Journal of Sociology* 104: 1704–1743.
Freidson, Eliot. 1970. *Professional Dominance: The Social Structure of Medical Care*. New York: Atherton Press.
———. 2001. *Professionalism, the Third Logic*. Chicago: The Third Logic.
Freire, Paulo. 2000. *Pedagogy of the Oppressed*. New York: Continuum International.
Freire, Paulo, and Donald Macedo. 1987. *Literacy: Reading the Word and the World*. New York: Routledge.
Freudenburg, William R., and Robert Gramling. 2010. *Blowout: The BP Oil Disaster and the Future of Energy in America*. Cambridge, MA: MIT Press.
Freudenburg, William R., Robert B. Gramling, Shirley Laska, and Kai Erikson. 2009. *Catastrophe in the Making: The Engineering of Katrina and Disasters of Tomorrow*. Washington, DC: Island Press.
Frezzo, Mark. 2008. "Sociology, Human Rights, and the World Social Forum." *Societies without Borders* 3: 35–47.
———. 2011. "Sociology and Human Rights in the Post Development Era." *Sociology Compass* 5, no. 3: 203–214.
Frickel, Scott, and Kelly Moore, eds. 2006. *The New Political Sociology of Science: Institutions, Networks, and Power*. Madison: University of Wisconsin Press.
Frickel, Scott, and M. Bess Vincent. 2007. "Katrina, Contamination, and the Unintended Organization of Ignorance." *Technology in Society* 29: 181–188.
Friedkin, Noah E. 1998. *A Structural Theory of Social Influence*. Cambridge, UK: Cambridge University Press.
Friedländer, Saul. 2007. *Nazi Germany and the Jews, 1939–1945: The Years of Extermination*. New York: Harper.
Friedman, E. L. 1977. *Industry and Labour: Class Struggle at Work and Monopoly Capitalism*, 18–35. London: Macmillan Press.
Friedman, Elisabeth J. 1995. "Women's Human Rights: The Emergence of a Movement." In *Women's Rights, Human Rights: International Feminist Perspectives*, edited by Julia Peters and Andrea Wolper. New York: Routledge.
———. 2003. "Gendering the Agenda: The Impact of the Transnational Women's Rights Movement at the UN Conferences of the 1990s." *Women's Studies International Forum* 26: 313–331.
Friedman, Lawrence Meir. 2002. *American Law in the 20th Century*. New Haven, CT: Yale University Press.
Friedman, Milton. 1962. *Capitalism and Freedom*. Chicago: University of Chicago Press.
Friedman, Neil A. 1986. "A Human Rights Approach to the Labor Rights of Undocumented Workers." *California Law Review* 74, no. 5: 1715–1745.
Friedman, Thomas L. 2005. *The World Is Flat: A Brief History of the Twenty-First Century*. New York: Farrar, Straus and Giroux.
Friedrichs, David O. 2009. "On Resisting State Crime: Conceptual and Contextual Issues." *Social Justice* 36: 4–27.
Fritz, J. M. 1989. "Dean Winternitz, Clinical Sociology and the Julius Rosenwald Fund." *Clinical Sociology Review* 7: 17–27.
———. 1991. "The Emergency of American Clinical Sociology: The First Courses." *Clinical Sociology Review* 9: 15–26.
———. 2004. "Derriere la magie: models, approaches et theories de mediation [Behind the Magic: Mediation, Models, Approaches and Theories]." *Esprit Critique* 6. http://www.espritcritique.fr/0603/esp0603article01.pdf (accessed September 6, 2012).

———. 2005. "The Scholar-Practitioners: The Development of Clinical Sociology in the United States." In *Diverse Histories of American Sociology*, edited by A. J. Blasi, 40-56. Leiden, the Netherlands: Brill.
———, ed. 2008. *International Clinical Sociology*. New York: Springer.
———. 2010. "Special Education Mediation in the United States." In *People with Health Limitations in Modern Society*, edited by O. Dikova-Favorskaya, 268-285. Zhitomar, Ukraine: DZHIVIES.
Fritz, J. M., P. Bistak, and C. Auffrey. 2000. "The Bumpy Road to a Tobacco-Free Community: Lessons from Well City." *Sociological Practice* 2: 113-126.
Fritz, J. M., S. Doering, and F. Belgin Gumru. 2011. "Women, Peace, Security, and the National Action Plans." *Journal of Applied Social Science* 5, no. 1 (spring): 1-23.
Frost, Jennifer. 2001. *An Interracial Movement of the Poor: Community Organizing and the New Left in the 1960s*. New York: New York University Press.
Fry, C. L. 2007. "Demographic Transitions, Age, and Culture." In *Social Structures: Demographic Changes and the Well-Being of Older Persons*, edited by K. W. Schaie and P. Uhlenberg, 283-300. New York: Springer Publishing Co.
Fukumura, Yoko, and Martha Matsuoka. 2002. "Redefining Security: Okinawa Women's Resistance to U.S. Militarism." In *Women's Activism and Globalization: Linking Local Struggles and Transnational Politics*, edited by Nancy A. Naples and Manisha Desai, 239-263. New York: Routledge.
Fulcomer, David. 1947. "Some Newer Methods of Teaching Sociology." *Journal of Educational Sociology* 21: 154-162.
Fuller, Robert W. 2003. *Somebodies and Nobodies: Overcoming the Abuse of Rank*. Gabriola Island, BC: New Society Publishers.
Fuller, Robert W., and T. Scheff. 2009. "Bleeding Heart Liberals Proven Right: Too Much Inequality Harms a Society." *Huffington Post*. June 18.
Fung, Archon, and Erik Olin Wright. 2003. *Deepening Democracy: Institutional Innovations in Empowered Participatory Governance*, with contributions by Rebecca Neaera Abers et al. London: Verso.
Furstenberg, Frank. 2010. "On a New Schedule: Transitions to Adulthood and Family Change." *Transition to Adulthood* 20, no. 1: 68-87.
Gaer, Felice. 1998. "And Never the Twain Shall Meet? The Struggle to Establish Women's Rights as International Human Rights." In *The International Human Rights of Women: Instruments of Change*, edited by Carol Lockwood et al., 41-69. Washington, DC: American Bar Association Section of International Law and Practice.
Gaines, Atwood D. 2011. "Millennial Medical Anthropology: From There to Here and Beyond, or the Problem of Global Health." *Culture, Medicine and Psychiatry* 35, no. 1: 83-89.
Galbraith, John Kenneth. 1983. *The Anatomy of Power*. Boston: Houghton Mifflin.
Gallahue, Patrick. 2010. "Targeted Killing of Drug Lords: Traffickers as Members of Armed Opposition Groups and/or Direct Participants in Hostilities." *International Yearbook on Human Rights and Drug Policy* 1.
Galtung, Johan. 1996. *Peace by Peaceful Means*. Thousand Oaks, CA: Sage Publications.
Gamson, William A. 1988. "Review: [untitled]." *American Journal of Sociology* 94: 436-438.
———. 1992. *Talking Politics*. Cambridge, UK: Cambridge University Press.
Gamson, William A., and David S. Meyer. 1996. "Framing Political Opportunity." In *Comparative Perspectives in Social Movements: Political Opportunities, Mobilizing Structures, and Cultural Framings*, edited by Doug McAdam, John D. McCarthy, and Mayer N. Zald, 275-290. Cambridge, UK: Cambridge University Press.
Gandhi, Mahatma. 1993a. *The Collected Works of Mahatma Gandhi* (electronic book). New Delhi: Publications Division Government of India.
———. 1993b. *Gandhi and the Gita*, edited by. J. I. (Hans) Bakker. Toronto: Canadian Scholars' Press.
———. 1999. *The Collected Works of Mahatma Gandhi* (electronic book). 98 vols. New Delhi: Publications Division Government of India. http://www.gandhiserve.org/cwmg/cwmg.html (accessed January 20, 2012).
———. 2002. *The Essential Gandhi: An Anthology of His Writings on His Life, Work and Ideas*. New York: Vintage Publishers.
Gans, H. J. 1997. "Toward a Reconciliation of 'Assimilation' and 'Pluralism': The Interplay of Acculturation and Ethnic Retention." *International Migration Review* 31: 875-892.
Gardner, G., and T. Prugh. 2008. "Seeding the Sustainable Economy." In *State of the World: Innovations for Sustainable Economy*, edited by Linda Starke, 3-17. New York: W. W. Norton.
Garey, A. 1999. *Weaving Work and Motherhood*. Philadelphia, PA: Temple University Press.
Garfinkel, Harold. 1967. *Studies in Ethnomethodology*. Englewood Cliffs, NJ: Prentice Hall.
———, ed. 1986. *Ethnomethodological Studies of Work*. London: Routledge and Kegan Paul.
———. 2002. *Ethnomethodology's Program: Working Out Durkheim's Aphorism*, edited and introduced by Anne Warfield Rawls. Lanham, MD: Rowman & Littlefield.

———. 2006. *Seeing Sociologically: The Routine Grounds of Social Action*, edited and introduced by Anne Warfield Rawls. Boulder, CO: Paradigm.
———. 2008. *Toward a Sociological Theory of Information*, edited and introduced by Anne Warfield Rawls. Boulder, CO: Paradigm.
Garfinkel, Harold, and Harvey Sacks. 1970. "On Formal Structures of Practical Action." In *Theoretical Sociology: Perspectives and Developments*, edited by J. C. McKinney and E. A. Tiryakian, 338-366. New York: Appleton-Century-Crofts.
Garfinkel, Harold, and D. Lawrence Wieder. 1992. "Two Incommensurable, Asymmetrically Alternate Technologies of Social Analysis." In *Text in Context: Contributions to Ethnomethodology*, edited by Graham Watson and Robert M. Seiler, 175-206. Newbury Park, CA: Sage.
Gargano, G. 2008. "Art and Science in Italian Clinical Sociology." In *International Clinical Sociology*, edited by J. M. Fritz, 153-169. New York: Springer.
Garland, David. 1990. *Punishment in Modern Society*. Chicago: University of Chicago Press.
Garnett, Richard A. 1988. "The Study of War in American Sociology: An Analysis of Selected Journals, 1936-1988." *American Sociologist* 19: 270-282.
Garrett, William R. 2001. "Religion, Law, and the Human Condition." In *Religion in the Process of Globalization*, edited by Peter Beyer, 289-340. Würzburg: Ergon.
Garroutte, Eva M. 2001. "The Racial Formation of American Indians: Negotiating Legitimate Identities within Tribal and Federal Law." *American Indian Quarterly* 25, no. 2: 224-239.
———. 2003. *Real Indians: Identity and the Survival of Native America*. Los Angeles: University of California Press.
Gaston, Alonso, Noel Anderson, Celina Su, and Jeanne Theoharis. 2009. *Our Schools Suck: Students Talk Back to a Segregated Nation on the Failures of Urban Education*. New York: New York University Press.
Gaulejac, V. de. 2008. "On the Origins of Clinical Sociology in France: Some Milestones." In *International Clinical Sociology*, edited by J. M. Fritz, 54-71. New York: Springer.
———. 2010. Personal communication with J. M. Fritz. December 15.
Gavey, N., K. McPhillips, and M. Doherty. 2001. "'If It's Not On, It's Not On'—or Is It? Discursive Constraints on Women's Condom Use." *Gender and Society* 15: 917-934.
Gecas, Viktor. 1991. "The Self-Concept as a Basis for a Theory of Motivation." In *The Self-Society Dynamic*, edited by Judith A. Howard and Peter L. Callero, 171-185. Cambridge, UK: Cambridge University Press.
Gecas, Viktor, and Peter Burke. 1995. "Self and Identity." In *Sociological Perspectives on Social Psychology*, edited by Karen S. Cook, Gary Alan Fine, and James T. House, 156-173. Boston: Allyn and Bacon.
Geiger, Roger. 1986. *To Advance Relevant Knowledge: The Growth of American Research Universities, 1900-1940*. Oxford: Oxford University Press.
Gendron, Richard, and G. William Domhoff. 2008. *The Leftmost City: Power and Progressive Politics in Santa Cruz*. Boulder, CO: Westview Press.
Gerhardt, U. 1989. *Ideas about Illness: An Intellectual and Political History of Medical Sociology*. New York: New York University Press.
Gerstenfeld, Phylis, Diana Grant, and Chau-Pu Chiang. 2003. "Hate Online: A Content Analysis of Extremist Internet Sites." *Analyses of Social Issues and Public Policy* 3: 29-44.
Ghosh, B. 1992. "Migration-Development Linkages: Some Specific Issues and Practical Policy Measures." *International Migration* 30: 423-452.
GID Reform Advocates. 2008. "GID Reform Advocates." Transgender Forum. http://www.transgender.org/gird (accessed November 11, 2011).
Giddens, Anthony. 1985. *The Nation-State and Violence*. Cambridge, UK: Polity Press.
———. 1998. *The Third Way: The Renewal of Social Democracy*. Cambridge, UK: Polity Press.
———. 1999. *Runaway World*. London: Profile Books.
———. 2009. *The Politics of Climate Change*. Malden, MA: Polity Press.
Giesen, Bernhard. 2004. *Triumph or Trauma*. Boulder, CO: Paradigm.
Gill, Aisha K., and Anitha Sundari. 2011. *Forced Marriage: Introducing a Social Justice and Human Rights Perspective*. Boston: Zed Books.
Gill, Anthony James. 2008. *The Political Origins of Religious Liberty*. Cambridge, UK, and New York: Cambridge University Press.
Gill, D. A., and J. S. Picou. 1998. "Technological Disasters and Chronic Community Stress." *Society and Natural Resources* 11: 795-815.
Gill, E. 2002. "Unlocking the Iron Cage: Human Agency and Social Organization." *Studies in Symbolic Interaction* 25: 109-128.
Gillum, R. F. 2005. "Religiosity and the Validity of Self-Reported Smoking: The Third National Health and Nutritional Examination Survey." *Review of Religious Research* 47, no. 2: 190-196.

Ginsberg, Morris. 1942. "The Individualist Basis of International Law and Morals: The Presidential Address." *Proceedings of the Aristotelian Society* 43: i–xxvi.
Ginsburg, Tom. 2009. "The Clash of Commitments at the International Criminal Court." *Chicago Journal of International Law* 9, no. 2: 499–514.
Giroux, Henry. 1983a. "Theories of Reproduction and Resistance in the New Sociology of Education: A Critical Analysis." *Harvard Educational Review* 55: 257–293.
——. 1983b. *Theories and Resistance in Education.* South Hadley, MA: Bergin and Garvey.
——. 1997. *Pedagogy and the Politics of Hope: Theory, Culture, and Schooling.* Boulder, CO: Westview.
Glazebrook, Susan. 2009. "Human Rights and the Environment." *Victoria University Wellington Law Review* 40: 293–350.
Glazebrook, Trish, and Anthony Kola-Olusanya. 2011. "Justice, Conflict, Capital and Care: Oil in the Niger Delta." *Environmental Ethics* 33, no. 2: 163–184.
Glenn, Evelyn Nakano. 1999. "The Social Construction and Institutionalization of Gender and Race: An Integrative Framework." In *Revisiting Gender*, edited by Myra Marx Ferree, Judith Lorber, and Beth B. Hess, 3–43. New York: Sage.
——. 2002. *Unequal Freedom: How Race and Gender Shaped American Citizenship and Labor.* Cambridge, MA: Harvard University Press.
Gluck, Sherna Berger, with Maylei Blackwell, Sharon Cotrell, and Karen S. Harper. 1997. "Whose Feminism, Whose History? Reflections on Excavating the History of (the) U.S. Women's Movement(s)." In *Community Activism and Feminist Politics: Organizing across Race, Gender, and Class*, edited by Nancy A. Naples, 31–56. New York: Routledge.
Goffman, Erving. 1955. "On Face-Work: An Analysis of Ritual Elements in Social Interaction." *Psychiatry* 18, no. 3: 213–231.
——. 1956a. "The Nature of Deference and Demeanor." *American Anthropologist* 58, no. 3: 473–502.
——. 1956b. "Embarrassment and Social Organization." *American Journal of Sociology* 62, no. 3: 264–271.
——. 1959. *The Presentation of Self in Everyday Life.* 1st ed. Garden City, NY: Anchor.
——. 1961. *Asylums: Essays on the Social Situation of Mental Patients and Other Inmates.* New York: Anchor Books.
——. 1963. *Stigma: Notes on the Management of Spoiled Identity.* Englewood Cliffs, NJ: Prentice Hall.
——. 1979. *Gender Advertisements.* New York: HarperCollins.
——. 1986. *Frame Analysis: An Essay on the Organization of Experience.* Boston: Northeastern University Press.
Golash-Boza, Tanya. 2009. "The Immigration Industrial Complex: Why We Enforce Immigration Policies Destined to Fail." *Sociology Compass* 3: 295–309.
——. 2011. *Immigration Nation: Raids, Detentions, and Deportations in Post-9/11 America.* Boulder, CO: Paradigm Publishers.
Goldberg, David Theo. 1990. *Anatomy of Racism.* Minneapolis: University of Minnesota Press.
Goldberg, Walter. 1986. Personal communication.
Goldfield, Michael. 1987. *The Decline of Organized Labor in the United States.* Chicago: University of Chicago Press.
——. 1989. "Worker Insurgency, Radical Organization, and New Deal Labor Legislation." *American Political Science Review* 83: 1257–1282.
Goldfrank, Walter L. 2000. "Paradigm Regained? The Rules of Wallerstein's World-System Method." *Journal of World-Systems Research* 6, no. 2: 150–195.
Goldfrank, Walter L., David Goodman, and Andrew Szasz. 1999. *Ecology and the World System.* Westport, CT: Greenwood Press.
Goldring, Luin. 1998. "The Power of Status in Transnational Social Fields." In *Transnationalism from Below*, edited by Michael Smith and Luis Guarnizo, 165–195. London: Transaction Publishers.
Goldsmith, Jack, and Stephen D. Krasner. 2003. "The Limits of Idealism." *Daedalus* 132: 47–63.
Goldstein, Joseph, Burke Marshall, and Jack Schwartz. 1976. *The My Lai Massacre and Its Cover-Up: Beyond the Reach of Law? The Peers Commission Report with a Supplement and an Introductory Essay on the Limits of Law.* New York: The Free Press.
Goldstein, Joshua S. 2001. *War and Gender: How Gender Shapes the War System and Vice Versa.* Cambridge, UK: Cambridge University Press.
Goldstone, Jack. 2001. "Towards a Fourth Generation of Revolutionary Theory." *Annual Review of Political Science* 4: 139–187.
Goldthorpe, J. 2007. *On Sociology.* Stanford, CA: Stanford University Press.
Gonzales, Roberto G. 2011. "Learning to Be Illegal." *American Sociological Review* 76: 602–619.
González-López, Gloria. 2005. *Erotic Journeys: Mexican Immigrants and Their Sex Lives.* Berkeley: University of California Press.

Goodale, Mark. 2009. *Surrendering to Utopia: Anthropology of Human Rights*. Stanford, CA: Stanford University Press.
Goode, William J. 1978. *The Celebration of Heroes: Prestige as a Control System*. Berkeley: University of California Press.
Goodhard, Michael. 2003. "Origins and Universality in the Human Rights Debates: Cultural Essentialism and the Challenge of Globalization." *Human Rights Quarterly* 25: 935–964.
Goodwin, Glenn. 1987. "Humanistic Sociology and the Craft of Teaching." *Teaching Sociology* 15, no. 1: 19.
Goodwin, Jeff. 2001. *No Other Way Out*. New York: Cambridge University Press.
Goodwin, Jeff, and James M. Jasper. 2004. *Rethinking Social Movements: Structure, Meaning, and Emotion*. Lanham, MD: Rowman & Littlefield.
Goodyear-Smith, F., and S. Buetow. 2001. "Power Issues in the Doctor-Patient Relationship." *Health Care Analysis* 9: 449–462.
Goonesekere, Savitri. 2000. "Human Rights as a Foundation for Family Law Reform." *International Journal of Children's Rights* 8: 83–99.
Gordon, B. O., and K. E. Rosenblum. 2001. "Bringing Disability into the Sociological Frame: A Comparison of Disability with Race, Sex, and Sexual Orientation Statuses." *Disability and Society* 16: 5–19.
Gordon, Milton. 1964. *Assimilation in American Life*. New York: Oxford University Press.
Gordon, N., J. Swanson, and J. Buttigieg. 2000. "Is the Struggle for Human Rights a Struggle for Emancipation?" *Rethinking Marxism* 12, no. 3: 1–22.
Gordon, Steven L. 1981. "The Sociology of Sentiments and Emotions." In *Social Psychology: Sociological Perspectives*, edited by M. Rosenberg and R. H. Turner, 562–592. New York: Basic Books.
———. 1989a. "Institutions and Impulsive Orientations in Selectively Appropriating Emotions to Self." In *The Sociology of Emotions: Original Essays and Research Papers*, edited by D. D. Franks and E. D. McCarthy, 115–135. Greenwich, CT: JAI Press.
———. 1989b. "The Socialization of Children's Emotions: Emotional Culture, Competence, and Exposure." In *Children's Understanding of Emotion*, edited by C. Saarni and P. L. Harris, 319–349. Cambridge, UK: Cambridge University Press.
———. 1990. "Social Structural Effects on Emotions." In *Research Agendas in the Sociology of Emotions*, edited by T. D. Kemper, 180–203. Albany: State University of New York Press.
Gottfried, Heidi. 2012. *Gender, Work, and Economy: Unpacking the Global Economy*. Cambridge, UK: Polity Press.
Gould, K. A. 2009. "Technological Change and the Environment." In *Twenty Lessons in Environmental Sociology*, edited by K. A. Gould and T. L. Lewis, 95–106. New York: Oxford University Press.
Gould, Stephen Jay. 1981. *The Mismeasure of Man*. New York: Norton.
Gouldner, A. 1955. "Explorations in Applied Social Science." *Social Problems* 3: 169–181.
Government Accountability Office (GAO). 2005. *Denial of Federal Benefits*. GAO-05-238. GAO. http://www.gao.gov/new.items/d05238.pdf (accessed January 1, 2011).
Gramsci, Antonio. 1971. *Selections from the Prison Notebooks*. New York: International Publishers Co.
———. 1982. *Selections from the Prison Notebooks*. London: Lawrence and Wishart.
Gran, Brian K. 2008. "Public or Private Management? A Comparative Analysis of Social Policies in Europe." *Sociology Compass* 2: 1–29.
———. 2010a. "A Comparative-Historical Analysis of Children's Rights." NSF Grant, Law and Social Science Program.
———. 2010b. "Comparing Children's Rights: Introducing the Children's Rights Index." *International Journal of Children's Rights* 18, no. 1: 1–17.
———. 2011. "The Roles of Independent Children's Rights Institutions in Implementing the CRC." In *Children's Rights: From 20th Century Visions to 21st Century Implementation?*, 219–237. Surrey, UK: Ashgate Publishing Group.
Gran, Brian K., and Dawn M. Aliberti. 2003. "The Office of Children's Ombudsperson: Children's Rights and Social-Policy Innovation." *International Journal of the Sociology of Law* 31, no. 2: 89–106.
Grande, Sandy. 2004. *Red Pedagogy: Native American Social and Political Thought*. Lanham, MD: Rowman & Littlefield.
Granovetter, Mark S. 1973. "The Strength of Weak Ties." *American Journal of Sociology* 78: 1360–1380.
Gready, P. 2008. "Rights-Based Approaches to Development: What Is the Value-Added?" *Development in Practice*. http://www.developmentinpractice.org/journals/rights-based-approaches-development-what-value-added (accessed July 17, 2012).
Greenberg, David F. 1988. *The Construction of Homosexuality*. Chicago: University of Chicago Press.
Grewal, Inderpal, and Caren Kaplan, eds. 1994. *Scattered Hegemonies: Postmodernity and Transnational Feminist Practices*. Minneapolis: University of Minnesota Press.

———. 2000. "Postcolonial Studies and Transnational Feminist Practices." *Jouvert: A Journal of Postcolonial Studies* 5. http://social.chass.ncsu.edu/jouvert/v5i1/con51.htm (accessed September 6, 2012).
Griffin, Larry J., Michael Wallace, and Beth A. Rubin. 1986. "Capitalist Resistance to the Organization of Labor before the New Deal: Why? How? Success?" *American Sociological Review* 51: 147–167.
Griswold, Wendy. 1995. *Cultures and Societies in a Changing World*. Los Angeles: Sage Pine Forge.
Grosfoguel, Ramon. 2008. "Transmodernity, Border Thinking, and Global Coloniality." *Eurozine.* http://www.eurozine.com/articles/2008-07-04-grosfoguel-en.html (accessed January 1, 2011).
Gross, James A. 2009. "Takin' It to the Man: Human Rights at the American Workplace." In *Human Rights in Labor and Employment Relations: International and Domestic Perspectives*, edited James A. Gross and Lance Compa, 13–41. Urbana-Champaign, IL: Labor and Employment Relations Association.
Gross, James A., and Lance Compa. 2009. "Introduction." In *Human Rights in Labor and Employment Relations: International and Domestic Perspectives*, edited James A. Gross and Lance Compa, 1–11. Urbana-Champaign, IL: Labor and Employment Relations Association.
Grossberg, Lawrence. 1992. *We Gotta Get Out of This Place: Popular Conservatism and Postmodern Culture*. 1st ed. London: Routledge.
Grouzet, Frederick M. E., Tim Kasser, Aaron Ahuvia, José Miguel Fernandez-Dols, Youngmee Kim, Sing Lau, Richard M. Ryan, Shaun Saunders, Peter Schmuck, and Kennon M. Sheldon. 2005. "The Structure of Goal Contents across 15 Cultures." *Journal of Personality and Social Psychology* 89: 800–816.
Grue, L. 2010. "Eugenics and Euthanasia—Then and Now." *Scandinavian Journal of Disability Research* 12: 33–45.
Grundmann, Reiner, and Nico Stehr. 2012. *Experts: The Knowledge and Power of Expertise*. London: Rutledge.
Guardian. 2010. "Xinjiang Riots: One Year On, Uighur and Han Fears Still Run Deep." *Guardian*, July 4. http://www.guardian.co.uk/world/2010/jul/05/xianjiang-riots-security-uighur-han (accessed September 6, 2012).
Guarnizo, Luis, Alejandro Portes, and William Haller. 2003. "Assimilation and Transnationalism: Determinants of Transnational Political Action among Contemporary Migrants." *American Journal of Sociology* 108: 1211–1248.
Guarnizo, Luis, and Michael Peter Smith. 1998. "The Locations of Transnationalism." In *Transnationalism from Below*, edited by Michael Smith and Luis Guarnizo. London: Transaction Publishers.
Gubrium, Jaber. 1997. *Living and Dying and Murray Manor*. Charlottesville: University Press of Virginia.
Gubrium, Jaber, and James A. Holstein. 2012. "Don't Argue with the Members." *American Sociologist* 43, no. 1 (March): 85–98.
Guillen, M. F. 2001. *The Limits of Convergence: Globalization and Organizational Change in Argentina, South Korea, and Spain*. Princeton, NJ: Princeton University Press.
Gunn, T. Jeremy. 2000. "A Preliminary Response to Criticisms of the International Religious Freedom Act of 1998." *Brigham Young University Education and Law Journal* 841–865.
Guo, Guang, Glen H. Elder, Tianji Cai, and Nathan Hamilton. 2009. "Gene-Environment Interactions: Peers' Alcohol Use Moderates Genetic Contribution to Adolescent Drinking Behavior." *Social Science Research* 38: 213–224.
Guo, Guang, Michael Roettger, and Tianji Cai. 2008. "The Integration of Genetic Propensities into Social Control Models of Delinquency and Violence among Male Youths." *American Sociological Review* 73: 543–568.
Guo, Guang, and Yuying Tong. 2006. "Age at First Sexual Intercourse, Genes, and Social and Demographic Context: Evidence from Twins and the Dopamine D4 Receptor Gene." *Demography* 43: 747–769.
Guo, Guang, Yuying Tong, and Tianji Cai. 2008. "Gene by Social-Context Interactions for Number of Sexual Partners among White Male Youths: Genetics-Informed Sociology." *American Journal of Sociology* 114: 36–66.
Guskin, Jane, and David Wilson. 2007. *The Politics of Immigration: Questions and Answers*. New York: St. Martin's Press.
Gutman, A., and D. Thompson. 2004. *Why Deliberative Democracy?* Princeton, NJ: Princeton University Press.
Gutman, Herbert G. 1961. "Trouble on the Railroads in 1873–1874: Prelude to the 1877 Crisis?" *Labor History* 2: 215–235.
———. 1962. "Reconstruction in Ohio: Negroes in the Hocking Valley Coal Mines in 1873 and 1874." *Labor History* 3: 243–264.
———. 1976. *Work, Culture, and Society in Industrializing America: Essays in American Working Class and Social History*. New York: Alfred A. Knopf.
Gwangju Metropolitan City, Republic of Korea. 2011. *The Vision of Gwangju as a Human Rights City: The Action Plan and Gwangju Human Rights Index*. Gwangju, Republic of Korea: Gwangju Metropolitan City.

Gwangju World Human Rights Cities Forum. 2011. "Gwangju Declaration." Human Rights Cities. http://humanrightscity.net/eng/subpage.php?pagecode=020301 (accessed July 17, 2012).
Habermas, Jürgen. 1979. *Communication and the Evolution of Society.* Boston: Beacon Press.
———. 1981. *The Theory of Communicative Action.* Vol. 1: *Reason and the Rationalization of Society.* Translated by Thomas McCarthy. Boston: Beacon Press.
———. 1989 [1981]. *The Theory of Communicative Action.* Vol. 2: *Lifeworld and System: A Critique of Functionalist Realism.* Translated by Thomas McCarthy. Boston: Beacon Press.
———. 1995. "Reconciliation through the Public Use of Reason: Remarks on John Rawls' Political Liberalism." *Journal of Philosophy* 92: 109–131.
Hackett, Edward J., Olga Amsterdamska, Michael Lynch, and Judy Wajcman, eds. 2007. *The Handbook of Science and Technology Studies.* 3rd ed. Cambridge, MA: MIT Press.
Hackworth, Jason. 2007. *The Neoliberal City: Governance, Ideology, and Development in American Urbanism.* Ithaca, NY: Cornell University Press.
Haddad, Yvonne Yazbeck. 2007. "The Post-9/11 Hijab as Icon." *Sociology of Religion* 68: 253–267.
Hafner-Burton, Emilie. 2005. "Right or Robust? The Sensitive Nature of Repression to Globalization." *Journal of Peace Research* 42: 679–698.
———. 2008. "'Sticks and Stones': Naming and Shaming the Human Rights Enforcement Problem." *International Organization* 62 (fall): 689–716.
———. 2009. *Forced to Be Good: Why Trade Agreements Boost Human Rights.* Ithaca, NY: Cornell University Press.
Hafner-Burton, Emilie M., and Alexander H. Montgomery. 2008. "Power Positions: International Organizations, Social Networks, and Conflict." *Journal of Conflict Resolution* 54, no. 2: 213–242.
Hafner-Burton, Emilie M., and Kiyoteru Tsutsui. 2005. "Human Rights in a Globalizing World: The Paradox of Empty Promises." *American Journal of Sociology* 110: 1373–1411.
Hafner-Burton, Emilie M., Kiyoteru Tsutsui, and John W. Meyer. 2008. "International Human Rights Law and the Politics of Legitimation: Repressive States and Human Rights Treaties." *International Sociology* 23, no. 1: 115–141.
Hagan, John. 1994. *Crime and Disrepute.* Thousand Oaks, CA: Pine Forge Press.
———. 2003. *Justice in the Balkans.* Chicago: University of Chicago Press.
Hagan, John, and Scott Greer. 2002. "Making War Criminal." *Criminology* 40: 231–264.
Hagan, John, and Sanja Kutnjak. 2006. "War Crimes, Democracy, and the Rule of Law in Belgrade, the Former Yugoslavia, and Beyond." *Annals of the American Academy of Political and Social Science* 605: 130–51.
Hagan, John, and Ron Levi. 2005. "Crimes of War and the Force of Law." *Social Forces* 3: 1499–1534.
———. 2007. "Justiciability as Field Effect: When Sociology Meets Human Rights." *Sociological Forum* 22: 372–384.
Hagan, John, and Ruth Peterson. 1995. "Criminal Inequality in America." In *Crime and Inequality*, edited by John Hagan and Ruth D. Peterson, 14–36. Stanford, CA: Stanford University Press.
Hagan, John, and Wenona Rymond-Richmond. 2008. "The Collective Dynamics of Racial Dehumanization and Genocidal Victimization in Darfur." *American Sociological Review* 6: 875–902.
———. 2009. *Darfur and the Crime of Genocide.* Cambridge, UK: Cambridge University Press.
Hagan, John, Wenona Rymond-Richmond, and Patricia Parker. 2005. "The Criminology of Genocide: The Death and Rape of Darfur." *Criminology* 43: 525–561.
Hagan, John, Heather Schoenfeld, and Alberto Palloni. 2006. "The Science of Human Rights, War Crimes and Humanitarian Emergencies." *Annual Review of Sociology* 32: 329–350.
Hagestad, Gunhild O. 2008. "The Book-Ends: Emerging Perspectives on Children and Old People." In *Families and Social Policy: Intergenerational Solidarity in European Welfare States*, edited by C. Saraceno, 20–37. London: Edward Elgar Publishing.
Hagestad, Gunhild O., and Peter Uhlenberg. 2005. "The Social Separation of Old and Young: A Root of Ageism." *Journal of Social Issues* 61: 343–360.
———. 2006. "Should We Be Concerned about Age Segregation? Some Theoretical and Empirical Explorations." *Research on Aging* 28: 638–653.
———. 2007. "The Impact of Demographic Changes on Relations between Age Groups and Generations: A Comparative Perspective." In *Social Structures: Demographic Changes and the Well-Being of Older Persons*, edited by K. W. Schaie and P. Uhlenberg, 239–261. New York: Springer Publishing Co.
Hagestad, Gunhild O., and Dale Dannefer. 2001. "Concepts and Theories of Aging: Beyond Microfication in Social Science Approaches." In *Handbook of Aging and Social Sciences*, edited by R. Binstock and L. George. 5th ed. San Diego: Academic Press.
Haiken, Elizabeth. 1999. *Venus Envy: A History of Cosmetic Surgery.* Baltimore: Johns Hopkins University Press.
Halbwachs, Maurice. 1992. *On Collective Memory.* Chicago: University of Chicago Press.

Hall, G. B., and G. Nelson. 1996. "Social Networks, Social Support, Personal Empowerment, and the Adaptation of Psychiatric Consumers: Survivors: Path Analytic Models." *Social Science and Medicine* 43: 1743-1754.
Hall, John R. 1987. *Gone from the Promised Land: Jonestown in American Cultural History.* New Brunswick, NJ: Transaction Books.
Hall, John R., Philip Daniel Schuyler, and Sylvaine Trinh. 2000. *Apocalypse Observed: Religious Movements and Violence in North America, Europe, and Japan.* London and New York: Routledge.
Hall, Peter A., and D. Soskice, eds. 2001. *Varieties of Capitalism: The Institutional Foundations of Comparative Advantage.* Oxford: Oxford University Press.
Hall, Peter M. 1987. "Interactionism and the Study of Social Organization." *Sociological Quarterly* 28, no. 1: 1-22.
Hall, Peter M., and Patrick J. W. McGinty. 1997. "Policy as the Transformation of Intentions." *Sociological Quarterly* 38: 439-467.
Hall, S., C. Critcher, T. Jefferson, J. Clarke, and B. Roberts. 1978. *Policing the Crisis: Mugging, the State, and Law and Order.* London: Macmillan.
Hall, Stuart. 1986. "Gramsci's Relevance for the Study of Race and Ethnicity." *Journal of Communication Inquiry* 10: 5-27.
Hall, Stuart, and Paul Du Gay. 1996. *Questions of Cultural Identity.* Thousand Oaks, CA: Sage.
Hall, Thomas. 2002. "World-Systems Analysis and Globalization Directions for the Twenty-First Century." *Research in Political Sociology* 11: 81-22.
Hall, Thomas D., and James V. Fenelon. 2009. *Indigenous Peoples and Globalization: Resistance and Revitalization.* Boulder, CO: Paradigm Publishers.
Haller, B., B. Dorries, and J. Rahn. 2006. "Media Labeling versus the US Disability Community Identity: A Study of Shifting Cultural Language." *Disability and Society* 21: 61-75.
Halliday, Terence C., and Pavel Osinsky. 2006. "Globalization of Law." *Annual Review of Sociology* 32: 447-470.
Hamilton, Laura, Simon Cheng, and Brian Powell. 2007. "Adoptive Parents, Adaptive Parents: Evaluating the Importance of Biological Ties for Parental Investment." *American Sociological Review* 72: 95-116.
Hammond, Michael. 2004. "The Enhancement Imperative and Group Dynamics in the Emergence of Religion and Ascriptive Inequality." *Advances in Group Processes* 21: 167-188.
Haney, Lynn. 2000. "Feminist State Theory: Applications to Jurisprudence, Criminology, and the Welfare State." *Annual Review of Sociology* 26: 641-666.
Hannan, Michael, and John Freeman. 1977. "The Population Ecology of Organizations." *American Journal of Sociology* 82: 929-964.
Hao, Lingxin, and Suet-ling Pong. 2008. "The Role of School in Upward Mobility of Disadvantaged Immigrants' Children." *Annals of the American Academy of Political and Social Sciences* 620, no. 1: 62-89.
Haraway, Donna. 1991. "A Cyborg Manifesto: Science, Technology, and Socialist-Feminism in the Late Twentieth Century." In *Simians, Cyborgs and Women: The Reinvention of Nature*, 149-181. New York; Routledge.
Harding, David J. 2007. "Cultural Context, Sexual Behavior, and Romantic Relationships in Disadvantage." *American Sociological Review* 72: 341-364.
Harding, Sandra. 2003. "How Standpoint Methodology Informs Philosophy of Social Science." In *The Blackwell Guide to the Philosophy of the Social Sciences*, edited by Stephen P. Turner and Paul A. Roth, 291-310. Malden, MA: Blackwell Publishing.
Harding, Sandra, and K. Norberg. 2005. "New Feminist Approaches to Social Science Methodologies: An Introduction." *Signs: Journal of Women in Culture and Society* 30: 2009-2015.
Hardt, Michael, and Antonio Negri. 2000. *Empire.* Cambridge, MA: Harvard University Press.
———. 2009. *Commonwealth.* Cambridge, MA: Belknap Press.
Hare, Richard M. 1981. *Moral Thinking: Its Levels, Method, and Point.* Oxford, UK: Clarendon Press.
Harmon, Katherine. 2009. "Deaths from Avoidable Medical Error More Than Double in Past Decade, Investigation Shows." *Scientific American.* http://www.scientificamerican.com/blog/post.cfm?id=deaths-from-avoidable-medical-error-2009-08-10 (accessed January 1, 2011).
Harper, A. Breeze, ed. 2010. *Sistah Vegan: Black Female Vegans Speak on Food, Identity, Health, and Society.* New York: Lantern Books.
Harris, Angela. 1990. "Race and Essentialism in Feminist Legal Theory." *Stanford Law Review* 42: 581-616.
Harrison, Bennett, and Barry Bluestone. 1988. *The Great U-Turn: Corporate Restructuring and the Polarizing of America.* New York: Basic Books.
Hartman, Chester, and Gregory Squires. 2009. *The Integration Debate: Competing Futures for American Cities.* New York: Routledge.
Harvey, David. 2005. *A Brief History of Neoliberalism.* New York: Oxford University Press.

———. 2008. "The Right to the City." *New Left Review* 53: 23-40.
Hastings, N. A. J., and J. B. Peacock. 1974. *Statistical Distributions*. London: Butterworths.
Hattery, Angela. 2001. *Women, Work, and Family: Balancing and Weaving*. Thousand Oaks, CA: Sage Publications.
———. 2009. *Intimate Partner Violence*. Lanham, MD: Rowman & Littlefield.
Hattery, Angela, and Earl Smith. 2006. "Teaching Public Sociologies." In *Public Sociologies Reader*, edited by Judith Blau and Keri E. Iyall Smith, 265-280. New York: Rowman & Littlefield.
———. 2007. *African American Families*. Thousand Oaks, CA: Sage Publishers.
Haugen, Hans M. 2008. "Human Rights and Technology—a Conflictual Relationship? Assessing Private Research and the Right to Adequate Food." *Journal of Human Rights* 7: 224-244.
Hayden, Tom. 2006. *Radical Nomad: C. Wright Mills and His Times*. Boulder, CO: Paradigm Publishers.
Hayner, Priscilla B. 2001. *Unspeakable Truths: Confronting State Terror and Atrocity*. London: Routledge.
Haynes, J. 2008. *Development Studies*. Malden, MA: Polity.
Hayward, T. 2005. *Constitutional Environmental Rights*. Oxford: Oxford University Press.
Hays, Sharon. 2003. *Flat Broke with Children*. New York: Oxford University Press.
Headrick, D. R. 2010. *Power over Peoples: Technology, Environments, and Western Imperialism, 1400 to the Present*. Princeton, NJ: Princeton University Press.
Heberer, Patricia, and Jürgen Matthäus, eds. 2008. *Atrocities on Trial*. Lincoln: University of Nebraska Press.
Hedström, P., and R. Swedberg. 1998. *Social Mechanisms. An Analytical Approach to Social Theory*. Cambridge, UK: Cambridge University Press.
Heinz, Walter R. 2003. "From Work Trajectories to Negotiated Careers: The Contingent Work Life Course." In *Handbook of the Life Course*, edited by Jeylan T. Mortimer and Michael J. Shanahan, 185-204. New York: Kluwer.
Held, David. 1995. *Democracy and the Global Order: From the Modern State to Cosmopolitan Governance*. Stanford, CA: Stanford University Press.
———. 2004. *Global Covenant: The Social Democratic Alternative to the Washington Consensus*. Cambridge, UK: Polity Press.
———. 2010. *Cosmopolitanism*. Cambridge, UK: Polity Press.
Hendawi, Hamza. 2011. "Egypt: Internet Down, Counterterror Unit Up." *Press-Register*, January 28. http://www.3news.co.nz/Egypt-internet-down-counterterror-unit-up/tabid/417/articleID/196288/Default.aspx (accessed September 6, 2012).
Henderson, Conway W. 1991. "Conditions Affecting the Use of Political Repression." *Journal of Conflict Resolution* 35: 120-142.
———. 1993. "Population Pressures and Political Repression." *Social Science Quarterly* 74: 322-333.
Herd, D. 1985. "Migration, Cultural Transformation, and the Rise of Black Liver Cirrhosis Mortality." *British Journal of Addiction* 80: 397-410.
———. 1988a. "A Review of Drinking Patterns and Alcohol Problems among US Blacks." Report of the Secretary's Task Force on Black and Minority Health. *Chemical Dependency and Diabetes* 7: 7-140. Washington, DC: U.S. Government Printing Office.
———. 1988b. "The Epidemiology of Drinking Patterns and Alcohol Problems among US Blacks." In *Alcohol Use among U.S. Ethnic Minorities*, edited by D. Spiegler, D. Tate, S. Aitken, and C. Christian, 3-51. Rockville, MD: National Institute on Alcohol Abuse and Alcoholism.
Herdt, Gilbert. 1994. *Third Sex, Third Gender*. New York: Zone Books.
———. 1997. *Same Sex, Different Cultures: Exploring Gay and Lesbian Lives*. Oxford: Westview.
Herek, Gregory M., and Kevin T. Berrill. 1992. *Hate Crimes: Confronting Violence against Lesbians and Gay Men*. Newbury Park, CA: Sage Publications.
Herek, Gregory M., and John P. Capitanio. 1996. "'Some of My Best Friends': Intergroup Contact, Concealable Stigma, and Heterosexuals' Attitudes toward Gay Men and Lesbians." *Personality and Social Psychology Bulletin* 22: 412-424.
Herek, Gregory M., and Eric K. Glunt. 1993. "Interpersonal Contact and Heterosexuals' Attitudes toward Gay Men: Results from a National Survey." *Journal of Sex Research* 30: 239-244.
Herkert, J. R. 2004. "Microethics, Macroethics, and Professional Engineering Societies." In *Emerging Technologies and Ethical Issues in Engineering*, edited by National Academy of Engineering, 107-114. Washington, DC: National Academies Press.
Hernan, R. E. 2010. *This Borrowed Earth: Lessons from the 15 Worst Environmental Disasters around the World*. New York: Palgrave Macmillan.
Hershock, Peter D. 2000. "Dramatic Intervention: Human Rights from a Buddhist Perspective." *Philosophy East and West* 50: 9-33.
Hertel, Shareen, and Kathryn Libal. 2011. *Human Rights in the United States: Beyond Exceptionalism*. New York: Cambridge University Press.

Hess, David J. 1997. *Science Studies: An Advanced Introduction*. New York: New York University Press.
Hesse-Biber, Sharlene Nagy. 2006. *The Cult of Thinness*. New York: Oxford University Press.
Hester, Stephen. 2009. "Ethnomethodology: Respecifying the Problem of Social Order." In *Encountering the Everyday: An Introduction to the Sociologies of the Unnoticed*, edited by Michael Hviid Jacobsen, 234–256. Basingstoke, UK: Palgrave Macmillan.
Hester, Stephen, and Peter Eglin, eds. 1997a. *Culture in Action: Studies in Membership Categorization Analysis*. Washington, DC: International Institute for Ethnomethodology and Conversation Analysis and University Press of America.
———. 1997b. "Membership Categorization Analysis: An Introduction." In *Culture in Action: Studies in Membership Categorization Analysis*, edited by Stephen Hester and Peter Eglin, 1–23. Washington, DC: International Institute for Ethnomethodology and Conversation Analysis and University Press of America.
———. 1997c. "Conclusion: Membership Categorization Analysis and Sociology." In *Culture in Action: Studies in Membership Categorization Analysis*, edited by Stephen Hester and Peter Eglin, 153–163. Washington, DC: International Institute for Ethnomethodology and Conversation Analysis and University Press of America.
Hewitt, Lyndi. 2008. "Feminists and the Forum: Is It Worth the Effort?" *Societies without Borders* 3: 118–135.
———. 2009. *The Politics of Transnational Feminist Discourse: Framing across Differences, Building Solidarities*. PhD diss., Vanderbilt University, Nashville, Tennessee.
Heydebrand, Wolf. 1977. "Organizational Contradictions in Public Bureaucracies, toward a Marxian Theory of Organizations." *Sociological Quarterly* 18, no. 1: 83–107.
———. 1983. "Technocratic Corporatism: Toward a Theory of Occupational and Organizational Transformation." In *Organizational Theory and Public Policy*, edited by Richard Hall and Robert Quinn, 93–114. Beverly Hills, CA: Sage.
Heyman, Josiah. 2002. "U.S. Immigration Officers of Mexican Ancestry as Mexican Americans, Citizens, and Immigration Police." *Current Anthropology* 43: 479–507.
———. 2010. "Human Rights and Social Justice Briefing 1: Arizona's Immigration Law–S.B. 1070." Society for Applied Anthropology. http://www.sfaa.net/committees/humanrights/AZImmigrationLawSB1070.pdf (accessed July 17, 2012).
Hidalgo, Myra L. 2007. *Sexual Abuse and the Culture of Catholicism: How Priests and Nuns Become Perpetrators*. New York: Haworth Maltreatment and Trauma Press.
Higgins, E. Tory. 1987. "Self-Discrepancy: A Theory Relating Self and Affect." *Psychological Review* 94: 319–340.
Hill, Herman. 1993. "The CIA in National and International Labor Movements. Review of *Compromised Campus: The Collaboration of Universities with the Intelligence Community, 1945–1955*, by Sigmund Diamond." *International Journal of Politics* 6: 405–407.
Hill, Jane H. 2008. *The Everyday Language of White Racism*. Malden, MA: Wiley-Blackwell.
Hinde, Andrew. 1998. *Demographic Methods*. London: Oxford University Press.
Hinton, Alexander L., and Kevin L. O'Neill. 2009. *Genocide: Truth, Memory, and Representation*. Durham, NC: Duke University Press.
Hinze, Susan W., Jielu Lin, and Tanetta Andersson. 2011. "Can We Capture the Intersections? Older Black Women, Education, and Health." *Women's Health Issues* 22, no. 1 (January): e91–e98.
Hinze, Susan W., Noah J. Webster, Heidi T. Chirayath, and Joshua H. Tamayo-Sarver. 2009. "Hurt Running from Police? No Chance of (Pain) Relief: The Social Construction of Deserving Patients in Emergency Departments." *Research in the Sociology of Health Care* 27: 235–261.
Hirschman, A. O. 1983. "Morality and the Social Sciences: A Durable Tension." In *Social Science as Moral Inquiry*, edited by N. Hann et al., 21–32. New York: Columbia University Press.
Hiskes, Richard P. 2010. "The Relational Foundations of Emergent Human Rights: From Thomas Hobbes to the Human Right to Water." *Zeitschrift für Menschenrechte [Journal for Human Rights]* 4, no. 2: 127–146.
Hitlin, Steven, and Jane A. Piliavin. 2004. "Values: A Review of Recent Research and Theory." *Annual Review of Sociology* 30: 359–393.
Hitt, L., ed. 2002. *Human Rights: Great Speeches in History*. San Diego, CA: Greenhaven Press.
Hlaing, Kyaw Y. 2004. "Myanmar in 2003: Frustration and Despair?" *Asian Survey* 44: 87–92.
———. 2005. "Myanmar in 2004: Another Year of Uncertainty." *Asian Survey* 45: 174–179.
Hoang, Nghia. 2009. "The 'Asian Values' Perspective of Human Rights: A Challenge to Universal Human Rights." Social Science Research Network. http://ssrn.com/abstract=1405436 (accessed July 17, 2012).
Hobhouse, L. T. 1922. *The Elements of Social Justice*. London: G. Allen and Unwin.

Hobsbawm, Eric J. 1962. *The Age of Revolution: Europe 1789–1848*. London: Weidenfeld and Nicolson.
———. 1964. *Labouring Men: Studies in the History of Labour*. London: Weidenfeld and Nicolson.
Hochschild, Arlie. 1979. "Emotion Work, Feeling Rules, and Social Structure." *American Journal of Sociology* 85: 551–575.
———. 1983. *The Managed Heart: Commercialization of Human Feeling*. Berkeley: University of California Press.
Hockenberry, J. 1995. *Moving Violations: War Zones, Wheelchairs, and Declarations of Independence*. New York: Hyperion.
Hoffman Plastic Compounds, Inc. v. NLRB. 2002. 122 S. Ct. 1275.
Hoffman, John P. 2006. "Extracurricular Activities, Athletic Participation, and Adolescent Alcohol Use: Gender-Differentiated and School-Contextual Effects." *Journal of Health and Social Behavior* 47, no. 3: 275–290.
Holland, J., C. Ramazanoglu, S. Sharpe, and R. Thomson. 1998. *The Male in the Head: Young People, Heterosexuality and Power*. London: The Tufnell.
Hollingshead, A. B., and F. C. Redlich. 1958. *Social Class and Mental Illness*. New York: Wiley.
Hollingsworth, J. Rogers, Philippe C. Schmitter, and Wolfgang Streeck, eds. 1994. *Governing Capitalist Economies: Performance and Control of Economic Sectors*. New York: Oxford University Press.
Holmes, Malcolm D. 2008. *Race and Police Brutality: Roots of an Urban Dilemma*. Albany: State University of New York Press.
Holstein, James A., and Jaber F. Gubrium. 1999. *The Self We Live By: Narrative Identity in a Postmodern World*. 1st ed. New York: Oxford University Press.
———, eds. 2003. *Inner Lives and Social Worlds: Readings in Social Psychology*. New York: Oxford University Press.
Homans, George C. 1974. *Social Behavior: Its Elementary Forms*. Rev. ed. New York: Harcourt, Brace, Jovanovich.
Hopcroft, Rosemary L. 2005. "Parental Status and Differential Investment in Sons and Daughters: Trivers-Willard Revisited." *Social Forces* 83: 169–193.
———. 2008. "Darwinian Conflict Theory: Alternative Theory or Unifying Paradigm for Sociology?" In *The New Evolutionary Science: Human Nature, Social Behavior and Social Change*, edited by Heinz-Jürgen Niedenzu, Tamás Meleghy, and Peter Meyer. Boulder, CO: Paradigm Publishers.
———. 2009. "Gender Inequality in Interaction: An Evolutionary Account." *Social Forces* 87: 1845–1872.
Hopcroft, Rosemary L., and Dana Burr Bradley. 2007. "The Sex Difference in Depression across 29 Countries." *Social Forces* 85: 1483–1507.
Hopgood, Stephen. 2006. *Keepers of the Flame*. Ithaca, NY: Cornell University Press.
Horkheimer, Max, and Theodor W. Adorno. 1993 [1944]. *Dialectic of Enlightenment*. Translated by John Cumming. New York: Continuum.
Hornburg, Alf. 1998. "Ecosystems and World Systems: Accumulation as an Ecological Process." *Journal of World-Systems Research* 4, no. 2: 169–177.
Horne, Christine. 2004. "Values and Evolutionary Psychology." *Sociological Theory* 22: 477–503.
Horne, Sharon, and Melanie J. Zimmer-Gembeck. 2005. "Female Sexual Subjectivity and Well-Being: Comparing Late Adolescents with Different Sexual Experiences." *Sexuality Research and Social Policy* 2: 25–40.
Horowitz, Louis Irving. 1980. *Taking Lives: Genocide and State Power*. New Brunswick, NJ: Transaction Books.
———. 2002. *Tanking Lives: Genocide and State Power*. 5th ed. New Brunswick, NJ: Transaction.
Horton, Hayward Derrick. 1999. "Critical Demography: The Paradigm of the Future?" *Sociological Forum* 14, no. 3: 363–367.
Hosken, Fran P. 1993. *The Hosken Report: Genital and Sexual Mutilation of Females*. 4th ed. Lexington, MA: Women's International Network News.
House, J. S. 1981. "Social Structure and Personality." In *Social Psychology, Sociological Perspectives*, edited by M. Rosenberg and R. H. Turner, 525–561. New York: Basic Books.
House, James S. 1977. "The Three Faces of Social Psychology." *Sociometry* 40: 161–177.
House, James S., James M. Lepkowski, Ann M. Kinney, Richard P. Mero, Ronald C. Kessler, and A. Regula Herzog. 1994. "The Social Stratification of Aging and Health." *Journal of Health and Social Behavior* 35: 213–234.
Hovenkamp, Herbert. 1991. *Enterprise and American Law, 1836–1937*. Cambridge, MA: Harvard University Press.
Hovey, Michael W. 1997. "Interceding at the United Nations: The Human Right of Conscientious Objection." In *Transnational Social Movements and Global Politics: Solidarity beyond the State*, edited by J. Smith, C. Chatfield, and R. Pagnucco. Syracuse, NY: Syracuse University Press.
Hovil, L., and E. Werker. 2005. "Portrait of a Failed Rebellion: An Account of Rational, Sub-Optimal Violence in Western Uganda." *Rationality and Society* 17: 5–34.

Howard, Jay. 2010. "2009 Hans O. Mauksch Address: Where Are We and How Did We Get Here? A Brief Examination of the Past, Present and Future of the Teaching and Learning Movement in Sociology." *Teaching Sociology* 38: 81-92.

Howard, Judith, and Carolyn Allen. 1996. "Reflections on the Fourth World Conference on Women and NGO Forum '95: Introduction." *Signs* 22: 181-185.

Howard, Rhoda E. 1985. "Legitimacy and Class Rule in Commonwealth Africa: Constitutionalism and the Rule of Law." *Third World Quarterly* 7, no. 2: 323-347.

———. 1995. *Human Rights and the Search for Community*. Boulder, CO: Westview Press.

Howard, Rhoda E., and Jack Donnelly. 1986. "Human Dignity, Human Rights and Political Regimes." *American Political Science Review* 80: 801-817.

Huber, Evelyn, and John Stephens. 2001. *Development and Crisis of the Welfare State*. Chicago: University of Chicago Press.

Huber, Joan. 2007. *On the Origins of Gender Inequality*. Boulder, CO: Paradigm Publishers.

Huda, S. 2006. "Sex Trafficking in South Asia." *International Journal of Gynecology and Obstetrics* 94: 374-381.

Hughes, Everett C. 1963. "Good People and Dirty Work." In *The Other Side*, edited by Howard Becker, 23-36. New York: The Free Press.

———. 1971. *The Sociological Eye: Selected Papers*. Chicago: Aldine-Atherton.

Hughes, Jason. 2003. *Learning to Smoke: Tobacco Use in the West*. Chicago: University of Chicago Press.

Hughes, John A., Peter J. Martin, and W. W. Sharrock. 1995. *Understanding Classical Sociology: Marx, Weber, Durkheim*. London: Sage.

Hughes, John A., and W. W. Sharrock. 2007. *Theory and Methods in Sociology: An Introduction to Sociological Thinking and Practice*. Basingstoke, UK: Palgrave Macmillan.

Hughs, Alex, and Ann Witz. 1997. "Feminism and the Matter of Bodies: From de Beauvoir to Butler." *Body and Society* 3: 47-60.

Huizinga, Johann. 2006 [1919]. *The Autumn of the Middle Ages*. Translated by Rodney J. Payton and Ulrich Mammitzsch. Chicago: University of Chicago Press.

Hulko, Wendy. 2009. "The Time- and Context-Contingent Nature of Intersectionality and Interlocking Oppressions." *Affilia: Journal of Women and Social Work* 24: 44-55.

Human Rights Watch (HRW). 2000. "Racial Disparities in the War on Drugs." HRW. http://www.hrw.org/legacy/reports/2000/usa/Rcedrg00.htm#P54_1086 (accessed January 1, 2011).

———. 2010. *World Report*. New York: HRW.

Hunt, Lynn. 2007. *Inventing Human Rights: A History*. New York: W. W. Norton and Co.

Huntington, Samuel. 1991. *The Third Wave*. Norman: University of Oklahoma Press.

Husak, Douglas. 2003. "The Criminalization of Drug Use." *Sociological Forum* 18, no. 3: 503-513.

Hutchinson, Phil, Rupert Read, and Wes Sharrock. 2008. *There Is No Such Thing as a Social Science: In Defence of Peter Winch*. Aldershot, UK: Ashgate.

Hynes, Patricia, Michele Lamb, Damien Short, and Matthew Waites. 2010. "Sociology and Human Rights: Confrontations, Evasions and New Engagements." *International Journal of Human Rights* 14, no. 6: 811-832.

Hynie, M., and J. E. Lydon. 1995. "Women's Perceptions of Female Contraceptive Behavior: Experimental Evidence of the Sexual Double Standard." *Psychology of Women Quarterly* 19: 563-581.

Ignatiev, N. 1995. *How the Irish Became White*. New York: Routledge.

Ikegami, Eiko. 2005. "Bringing Culture into Macrostructural Analysis in Historical Sociology." *Poetics* 33: 15-32.

Illich, Ivan. 1971. *Deschooling Society*. London: Calder and Boyars.

Inglehart, Ronald. 1977. *The Silent Revolution Changing Values and Political Styles among Western Publics*. Princeton, NJ: Princeton University Press.

Inglehart, Ronald, and Wayne E. Baker. 2000. "Modernization, Cultural Change, and the Persistence of Traditional Values." *American Sociological Review* 65, no. 1: 19-51.

Ingraham, Chrys. 2008. *White Weddings: Romancing Heterosexuality in Popular Culture*. New York: Routledge.

International Criminal Court (ICC). 2011. "Rome Statute." ICC. http://www.icc-cpi.int/Menus/ICC/Legal+Texts+and+Tools/Official+Journal/Rome+Statute.htm (accessed August 15, 2012).

International Federation of Red Cross and Red Crescent Societies. 2004. *World Disaster Report: Focus on Community Resilience*. Bloomfield, CT: Kumarian Press.

International Gay and Lesbian Human Rights Commission (IGLHRC). 2011. "Our Issues." IGLHRC. http://www.iglhrc.org/cgi-bin/iowa/theme/1.html (accessed November 11, 2011).

International Labour Office. 1973. Minimum Age Convention. http://www.ilocarib.org.tt/projects/cariblex/conventions_6.shtml (accessed September 6, 2012).

Irvine, Janice M. 2002. *Talk about Sex: The Battles over Sex Education in the United States*. Berkeley: University of California Press.

Irwin, Alan, and Brian Wynne, eds. 1996. *Misunderstanding Science? The Public Reconstruction of Science and Technology*. Cambridge, UK: Cambridge University Press.
Ishay, Micheline R., ed. 1997. *The Human Rights Reader: Major Political Essays, Speeches, and Documents from the Bible to the Present*. New York: Routledge.
———. 2004a. *The History of Human Rights: From Ancient Times to the Globalization Era*. Berkeley: University of California Press.
———. 2004b. "What Are Human Rights? Six Historical Controversies." *Journal of Human Rights* 3: 359-371.
Israel, Jonathan. 2011. *Democratic Enlightenment: Philosophy, Revolution, and Human Rights*. Oxford: Oxford University Press.
Ito, Mizuko, Sonja Baumer, Matteo Bittanti, Danah Boyd, Rachel Cody, Becky Herr-Stephenson, Heather A. Horst, Patricia G. Lange, Dilan Mahendran, Katynka Z. Martinez, C. J. Pascoe, Dan Perkel, Laura Robinson, Christo Sims, and Lisa Tripp, with Judd Antin, Megan Finn, Arthur Law, Annie Manion, Sarai Mitnick, David Scholssberg, and Sarita Yardi. 2009. *Hanging Out, Messing Around, and Geeking Out*. Cambridge, MA: Massachusetts Institute of Technology Press.
Jacobs, David, Zenchao Qian, Jason T. Carmichael, and Stephanie L. Kent. 2007. "Who Survives on Death Row? An Individual and Contextual Analysis." *American Sociological Review* 72: 610-632.
Jacobs, Mark D. 2012. "Financial Crises as Symbols and Rituals." In *The Oxford Handbook of the Sociology of Finance*, edited by Karin Knorr Cetina and Alex Preda. New York: Oxford University Press.
Jacobs, Mark D., and Nancy Weiss Hanrahan. 2005. Introduction to *The Blackwell Companion to the Sociology of Culture*, edited by Mark D. Jacobs and Nancy Weiss Hanrahan. Malden, MA: Blackwell.
Jacobs, Mark D., and Lyn Spillman. 2005. "Cultural Sociology at the Crossroads of the Discipline." *Poetics* 33: 1-14.
Jaeger, Gertrude, and Philip Selznick. 1964. "A Normative Theory of Culture." *American Sociological Review* 29: 653-669.
Jain, D. 2005. *Women, Development, and the UN: A Sixty-Year Quest for Equality and Justice*. Bloomington: Indiana University Press.
Jalata, Asafa. 2005. "State Terrorism and Globalization: The Cases of Ethiopia and Sudan." *International Journal of Comparative Sociology* 46, no. 1-2: 79-102.
———. 2008. "Struggling for Social Justice in the Capitalist World System: The Cases of African Americans, Oromos, and Southern and Western Sudanese." *Social Identities* 14, no. 3: 363-388.
James, Helen. 2006. "Myanmar in 2005: In a Holding Pattern." *Asian Survey* 46: 162-167.
Jamieson, Dale. 2003. *Morality's Progress: Essays on Humans, Other Animals, and the Rest of Nature*. London: Oxford University Press.
Janoski, Thomas. 1998. *Citizenship and Civil Society*. New York: Cambridge University Press.
Jasper, James. 1997. *The Art of Moral Protest: Culture, Biography, and Creativity in Social Movements*. Chicago: University of Chicago Press.
———. 2004. "A Strategic Approach to Collective Action: Looking for Agency in Social Movement Choices." *Mobilization* 9, no. 1: 1-16.
Jasso, Guillermina. 1978. "On the Justice of Earnings: A New Specification of the Justice Evaluation Function." *American Journal of Sociology* 83: 1398-1419.
———. 1980. "A New Theory of Distributive Justice." *American Sociological Review* 45: 3-32.
———. 1988a. "Distributive-Justice Effects of Employment and Earnings on Marital Cohesiveness: An Empirical Test of Theoretical Predictions." In *Status Generalization: New Theory and Research*, edited by Murray Webster and Martha Foschi, 123-162 (references, 490-493). Stanford, CA: Stanford University Press.
———. 1988b. "Principles of Theoretical Analysis." *Sociological Theory* 6: 1-20.
———. 1990. "Methods for the Theoretical and Empirical Analysis of Comparison Processes." *Sociological Methodology* 20: 369-419.
———. 2001. "Studying Status: An Integrated Framework." *American Sociological Review* 66: 96-124.
———. 2008. "A New Unified Theory of Sociobehavioral Forces." *European Sociological Review* 24: 411-434.
———. 2009. "A New Model of Wage Determination and Wage Inequality." *Rationality and Society* 21: 113-168.
———. 2010. "Linking Individuals and Societies." *Journal of Mathematical Sociology* 34: 1-51.
Jasso, Guillermina, and Samuel Kotz. 2007. "A New Continuous Distribution and Two New Families of Distributions Based on the Exponential." *Statistica Neerlandica* 61: 305-328.
———. 2008. "Two Types of Inequality: Inequality between Persons and Inequality between Subgroups." *Sociological Methods and Research* 37: 31-74.
Jayasree, A. K. 2004. "Searching for Justice for Body and Self in a Coercive Environment: Sex Work in Kerala, India." *Reproductive Health Matters* 12: 58-67.
Jayyusi, Lena. 1984. *Categorization and the Moral Order*. London: Routledge and Kegan Paul.

———. 1991. "Values and Moral Judgment: Communicative Praxis as a Moral Order." In *Ethnomethodology and the Human Sciences*, edited by Graham Button, 227-251. Cambridge, UK: Cambridge University Press.
Jenkins, Alan, and Kevin Shawn Hsu. 2008. "American Ideals and Human Rights: Findings from New Public Opinion Research by the Opportunity Agenda." *Fordham Law Review* 77, no. 2: 439-458.
Jenkins, J. Craig. 1983. "Resource Mobilization Theory and the Study of Social Movements." *Annual Review of Sociology* 9: 527-553.
Jenkins, J. Craig, and Craig Eckert. 1986. "Channeling Black Insurgency: Elite Patronage and the Development of the Civil Rights Movement." *American Sociological Review* 51: 812-830.
Jensen, Gary. 2007. *The Path of the Devil: Early Modern Witch Hunts*. Lanham, MD: Rowman & Littlefield.
Jessop, Robert D. 2002. *The Future of the Capitalist State*. Cambridge, MA: Polity.
Jo, Moon Ho. 1984. "The Putative Political Complacency of Asian Americans." *Political Psychology* 5: 583-605.
Joachim, Jutta. 2003. "Framing Issues and Seizing Opportunities: Women's Rights and the UN." *International Studies Quarterly* 47: 247-274.
Joas, Hans. 2000. *The Genesis of Values*. Cambridge, UK: Polity Press.
———. 2003. *War and Modernity*. Cambridge, UK: Polity Press.
Jochnick, Chris. 1999. "Confronting the Impunity of Non-State Actors: New Fields for the Promotion of Human Rights." *Human Rights Quarterly* 21, no. 1: 56-79.
Johansen, Bruce. 2003. *The Dirty Dozen: Toxic Chemicals in the Earth's Future*. Westport, CT: Praeger.
Johnson, C., and T. Forsyth. 2002. "In the Eyes of the State: Negotiating a 'Rights-Based Approach' to Forest Conservation in Thailand." *World Development* 20: 1591-1605.
Johnson, E. Patrick. 2003. *Appropriating Blackness: Performance and the Politics of Authenticity*. Durham, NC: Duke University Press.
Johnson, Eric A., and Eric H. Monkkonen, eds. 1996. *The Civilization of Crime*. Urbana: University of Illinois Press.
Johnson, Heather Beth. 2006. *The American Dream and the Power of Wealth: Choosing Schools and Inheriting Inequality in the Land of Opportunity*. New York: Routledge.
Johnson, J. 2001. "In-depth Interviewing." In *Handbook of Interview Research: Context and Method*, edited by Jay Gubrium and James Holstein, 103-119. Thousand Oaks, CA: Sage.
Johnson, Jim (aka Bruno Latour). 1988. "Mixing Humans and Nonhumans Together: The Sociology of a Door-Closer." *Social Problems* 35, no. 3: 298-310.
Johnson, Norman L., and Samuel Kotz. 1969-1972. *Distributions in Statistics*. 4 vols. New York: Wiley.
Johnson, Norman L., Samuel Kotz, and N. Balakrishnan. 1994. *Continuous Univariate Distributions*. Vol. 1. 2nd ed. New York: Wiley.
———. 1995. *Continuous Univariate Distributions*. Vol. 2. 2nd ed. New York: Wiley.
Johnson, Victoria. 2011. "Everyday Rituals of the Master Race: Fascism, Stratification, and the Fluidity of 'Animal' Domination." In *Critical Theory and Animal Liberation*, edited by John Sanbonmatsu, 203-218. Lanham, MD: Rowman & Littlefield.
Johnston, Barbara R. 1995. "Human Rights and the Environment." *Human Ecology* 23: 111-123.
Johnston, Hank, and Bert Klandermans, eds. 1995. *Social Movements and Culture*. Minneapolis: University of Minnesota Press.
Johnston, Hank, and John A. Noakes, eds. 2005. *Frames of Protest: Social Movements and the Framing Perspective*. Lanham, MD: Rowman & Littlefield Publishers.
Jordan, Kathleen Casey. 1997. "The Effect of Disclosure on the Professional Life of Lesbian Police Officers." PhD diss., City University of New York.
Jordan-Zachary, Julia S. 2007. "Am I a Black Woman or a Woman Who Is Black? A Few Thoughts on the Meaning of Intersectionality." *Politics and Gender* 3: 254-263.
Jorgensen, Anja, and Dennis Smith. 2009. "The Chicago School of Sociology: Survival in the Urban Jungle." In *Encountering the Everyday: An Introduction to the Sociologies of the Unnoticed*, edited by Michael Hviid Jacobsen, 45-69. New York: Macmillan.
Jorgenson, Andrew. 2003. "Consumption and Environmental Degradation: A Cross-National Analysis of the Ecological Footprint." *Social Problems* 50, no. 3: 374-394.
Joseph, Paul. 1993. *Peace Politics: The United States between the Old and New World Orders*. Philadelphia: Temple University Press.
Jost, Timothy S. 2003. *Disentitlement? The Threats Facing Our Public Health Care Programs and a Rights-Based Response*. Oxford: Oxford University Press.
Jotkowitz, A., S. Glick, and B. Gesundheit. 2008. "A Case against Justified Non-Voluntary Active Euthanasia (The Groningen Protocol)." *American Journal of Bioethics* 8: 23-26.
Juris, Jeffrey. 2008. *Networking Futures*. Durham, NC: Duke University Press.
Kaiser Family Foundation. 2002. *Sex Smarts Survey: Gender Roles*. Menlo Park, CA: Kaiser Family Foundation.

Kalberg, Stephen. 1994. *Max Weber's Comparative-Historical Sociology.* Chicago: University of Chicago Press.
———. 2011. Introduction to *The Protestant Ethic and the Spirit of Capitalism* by Max Weber. Translated by Stephen Kalberg. Rev. 1920 ed. New York: Oxford University Press.
Kaldor, Mary. 1999. *New and Old Wars: Organized Violence in a Global Era.* Stanford, CA: Stanford University Press.
———. 2003. *Global Civil Society: An Answer to War.* Cambridge, UK: Polity Press.
Kang, Miliann. 2003. "The Managed Hand: The Commercialization of Bodies and Emotions in Korean Immigrant-Owned Nail Salons." *Gender and Society* 17: 820–839.
Kant, Immanuel. 1933 [1788]. *Critique of Practical Reason.* Upper Saddle River, NJ: Prentice Hall.
———. 1939. *Perpetual Peace.* New York: Columbia University Press.
Kapur, Ratna. 2002. "The Tragedy of Victimization Rhetoric: Resurrecting the 'Native' Subject in International/Post-Colonial Feminist Legal Politics." *Harvard Law School Human Rights Journal of Law* 15: 1–38.
———. 2005. *Erotic Justice: Law and the New Politics of Postcolonialism.* London: Glasshouse Press.
Kara, Karel. 1968. "On the Marxist Theory of War and Peace." *Journal of Peace Research* 5: 1–27.
Karger, Howard. 1989. "The Common and Conflicting Goals of Labor and Social Work." *Administration in Social Work* 13: 1–17.
Karp, David. 1996. *Speaking of Sadness: Depression, Disconnection, and the Meanings of Illness.* New York: Oxford University Press.
Karpik, Lucien. 1977. "Technological Capitalism." In *Critical Issues in Organizations,* edited by S. Clegg and D. Dunkerley, 41–71. London: Routledge and Kegan Paul.
Karstedt, Susanne. 2007. "Human Rights." In *The Blackwell Encyclopedia of Sociology,* edited by George Ritzer, 2182–2185. Malden, MA: Blackwell Publishing.
———. 2011. "Human Rights." In *The Concise Encyclopedia of Sociology,* edited by George Ritzer and J. Michael Ryan, 294–295. Malden, MA: Wiley-Blackwell.
Kasinitz, Philip, Mary Waters, John H. Mollenkopf, and Jennifer Holdaway. 2009. *Inheriting the City: The Children of Immigrants Come of Age.* New York: Russell Sage Foundation.
Kass, Leon R. 1971. "The New Biology: What Price Relieving Man's Estate?" *Science* 174: 779–788.
Kasser, Tim. 2011. "Cultural Values and the Well-Being of Future Generations: A Cross-National Study." *Journal of Cross-Cultural Psychology* 42, no. 2 (March): 206–215.
Katsui, H., and J. Kumpuvuori. 2008. "Human Rights Based Approach to Disability in Development in Uganda: A Way to Fill the Gap between Political and Social Spaces?" *Scandinavian Journal of Disability Research* 10: 227–236.
Katz, Jonathan. 2007. *The Invention of Heterosexuality.* Chicago: University of Chicago Press.
Kausikan, Bilahari. 1995. "An East Asian Approach to Human Rights." *Buffalo Journal of International Law* 2: 263–283.
Kautsky, Karl. 1931. *Bolshevism at a Deadlock.* London: G. Allen and Unwin.
Keck, Margaret E., and Kathryn Sikkink. 1998. *Activists beyond Borders: Advocacy Networks in International Politics.* Ithaca, NY: Cornell University Press.
Keith, Michael, and Steve Pile. 1993. *Place and the Politics of Identity.* London: Psychology Press.
Keller, C., and M. Siegrist. 2010. "Psychological Resources and Attitudes toward People with Physical Disabilities." *Journal of Applied Social Psychology* 40: 389–401.
Kelman, Herbert C., and V. Lee Hamilton. 2002. "The My Lai Massacre: Crimes of Obedience and Sanctioned Massacres." In *Corporate and Governmental Deviance: Problems of Organizational Behavior in Contemporary Society,* edited by M. David Ermann and Richard J. Lundman, 195–221. Oxford: Oxford University Press.
Kempadoo, Kamala, ed. 2005. *Trafficking and Prostitution Reconsidered: New Perspectives on Migration, Sex Work, and Human Rights.* Boulder, CO: Paradigm Publishers.
Kemper, Theodore D. 1990. "Social Relations and Emotions: A Structural Approach." In *Research Agendas in the Sociology of Emotions,* edited by T. D. Kemper, 207–237. Albany: State University of New York Press.
Kemper, Theodore D., and Randall Collins. 1990. "Dimensions of Microinteraction." *American Journal of Sociology* 93: 32–68.
Kendall, Maurice G. 1943. *The Advanced Theory of Statistics.* Vol. 1: *Distribution Theory.* Original 2-vol. ed. London: Charles Griffin.
Kendall, Maurice G., and Alan Stuart. 1958. *The Advanced Theory of Statistics.* Vol. 1: *Distribution Theory.* First 3-vol. ed. New York: Hafner.
Kendler, Kenneth S., Sara Jaffee, and Dan Romer, eds. 2010. *The Dynamic Genome and Mental Health: The Role of Genes and Environments in Development.* Oxford: Oxford University Press.

Kennedy, David. 2002. "Boundaries in the Field of Human Rights: The International Human Rights Movement: Part of the Problem?" *Harvard Law School Human Rights Journal* 15: 101-25.
Kessler R. C., and J. McLeod. 1984. "Sex Differences in Vulnerability to Undesirable Life Events." *American Sociological Review* 49: 620-631.
Kessler, Suzanne J. 1990. *Lessons from the Intersexed*. New Brunswick, NJ: Rutgers University Press.
Kestnbaum, Meyer. 2009. "The Sociology of War and the Military." *Annual Review of Sociology* 35: 235-254.
Khalili-Borna, C. A. 2007. "Technological Advancement and International Human Rights: Is Science Improving Human Life or Perpetuating Human Rights Violations?" *Michigan Journal of International Law* 29: 95-125.
Kick, Edward, and Andrew Jorgenson. 2003. "Globalization and the Environment." *Journal of World-Systems Research* 9, no. 2: 195-203.
Kikuzawa, Saeko, Sigrun Olafsdottir, and Bernice Pescosolido. 2008. "Similar Pressures, Different Contexts: Public Attitudes toward Government Intervention for Health Care in 21 Nations." *Journal of Health and Social Behavior* 49: 385-399.
Kilbourne, Jean. 1999. *Deadly Persuasion: Why Women and Girls Must Fight the Addictive Power of Advertising*. New York: The Free Press.
Kim, Hyun Sik. 2011. "Consequences of Parental Divorce for Child Development." *American Sociological Review* 76, no. 3: 487-511.
Kimeldorf, Howard. 1991. "Bringing Unions Back In (or Why We Need a New Old Labor History)." *Labor History* 32: 91-103.
Kimeldorf, Howard, and Judith Stepan-Norris. 1992. "Historical Studies of Labor Movements in the United States." *Annual Review of Sociology* 18: 495-517.
Kimmel, Michael S. 2001. "The Kindest Un-Cut: Feminism, Judaism, and My Son's Foreskin." *Tikkun* 16, no. 1. http://www.cirp.org/pages/cultural/kimmel1/ (accessed September 6, 2012).
———. 2005. *Manhood in America: A Cultural History*. New York: Oxford University Press.
Kincaid, Jamaica. 2000. *A Small Place*. 1st ed. New York: Farrar, Straus and Giroux.
Kincheloe, Joe, and Peter McLaren. 1994. "Rethinking Critical Theory and Qualitative Research." In *Handbook of Qualitative Research*, edited by Norman Denzin and Yvonna Lincoln, 138-157. Thousand Oaks, CA: Sage.
Kindleberger, Charles Poor, and Robert Z. Aliber. 2005. *Manias, Panics and Crashes: A History of Financial Crises*. Hoboken, NJ: John Wiley and Sons.
King, Deborah K. 1988. "Multiple Jeopardy, Multiple Consciousnesses: The Context of a Black Feminist Ideology." *Signs: Journal of Women in Culture and Society* 14: 42-72.
King, Martin Luther, Jr. 1986. "If the Negro Wins, Labor Wins." In *A Testament of Hope: The Essential Writings and Speeches of Martin Luther King, Jr.*, edited by James M. Washington. New York: HarperCollins.
Kingsbury, Benedict, Nico Krisch, and Richard Stewart. 2005. "The Emergence of Global Administrative Law." *Law and Contemporary Problems* 68: 15-61.
Kinney, Eleanor D., and Brian Alexander Clark. 2004. "Provisions for Health and Health Care in the Constitutions of the Countries of the World." *Cornell International Law Journal* 37: 285-355.
Kinsey, Alfred, Wardell B. Pomeroy, and Clyde E. Martin. 1948. *Sexual Behavior in the Human Male*. Philadelphia: W. B. Saunders Company.
Kiser, Edgar, and Howard T. Welser. 2010. "The Relationship between Theory and History in Revolutionary Biology: A Model for Historical Sociology?" Unpublished manuscript, University of Washington.
Kitano, Harry H. L. 1988. "Asian Americans and Alcohol: The Chinese, Japanese, Koreans and Filipinos in Los Angeles." In *Alcohol Use among U.S. Ethnic Minorities*, edited by D. Spiegler, D. Tate, S. Aitken, and C. Christian, 373-382. Rockville, MD: National Institute on Alcohol Abuse and Alcoholism.
Kitschelt, Herbert P. 1986. "Political Opportunity Structures and Political Protest: Anti-Nuclear Movements in Four Democracies." *British Journal of Political Science* 16, no. 1: 57-85.
Klandermans, Bert, and Suzanne Staggenborg, eds. 2002. *Methods of Social Movement Research*. Minneapolis: University of Minnesota Press.
Klare, Karl E. 1978. "Judicial Deradicalization of the Wagner Act and the Origins of Modern Legal Consciousness, 1937-1941." *Minnesota Law Review* 62: 265.
Kleiber, Christian, and Samuel Kotz. 2003. *Statistical Size Distributions in Economics and Actuarial Sciences*. Hoboken, NJ: Wiley.
Knights, David, and Hugh Wilmott, eds. 1990. *Labour Process Theory*. London: Macmillan.
Knoke, D., and E. O. Laumann. 1987. *The Organizational State: Social Choice in National Policy Domains*. Madison: University of Wisconsin Press.
Koch, T. 2004. "The Difference that Difference Makes: Bioethics and the Challenge of 'Disability.'" *Journal of Medicine and Philosophy* 29: 697-716.

Kohler, Hans-Peter, J. L. Rodgers, and Kaare Christensen. 1999. "Is Fertility Behavior in Our Genes? Findings from a Danish Twin Study." *Population and Development Review* 25: 253-288.

———. 2002. "Between Nurture and Nature: The Shifting Determinants of Female Fertility in Danish Twin Cohorts." *Social Biology* 49: 218-248.

Kohli, M., and J. W. Meyer. 1986. "Social Structure and Social Construction of Life Stages." *Human Development* 29, no. 3: 145-149.

Kohli, Martin. 1986. "Social Organization and Subjective Construction of the Life Course." In *Human Development and the Life Course*, edited by A. Sorensen, F. Weinert, and L. Sherrod, 271-292. Cambridge, MA: Harvard University Press.

———. 2007. "The Institutionalization of the Life Course: Looking Back to Look Ahead." *Research in Human Development* 4, no. 3-4: 253-271.

Kohn, Melvin L. 1981. "Social Class and Schizophrenia: A Critical Review and a Reformulation." In *The Sociology of Mental Illness: Basic Studies*, edited by O. Grusky and Pollner M. Holt, 127-143. New York: Rinehart and Winston.

Kohn, Melvin L., and Carmi Schooler. 1983. *Work and Personality: An Inquiry into the Impact of Social Stratification*. Norwood, NJ: Ablex Publishing Corporation.

Kohn, Melvin L., Kazimierz M. Slomczynski, Krystyna Janicka, Valeri Khmelko, Bogdan W. Mach, Vladimir Paniotto, Wojciech Zaborowski, Roberto Gutierrez, and Cory Heyman. 1997. "Social Structure and Personality under Conditions of Radical Social Change: A Comparative Analysis of Poland and Ukraine." *American Sociological Review* 62: 614-638.

Kohn, P. M., and R. G. Smart. 1987. "Wine, Women and Suspiciousness and Advertising." *Journal Studies of Alcohol and Drugs* 48: 161-166.

Kolakowski, Leszek. 1983. "Marxism and Human Rights." *Daedalus* 112, no. 4: 81-92.

Kolben, Kevin. 2010. "Labor Rights as Human Rights?" *Virginia Journal of International Law* 50: 449-484.

Komarovsky, Mirra. 1951. "Editorial: Teaching College Sociology." *Social Forces* 30: 252-256.

Koo, Jeong-Woo, and Francisco O. Ramirez. 2009. "National Incorporation of Global Human Rights: Worldwide Adoptions of National Human Rights Institutions, 1966-2004." *Social Forces* 87: 1321-1354.

Korgen, Kathleen, and Jonathan White. 2010. *The Engaged Sociologist: Connecting the Classroom to the Community*. 3rd ed. Thousand Oaks, CA: Pine Forge.

Kornbluh, Joyce. 1987. *A New Deal for Workers' Education: The Workers' Service Program, 1933-1942*. Urbana: University of Illinois Press.

Korpi, Walter. 1983. *The Democratic Class Struggle*. London: Routledge and Kegan Paul.

Kostecki, Marian, and Krzysztof Mrela. 1984. "Collective Solidarity in Poland's Powdered Society." *Critical Sociology* 12: 131-141.

Koven, Seth, and Sonya Michel, eds. 1993. *Mothers of a New World: Maternalist Politics and the Origins of Welfare States*. New York: Routledge.

Krahe, B., and C. Altwasser. 2006. "Changing Negative Attitudes towards Persons with Physical Disabilities: An Experimental Intervention." *Journal of Community and Applied Social Psychology* 16: 59-69.

Krain, Matthew, and Anne Nurse. 2004. "Teaching Human Rights through Service Learning." *Human Rights Quarterly* 26: 189-207.

Krieger, Nancy. 2000. "Discrimination and Health." In *Social Epidemiology*, edited by L. Berkman and I. Kawachi, 36-75. Oxford: Oxford University Press.

———. 2011. *Epidemiology and the People's Health*. Oxford: Oxford University Press.

Krieger, Nancy, D. L. Rowley, A. A. Herman, B. Avery, and M. T. Philips. 1993. "Racism, Sexism and Social Class: Implications for Studies of Health, Disease, and Well-Being." *American Journal of Preventive Medicine* 9: 82-122.

Krieger, Nancy, and Stephen Sidney. 1997. "Prevalence and Health Implications of Anti-Gay Discrimination: A Study of Black and White Women and Men in the Cardia Cohort." *International Journal of Health Services* 27, no. 1: 157-176.

Krieger, Nancy, Pamela D. Waterman, Cathy Hartman, Lisa M. Bates, Anne M. Stoddard, Margaret M. Quinn, Glorian Sorensen, and Elizabeth M. Barbeau. 2006. "Social Hazards on the Job: Workplace Abuse, Sexual Harassment, and Racial Discrimination—a Study of Black, Latino, and White Low-Income Women and Men Workers in the United States." *International Journal of Health Services* 36: 51-85.

Kriesi, Hanspeter. 2004. "Political Context and Opportunity." In *The Blackwell Companion to Social Movements*, edited by David A. Snow, Sarah A. Soule, and Hanspeter Kreisi, 67-90. Oxford, UK: Blackwell.

Kreisler, Harry. 2005. "Lakhdar Brahimi Interview: Conversations with History; Institute of International Studies. UC Berkeley." Institute of International Studies. April 5. http://globetrotter.berkeley.edu/people5/Brahimi/brahimi-con4.html.

Krippner, Greta. 2010. "Democracy of Credit: Transformations in Economic Citizenship." Paper presented at the annual meeting of the American Sociological Association, Atlanta, Georgia, August.
Kristoff, Nicholas. 2010. "Our Banana Republic." *New York Times*. November 6. http://www.nytimes.com/2010/11/07/opinion/07kristof.html (accessed December 18, 2010).
Krog, Antjie. 2010. "In the Name of Human Rights: I Say (How) You (Should) Speak (before I Listen)." In *Qualitative Inquiry and Human Rights*, edited by Norman Denzin and Michael Giardina, 66–81. Walnut Creek, CA: Left Coast Press.
Krugman, Paul R. 2007. *The Conscience of a Liberal*. New York: W. W. Norton and Co.
Kuhn, Thomas S. 1996. *The Structure of Scientific Revolutions*. Chicago: University of Chicago Press.
Kulick, Don. 1998. *Travesti: Sex, Gender, and Culture among Brazilian Transgendered Prostitutes*. Chicago: University of Chicago Press.
Kunioka, Todd T., and Karen M. McCurdy. 2006. "Relocation and Internment: Civil Rights Lessons from World War II." *PS: Political Science and Politics* 39: 503–511.
Kurashige, Scott. 2002. "Detroit and the Legacy of Vincent Chin." *Amerasia Journal* 28: 51–55.
Kuroiwa, Yoko, and Maykel Verkuyten. 2008. "Narratives and the Constitutions of Common Identity: The Karen in Burma." *Identities: Global Studies in Power and Culture* 15: 391–412.
Kurtz, Lester R. 2008. "Gandhi and His Legacies." *Encyclopedia of Violence, Peace and Conflict*, edited by Lester R. Kurtz, 837–851. 2nd ed. Amsterdam: Elsevier.
———. 2010. "Repression's Paradox in China." OpenDemocracy. November 17. http://www.opendemocracy.net/lester-r-kurtz/repression's-paradox-in-china (accessed January 20, 2012).
———. 2012. *Gods in the Global Village*. Los Angeles: Sage Pine Forge.
Laclau, Ernesto, and Chantal Mouffe. 1985. *Hegemony and Socialist Strategy: Towards a Radical Democratic Politics*. Translated by Winston Moore and Paul Cammack. London: Verso.
Lamb, H. R. 1998. "Mental Hospitals and Deinstitutionalization." In *Encyclopedia of Mental Health*, edited by H. S. Friedman, 2: 665–676. San Diego: Academic Press.
Lamont, Michèle. 2000. *The Dignity of Working Men: Morality and the Boundaries of Race, Class, and Immigration*. Cambridge, MA: Harvard University Press.
Landry, Bart. 2007. *Race, Gender, and Class: Theory and Methods of Analysis*. Upper Saddle River, NJ: Pearson.
Landsman, Stephen. 2005. *Crimes of the Holocaust: The Law Confronts Hard Cases*. Philadelphia: University of Pennsylvania Press.
Langer, Suzanne K. 1953. *Feeling and Form: A Theory of Art*. New York: Scribner.
Langevoort, Donald C. 1996. "Selling Hope, Selling Risk: Some Lessons for Law from Behavioral Economics about Stockbrokers and Sophisticated Customers." *California Law Review* 84: 627.
Langlois, Anthony J. 2002. "Human Rights: The Globalization and Fragmentation of Moral Discourse." *Review of International Studies* 28, no. 3: 479–496.
Lareau, Annette. 2003. *Unequal Childhoods: Class, Race, and Family Life*. Berkeley: University of California Press.
Larson, Heidi. 1999. "Voices of Pacific Youth: Video Research as a Tool for Youth Expression." *Visual Sociology* 14: 163–172.
Laslett, John H. M. 1970. *Labor and the Left: A Study of Socialist and Radical Influences in the American Labor Movement*. New York: Basic Books.
Laslett, John H. M., and Seymour Martin Lipset, eds. 1974. *Failure of a Dream? Essays on the History of American Socialism*. Garden City, NY: Doubleday.
Latour, Bruno. 2007. *Reassembling the Social*. New York: Oxford University Press.
Laumann, Edward O., John H. Gagnon, Robert T. Michael, and Stuart Michaels. 2000. *The Social Organization of Sexuality: Sexual Practices in the United States*.
Lauren, Paul Gordon. 1998. *The Evolution of International Human Rights: Visions Seen*. Philadelphia: University of Pennsylvania Press.
———. 2008. "History and Human Rights: People and Forces in Paradoxical Interaction." *Journal of Human Rights* 7: 91–103.
LaVeist, Thomas A. 2002. "Segregation, Poverty and Empowerment: Health Consequences for African Americans." In *Race, Ethnicity and Health*, edited by Thomas A. LaVeist, 76–96. San Francisco: Jossey-Bass.
Law, Joan, and John Hassard, eds. 1999. *Actor Network Theory and After*. Oxford and Keele, UK: Blackwell and the Sociological Review.
Leary, Virginia A. 1996. "The Paradox of Workers' Rights as Human Rights." In *Human Rights, Labor Rights, and International Trade*, edited by Lance A. Compa and Stephen F. Diamond. Philadelphia: University of Pennsylvania Press.
Leasher, M. K., C. E. Miller, and M. P. Gooden. 2009. "Rater Effects and Attitudinal Barriers Affecting People with Disabilities in Personnel Selection." *Journal of Applied Social Psychology* 39: 2236–2274.

Lebovic, James H., and Erik Voeten. 2006. "The Politics of Shame: The Condemnation of Country Human Rights Practices in the UNHCR." *International Studies Quarterly* 50, no. 4: 861–888.
Lebowitz, Michael. 2010. "Socialism: The Goal, the Paths and the Compass. The Bullet. Socialist Project." *E-Bulletin* 315 (February 20).
Lechner, Frank. 2005. "Religious Rejections of Globalization and Their Directions." In *Religion in Global Civil Society*, edited by M. Juergensmeyer. Oxford: Oxford University Press.
Lechner, Frank, and John Boli. 2005. *World Culture: Origins and Consequences*. Malden, MA: Blackwell Publishing.
Lee, Alfred McClung. 1973. *Toward Humanist Sociology*. Englewood-Cliffs, NJ: Prentice Hall.
———. 1979. "The Services of Clinical Sociology." *American Behavioral Scientist* 22: 487–511.
Lee, Angela Y. 2001. "The Mere Exposure Effect: An Uncertainty Reduction Explanation Revisited." *Personality and Social Psychology Bulletin* 27: 1255–1266.
Lee, Everett S. 1966. "A Theory of Migration." *Demography* 3: 47–57.
Lefebvre, Henri. 1968. *The Sociology of Marx*. Translated by Norbert Guterman. New York: Pantheon Books.
———. 1971. *Everyday Life in the Modern World*. Translated by Sacha Rabinovitch. New York: Harper and Row.
Lefort, Claude. 1986. "Politics and Human Rights." In *The Political Forms of Modern Society* 239. http://www.geocities.com/~johngray/impl13.htm (accessed September 6, 2012).
Leibovitz, Joseph. 2007. "Faultline Citizenship: Ethnonational Politics, Minority Mobilisation, and Governance in the Israeli 'Mixed Cities' of Haifa and Tel Aviv-Jaffa." *Ethnopolitics* 6: 235–263.
Leigh, Gillian, and Robin Gerrish. 1986. "Attitudes toward Alcoholism in Volunteer Therapist Aides: Do They Change?" *Drug and Alcohol Dependence* 17, no. 4: 381–390.
Leik, Robert K., and Barbara F. Meeker. 1975. *Mathematical Sociology*. Englewood Cliffs, NJ: Prentice Hall.
Lekachman, Robert. 1966. *The Age of Keynes*. New York: Random House.
Lembcke, Jerry. 1984. "Labor and Education: Portland Labor College, 1921–1929." *Oregon Historical Quarterly* 85: 117–134.
Lemus, Maria, Kimberly Stanton, and John Walsh. 2005. "Colombia: A Vicious Cycle of Drugs and War." In *Drugs and Democracy in Latin America*, edited by Eileen Rosin and Coletta Youngers, 112–120. Boulder, CO: Lynne Rienner Publishers.
Lengerman, Patricia, and Jill Niebrugge-Brantley. 1998. *The Women Founders: Sociology and Social Theory, 1830–1930*. Boston, MA: McGraw-Hill.
———. 2002. "Back to the Future: Settlement Sociology, 1885–1930." *American Sociologist* 33: 5–20.
———. 2007. "Thrice Told: Narratives of Sociology's Relation to Social Work." In *Sociology in America*, edited by Craig Calhoun, 63–114. Chicago: University of Chicago Press.
Lenin, Vladimir I. 1939. *Imperialism, the Highest Stage of Capitalism*. New York: International Publishers.
———. 2007. *The State and Revolution*. Synergy International of the Americas.
Lenski, Gerhard. 1966. *Power and Privilege: A Theory of Social Stratification*. New York: McGraw-Hill.
———. 2005. *Ecological-Evolutionary Theory: Principles and Applications*. Boulder, CO, and London: Paradigm Publishers.
Lenski, Gerhard, and Patrick Nolan. 2005. "Trajectories of Development among Third World Societies." In *Evolutionary Theory: Principles and Applications*, edited by Gerhard Lenski, 187–201. Boulder, CO: Paradigm Publishers.
Lenzer, Gertrud, and Brian K. Gran. 2011. "Rights and the Role of Family Engagement in Child Welfare: An International Treaties Perspective on Family's Rights, Parents' Rights, and Children's Rights." In "Taking Child and Family Rights Seriously: Family Engagement and Its Evidence in Child Welfare," special issue, *Child Welfare* 90, no. 4: 157–179.
Lerner, S. 2010. *Sacrifice Zones: The Frontlines of Toxic Chemical Exposure in the United States*. Cambridge, MA: MIT Press.
Levels, M., J. Dronkers, and G. Kraaykamp. 2008. "Educational Achievement of Immigrants in Western Countries: Origin, Destination, and Community Effects on Mathematical Performance." *American Sociological Review* 73, no. 5: 835–853.
Levine, Donald Nathan. 1985. "Rationality and Freedom: Inveterate Multivocals." In *The Flight from Ambiguity: Essays in Social and Cultural Theory*, 142–178. Chicago: University of Chicago Press.
Levine, J. 2002. *Harmful to Minors: The Perils of Protecting Children from Sex*. Minneapolis: University of Minnesota Press.
Levine, Judith A., Clifton R. Emery, and Harold Pollack. 2007. "The Well-Being of Children Born to Teen Mothers." *Journal of Marriage and Family* 69 (February): 105–122.
Levit, Nancy. 2002. "Theorizing the Connections among Systems of Subordination." *University of Missouri-Kansas City Law Review* 77: 227–249.
Levitt, Peggy. 2001. *Transnational Villagers*. Berkeley: University of California Press.

———. 2005. "Building Bridges: What Migration Scholarship and Cultural Sociology Have to Say to Each Other." *Poetics* 33: 49–62.
Levitt, Peggy, and Sally Merry. 2009. "Vernacularization on the Ground: Local Uses of Global Women's Rights in Peru, China, India and the United States." *Global Networks* 9, no. 4: 441–461.
Levy, Daniel, and Natan Sznaider. 2006. "Sovereignty Transformed: A Sociology of Human Rights." *British Journal of Sociology* 57: 657–676.
Lewack, Howard. 1953. *Campus Rebels: A Brief History of the Student League for Industrial Democracy*. New York: Student League for Industrial Democracy.
Lewis, L. 2009a. "Introduction: Mental Health and Human Rights: Social Policy and Sociological Perspectives." *Social Policy and Society* 8: 211–214.
———. 2009b. "Politics of Recognition: What Can a Human Rights Perspective Contribute to Understanding Users' Experiences of Involvement in Mental Health Services?" *Social Policy and Society* 8: 257–274.
Lewis, Tammy. 2004. "Service Learning for Social Change? Lessons from a Liberal Arts College." *Teaching Sociology* 32: 94–108.
Leydesdorff, L., and T. Schank. 2008. "Dynamic Animations of Journal Maps: Indicators of Structural Change and Interdisciplinary Developments." *Journal of the American Society for Information Science and Technology* 59, no. 11: 1810–1818.
Liao, Tim Futing. 2006. "Measuring and Analyzing Class Inequality with the Gini Index Informed by Model-Based Clustering." *Sociological Methodology* 36: 201–224.
Lichtenstein, B. 2003. "Stigma as a Barrier to Treatment of Sexually Transmitted Infection in the American Deep South: Issues of Race, Gender, and Poverty." *Social Science & Medicine* 57: 2435–2445.
Liebow, Elliot. 1993. *Tell Them Who I Am: The Lives of Homeless Women*. New York: Penguin.
———. 2003. *Tally's Corner: A Study of Negro Streetcorner Men*. 2nd ed. New York: Rowman & Littlefield.
Liebowitz, Deborah. 2008. *Respect, Protect, and Fulfill: Raising the Bar on Women's Rights in San Francisco*. San Francisco: Women's Institute for Leadership Development for Human Rights.
Light, Donald W. 2001. "Comparative Models of Health Care Systems." In *The Sociology of Health and Illness: Critical Perspectives*, edited by Peter Conrad, 464–479. 6th ed. New York: Worth Publishers.
Lindenberg, S. 2006a. "Rational Choice Theory." In *International Encyclopedia of Economic Sociology*, edited by J. Beckert and M. Zafirovski, 548–552. New York: Routledge.
———. 2006b. "Social Rationality." In *International Encyclopedia of Economic Sociology*, edited by J. Beckert and M. Zafirovski, 16–618. New York: Routledge.
Lindsay, Jo. 2009. "Young Australians and the Staging of Intoxification and Self-Control." *Journal of Youth Studies* 12, no. 4: 371–384.
Link, B. G., B. Dohrenwend, and A. Skodol. 1986. "Socioeconomic Status and Schizophrenia: Noisome Occupational Characteristics as a Risk Factor." *American Sociological Review* 51: 242–258.
Link, B. G., E. L. Struening, M. Rahav, J. C. Phelan, and L. Nuttbrock. 1997. "On Stigma and Its Consequences: Evidence from a Longitudinal Study of Men with Dual Diagnosis of Mental Illness and Substance Abuse." *Journal of Health and Social Behavior* 38: 177–190.
Link, Bruce, and Jo Phelan. 1995. "Social Conditions and Fundamental Causes of Illness." *Journal of Health and Social Behavior* (extra issue) 35: 80–94.
———. 2001. "Conceptualizing Stigma." *Annual Review of Sociology* 27: 363–385.
———. 2010. "Social Conditions as Fundamental Causes of Health Inequalities." In *Handbook of Medical Sociology*, edited by Chloe Bird, Peter Conrad, Allen Fremont, and Stephan Timmermans, 3–17. 6th ed. Nashville, TN: Vanderbilt University Press.
Linzey, Andrew. 2009. *The Link between Animal Abuse and Human Violence*. East Sussex, UK: Sussex Academic Press.
Lippett, R., J. Watson, and B. Westley. 1958. *The Dynamics of Planned Change*. New York: Harcourt, Brace and World.
Lippman, Abby. 1991. "Prenatal Genetic Testing and Screening: Constructing Needs and Reinforcing Tendencies." *American Journal of Law and Society* 17: 15–50.
Lipset, Seymour Martin. 1960. "The Political Process in Trade Unions: A Theoretical Statement." In *Labor and Trade Unionism*, edited by W. Galenson and S. M. Lipset. New York: Wiley.
———. 1981. *Political Man*. Baltimore: John Hopkins University Press.
Lipsitz, George. 2006. *The Possessive Investment in Whiteness: How White People Profit from Identity Politics*. Philadelphia: Temple University Press.
Lipton, M. 1980. "Migration from Rural Areas of Poor Countries: The Impact on Rural Productivity and Income Distribution." *World Development* 8: 1–24.
Lisborg, Russell, S. 1993. "Migrant Remittances and Development." *International Migration* 31: 267–287.
Little, David. 1991. *Varieties of Social Explanation*. Boulder, CO: Westview.

———. 1999. "Review: Rethinking Human Rights: A Review Essay on Religion, Relativism, and Other Matters." *Journal of Religious Ethics* 27: 149–177.
Lo, Clarence Y. H. 2008. "State Capitalism." In *International Encyclopedia of the Social Sciences*, edited by William A. Darity Jr. 2nd ed. Detroit, MI: Macmillan Reference.
———. Forthcoming. *Politics of Justice for Corporate Wrongdoing–Equality, Market Fairness, and Retribution in Enron and Beyond*.
Locke, J. 1970 [1689]. *Two Treatises of Government*. Cambridge, UK: Cambridge University Press.
Lockwood, Elizabeth, Daniel Barstow Magraw, Margaret Faith Spring, and S. I. Strong. 1998. *The International Human Rights of Women: Instruments of Change*. Washington, DC: American Bar Association Section of International Law and Practice.
Loe, Meika. 2006. *The Rise of Viagra: How the Little Blue Pill Changed Sex in America*. New York: New York University Press.
Logan, John R., and Harvey L. Molotch. 2007. *Urban Fortunes: The Political Economy of Place*. 2nd ed. Berkeley: University of California Press.
London, L. 2008. "What Is a Human Rights-Based Approach to Health and Does It Matter?" *Health and Human Rights* 10: 65–80.
Long, A. B. 2008. "Introducing the New and Improved Americans with Disabilities Act: Assessing the ADA Amendments Act of 2008." *Northwestern University Law Review Colloquy* 103: 217–229.
Longmore, P. K. 2003. *Why I Burned My Book and Other Essays on Disability*. Philadelphia: Temple University Press.
López, Ian Haney. 2006. *White by Law: The Legal Construction of Race*. Rev. and updated 10th anniv. ed. New York: New York University Press.
Lopez, Iris. 1993. "Agency and Constraint: Sterilization and Reproductive Freedom among Puerto Rican Women in New York City." *Urban Anthropology* 22: 299–323.
———. 2008. *Matters of Choice: Puerto Rican Women's Struggle for Reproductive Freedom*. New Brunswick, NJ: Rutgers University Press.
Lorber, Judith. 2002. *Gender and the Construction of Illness*. Lanham, MD: AltaMira Press.
Lorber, Judith, and Lisa Jean Moore. 2002. *Gender and the Social Construction of Illness*. Newbury Park, CA: Sage Publications.
———. 2007. *Gendered Bodies: Feminist Perspectives*. New York: Oxford.
Los Angeles Times. 2011. "Mexico under Siege: The Drug War at Our Doorstop." *Los Angeles Times*. http://projects.latimes.com/mexico-drug-war (accessed January 1, 2011).
Lounsbury, Michael, and Paul M. Hirsch, eds. 2010. *Markets on Trial: The Economic Sociology of the U.S. Financial Crisis*. Research in the Sociology of Organizations 30A. London: Emerald Group Publishing.
Low, Petra. 2010. "Devastating Natural Disasters Continue Steady Rise." *Vital Signs: Global Trends that Shape Our Future* (March): 38–41.
Ludvig, Alice. 2006. "'Differences between Women' Intersecting Voices in a Female Narrative." *European Journal of Women's Studies* 13: 245–258.
Lukács, Georg. 1971. *History and Class Consciousness: Studies in Marxist Dialectics*. Translated by Rodney Livingstone. Cambridge, MA: MIT Press.
Luker, Kristin. 2006. *When Sex Goes to School: Warring Views on Sex and Sex Education since the Sixties*. New York: W. W. Norton.
Lukes, Steven. 1972. *Émile Durkheim: His Life and Work*. New York: Harper and Row Publishers.
———. 2005 [1974]. *Power: A Radical View*. Houndsmill, UK: Palgrave Macmillan.
Lupton, D. 1999. *Risk*. New York: Routledge.
Lynch, Michael. 1996. "Ethnomethodology." In *The Social Science Encyclopaedia*, edited by Adam Kuper and Jessica Kuper, 266–267. 2nd ed. London: Routledge.
Lynch, Michael, and Wes Sharrock, eds. 2003. *Harold Garfinkel*. 4 vols. Sage Masters in Modern Social Thought Series. London: Sage.
Lynd, Robert S. 1939. *Knowledge for What? The Place of the Social Sciences in American Culture*. Princeton, NJ: Princeton University Press.
Lynd, Robert S., and Helen Merrell Lynd. 1929. *Middletown: A Study in Modern American Culture*. New York: Harcourt, Brace and World.
Maas, Peter. 2009. *Crude World: The Violent Twilight of Oil*. New York: Alfred Knopf.
Mackelprang, R. W., and R. D. Mackelprang. 2005. "Historical and Contemporary Issues in End-of-Life Decisions: Implications for Social Work." *Social Work* 40: 315–324.
MacKinnon, Catherine. 1993. "On Torture: A Feminist Perspective on Human Rights." In *Human Rights in the Twenty-First Century: A Global Challenge*, edited by Kathleen E. Mahoney and Paul Mahoney. Boston: Springer Publishing.

MacLean, Vicky, and Joyce Williams. 2009. "US Settlement Sociology in the Progressive Era: Neighborhood Guilds, Feminist Pragmatism and the Social Gospel." Paper presented at the annual meeting for the American Sociological Association, San Francisco, California.

Macy, M. W., and A. Flache. 1995. "Beyond Rationality in Models of Choice." *Annual Review of Sociology* 21: 73–91.

Mahler, Sarah. 1998. "Theoretical and Empirical Contributions toward a Research Agenda for Transnationalism." In *Transnationalism from Below*, edited by Michael Smith and Luis Guarnizo. London: Transaction Publishers.

Mahoney, Jack. 2006. *The Challenge of Human Rights: Origin, Development and Significance*. Malden, MA: Wiley-Blackwell.

Maier-Katkin, Daniel, Daniel P. Mears, and Thomas J. Bernard. 2011. "Toward a Criminology of Crimes against Humanity." *Theoretical Criminology* 13: 227–255.

Maira, Sunaina. 2004. "Youth Culture, Citizenship and Globalization: South Asian Muslim Youth in the United States after September 11th." *Comparative Studies of South Asia, Africa and the Middle East* 24: 219–231.

Maldonado-Torres, Nelson. 2007. "On the Coloniality of Being." *Cultural Studies* 21, no. 2–3: 240–270.

Malešević, Siniša. 2010. *The Sociology of War and Violence*. Cambridge, UK: Cambridge University Press.

Mallett, Robin K., Timothy D. Wilson, and Daniel T. Gilbert. 2008. "Expect the Unexpected: Failure to Anticipate Similarities Leads to an Intergroup Forecasting Error." *Journal of Personality and Social Psychology* 94: 265–277.

Mallinder, Louise. 2008. *Amnesties, Human Rights and Political Transitions*. Oxford: Hart.

Mamo, Laura. 2007. *Queering Reproduction: Achieving Pregnancy in the Age of Technoscience*. Durham, NC: Duke University Press.

Maney, Gregory M. 2011. "Of Praxis and Prejudice: Enhancing Scholarship and Empowering Activists through Movement-Based Research." Plenary address, Collective Behavior and Social Movements Workshop, Las Vegas, Nevada.

Mann, Abby. 1961. "Judgment at Nuremberg Script—Dialogue Transcript." Drew's Script-O-Rama. http://www.script-o-rama.com/movie_scripts/j/judgment-at-nuremburg-script-transcript.html (accessed July 20, 2012).

Mann, Jonathan M. 1996. "Health and Human Rights." *British Medical Journal* 312: 924.

Mann, Michael. 1987. "War and Social Theory: Into Battle with Classes, Nations and States." In *Sociology of War and Peace*, edited by Colin Creighton and Martin Shaw. Dobbs Ferry, NY: Sheridan House.

———. 1988. *States, War and Capitalism: Studies in Political Sociology*. Oxford: Blackwell.

Mannheim, Karl. 1936. *Ideology and Utopia*. London: Routledge.

Mansbridge, Jane. 1994. "Feminism and the Forms of Freedom." In *Critical Studies in Organization and Bureaucracy*, edited by Frank Fischer and Carmen Sirianni, 544–543. Rev. ed. Philadelphia: Temple University Press.

Manza, Jeff, and Christopher Uggen. 2006. *Locked Out: Felon Disenfranchisement and American Democracy*. New York: Oxford University Press.

March, James G., and Johan P. Olsen. 1984. "The New Institutionalism: Organizational Factors in Political Life." *American Political Science Review* 78, no. 3: 734–749.

March, James G., and Herbert Simon. 1958. *Organizations*. New York: Wiley.

———. 1976. *Ambiguity and Choice in Organizations*. Bergen, Norway: Universitetsforlaget.

Margolis, Eric. 1999. "Class Pictures: Representations of Race, Gender and Ability in a Century of School Photography." *Visual Sociology* 14, no. 1: 7–38.

Markovic, Mihailo. 1974. *From Affluence to Praxis*. Ann Arbor: University of Michigan Press.

Marks, Stephen P., and Kathleen A. Modrowski. 2008. *Human Rights Cities: Civic Engagement for Societal Development*. New York: UN-HABITAT and PDHRE.

Marmot, Michael G. 2004. *The Status Syndrome: How Your Social Standing Directly Affects Your Health and Life Expectancy*. London: Bloomsbury.

Marriage Project. 2010. *When Marriage Disappears: The New Middle America*. Charlottesville, VA: Institute for American Values.

Marshall, Brent K., and J. Steven Picou. 2008. "Post-Normal Science, Precautionary Principle and Worst Cases: The Challenge of Twenty-First Century Catastrophes." *Sociological Inquiry* 78: 230–247.

Marshall, S. L. A. 1947. *Men against Fire: The Problem of Battle Command*. New York: Morrow.

Marshall, T. H. (Thomas Humphrey). 1964. *Class, Citizenship, and Social Development*. Garden City, NY: Doubleday.

Martin, David. 1978. *A General Theory of Secularization*. New York: Harper and Row.

Martin, Karin A. 1996. *Puberty, Sexuality, and the Self: Boys and Girls at Adolescence*. New York: Routledge.

Martino, George. 2000. *Global Economy, Global Justice: Theoretical Objections and Policy Alternatives to Neo-Liberalism*. New York: Routledge.
Marx Ferree, Myra, and Aili Mari Tripp, eds. 2006. *Global Feminism: Transnational Women's Activism, Organizing, and Human Rights*. New York and London: New York University Press.
Marx, Karl. 1843a. "On the Jewish Question." Marxists Internet Archive. http://www.marxists.org/archive/marx/works/1844/jewish-question (accessed July 18, 2012).
———. 1843b. "Introduction to a Contribution to the Critique of Hegel's Philosophy of Right." Marxists Internet Archive. http://www.marxists.org/archive/marx/works/1843/critique-hpr/intro.htm (accessed July 18, 2012).
———. 1956. *The Holy Family*. Moscow: Foreign Language Publishing House.
———. 1967 [1867]. *Capital: A Critique of Political Economy*. Vol. 1: *The Process of Capitalist Production*. New York: International Publishers.
———. 1978 [1844]. "Economic and Philosophic Manuscripts of 1844." In *The Marx-Engels Reader*, edited by Robert C. Tucker, 56–67. New York: W. W. Norton.
Marx, Karl, and Friedrich Engels. 1848. *The Communist Manifesto*. http://www.anu.edu.au/polsci/marx/classics/manifesto.html (accessed September 5, 2012).
———. 1976 [1846]. *The German Ideology*. Moscow: Progress Publishers.
Mason-Schrock, Douglas. 1996. "Transsexuals' Narrative Construction of the 'True Self.'" *Social Psychology Quarterly* 59: 176–192.
Massey, Douglas S. 1988. "Economic Development and International Migration in Comparative Perspective." *Population and Development Review* 14: 383–413.
———. 2004. "Segregation and Stratification: A Biosocial Perspective." *Du Bois Review: Social Science Research on Race* 1: 7–25.
Massey, Douglas, and Nancy Denton. 1993. *American Apartheid: Segregation and the Making of the Underclass*. Cambridge, MA: Harvard University Press.
Massey, Douglas, Jorge Durand, and Nolan J. Malone. 2002. *Beyond Smoke and Mirrors: Mexican Immigration in an Era of Economic Integration*. New York: Russell Sage Foundation.
Massey, Douglas, and Rene Zenteno. 2000. "A Validation of the Ethnosurvey: The Case of Mexico-U.S. Migration." *International Migration Review* 34: 766–793.
Matcha, Duane A. 2003. *Health Care Systems of the Developed World: How the United States' System Remains an Outlier*. Westport, CT: Praeger.
Matsueda, Ross. 2006. "Differential Social Organization, Collective Action, and Crime." *Crime, Law, and Social Change* 46: 3–33.
Matsueda, Ross, Derek A. Kreager, and David Huizinga. 2006. "Deterring Delinquents: A Rational Choice Model of Theft and Violence." *American Sociological Review* 71: 95–122.
Matthews, N. 2009. "Contesting Representations of Disabled Children in Picture-Books: Visibility, the Body and the Social Model of Disability." *Children's Geographies* 7: 37–49.
Matthus, Jürgen. 2009. *Approaching an Auschwitz Survivor: Holocaust Testimony and Its Transformations*. New York: Oxford University Press.
Mayer, Karl Ulrich, and W. Müller. 1986. "The State and the Structure of the Life Course." In *Human Development and the Life Course: Multidisciplinary Perspectives*, edited by A. B. Sorensen, F. E. Weinert, and L. R. Sherrod, 217–245. Hillsdale, NJ: Lawrence Erlbaum Associates.
Mayer, Karl Ulrich. 2009. "New Directions in Life Course Research." *Annual Review of Sociology* 35: 413–433.
Maynard, Douglas W., and Stephen E. Clayman. 1991. "The Diversity of Ethnomethodology." *Annual Review of Sociology* 17: 385–418.
Mayo, E. 1933. *The Human Problems of an Industrial Civilization*. New York: Macmillan.
Mazower, Mark. 2004. "The Strange Triumph of Human Rights, 1933–1950." *Historical Journal* 47: 379–398.
Mazur, Allan. 2004. *Biosociology of Dominance and Deference*. Lanham, MD: Rowman & Littlefield.
Mazur, Allan, and A. Booth. 1998. "Testosterone and Dominance in Men." *Behavioral and Brain Sciences* 21: 353–363.
McAdam, Doug. 1982. *Political Process and the Development of Black Insurgency, 1930–1970*. Chicago: University of Chicago Press.
———. 1994. "Social Movements and Culture." In *Ideology and Identity in Contemporary Social Movements*, edited by Joseph R. Gusfield, Hank Johnston, and Enrique Laraña, 36–57. Philadelphia: Temple University Press.
———. 1999. *Political Process and Black Insurgency, 1930–1970*. 2nd ed. Chicago: University of Chicago Press.
McAdam, Doug, John D. McCarthy, and Mayer N. Zald. 1996. *Comparative Perspectives on Social Movements: Political Opportunities, Mobilizing Structures, and Cultural Framings*. Cambridge, UK: Cambridge University Press.

McAdoo, Harriette P. 1998. "African-American Families." In *Ethnic Families in America: Patterns and Variations*, edited by Charles H. Mindel, Robert W. Haberstein, and Roosevelt Wright Jr. Upper Saddle River, NJ: Prentice Hall.
McCall, Leslie. 2001. *Complex Inequality: Gender, Class and Race in the New Economy*. New York: Routledge.
——. 2005. "The Complexity of Intersectionality." *Signs* 30: 1771–1800.
McCammon, Holly J. 1990. "Legal Limits on Labor Militancy: U.S. Labor Law and the Right to Strike since the New Deal." *Social Problems* 37: 206–229.
——. 2001. "Stirring Up Suffrage Sentiment: The Formation of the State Woman Suffrage Organizations, 1866–1914." *Social Forces* 80: 449–480.
——. 2012. *A More Just Verdict: The U.S. Women's Jury Movements and Strategic Adaptation*. New York: Cambridge University Press.
McCammon, Holly J., Soma Chaudhuri, Lyndi Hewitt, Courtney Sanders Muse, Harmony D. Newman, Carrie Lee Smith, and Teresa M. Terrell. 2008. "Becoming Full Citizens: The U.S. Women's Jury Rights Campaigns, the Pace of Reform, and Strategic Adaptation." *American Journal of Sociology* 113: 1104–1148.
McCammon, Holly J., Courtney Sanders Muse, Harmony D. Newman, and Teresa M. Terrell. 2007. "Movement Framing and Discursive Opportunity Structures: The Political Successes of the U.S. Women's Jury Movements." *American Sociological Review* 72: 725–749.
McCarthy, John D., and Mayer N. Zald. 1977. "Resource Mobilization and Social Movements: A Partial Theory." *American Sociological Review* 82: 1212–1241.
McClain, Linda. 1994. "Rights and Responsibilities." *Duke Law Journal* 43, no. 5: 989–1088.
McConnell, Eileen Diaz. 2011. "An 'Incredible Number of Latinos and Asians': Media Representations of Racial and Ethnic Population Change in Atlanta, Georgia." In "Latino/as and the Media," special issue, *Latino Studies* 9 (summer/autumn): 177–197.
McDew, Charles. 1966. "Spiritual and Moral Aspects of the Student Nonviolent Struggle in the South." In *The New Student Left*, edited by Mitchell Cohen and Dennis Hale, 51–57. Boston, MA: Beacon Press.
McFarland, Sam. 2010. "Personality and Support for Human Rights: A Review and Test of a Structural Model." *Journal of Personality* 78: 1–29.
McIntyre, Alice. 1997. *Making Meaning of Whiteness: Exploring Racial Identity with White Teachers*. Albany: State University of New York Press.
McIntyre, Richard P. 2003. "Globalism, Human Rights and the Problem of Individualism." *Human Rights and Human Welfare* 3, no. 1: 1–14.
——. 2008. *Are Worker Rights Human Rights?* Ann Arbor: University of Michigan Press.
McKinlay, John B. 1974. "A Case for Refocusing Upstream: The Political Economy of Illness." Reprinted in *The Sociology of Health and Illness: Critical Perspectives*, edited by Peter Conrad, 519–529. 5th ed. New York: Worth Publishers.
——. 1996. "Some Contributions from the Social System to Gender Inequalities in Heart Disease." *Journal of Health and Social Behavior* 37: 1–26.
McKinney, Kathleen, and Carla Howery. 2006. "Teaching and Learning in Sociology: Past, Present and Future." In *21st Century Sociology: A Reference Handbook*, edited by Clifton D. Bryant and Dennis L. Peck, 2: 379–388. Thousand Oaks, CA: Sage.
McLaren, Peter. 1989. *Life in Schools: An Introduction to Critical Pedagogy in the Foundations of Education*. New York: Longman.
——. 1999. *Schooling as Ritual Performance*. London: Routledge.
——. 2005. *Capitalists and Conquerors: A Critical Pedagogy against Empire*. New York: Rowman & Littlefield.
McLaren, Peter, and Nathalia E. Jaramillo. 1999. "Medicine and Public Health, Ethics and Human Rights." In *Health and Human Rights: A Reader*, edited by Jonathan Mann, Michael A. Grodin, Sofia Gruskin, and George J. Annas, 439–452. New York: Routledge.
——. 2007. *Pedagogy and Praxis in the Age of Empire: Towards a New Humanism*. Rotterdam: Sense Publishers.
McLeod, Jane D., and Kathryn J. Lively. 2003. "Social Structure and Personality." In *Handbook of Social Psychology*, edited by John DeLamater, 77–102. New York: Kluwer.
McNally, David. 2001. *Bodies of Meaning: Studies on Language, Labor and Liberation*. Albany: State University of New York Press.
McWhorter, John. 2011. "How the War on Drugs Is Destroying Black America." *Cato's Letter* 9, no. 1. http://www.cato.org/pubs/catosletter/catosletterv9n1.pdf.
Mead, George Herbert. 1934. *Mind, Self, and Society*. Chicago: University of Chicago Press.
——. 1967. *Mind, Self, and Society: From the Standpoint of a Social Behaviorist*. Chicago: University of Chicago Press.
——. 2008 [1918]. "Immanuel Kant on Peace and Democracy." In *Self, War and Society: George Herbert Mead's Macrosociology*, edited by Mary Jo Deegan, 159–174. New Brunswick, NJ: Transaction Publishers.

Mead, S., and M. E. Copeland. 2001. "What Recovery Means to Us: Consumers' Perspectives." In *The Tragedy of Great Power Politics*, edited by John J. Mearsheimer. New York: Norton.
Mearsheimer, John J. 2001. *The Tragedy of Great Power Politics*. New York: Norton.
Mechanic, David. 1997. "Muddling through Elegantly: Finding the Proper Balance in Rationing." *Health Affairs* 16: 83-92.
Mechanic, David, and Donna D. McAlpine. 2010. "Sociology of Health Care Reform: Building on Research and Analysis to Improve Health Care." *Journal of Health and Social Behavior* 51: S137-S159.
Mele, A., and P. Rawling. 2004. *The Oxford Handbook of Rationality*. Oxford: Oxford University Press.
Melucci, Alberto. 1989. *Nomads of the Present: Social Movements and Individual Needs in Contemporary Society*. Philadelphia: Temple University Press.
Mendez, Jennifer Bickham. 2005. *From the Revolution to the Maquiladoras: Gender, Labor, and Globalization in Nicaragua*. Durham, NC: Duke University Press.
Menjívar, Cecilia, and Leisy Abrego. 2009. "Parents and Children across Borders: Legal Instability and Intergenerational Relations in Guatemalan and Salvadoran Families." In *Across Generations: Immigrant Families in America*, edited by N. Foner, 160-189. New York: New York University Press.
Menon, Anu. 2010. *Human Rights in Action: San Francisco's Local Implementation of the United Nations' Women's Treaty (CEDAW)*. San Francisco: City and County of San Francisco, Department on the Status of Women.
Mental Health Advisory Team IV. 2006. "Operation Iraqi Freedom 05-07." Final Report of November 17. Office of the Surgeon, Multinational Force—Iraq, and Office of the Surgeon General, United States Army Medical Command.
Merenstein, Beth Frankel. 2008. *Immigrants and Modern Racism: Reproducing Inequality*. Boulder, CO: Lynne Rienner Publishers.
Merry, Sally Engle. 2006. *Human Rights and Gender Violence: Translating International Law into Local Justice*. Chicago: University of Chicago Press.
Merton, Robert K. 1938. "Social Structure and Anomie." *American Sociological Review* 3: 672-682.
———. 1968. *Social Theory and Social Structure*. New York: The Free Press.
———. 1973. *The Sociology of Science: Theoretical and Empirical Investigations*, edited by Norman Storer. Chicago: University of Chicago Press.
Mertus, Julie. 2007. "The Rejection of Human Rights Framings: The Case of LGBT Advocacy in the US." *Human Rights Quarterly* 29: 1036-1064.
Messner, Michael A. 1992. *Power at Play: Sports and the Problem of Masculinity*. Boston: Beacon Press.
Messner, Steven F., and Richard Rosenfeld. 2007. *Crime and the American Dream*. 4th ed. Belmont, CA: Wadsworth.
Mesthene, E. 2000. "The Role of Technology in Society." In *Technology and the Future*, edited by A. H. Teich, 61-70. 8th ed. New York: Bedford/St. Martin's.
Metzger, Barbara. 2007. "Towards an International Human Rights Regime during the Inter-War Years: The League of Nations' Combat of Traffic in Women and Children." In *Beyond Sovereignty: Britain, Empire and Transnationalism, 1880-1950*, edited by Kevin Grant, Philippa Levine, and Frank Trentmann. New York: Palgrave Macmillan.
Meyer, David S. 2004. "Protest and Political Opportunities." *Annual Review of Sociology* 30: 125-145.
Meyer, Jean-Baptiste. 2001. "Network Approach versus Brain Drain: Lessons from the Diaspora." *International Migration* 39: 1468-2435. doi.10.1111/1468-2435.00173.
Meyer, John W., John Boli, George Thomas, and Francisco Ramirez. 1997. "World Society and the Nation-State." *American Journal of Sociology* 103: 144-181.
Meyer, John W. 2010. "World Society, Institutional Theories and the Actor." *Annual Review of Sociology* 36: 1-20.
Meyer, John W., and Brian Rowan. 1977. "Institutionalized Organizations: Formal Structure as Myth and Ceremony." *American Journal of Sociology* 83, no. 2: 340-363.
Meyer, Marshall W., and Lynn G. Zucker. 1989. *Permanently Failing Organizations*. Newbury Park, CA: Sage.
Meyer, William H. 1996. "Human Rights and MNCs: Theory versus Quantitative Analysis." *Human Rights Quarterly* 18: 368-397.
Michels, Robert. 1962 [1915]. *Political Parties*. New York: The Free Press.
Micklin, Michael, and Dudley L. Poston. 1995. *Continuities in Social Human Ecology*. New York: Plenum.
Middelstaedt, Emma. 2008. "Safeguarding the Rights of Sexual Minorities: Incremental and Legal Approaches to Enforcing International Human Rights Obligations." *Chicago Journal of International Law* 9: 353-386.
Midgley, Mary. 1995. *Beast and Man: The Roots of Human Nature*. London: Routledge.

Miech, R. A., A. Caspi, T. E. Moffitt, B. R. E. Wright, and P. A. Silva. 1999. "Low Socioeconomic Status and Mental Disorders: A Longitudinal Study of Selection and Causation during Young Adulthood." *American Journal of Sociology* 104: 1096–1131.

Mignolo, Walter. 2010. "De-Coloniality: Decolonial Thinking and Doing in the Andes: A Conversation by Walter Mignolo with Catherine Walsh." *Reartikulacija* 10–13. http://www.reartikulacija.org/?p=1468 (accessed July 18, 2012).

Milkman, Ruth. 1987. *Gender at Work: The Dynamics of Job Segregation by Sex during World War II*. Urbana: University of Illinois Press.

Miller, Alan S., and Rodney Stark. 2002. "Gender and Religiousness: Can Socialization Explanations Be Saved?" *American Journal of Sociology* 107: 1399–1423.

Miller, Francesca. 1999. "Feminism and Transnationalism." In *Feminisms and Internationalism*, edited by Mrinalini Sinha, Donna Guy, and Angela Woollacott. Oxford, UK: Blackwell Publishers.

Millet, Kris. 2008. "The Naxalite Movement: Exposing Scrapped Segments of India's Democracy." *Culture Magazine*. January 5. http://culturemagazine.ca/politics/the_naxalite_movement_exposing_scrapped_segments_of_indias_democracy.html (accessed July 18, 2012).

Mills, C. Wright. 1948. *The New Men of Power*. New York: Harcourt, Brace.

———. 1956. *The Power Elite*. New York: Oxford University Press.

———. 1959. *The Sociological Imagination*. New York: Oxford University Press.

Mills, Charles W. 1997. *The Racial Contract*. Ithaca, NY: Cornell University Press.

Minh-ha, Trinh T. 2009. *Woman, Native, Other: Writing Postcoloniality and Feminism*. 1st ed. Bloomington: Indiana University Press.

Mink, Gwendolyn. 1986. *Old Labor and New Immigrants in American Political Development: Union, Party, and the State, 1875–1920*. Ithaca, NY: Cornell University Press.

Minkov, Anton. 2009. *Counterinsurgency and Ethnic/Sectarian Rivalry in Comparative Perspective: Soviet Afghanistan and Iraq*. Ottawa, Canada: Centre for Operational Research and Analysis, Defense Research and Development Canada.

Minow, Martha. 1998. *Between Vengeance and Forgiveness: Facing History after Genocide and Mass Violence*. Boston: Beacon Press.

———. 2002. *Breaking the Cycles of Hatred: Memory, Law, and Repair*. Introduced and with commentaries by N. L. Rosenblum. Princeton, NJ: Princeton University Press.

Mirowsky, J., C. E. Ross, and J. R. Reynolds. 2000. "Links between Social Status and Health Status." In *Handbook of Medical Sociology*, edited by Chloe Bird, Peter Conrad, and Alan M. Fremont, 47–67. 5th ed. Upper Saddle River, NJ: Prentice Hall.

Mishel, Lawrence, and Matthew Walters. 2003. "How Unions Help All Workers." Economic Policy Institute Briefing Paper 143. Economic Policy Institute. August. http://www.epi.org/publications/entry/briefingpapers_bp143.

Mishra, Ramesh. 1984. *Welfare State in Crisis*. New York: St. Martin's Press.

Mitchell, Neil, and James McCormick. 1988. "Economic and Political Explanations of Human Rights Violations." *World Politics* 40: 476–498.

Modic, Dolores. 2008. "Stigma of Race." *Raziskave and Razprave/Research and Discussion* 1: 153–185.

Moghadam, Valentine M. 2005. *Globalizing Women: Transnational Feminist Networks*. Baltimore: Johns Hopkins University Press.

Mohanty, Chandra Talpade. 2006. *Feminism without Borders: Decolonizing Theory, Practicing Solidarity*. Durham, NC: Duke University Press.

Mohanty, Chandra Talpade, Ann Russo, and Lourdes Torres, eds. 1991. *Third World Women and the Politics of Feminism*. Bloomington: Indiana University Press.

Mojab, Shahrzad. 2009. "'Post-War Reconstruction,' Imperialism and Kurdish Women's NGOs." In *Women and War in the Middle East*, edited by Nadje Al-Ali and Nicola Pratt, 99–128. London: Zed Books.

Moncada, Alberto, and Judith Blau. 2006. "Human Rights and the Role of Social Scientists." *Societies without Borders* 1: 113–122.

Moody, Kim. 1997. *Workers in a Lean World: Unions in the International Economy*. New York: Verso.

Moore, D. 2003. "A Signaling Theory of Human Rights Compliance." *Northwestern University Law Review* 97: 879–910.

Moore, Jason. 2000. "Sugar and the Expansion of the Early Modern World-Economy." *Review: A Journal of the Fernand Braudel Center* 23, no. 33: 409–433.

Moore, Kelly. 2008. *Disrupting Science: Social Movements, American Scientists, and the Politics of the Military, 1945–1975*. Princeton, NJ: Princeton University Press.

Moore, S. F. 1978. "Law and Social Change: The Semi-Autonomous Social Field as an Appropriate Field of Study." In *Law as Process: An Anthropological Approach*, edited by S. F. Moore, 54–81. London: Routledge.

Moore, Wendy Leo. 2008. *Reproducing Racism: White Space, Elite Law Schools, and Racial Inequality.* Lanham, MD: Rowman & Littlefield.

Morales, Maria Cristina. 2009. "Ethnic-Controlled Economy or Segregation? Exploring Inequality in Latina/o Co-Ethnic Jobsites." *Sociological Forum* 24: 589-610.

Morales, Maria Cristina, and Cynthia Bejarano. 2009. "Transnational Sexual and Gendered Violence: An Application of Border Sexual Conquest at a Mexico-U.S. Border." *Global Networks* 9: 420-439.

Morin, Alain, and James Everett. 1990. "Inner Speech as a Mediator of Self-Awareness, Self-Consciousness, and Self-Knowledge: An Hypothesis." *New Ideas in Psychology* 8: 337-356.

Morrell, Ernest. 2008. *Critical Literacy and Urban Youth: Pedagogies of Access, Dissent, and Liberation.* New York: Routledge.

Morris, Lydia. 2010. *Asylum, Welfare and the Cosmopolitan Ideal.* London: Routledge.

Morse, Janice M., and Linda Niehaus. 2009. *Mixed-Method Design: Principles and Procedures.* Walnut Creek, CA: Left Coast Press.

Morsink, Johannes. 1999. *The Universal Declaration of Human Rights: Origins, Drafting and Intent.* Philadelphia: University of Pennsylvania Press.

Moser, Annalise. 2007. *Gender and Indicators: Overview Report.* Brighton, UK: Institute of Development Studies.

Mossakowski, K. N. 2008. "Dissecting the Influence of Race, Ethnicity, and Socioeconomic Status on Mental Health in Young Adulthood." *Research on Aging* 30: 649-671.

Motley, Susan. 1987. "Burning the South: U.S. Tobacco Companies in the Third World." *Multinational Monitor* 8, no. 7-8: 7-10.

Moulier Boutang, Yann. 1998. *De l'esclavage au salariat: economie histoire du salariat bride.* Paris: Partner University Fund.

Mousin, Craig B. 2003. "Standing with the Persecuted: Adjudicating Religious Asylum Claims after the Enactment of the International Religious Freedom Act of 1998." *Brigham Young University Law Review* 2003: 541-592.

Moyn, Samuel. 2010. *The Last Utopia: Human Rights in History.* Cambridge, MA: Belknap Press.

Mueller, John. 1989. *Retreat from Doomsday: The Obsolescence of Major War.* New York: Basic Books.

Muller, Mike. 1983. "Preventing Tomorrow's Epidemic: The Control of Smoking and Tobacco Production in Developing Countries." *New York State Journal of Medicine* 83, no. 13: 1304-1309.

Mullins, Christopher W., David Kauzlarich, and Dawn L. Rothe. 2004. "The International Criminal Court and the Control of State Crime: Prospects and Problems." *Critical Criminology* 12: 285-308.

Muraven, Mark, Dianne M. Tice, and Roy F. Baumeister. 1998. "Self-Control as Limited Resource: Regulatory Depletion Patterns." *Journal of Personality and Social Psychology* 74: 774-789.

Myers, Kristen, and Laura Raymond. 2010. "Elementary School Girls and Heteronormativity: The Girl Project." *Gender & Society* 24: 167-188.

Nadarajah, Saralees. 2002. "A Conversation with Samuel Kotz." *Statistical Science* 17: 220-233.

Nagarjuna. 2007 [1300]. *In Praise of Dharmadh tu.* With commentary by the Third Karmapa. Translated by Karl Brunnhölzl. Ithaca, NY: Snow Lion Publications.

Nagel, Joane. 2003. *Race, Ethnicity, and Sexuality: Intimate Intersections, Forbidden Frontiers.* New York: Oxford University Press.

Naples, Nancy A. 1991, "Socialist Feminist Analysis of the Family Support Act of 1988."*AFFILIA: Journal of Women and Social Work* 6: 23-38.

———. 1998. *Community Activism and Feminist Politics: Organizing across Race, Gender and Class.* New York: Routledge.

———. 2009. "Teaching Intersectionality Intersectionally." *International Feminist Journal of Politics* 11: 566-577.

———. 2011. "Women's Leadership, Social Capital and Social Change." In *Activist Scholar: Selected Works of Marilyn Gittell*, edited by Kathe Newman and Ross Gittell, 263-278. Thousand Oaks, CA: Sage Publications.

Naples, Nancy A., and Manisha Desai. 2002. *Women's Activism and Globalization: Linking Local Struggles and Transnational Politics.* New York: Routledge.

Narayan, Uma. 1997. *Dislocating Cultures: Identities, Traditions, and Third World Feminism.* New York: Routledge.

———. 1998. "Essence of Culture and a Sense of History: A Feminist Critique of Cultural Essentialism." *Hypatia* 13: 86-106.

Nash, J. C. 2008. "Re-thinking Intersectionality." *Feminist Review* 89: 1-15.

National Center on Addiction and Substance Abuse (CASA) at Columbia University. 2001. "Malignant Neglect: Substance Abuse and America's Schools." CASA. http://www.casacolumbia.org/templates/Publications.aspx?articleid=320&zoneid=52.

National Drug Strategy Network. 1997. "18-Year-Old Texan, Herding Goats, Killed by U.S. Marine Corps Anti-Drug Patrol; Criminal Investigation of Shooting Underway." National Drug Strategy Network News Briefs. July. http://www.ndsn.org/july97/goats.html (accessed March 23, 2011).

Navarro, Vicente. 2004. "The Politics of Health Inequalities Research in the United States." *International Journal of Health Services* 34, no. 1: 87–99.
Neckerman, Kathryn. 2010. *Schools Betrayed: Roots of Failure in Inner-City Education.* Chicago: University of Chicago Press.
Nee, Victor. 2005. "The New Institutionalisms in Economics and Sociology." In *The Handbook of Economic Sociology,* edited by N. J. Smelser and R. Swedberg, 49–74. Princeton, NJ: Princeton University Press and Russell Sage Foundation
Neilson, Brett, and Mohammed Bamyeh. 2009. "Drugs in Motion: Toward a Materialist Tracking of Global Mobilities." *Cultural Critique* 71: 1–12.
Nettle, Daniel, and Thomas V. Pollet. 2008. "Natural Selection on Male Wealth in Humans." *American Naturalist* 172: 658–666.
Nevins, Joseph. 2003. "Thinking Out of Bounds: A Critical Analysis of Academic and Human Rights: Writings on Migrant Deaths in the U.S.-Mexico Border Region." *Migraciones Internacionales* 2: 171–190.
New York City Human Rights Initiative. 2011. http://www.nychri.org (accessed May 25, 2011).
Newman, Katherine S. 2008. *Chutes and Ladders: Navigating the Low-Wage Labor Market.* Cambridge, MA: Harvard University Press.
Ngai, Mae M. 2004. *Impossible Subjects: Illegal Aliens and the Making of Modern America.* Princeton, NJ: Princeton University Press.
Niazi, Tarique. 2002. "The Ecology of Genocide in Rwanda." *International Journal of Contemporary Sociology* 39, no. 2: 219–247.
——. 2005. "Democracy, Development, and Terrorism: The Case of Baluchistan (Pakistan)." *International Journal of Contemporary Sociology* 42, no. 2: 303–337.
——. 2008. "Toxic Waste." In *International Encyclopedia of the Social Sciences,* edited by William A. Darity, 407–409. 2nd ed. Farmington Hills, MI: Gale.
Nibert, David. 2002. *Animal Rights/Human Rights.* Lanham, MD: Rowman & Littlefield.
——. 2006. "The Political Economy of Beef: Oppression of Cows and Other Devalued Groups in Latin America." Paper presented at the annual meeting of the American Sociological Association, Montreal, Quebec, August 11, 2006.
Nichter, Mark, and Elizabeth Cartwright. 1991. "Saving the Children for the Tobacco Industry." *Medical Anthropology Quarterly,* New Series 5, no. 3: 236–256.
Nickel, James. 2010. "Human Rights." Stanford Encyclopedia of Philosophy. http://plato.stanford.edu/entries/rights-human (accessed July 18, 2012).
Nielsen, Francois. 2004. "The Ecological-Evolutionary Typology of Human Societies and the Evolution of Social Inequality." *Sociological Theory* 22: 292–314.
——. 2006. "Achievement and Ascription in Educational Attainment: Genetic and Environmental Influences on Adolescent Schooling." *Social Forces* 85: 193–216.
Nobis, Nathan. 2004. "Carl Cohen's 'Kind' Arguments for Animal Rights and against Human Rights." *Journal of Applied Philosophy* 21: 43–49.
Noguchi, Y. 2008. "Clinical Sociology in Japan." In *International Clinical Sociology,* edited by J. M. Fritz, 72–81. New York: Springer.
Nolan, James. 2001. *Reinventing Justice: The American Drug Court Movement.* Princeton, NJ: Princeton University Press.
Nolan, P., and G. Lenski. 2011. *Human Societies: An Introduction to Macrosociology.* Boulder, CO: Paradigm Publishers.
Nordberg, Camilla. 2006. "Claiming Citizenship: Marginalised Voices on Identity and Belonging." *Citizenship Studies* 10: 523–539.
Nöth, Winfried. 1995. *Handbook of Semiotics.* Bloomington: Indiana University Press.
Nouwen, S., and W. Werner. 2010. "Doing Justice to the Political: The International Criminal Court in Uganda and Sudan." *European Journal of International Law* 21: 941–965.
Núñez, Guillermina, and Josiah McC. Heyman. 2007. "Entrapment Processes and Immigrant Communities in a Time of Heightened Border Vigilance." *Human Organization* 66: 354–365.
Nyland, Chris, and Mark Rix. 2000. "Mary van Kleeck, Lillian Gilbreth and the Women's Bureau Study of Gendered Labor Law." *Journal of Management History* 6: 306–322.
Nystrom, P. C. 1981. "Designing Jobs and Assigning Employees." In *Handbook of Organizational Design.* Vol. 2: *Remodelling Organizations and Their Environments,* edited by P. C. Nystrom and William Starbuck, 272–301. New York: Oxford University Press.
O'Connor, Alice. 2002. *Poverty Knowledge: Social Science, Social Policy and the Poor in Twentieth-Century U.S. History.* Princeton, NJ: Princeton University Press.
O'Connor, Alice, Chris Tilly, and Lawrence D. Bobo. 2001. *Urban Inequality: Evidence from Four Cities.* New York: Russell Sage Foundation.

Offe, Claus. 1984. *Contradictions of the Welfare State.* Cambridge, MA: MIT Press.
———. 1985. *Disorganized Capitalism.* Cambridge, MA: MIT Press.
Office of the High Commissioner for Human Rights (OHCHR). 1998. *Basic Human Rights Instruments.* 3rd ed. Geneva: Office of the High Commissioner for Human Rights.
———. 2010. *2009 OHCHR Report on Activities and Results.* New York: United Nations.
———. 2011. "Human Rights at the Centre of Climate Change Policy." OHCHR. www.ohchr.org/EN/NewsEvents/pages/climate change policy (accessed January 1, 2011).
Ogien, A. 1994. "L'usage de drogues peut-il etre un object de recherché?" In *La Demande sociale de drogues,* edited by A. Ogien and P. Mignon, 7-12. Paris: La Documentation Française.
Okin, Susan Moller. 1989. *Justice, Gender, and the Family.* New York: Basic Books.
Okonta, I., and O. Douglas. 2001. *Where Vultures Feast: Shell, Human Rights, and Oil in the Niger Delta.* San Francisco: Sierra Club Books.
Oliver, Kelly. 2009. *Animal Lessons: How They Teach Us to Be Human.* New York: Columbia University Press.
Olshansky, S. Jay, and A. Brian Ault. 1986. "The Fourth Stage of the Epidemiologic Transition: The Age of Delayed Degenerative Disease." *Milbank Memorial Fund Quarterly* 64: 355-391.
Olson, Mancur. 1982. *The Rise and Decline of Nations: Economic Growth, Stagflation, and Social Rigidities.* New Haven, CT: Yale University Press.
Omi, M., and H. Winant. 1986. *Racial Formation in the United States: From the 1960s to the 1980s.* New York: Routledge.
———. 1994. *Racial Formation in the United States: From the 1960s to the 1980s.* 2nd ed. New York: Routledge.
Omran, Abdel R. 1971. "The Epidemiological Transition." *Milbank Memorial Fund Quarterly* 49: 509-538.
Oneal, John, and Bruce Russett. 2011. *Triangulating Peace: Democracy, Interdependence, and International Organizations.* New York: Norton.
Onken, S. J., and E. Slaten. 2000. "Disability Identity Formation and Affirmation: The Experiences of Persons with Severe Mental Illness." *Sociological Practice: A Journal of Clinical and Applied Sociology* 2: 99-111.
Ontario Human Rights Commission (OHRC). 2001. *An Intersectional Approach to Discrimination, Addressing Multiple Grounds in Human Rights Claims.* OHRC. http://www.ohrc.on.ca/sites/default/files/attachments/An_intersectional_approach_to_discrimination%3A_Addressing_multiple_grounds_in_human_ rights_claims.pdf (accessed July 18, 2012).
Oppenheimer, Gerald. 1991. "To Build a Bridge: The Use of Foreign Models by Domestic Critics of US Drug Policy." *Milbank Quarterly* 69, no. 3: 495-526.
Oppenheimer, Martin, Martin Murray, and Rhonda Levine. 1991. *Radical Sociologists and the Movement: Experiences, Legacies, and Lessons.* Philadelphia: Temple University Press.
Orellana, Marjorie Faulstich. 1999. "Space and Place in an Urban Landscape: Learning from Children's Views of Their Social Worlds." *Visual Sociology* 14: 73-89.
Orentlicher, Diane F. 1990. "Bearing Witness: The Art and Science of Human Rights Fact-Finding." *Harvard Law School Human Rights Journal* 3: 83-136.
Orr, David W. 1979. "Catastrophe and Social Order." *Human Ecology* 7: 41-52.
Ortiz, Victor M. 2001. "The Unbearable Ambiguity of the Border." *Social Justice* 28: 96-112.
Osiel, Mark J. 1997. *Mass Atrocities, Collective Memory, and the Law.* New Brunswick, NJ: Transaction Publishers.
Ostrom, Elinor. 1990. *Governing the Commons: The Evolution of Institutions for Collective Action.* Cambridge, UK: Cambridge University Press.
Ouellette-Kuntz, H., P. Burge, H. K. Brown, and E. Arsenault. 2010. "Public Attitudes towards Individuals with Intellectual Disabilities as Measured by the Concept of Social Distance." *Journal of Applied Research in Intellectual Disabilities* 23: 132-142.
Oxtoby, Willard G., and Allan F. Segal, eds. *A Concise Introduction to World Religions.* New York: Oxford University Press.
Page, Charles Hunt. 1982. *Fifty Years in the Sociological Enterprise: A Lucky Journey.* Amherst: University of Massachusetts Press.
Park, Robert E. 1914. "Racial Assimilation in Secondary Groups with Particular Reference to the Negro." *American Journal of Sociology* 19: 606-623.
———. 1928a. "Human Migration and the Marginal Man." *American Journal of Sociology* 33: 881-893.
———. 1928b. "The Bases of Race Prejudice." *Annals of the American Academy of Political and Social Science* 140: 11-20.
Parker, Karen. 2008. *Unequal Crime Decline: Theorizing Race, Urban Inequality, and Criminal Violence.* New York: New York University Press.

Parreñas, Rhacel Salazar. 1998. "The Global Servants: (Im)Migrant Filipina Domestic Workers in Rome and Los Angeles." Unpublished PhD diss., Department of Ethnic Studies, University of California, Berkeley.
Parsons, Talcott. 1951. *The Social System*. New York: The Free Press.
———. 1959. "The School as a Social System." *Harvard Educational Review* 29: 297–318.
Pascal, Celine-Marie. 2007. *Making Sense of Race, Class and Gender: Commonsense, Power and Privilege in the United States*. New York: Routledge.
Pascoe, C. J. 2007. *Dude, You're a Fag: Masculinity and Sexuality in High School*. Berkeley: University of California Press.
Pastor, Eugenia Relaño. 2005. "The Flawed Implementation of the International Religious Freedom Act of 1998: A European Perspective." *Brigham Young University Law Review* 2005: 711–746.
Patai, Raphael. 2002. *The Arab Mind*. New York: Hatherleigh Press.
Patterson, Charles. 2002. *Eternal Treblinka: Our Treatment of Animals and the Holocaust*. New York: Lantern Books.
Pattillo, Mary. 2007. *Black on the Block: The Politics of Race and Class in the City*. Chicago: University of Chicago Press.
Paust, Jordan J. 2004. "Post 9/11 Overreaction and Fallacies Regarding War and Defense, Guantanamo, the Status of Persons, Treatment, Judicial Review of Detention, and Due Process in Military Commissions." *Notre Dame Law Review* 79: 1335–1364.
Payne, Leigh. 2009. "Consequences of Transitional Justice." Paper presented at the Department of Political Science, University of Minnesota, Minneapolis.
PDHRE (People's Movement for Human Rights Learning). 2011. http://www.pdhre.org (accessed May 24, 2011).
Pearlin, L., and C. Schooler. 1978. "The Structure of Coping." *Journal of Health and Social Behavior* 19: 2–21.
Pécoud, Antoine, and Paul de Guchteneire. 2006. "International Migration, Border Controls and Human Rights: Assessing the Relevance of a Right to Mobility." *Journal of Borderlands Studies* 21: 69–86.
Peffley, Mark, and John Hurwitz. 2007. "Persuasion and Resistance: Race and the Death Penalty in America." *American Journal of Political Science* 51: 996–1012.
Pellow, D. N. 2007. *Resisting Global Toxics: Transnational Movements for Environmental Justice*. Cambridge, MA: MIT Press.
Penn, Michael, and Aditi Malik. 2010. "The Protection and Development of the Human Spirit: An Expanded Focus for Human Rights Discourse." *Human Rights Quarterly* 32, no. 3: 665–688.
Penna, David R., and Patricia J. Campbell. 1998. "Human Rights and Culture: Beyond Universality and Relativism." *Third World Quarterly* 19: 7–27.
Pennebaker, James W. 1997. "Writing about Emotional Experiences as a Therapeutic Process." *Psychological Science* 8: 162–166.
Perelman, Michael. 1978. "Karl Marx's Theory of Science." *Journal of Economic Issues* 12, no. 4: 859–870.
Peretti-Watel, Patrick. 2003. "How Does One Become a Cannabis Smoker? A Quantitative Approach." *Revue Française de Sociologie* 44: 3–27.
Peritz, Rudolph J. R. 1996. *Competition Policy in America, 1888–1992: History, Rhetoric, Law*. New York: Oxford University Press.
Perlman, Selig. 1922. *History of Trade Unionism in the United States*. New York: Macmillan.
———. 1928. *A Theory of the Labor Movement*. New York: Macmillan.
Perrin, Andrew J., and Lee Hedwig. 2007. "The Undertheorized Environment: Sociological Theory and the Ontology of Behavioral Genetics." *Sociological Perspectives* 50: 303–322.
Perrow, Charles. 1967. *Complex Organizations: A Critical Essay*. New York: Random House.
———. 1999. *Normal Accidents: Living with High-Risk Technologies*. Princeton, NJ: Princeton University Press.
———. 2002. *Organizing America, Wealth, Power, and the Origins of Corporate Capitalism*. Princeton, NJ, and Oxford, UK: Princeton University Press.
———. 2008. "Complexity, Catastrophe, and Modularity." *Sociological Inquiry* 78: 162–173.
Perrucci, Robert, and Carolyn C. Perrucci. 2009. *America at Risk: The Crisis of Hope, Trust, and Caring*. Lanham, MD: Rowman & Littlefield.
Perry, Michael J. 1997. "Are Human Rights Universal? The Relativist Challenge and Related Matters." *Human Rights Quarterly* 19, no. 3: 461–509.
Pescosolido, Bernice A., Brea L. Perry, J. Scott Long, Jack K. Martin, John I. Nurnberger Jr., and Victor Hesselbrock. 2008. "Under the Influence of Genetics: How Transdisciplinarity Leads Us to Rethink Social Pathways to Illness." *American Journal of Sociology* 114: S171–S201.
Peters, Julie, and Andrea Wolper. 1995. *Women's Rights, Human Rights: International Feminist Perspectives*. New York: Routledge.

Petersen, W. 1978. "International Migration." *Annual Review of Sociology* 4: 533–575.
Peterson, Ruth D., and Lauren J. Krivo. 2010. *Neighborhood Crime and the Racial-Spatial Divide*. New York: Russell Sage Foundation.
Pettigrew, T. F., and L. R. Tropp. 2006. "A Meta-Analytic Test of Intergroup Contact Theory." *Journal of Personality and Social Psychology* 90: 751–783.
PEW Forum on Religion in Public Life. 2009. "Global Restrictions on Religion." PEW Forum on Religion and Public Life, Washington, DC. http://www.pewforum.org/uploadedFiles/Topics/Issues/Government/restrictions-fullreport.pdf (accessed July 18, 2012).
PEW Research Center for the People and the Press. 2010. "Favorability Ratings of Labor Unions Fall Sharply." PEW Research Center for the People and the Press. http://pewresearch.org/pubs/1505/labor-unions-support-falls-public-now-evenly-split-on-purpose-power (accessed February 23, 2010).
Pfeiffer, D. 1993. "Overview of the Disability Movement: History, Legislative Record, and Political Implications." *Policy Studies Journal* 21: 724–734.
———. 2001. "The Conceptualization of Disability." In *Exploring Theories and Expanding Methodologies: Where We Are and Where We Need to Go*, edited by S. N. Barnartt and B. M. Altman, 2:29–52. Oxford: Elsevier Science.
Phemister, A. A., and N. M. Crewe. 2004. "Objective Self-Awareness and Stigma: Implications for Persons with Visible Disabilities." *Journal of Rehabilitation* 70: 33–37.
Picou, J. S., D. A. Gill, and M. J. Cohen, eds. 1997. *The Exxon-Valdez Disaster: Readings on a Modern Social Problem*. Dubuque, IA: Kendall-Hunt Publishers.
Picq, Ardant du. 2006. *Battle Studies*. Charleston, SC: BiblioBazaar.
Pierce, Jennifer L. 1995. *Gender Trials: Emotional Lives in Contemporary Law Firms*. Berkeley and Los Angeles: University of California Press.
Pilgrim, D., and A. A. Rogers. 1999. *A Sociology of Mental Health and Illness*. 2nd ed. Buckingham, UK: Open University Press.
Piven, Frances Fox, and Richard P. Cloward. 1977. *Poor People's Movements: Why They Succeed, How They Fail*. New York: Vintage Books.
Playle, J., and P. Keeley. 1998. "Non-Compliance and Professional Power." *Journal of Advanced Nursing* 27: 304–311.
Poe, Steven C., C. Neal Tate, and Linda Camp Keith. 1999. "Repression of the Human Right to Personal Integrity Revisited: A Global Cross-National Study Covering the Years 1976–1993." *International Studies Quarterly* 43: 291–313.
Polanyi, Karl. 1944. *The Great Transformation*. New York: Farrar and Rinehart.
Polletta, Francesca, and James M. Jasper. 2001. "Collective Identity and Social Movements." *Annual Review of Sociology* 27: 283–305.
Pollis, Adamantia. 2004. "Human Rights and Globalization." *Journal of Human Rights* 3, no. 3: 343–358.
Pollner, Melvin. 1987. *Mundane Reason: Reality in Everyday and Sociological Discourse*. Cambridge, UK: Cambridge University Press.
Ponse, Barbara. 1978. *Identities in the Lesbian World: The Social Construction of Self*. Westport, CT: Greenwood Press.
Poole, Michael. 1975. *Workers' Participation in Industry*. London: Routledge & K. Paul.
Popkin, Eric. 1999. "Guatemalan Mayan Migration to Los Angeles: Constructing Transnational Linkages in the Context of the Settlement Process." *Ethnic and Racial Studies* 22: 267–289.
Popper, Karl R. 1963. *Conjectures and Refutations: The Growth of Scientific Knowledge*. New York: Basic Books.
Population Research Bureau (PRB). 2007. "Is Low Birth Weight a Cause of Problems, or a Symptom of Them?" PBR. http://www.prb.org/Journalists/Webcasts/2007/LowBirthWeight.aspx (accessed January 25, 2012).
Porio, E. 2010. Personal communication with J. M. Fritz. December 12.
Portes, Alejandro, and Rubén Rumbaut. 2001. *Legacies: The Story of the Immigrant Second Generation*. Berkeley: University of California Press.
Poussaint, Alvin F. 1967. "A Negro Psychiatrist Explains the Negro Psyche." *New York Times Magazine*. August 20, 52.
Powell, Walter W., and Paul J. DiMaggio, eds. 1991. *The New Institutionalism in Organizational Analysis*. Chicago: University of Chicago Press.
Power, Samantha. 2002. *A Problem from Hell*. New York: Basic Books.
Prechel, Harland. 2000. *Big Business and the State: Historical Transitions and Corporate Transformation, 1880s–1990s*. Albany: State University of New York Press.
Preeves, Sharon E. 2003. *Intersex and Identity: The Contested Self*. New Brunswick, NJ: Rutgers University Press.

Preis, Ann-Belinda S. 1996. "Human Rights as Cultural Practice: An Anthropological Critique." *Human Rights Quarterly* 18, no. 2: 286-315.
Preston, Julia. 2011. "Risks Seen for Children of Illegal Immigrants." *New York Times*. September 20.
Prew, Paul. 2003. "The 21st Century World-Ecosystem: Dissipation, Chaos, or Transition?" In *Emerging Issues in the 21st Century World-System. Vol. 2: New Theoretical Directions for the 21st Century World System*, edited by Wilma A. Dunaway, 203-219. Westport, CT: Praeger Publishers.
Prior, L. 1996. *The Social Organization of Mental Illness*. London: Sage Publications.
Prunier, Gérard. 1997. *The Rwanda Crisis: History of a Genocide*. New York: Columbia University Press.
———. 2005. *Darfur: The Ambiguous Genocide*. Ithaca: Cornell University Press.
Pubantz, Jerry. 2005. "Constructing Reason: Human Rights and the Democratization of the United Nations." *Social Forces* 84: 1291-1302.
Pugh, Allison J. 2009. *Longing and Belonging: Parents, Children, and Consumer Culture*. Berkeley: University of California Press.
Purdy, Laura. 1989. "Surrogate Mothering: Exploitation or Empowerment?" *Bioethics* 3: 18-34.
Putnam, Robert D. 2000. *Bowling Alone: The Collapse and Revival of American Community*. New York: Simon and Schuster.
Quadagno, Jill. 1988. *The Transformation of Old Age Security*. Chicago: University of Chicago Press.
———. 2005. *One Nation, Uninsured: Why the U.S. Has No National Health Insurance*. New York: Oxford University Press.
Quadagno, Jill, and Debra Street, eds. 1995. *Aging for the Twenty-First Century*. New York: St. Martin's Press.
Quataert, Jean H. 2009. *Advocating Dignity: Human Rights Mobilizations in Global Politics*. Philadelphia: University of Pennsylvania Press.
———. 2010. "Women, Development, and Injustice: The Circuitous Origins of the New Gender Perspectives in Human Rights Visions and Practices in the 1970s." Paper presented at a conference titled "A New Global Morality? Human Rights and Humanitarianism in the 1970s," Freiburg Institute for Advanced Studies, Freiburg, Germany, June 10-12.
Queen, Stuart. 1981. "Seventy-Five Years of American Sociology in Relation to Social Work." *American Sociologist* 16: 34-37.
Quesnel-Vallee, Amelie. 2004. "Is It Really Worse to Have Public Health Insurance Than to Have No Insurance at All?" *Journal of Health and Social Behavior* 45, no. 4: 376-392.
Quigley, John. 2009. "The US Withdrawal from the ICJ Jurisdiction in Consular Cases." *Duke Journal of Comparative and International Law* 19, no. 2: 263-305.
Quinney, Richard. 1970. *The Social Reality of Crime*. Boston: Little, Brown and Co.
Rabben, Linda. 2002. *Fierce Legion of Friends: A History of Human Rights Campaigns and Campaigners*. Hyattsville, MD: Quixote Center.
Rainwater, Lee, and Timothy M. Smeeding. 2005. *Poor Kids in a Rich Country*. New York: Russell Sage Foundation.
Raskoff, Sally. 2011. "Welcome Back: Adjusting to Life after Military Service." Everday Sociology Blog. www.everydaysociologyblog.com/2011/12/welcome-back-adjusting-to-civilian-life-after-military-service.html (accessed December 17, 2011).
Ratner, S. R., J. S. Abrams, and J. L. Bischoff. 2009. *Accountability for Human Rights Atrocities in International Law: Beyond the Nuremberg Legacy*. 3rd ed. Oxford: Oxford University Press.
Rawls, A. 2000. "Harold Garfinkel." In *The Blackwell Companion to Major Social Theorists*, edited by George Ritzer, 545-576. Oxford: Blackwell.
———. 2003. "Conflict as a Foundation for Consensus: Contradictions of Industrial Capitalism in Book III of Durkheim's Division of Labor." *Critical Sociology* 29: 195-335.
———. 2006. "Respecifying the Study of Social Order: Garfinkel's Transition from Theoretical Conceptualization to Practices in Details." In *Seeing Sociologically: The Routine Grounds of Social Action* by Harold Garfinkel, 1-97. Boulder, CO: Paradigm.
Rawls, John. 1971. *A Theory of Justice*. Cambridge, MA: Belknap Press.
———. 1995. "Reply to Habermas." *Journal of Philosophy* 92: 132-180. Reprinted in *Political Liberalism*, edited by John Rawls, 372-434. New York: Columbia University Press.
———. 1996. *Political Liberalism*. New York: Columbia University Press.
Ray, Raka, and A. C. Korteweg. 1999. "Women's Movements in the Third World: Identity, Mobilization, and Autonomy." *Annual Review of Sociology* 25: 47-71.
Razack, Sherene. 1998. *Looking White People in the Eye: Gender, Race, and Culture in Courtrooms and Classrooms*. Toronto: University of Toronto Press.
Read, Jen'nan Ghazal. 2007. "Introduction: The Politics of Veiling in Comparative Perspective." *Sociology of Religion* 68: 231-236.

Reading, R., S. Bissell, J. Goldhagen, J. Harwin, J. Masson, S. Moynihan, N. Parton, M. S. Pais, J. Thoburn, and E. Webb. 2009. "Promotion of Children's Rights and Prevention of Child Maltreatment." *The Lancet* 373: 322-343.
Readings, Bill. 1996. *The University in Ruins.* Cambridge, MA: Harvard University Press.
Reardon, Betty. 1985. *Sexism and the War System.* New York: Teachers College Press.
Redwood, Loren K. 2008. "Strong-Arming Exploitable Labor: The State and Immigrant Workers in the Post-Katrina Gulf Coast." *Social Justice* 35: 33-50.
Reed, Michael. 1985. *Redirections in Organizational Analysis.* London: Tavistock.
Regan, Tom. 2004. *The Case for Animal Rights.* Berkeley: University of California Press.
Regnerus, Mark D. 2007. *Forbidden Fruit: Sex and Religion in the Lives of American Teenagers.* New York: Oxford University Press.
Reilly, Niamh. 2007. "Cosmopolitan Feminism and Human Rights." *Hypatia* 22: 180-198.
———. 2009. *Women's Human Rights: Seeking Gender Justice in a Globalizing Age.* Cambridge, MA: Polity Press.
Reimann, Kim. 2006. "A View from the Top: International Politics, Norms and the Worldwide Growth of NGOs." *International Studies Quarterly* 50: 45-67.
Reinarman, Craig, and Harry Levine. 1997. *Crack in America: Demon Drugs and Social Justice.* Berkeley: University of California Press.
Reisch, Michael. 2009. "Social Workers, Unions, and Low Wage Workers: A Historical Perspective." *Journal of Community Practice* 17: 50-72.
Renteln, Alison Dundes. 1985. "The Unanswered Challenge of Relativism and the Consequences for Human Rights." *Human Rights Quarterly* 7, no. 4: 514-540.
———. 1988. "The Concept of Human Rights." *Anthropos* 83: 343-364.
Rheaume, J. 2008. "Clinical Sociology in Quebec: When Europe Meets America." In *International Clinical Sociology*, edited by J. M. Fritz, 36-53. New York: Springer.
———. 2010. Personal communication with J. M. Fritz. December 16.
Rhoades, Lawrence. 1981. "A History of the American Sociological Association, 1905-1980." American Sociological Association. www.asanet.org/about/Rhoades_Chapter3.cfm (accessed December 10, 2011).
Rice, James. 2009. "The Transnational Organization of Production and Uneven Environmental Degradation and Change in the World Economy." *International Journal of Comparative Sociology* 50, no. 3/4: 215-236.
Rich, Adrienne. 1980. "Compulsory Heterosexuality." In *Powers of Desire: The Politics of Sexuality*, edited by Ann Snitow, Christine Stansell, and Sharon Thompson, 177-205. New York: Monthly Review Press.
Rich, Michael, and Richard Chalfen. 1999. "Showing and Telling Asthma: Children Teaching Physicians with Visual Narratives." *Visual Sociology* 14: 51-71.
Richards, Patricia. 2005. "The Politics of Gender, Human Rights, and Being Indigenous in Chile." *Gender and Society* 19: 199-220.
Richardson, L., and T. Brown. 2011. "Intersectionality of Race, Gender and Age in Hypertension Trajectories across the Life Course." Presented at the eighty-first annual meeting of the Eastern Sociological Society, Philadelphia, Pennsylvania, February.
Ridge, D., C. Emslie, and A. White. 2011. "Understanding How Men Experience, Express and Cope with Mental Distress: Where Next?" *Sociology of Health and Illness* 33: 145-159.
Rieker, Patricia P., Chloe E. Bird, and Martha E. Lang. 2010. "Understanding Gender and Health." In *Handbook of Medical Sociology*, edited by Chloe Bird, Peter Conrad, Allen Fremont, and Stephan Timmermans, 52-74. 6th ed. Nashville, TN: Vanderbilt University Press.
Right to the City Alliance. 2011. http://www.righttothecity.org (accessed May 28, 2011).
Riley, J. 2004. "Some Reflections on Gender Mainstreaming and Intersectionality." *Development Bulletin* 64: 82-86.
Riley, M. W., M. E. Johnson, and A. Foner. 1972. *Aging and Society.* Vol. 3: *A Sociology of Age Stratification.* New York: Russell Sage Foundation.
Riley, M. W., R. L. Kahn, and A. Foner. 1994. *Age and Structural Lag: Society's Failure to Provide Meaningful Opportunities in Work, Family, and Leisure.* New York: Wiley.
Riley, M. W., and J. W. Riley Jr. 1994. "Age Integration and the Lives of Older People." *Gerontologist* 3-4, no. 1: 110-115.
Ringelheim, Julie. 2011. "Ethnic Categories and European Human Rights Law." *Ethnic and Racial Studies* 34: 1682-1696.
Rios, Victor M. 2010. "Navigating the Thin Line between Education and Incarceration: An Action Research Case Study on Gang-Associated Latino Youth." *Journal of Education for Students Placed At-Risk* 15, no. 1-2: 200-212.

Risse, Thomas. 2000. "The Power of Norms versus the Norms of Power: Transnational Civil Society and Human Rights." In *The Third Force: The Rise of Transnational Civil Society*, edited by A. Florini, N. Kokusai, K. Senta, and Carnegie Endowment for International Peace. Tokyo: Japan Center for International Exchange, Washington Carnegie Endowment for International Peace, and Brookings Institution Press (distributor).

Risse, Thomas, S. C. Ropp, and K. Sikkink, eds. 1999. *The Power of Human Rights: International Norms and Domestic Change*. Cambridge, UK: Cambridge University Press.

Rist, Ray. 1970. "Student Social Class and Teacher Expectations: The Self-Fulfilling Prophecy in Ghetto Education." *Harvard Educational Review* 40: 411–451.

———. 1973. *The Urban School: Factory for Failure*. Cambridge, MA: MIT Press.

———. 1977. "On Understanding the Processes of Schooling: The Contributions of Labeling Theory." In *Power and Ideology in Education*, edited by Jerome Karabel and A. H. Halsey, 292–305. New York: Oxford University Press.

Rivera Vargas, Maria Isabel. 2010. "Government Influence and Foreign Direct Investment: Organizational Learning in an Electronics Cluster." *Critical Sociology* 36, no. 4: 537–553.

Robert, Stephanie A., and James S. House. 2000. "Socioeconomic Inequalities in Health: An Enduring Sociological Problem." In *Handbook of Medical Sociology*, edited by C. E. Bird, P. Conrad, and A. M. Fremont, 79–97. 5th ed. Upper Saddle River, NJ: Prentice Hall.

Roberts, Christopher N. J. Forthcoming. Untitled Work. Cambridge, UK: Cambridge University Press.

Roberts, Dorothy. 2010. "The Social Immorality of Health in the Gene Age: Race, Disability, and Inequality." In *Against Health: How Health Became the New Morality*, edited by Jonathan M. Metzl and Anna Kirkland, 61–71. New York: New York University Press.

Robertson, Roland. 1992. *Globalization: Social Theory and Global Culture*. London: Sage.

Robinson, Dawn T., Christabel L. Rogalin, and Lynn Smith-Lovin. 2004. "Physiological Measures of Theoretical Concepts: Some Ideas for Linking Deflection and Emotion to Physical Responses during Interaction." *Advances in Group Processes* 21: 77–115.

Rodan, Garry. 2006. "Singapore in 2005: 'Vibrant and Cosmopolitan' without Political Pluralism." *Asian Survey* 46: 180–186.

Rodríguez, Havidán, Rogelio Sáenz, and Cecilia Menjívar, eds. 2008. *Latina/os in the United States: Changing the Face of América*. New York: Springer.

Rodríguez, Nestor. 2008. "Theoretical and Methodological Issues of Latina/o Research." In *Latina/os in the United States: Changing the Face of América*, edited by H. Rodríguez, R. Sáenz, and C. Menjívar, 3–15. New York: Springer.

Roediger, D. R. 1991. *Wages of Whiteness: Race and the Making of the American Working Class*. London: Verso.

Roethlisberger, F. J., and W. J. Dickson. 1947. *Management and the Worker*. Cambridge, MA: Harvard University Press.

Rogers, Leslie. 1998. *Mind of Their Own: Thinking and Awareness in Animals*. Boulder, CO: Westview Press.

Rogoff, Barbara. 2003. *The Cultural Name of Human Development*. Oxford: Oxford University Press.

Rojas, Fabio. 2007. *From Black Power to Black Studies: How a Radical Social Movement Became an Academic Discipline*. Baltimore: Johns Hopkins University Press.

Rokeach, Milton. 1973. *The Nature of Human Values*. New York: The Free Press.

Romero, Mary. 1988. "Sisterhood and Domestic Service: Race, Class and Gender in the Mistress-Maid Relationship." *Humanity and Society* 12: 318–346.

———. 2006. "Racial Profiling and Immigration Law Enforcement: Rounding Up of Usual Suspects in the Latino Community." *Critical Sociology* 32: 449–475.

———. 2011. "Are Your Papers in Order? Racial Profiling, Vigilantes and 'America's Toughest Sheriff.'" *Harvard Latino Law Review* 14: 337–357.

Romero-Ortuno, Roman. 2004. "Access to Health Care for Illegal Immigrants in the EU: Should We Be Concerned?" *European Journal of Health Law* 11: 245–272.

Roschelle, Anne R., Jennifer Turpin, and Robert Elias. 2000. "Who Learns from Service Learning." *American Behavioral Scientist* 43: 839–847.

Rosenfield, S. 1999. "Gender and Mental Health: Do Women Have More Psychopathology, Men More, or Both the Same (and Why)?" In *Handbook for the Study of Mental Health*, edited by A. Horwitz and T. Scheid, 348–361. Cambridge, UK: Cambridge University Press.

Rosenhan, D. L. 1991. "On Being Sane in Insane Places." In *Down to Earth Sociology*, edited by J. M. Henslin, 294–307. New York: The Free Press.

Ross, J. S. Robert. 1991. "At the Center and the Edge: Notes on a Life in and out of Sociology and the New Left." In *Radical Sociologists and the Movement: Experiences, Lessons, and Legacies*, edited by Martin Oppenheimer, Martin J. Murray, and Rhonda F. Levine, 197–215. Philadelphia: Temple University Press.

Ross, Lauren. 2009. "Contradictions of Power, Sexuality, and Consent: An Institutional Ethnography of the Practice of Male Neonatal Circumcision." PhD diss., University of Connecticut, Storrs.
Rossi, Alice S. 1970. "Status of Women in Graduate Departments of Sociology, 1968-1969." *American Sociologist* (February): 1-12.
———. 1983. "Beyond the Gender Gap: Women's Bid for Political Power." *Social Science Quarterly* 64: 718-733.
———. 1984. "Gender and Parenthood." *American Sociological Review* 49, no. 1: 1-19.
Rossi, Federico M. 2009. "Youth Political Participation: Is This the End of Generational Cleavage?" *International Sociology* 24, no. 4: 467-497.
Roth, Brad. 2004. "Retrieving Marx for the Human Rights Project." *Leiden Journal of International Law* 17: 31-66.
Roth, Wendy D., and Gerhard Sonnert. 2011. "The Costs and Benefits of 'Red-Tape': Anti-Bureaucratic Structure and Gender Inequity in a Science Research Organization." *Social Studies of Science*. January 17. http://sss.sagepub.com/content/early/2011/01/15/0306312710391494 (accessed July 19, 2012).
Rothschild, Joyce. 1979. "The Collectivist Organization: An Alternative to Rational-Bureaucratic Models." *American Sociological Review* 44: 509-527.
Rowe, John, Lisa Berkman, Robert Binstock, Axel Boersch-Supan, John Cacioppo, Laura Carstensen, Linda Fried, Dana Goldman, James Jackson, Matin Kohli, Jay Olshansky, and John Rother. 2010. "Policies and Politics for an Aging America." *Contexts* 9, no. 1: 22-27.
Rowland, Robyn. 1995. "Symposium: Human Rights and the Sociological Project (Human Rights Discourse and Women: Challenging the Rhetoric with Reality)." *Australian and New Zealand Journal of Sociology* 31: 8-25.
Roy, William G. 1997. *Socializing Capital: The Rise of the Large Industrial Corporation in America*. Princeton, NJ: Princeton University Press.
Rubin, Gayle. 1984. "Thinking Sex: Notes for a Radical Theory of the Politics of Sexuality." In *Pleasure and Danger: Exploring Female Sexuality*, edited by Carol Vance, 267-319. London: Pandora Press.
Rumbaut, Rubén. 1994. "Origins and Destinies: Immigration to the United States since World War II." *Sociological Forum* 9: 583-621.
Rumbaut, Rubén, and Walter A. Ewing. 2007. "The Myth of Immigrant Criminality." Border Battles. May 23. http://borderbattles.ssrc.org/Rumbault_Ewing/index.html (accessed November 9, 2010).
Rumbaut, Rubén, and Alejandro Portes. 2001. *Ethnicities: Children of Immigrants in America*. Berkeley: University of California Press.
Rummel, R. J. 1994. *Death by Government*. New Brunswick, NJ: Transaction.
Rupp, Leila J. 1997. *Worlds of Women: The Making of an International Women's Movement*. Princeton, NJ: Princeton University Press.
———. 2009. *Sapphistries: A Global History of Love between Women*. New York: New York University Press.
Ruppel, Oliver C. 2009. "Third Generation Human Rights and the Protection of the Environment in Namibia." Konrad-Adenauer-Stiftung. http://www.kas.de/namibia/en/publications/16045 (accessed December 2, 2010).
Russon, John. 1997. *The Self and Its Body in Hegel's Phenomenology of Spirit*. Toronto: University of Toronto Press.
Rutherford, Markella B. 2011. *Adult Supervision Required*. Piscataway, NJ: Rutgers University Press.
Rytina, Nancy, Michael Hoefer, and Bryan Baker. 2010. "Estimates of the Unauthorized Immigrant Population Residing in the United States: January 2009." Department of Homeland Security. January. http://www.dhs.gov/xlibrary/assets/statistics/publications/ois_ill_pe_2009.pdf (accessed October 12, 2010).
Sabel, Charles, and Jonathan Zeitlin. 1997. *World of Possibilities: Flexibility and Mass Production in Western Industrialization*. Cambridge, UK: Cambridge University Press.
Sachs, A. 1996. "Upholding Human Rights and Environmental Justice." In *State of the World*, edited by Lester Brown, 133-151. New York: W. W. Norton.
Sacks, Harvey. 1972a. "An Initial Investigation of the Usability of Conversational Data for Doing Sociology." In *Studies in Social Interaction*, edited by David Sudnow, 31-74. New York: The Free Press.
———. 1972b. "On the Analyzability of Stories by Children." In *Directions in Sociolinguistics: The Ethnography of Communication*, edited by John J. Gumperz and Dell Hymes, 325-345. New York: Holt, Rinehart and Winston.
———. 1984. "Notes on Methodology." In *Structures of Social Action: Studies in Conversation Analysis*, edited by J. Maxwell Atkinson and John Heritage, 21-27. Cambridge, UK: Cambridge University Press; Paris: Les Éditions de la Maison des Sciences de l'Homme.
———. 1992. *Lectures on Conversation*, edited by Gail Jefferson with introductions by Emanuel A. Schegloff. 2 vols. Oxford: Basil Blackwell.

Sacks, Harvey, Emanuel A. Schegloff, and Gail Jefferson. 1974. "A Simplest Systematics for the Organization of Turn Taking for Conversation." *Language* 50, no. 4: 696-735.
Sadovnik, A. R., ed. 2007. *Sociology of Education: A Critical Reader.* New York: Routledge.
Sáenz, Rogelio. 2010a. "Latinos in the United States 2010." Population Reference Bureau. http://www.prb.org/pdf10/latinos-update2010.pdf (accessed July 19, 2012).
———. 2010b. "Latinos, Whites, and the Shifting Demography of Arizona." Population Reference Bureau. http://www.prb.org/Articles/2010/usarizonalatinos.aspx (accessed March 24, 2011).
Sáenz, Rogelio, Cynthia M. Cready, and Maria Cristina Morales. 2007. "Adios Aztlan: Mexican American Outmigration from the Southwest." In *The Sociology of Spatial Inequality*, edited by L. Lobao, G. Hooks, and A. Tickamyer, 189-214. Albany: State University of New York Press.
Sáenz, Rogelio, Cecilia Menjívar, and San Juanita Edilia Garcia. 2011. "Arizona's SB 1070: Setting Conditions for Violations of Human Rights Here and Beyond." In *Sociology and Human Rights: A Bill of Rights for the Twenty-First Century*, edited by J. Blau and M. Frezzo. Newbury Park, CA: Pine Forge Press.
Sáenz, Rogelio, Maria Cristina Morales, and Maria Isabel Ayala. 2004. "United States: Immigration to the Melting Pot of the Americas." In *Migration and Immigration: A Global View*, edited by M. I. Toro-Morn and M. Alicea, 211-232. Westport, CT: Greenwood Press.
Sáenz, Rogelio, and Lorena Murga. 2011. *Latino Issues: A Reference Handbook.* Santa Barbara, CA: ABC-CLIO.
Safran, S. P. 2001. "Movie Images of Disability and War: Framing History and Political Ideology." *Remedial and Special Education* 22: 223-232.
Said, Edward W. 1979. *Orientalism.* 1st ed. Vintage.
Saito, Leland T. 1998. *Race and Politics: Asian Americans, Latinos, and Whites in a Los Angeles Suburb.* Chicago: University of Illinois Press.
———. 2009. *The Politics of Exclusion: The Failure of Race-Neutral Policies in Urban America.* Palo Alto, CA: Stanford University Press.
Salvo, J. J., M. G. Powers, and R. S. Cooney. 1992. "Contraceptive Use and Sterilization among Puerto Rican Women." *Family Planning Perspectives* 24, no. 5: 219-223.
Salzinger, Leslie. 2005. *Genders in Production: Making Workers in Mexico's Global Factories.* Berkeley: University of California Press.
Sampson, Robert J., and Stephen W. Raudenbush. 1999. "Systematic Social Observation of Public Spaces: A New Look at Disorder in Urban Neighborhoods." *American Journal of Sociology* 105: 603-651.
Sampson, Robert J., Patrick Sharkey, and Stephen W. Raudenbush. 2008. "Durable Effects of Concentrated Disadvantage on Verbal Ability among African-American Children." *Proceedings of the National Academy of Sciences of the United States of America* 105, no. 3: 845-852.
Sampson, Robert J., and William J. Wilson. 1995. "Toward a Theory of Race, Crime, and Urban Inequality." In *Crime and Inequality*, edited by John Hagan and Ruth D. Peterson, 37-54. Stanford, CA: Stanford University Press.
San Miguel, Guadalupe. 2005. *Brown, Not White: School Integration and the Chicano Movement in Houston.* College Station: Texas A&M University Press.
Sanbonmatsu, John, ed. 2011. *Critical Theory and Animal Liberation.* Lanham, MD: Rowman & Littlefield.
Sanchez-Jankowski, Martin. 2008. *Cracks in the Pavement: Social Change and Resilience in Poor Neighborhoods.* Berkeley: University of California Press.
Sanders, Joseph. 1990. "The Interplay of Micro and Macro Processes in the Longitudinal Study of Courts: Beyond the Durkheimian Tradition." *Law and Society Review* 24, no. 2: 241-256.
Sanderson, Matthew R., and Jeffrey D. Kentor. 2008. "Foreign Direct Investment and International Migration: A Cross-National Analysis of Less-Developed Countries, 1985-2000." *International Sociology* 23, no. 4: 514-539.
Sanderson, Stephen K. 2001. *The Evolution of Human Sociality.* Lanham, MD: Rowman & Littlefield.
———. 2007. "Marvin Harris, Meet Charles Darwin: A Critical Evaluation and Theoretical Extension of Cultural Materialism." In *Studying Societies and Cultures: Marvin Harris's Cultural Materialism and Its Legacy*, edited by Lawrence A. Kuznar and Stephen K. Sanderson, 194-228. Boulder, CO: Paradigm Publishers.
———. 2008. "Adaptation, Evolution, and Religion." *Religion* 38: 141-156.
Sanford, Victoria. 2003. *Buried Secrets: Truth and Human Rights in Guatemala.* New York: Palgrave Macmillan.
Santos, B. S. 2009. "A Non-Occidentalist West? Learned Ignorance and Ecology of Knowledge." *Theory, Culture and Society* 26, no. 7-8: 103-125.
Sarbin, T. R., and E. Keen. 1998. "Classifying Mental Disorders: Nontraditional Approaches." In *Encyclopedia of Mental Health*, edited by H. S. Friedman, 2:461-473. San Diego: Academic Press.

Sarver, Joshua H., Susan W. Hinze, Rita K. Cydulka, and David W. Baker. 2003. "Racial/Ethnic Disparities in Emergency Department Analgesic Prescription." *American Journal of Public Health* 93, no. 12: 2067-2073.
Sassen, Saskia, ed. 1989. "America's 'Immigration Problem.'" *World Policy* 6: 811-832.
———. 1999. *Globalization and Its Discontents: Essays on the New Mobility of People and Money.* New York: The New Press.
———. 2001. *The Global City: New York, London, Tokyo.* Updated ed. Princeton, NJ: Princeton University Press.
———. 2006a. *Cities in a World Economy.* 3rd ed. Boulder, CO: Pine Forge Press.
———. 2006b. *Territory, Authority, Rights: From Medieval to Global Assemblages.* Princeton, NJ: Princeton University Press.
———, ed. 2007. *Deciphering the Global: Its Spaces, Scales and Subjects.* New York: Routledge.
Satterthwaite, Margaret L. 2005. "Crossing Borders, Claiming Rights: Using Human Rights Law to Empower Women Migrant Workers." *Yale Human Rights and Development Law Journal* 8: 1-66.
Savage, Joanne, and Bryan J. Vila. 2003. "Human Ecology, Crime, and Crime Control: Linking Individual Behavior and Aggregate Crime." *Social Biology* 50: 77-101.
Savelsberg, Joachim J. 2010. *Crime and Human Rights: Criminology of Genocide and Atrocities.* London: Sage.
Savelsberg, Joachim J., and Ryan D. King. 2007. "Law and Collective Memory." *Annual Review of Law and Social Science* 3: 189-211.
———. 2011. *American Memories: Atrocities and the Law.* New York: Russell Sage.
Scambler, Graham. 2004. *Medical Sociology, Major Themes in Health and Social Welfare.* New York: Taylor and Francis.
Scarritt, James R. 1985. "Socialist States and Human Rights Measurement in Africa." *Africa Today* 32, no. 1/2: 25-36.
Scheff, Thomas J. 1988. "Shame and Conformity: The Deference-Emotion System." *American Sociological Review* 53: 395-406.
———. 1990a. *Microsociology: Discourse, Emotion, and Social Structure.* Chicago: University of Chicago Press.
———. 1990b. "Socialization of Emotions: Pride and Shame as Causal Agents." In *Research Agendas in the Sociology of Emotions,* edited by T. D. Kemper, 281-304. Albany: State University of New York Press.
———. 1994. *Bloody Revenge: Emotions, Nationalism, and War.* Boulder, CO: Westview.
———. 1999. *Being Mentally Ill: A Sociological Theory.* 3rd ed. New York: Aldine De Gruyter.
———. 2000. "Shame and the Social Bond: A Sociological Theory." *Sociological Theory* 18, no. 1: 84-99.
Scheff, Thomas J., and Suzanne M. Retzinger. 1991. *Emotions and Violence: Shame and Rage in Destructive Conflicts.* Lexington, MA: Lexington Books.
Schegloff, Emanuel A. 2007a. "A Tutorial on Membership Categorization." *Journal of Pragmatics* 39: 462-482.
———. 2007b. "Categories in Action: Person-Reference and Membership Categorization." *Discourse Studies* 9: 433-461.
———. 2007c. *Sequence Organization in Interaction: A Primer in Sequential Analysis.* Vol. 1. Cambridge, UK: Cambridge University Press.
Schegloff, Emanuel A., Gail Jefferson, and Harvey Sacks. 1977. "The Preference for Self-Correction in the Organization of Repair in Conversation." *Language* 53, no. 2: 361-382.
Scheid, T. L. 2005. "Stigma as a Barrier to Employment: Mental Disability and the Americans with Disabilities Act." *International Journal of Law and Psychiatry* 28: 670-690.
Schenkein, Jim. 1978. "Sketch of an Analytic Mentality for the Study of Conversational Interaction." In *Studies in the Organization of Conversational Interaction,* edited by Jim Schenkein, 1-6. New York: Academic.
Schnittker, Jason. 2008. "Happiness and Success: Genes, Families, and the Psychological Effects of Socioeconomic Position and Social Support." *American Journal of Sociology* 114: S233-S259.
Schofer, Evan, and John W. Meyer. 2005. "The Worldwide Expansion of Higher Education in the Twentieth Century." *American Sociological Review* 70: 898-920.
Schrag, Peter. 2002. "A Quagmire for Our Time: The War on Drugs." *Journal of Public Health Policy* 23, no. 3: 286-298.
Schrecker, Ellen. 1986. *No Ivory Tower: McCarthyism and the Universities.* Oxford: Oxford University Press.
Schulz, William F. 2009. *Power of Justice: Applying International Human Rights Standards to American Domestic Practices.* Washington, DC: Center for American Progress.
Schulze, B., and M. C. Angermeyer. 2003. "Subjective Experiences of Stigma: Schizophrenic Patients, Their Relatives and Mental Health Professionals." *Social Science and Medicine* 56: 299-312.
Schwalbe, Michael L., and Douglas Mason-Schrock. 1996. "Identity Work as Group Process." In *Advances in Group Processes,* edited by Barry Markovsky, Michael J. Lovaglia, and Robin Simon, 13:113-147. Greenwich, CT: JAI Press.

Schwartz, Pepper, and Virginia Rutter. 1998. *The Gender of Sexuality.* Lanham, MD: AltaMira Press.
Schwartz, Shalom H. 1992. "Universals in the Content and Structure of Values: Theoretical Advances and Empirical Tests in 20 Countries." In *Advances in Experimental Social Psychology,* edited by Mark P. Zanna, 24: 1-65. San Diego: Academic Press.
———. 2006. "Basic Human Values: Theory, Measurement, and Applications." *Revue Française de Sociologie* 47: 249-288.
Schwartz, Shalom H., and Galit Sagie. 2000. "Value Consensus and Importance: A Cross-National Study." *Journal of Cross-Cultural Psychology* 31, no. 4: 465-497.
Schwed, Uri, and Peter Bearman. 2010. "The Temporal Structure of Scientific Consensus Formation." *American Sociological Review* 75: 817-840.
Schwerner, Cassie. 2005. "Building the Movement for Education Equity." In *Rhyming Hope and History: Activists, Academics, and Social Movement Scholarship,* edited by David Croteau, William Hoynes, and Charlotte Ryan, 157-175. Minneapolis: University of Minnesota Press.
Scimecca, Joseph A. 1976. "Paying Homage to the Father: C. Wright Mills and Radical Sociology." *Sociological Quarterly* 17: 180-196.
Scott, J. 2000. "Rational Choice Theory." In *Understanding Contemporary Society: Theories of the Present,* edited by G. Browning, A. Halcli, and F. Webster, 126-138. London: Sage.
Scott, W. Richard. 1998. *Organizations: Rational, Natural and Open Systems.* 4th ed. New Brunswick, NJ: Prentice Hall.
———. 2001. *Institutions and Organizations.* 2nd ed. Thousand Oaks, CA: Sage.
Scott, Tony. 2004. "Teaching the Ideology of Assessment." *Radical Teacher* 71: 30-37.
Scruton, Roger. 2000. *Animal Rights and Wrongs.* London: Claridge Press.
Scull, A. T. 1984. *Decarceration: Community Treatment and the Deviant–a Radical View.* Cambridge, UK: Polity Press.
Segura, Denise. 1989. "Chicana and Mexican Immigrant Women at Work: The Impact of Class, Race, and Gender on Occupational Mobility." *Gender and Society* 3: 37-52.
Seiwert, Hubert. 1999. "The German Enquete Commission on Sects: Political Conflicts and Compromises." *Social Justice Research* 12: 323-340.
———. 2003. "Freedom and Control in the Unified Germany: Governmental Approaches to Alternative Religions since 1989." *Sociology of Religion* 64: 367-375.
Sekulic, D., G. Massey, and R. Hodson. 2006. "Ethnic Intolerance and Ethnic Conflict in the Dissolution of Yugoslavia." *Ethnic and Racial Studies* 29: 797-827.
Selmi, Patrick, and Richard Hunter. 2001. "Beyond the Rank and File Movement: Mary Van Kleeck and Social Work Radicalism in the Great Depression, 1931-1942." *Journal of Sociology and Social Welfare* 28: 75-100.
Seltzer, William, and Margo Anderson. 2002. "Using Population Data Systems to Target Vulnerable Population Subgroups and Individuals: Issues and Incidents." In *Statistical Methods for Human Rights,* edited by Jana Asher, David Banks, and Fritz J. Scheuren, 273ff. New York: Springer.
Selznick, Philip. 1947. *TVA and the Grass Roots.* Berkeley and Los Angeles: University of California Press.
———. 1957. *Leadership in Administration: A Sociological Interpretation.* New York: Harper and Row.
———. 1959. "The Sociology of the Law." In *Sociology Today: Problems and Prospects,* edited by Robert K. Merton, Leonard Broom, and Leonard Cottrell Jr., 115-127. New York: Basic Books.
Sen, Amartya. 1981. *Poverty and Famines: An Essay on Entitlement and Deprivation.* New York: Oxford University Press.
———. 1992. *Inequality Reexamined.* New York: Russell Sage Foundation.
———. 1999a. "Democracy as a Universal Value." *Journal of Democracy* 10: 3-17.
———. 1999b. *Development as Freedom.* New York: Random House.
———. 2006. *Identity and Violence: The Illusion of Destiny.* New York: W. W. Norton and Co.
Sengupta, Amit. 2003. "Health in the Age of Globalization." *Social Scientist* 31, no. 11-12: 66-85.
Serrano, P. A., and L. Magnusson, eds. 2007. *Reshaping Welfare States and Activation Regimes in Europe.* Brussels and New York: PIE-Peter Lang.
Serrano, Susan K., and Dale Minami. 2003. "*Korematsu vs. United States*: A 'Constant Caution' in a Time of Crisis." *Asian Law Journal* 10: 37-50.
Settersten, R. A., Jr. 2005. "Linking the Two Ends of Life: What Gerontology Can Learn from Childhood Studies." *Journals of Gerontology, Series B: Psychological Sciences* 60B, no. 4: 173-180.
Settersten, R. A., Jr., and J. L. Angel, eds. 2011. *Handbook of Sociology of Aging.* New York: Springer.
Settersten, R. A., Jr., and G. Hagestad. 1996a. "What's the Latest? Cultural Age Deadlines for Family Transitions." *Gerontologist* 36, no. 2: 178-188.
———. 1996b. "What's the Latest II: Cultural Age Deadlines for Educational and Work Transitions." *Gerontologist* 36, no. 5: 602-613.

Settersten, Richard, and Barbara E. Ray. 2010. *Not Quite Adults: Why 20-Somethings Are Choosing a Slower Path to Adulthood, and Why It's Good for Everyone*. New York: Bantam.
Sevigny, R. 2010. Personal communication with J. M. Fritz. December 14.
Shah, Natubhai. 1998. *Jainism: The World of Conquerors*. Sussex, UK: Sussex Academic Press.
Shakespeare, T., and N. Watson. 2001. "The Social Model of Disability: An Outdated Ideology?" In *Exploring Theories and Expanding Methodologies: Where We Are and Where We Need to Go*, edited by S. N. Barnartt and B. M. Altman, 2:9-28. Oxford, UK: Elsevier Science.
Shakespeare, Tom. 2006. *Disability Rights and Wrongs*. New York: Routledge.
Shanahan, Michael J., Shawn Bauldry, and Jason Freeman. 2010. "Beyond Mendel's Ghost." *Contexts* 9: 34-39.
Shanahan, Michael J., Stephen Vaisey, Lance D. Erickson, and Andrew Smolen. 2008. "Environmental Contingencies and Genetic Propensities: Social Capital, Educational Continuation, and Dopamine Receptor Gene DRD2." *American Journal of Sociology* 114: S260-S286.
Shanks, Cheryl, Harold K. Jacobson, and Jeffrey H. Kaplan. 1996. "Inertia and Change in the Constellation of International Governmental Organizations, 1981-1992." *International Organization* 50: 593-627.
Sharrock, W. W. 1980. "The Possibility of Social Change." In *The Ignorance of Social Intervention*, edited by D. C. Anderson, 117-133. London: Croom Helm.
———. 2001. "Fundamentals of Ethnomethodology." In *Handbook of Social Theory*, edited by George Ritzer and Barry Smart, 250-259. London: Sage.
Sharrock, W. W., and D. R. Watson. 1988. "Autonomy among Social Theories: The Incarnation of Social Structures." In *Actions and Structure: Research Methods and Social Theory*, edited by Nigel Fielding, 56-77. London: Sage.
Sharrock, Wes, and Bob Anderson. 1991. "Epistemology: Professional Skepticism." In *Ethnomethodology and the Human Sciences*, edited by Graham Button, 51-76. Cambridge, UK: Cambridge University Press.
Sharrock, Wes, and Graham Button. 1991. "The Social Actor: Social Action in Real Time." In *Ethnomethodology and the Human Sciences*, edited by Graham Button, 137-175. Cambridge, UK: Cambridge University Press.
Shaw, Martin. 2000. *The Theory of the Global State: Globality as Unfinished Revolution*. Oxford: Cambridge University Press.
Shell-Duncan, B. 2008. "From Health to Human Rights: Female Genital Cutting and the Politics of Intervention." *American Anthropologist* 110: 225-236.
Shergill, S. S., D. Barker, and M. Greenberg. 1998. "Communication of Psychiatric Diagnosis." *Social Psychiatry and Psychiatric Epidemiology* 33: 32-38.
Shevelow, Kathryn. 2008. *For the Love of Animals: The Rise of the Animal Protection Movement*. New York: Henry Holt and Co.
Shields, Joseph, Kirk M. Broome, Peter J. Delany, Bennett W. Fletcher, and Patrick M. Flynn. 2007. "Religion and Substance Abuse Treatment: Individual and Program Effects." *Journal for the Scientific Study of Religion* 46, no. 3: 355-371.
Shils, Edward. 1968. "Deference." In *Social Stratification*, edited by John A. Jackson, 104-132. Cambridge, UK: Cambridge University Press.
———. 1975. *Center and Periphery: Essays in Macrosociology*. Chicago: University of Chicago Press.
Shin, Y., and S. Raudenbush. 2011. "The Causal Effect of Class Size on Academic Achievement: Multivariate Instrumental Variable Estimators with Data Missing at Random." *Journal of Educational and Behavioral Statistics* 34, no. 2: 154-185.
Shirazi, Farid, Ojelanki Ngwenyama, and Olga Morawczynski. 2010. "ICT Expansion and the Digital Divide in Democratic Freedoms: An Analysis of the Impact of ICT Expansion, Education and ICT Filtering on Democracy." *Telematics and Informatics* 27: 21-31.
Shiva, Vandana. 1997. *Biopiracy: The Plunder of Nature and Knowledge*. Cambridge, MA: South End Press.
Shor, Eran. 2008. "Conflict, Terrorism, and the Socialization of Human Rights Norms: The Spiral Model Revisited." *Social Problems* 55, no. 1: 117-138.
Shor, Ira. 1992. *Empowering Education: Critical Teaching for Social Change*. Portsmouth, NH: Heinemann.
Shorter, Edward. 1977. *The Making of the Modern Family*. New York: Basic Books.
Shostak, Sara, and Jeremy Freese. 2010. "Gene-Environment Interaction and Medical Sociology." In *Handbook of Medical Sociology*, edited by Chloe Bird, Peter Conrad, Allen Fremont, and Stephan Timmermans, 418-434. 6th ed. Nashville, TN: Vanderbilt University Press.
Shukin, Sharon. 2009. *Animal Capital: Rendering Life in Biopolitical Times*. Minneapolis: University of Minnesota Press.
Shupe, Anson D. 1998. *Wolves within the Fold: Religious Leadership and Abuses of Power*. New Brunswick, NJ: Rutgers University Press.

———. 2007. *Spoils of the Kingdom: Clergy Misconduct and Religious Community.* Urbana: University of Illinois Press.
Shura, Robin, Rebecca A. Siders, and Dale Dannefer. 2010. "Culture Change in Long-Term Care: Participatory Action Research and the Role of the Resident." *Gerontologist* 51, no. 2: 212–225.
Shuval, Judith T. 2001. "Migration, Health and Stress." In *The Blackwell Companion to Medical Sociology*, edited by W. Cockerham, 126–143. Oxford, UK: Blackwell.
Shwed, U., and Peter Bearman. 2010. "The Temporal Structure of Scientific Consensus Formation." *American Sociological Review* 75, no. 6: 817–840.
Sibley, David. 1995a. "Gender, Science, Politics and Geographies of the City." *Gender, Place and Culture: A Journal of Feminist Geography* 2: 37–50.
———. 1995b. "Women's Research on Chicago in the Early 20th Century." *Women and Environments* 14, no. 2: 6–8.
SIECUS. 1917. *Der Krieg und die Geistigen Entscheidungen.* Munich: Duncker and Humblot.
———. 1950. *The Sociology of Georg Simmel.* Translated by Kurt H. Wolff. New York: The Free Press.
———. 1955. *Conflict and the Web of Group Affiliations.* Glencoe, IL: The Free Press.
———. 2010. "Fact Sheet: State by State Decisions: The Personal Responsibility Education Program and Title V Abstinence-Only Program." http://www.siecus.org/index.cfm?fuseaction=Page.ViewPage&PageID=1272 (accessed September 5, 2012).
Sienkiewicz, Dorota. 2010. "Access to Health Services in Europe." *European Social Watch Report* 2010: 17–20.
Sigmon, Robert. 1990. "Service Learning: Three Principles." In *Combining Service and Learning: A Resource Book for Community and Public Service*, edited by Jane Kendall and Associates, 1: 56–64. Raleigh, NC: National Society for Internships and Experiential Education.
Sikkink, Kathryn. 2011. *Justice Cascade.* New York: Knopf.
Sikkink, Kathryn, and Hunjoon Kim. 2009. "Explaining the Deterrence Effect of Human Rights Prosecutions in Transitional Countries." *International Studies Quarterly*.
Silbey, Susan. 2005. "Everyday Life and the Constitution of Legality." In *The Blackwell Companion to the Sociology of Culture*, edited by Mark D. Jacobs and Nancy Weiss Hanrahan, 332–345. Malden, MA: Blackwell.
Silvers, A. 1998a. "Formal Justice." In *Disability, Difference, Discrimination: Perspectives on Justice in Bioethics and Public Policy*, edited by A. Silvers, D. Wasserman, and M. B. Mahowald, 13–145. Lanham, MD: Rowman & Littlefield.
———. 1998b. "Introduction." In *Disability, Difference, Discrimination: Perspectives on Justice in Bioethics and Public Policy*, edited by A. Silvers, D. Wasserman, and M. B. Mahowald, 1–12. Lanham, MD: Rowman & Littlefield.
Simmel, Georg. 1968. "The Conflict in Modern Culture." In *The Conflict in Modern Culture and Other Essays*, edited and translated by K. Peter Etzkorn. New York: Teachers College Press.
———. 1990. *The Philosophy of Money.* London: Routledge.
Simon, H. 1957. *Models of Man, Social and Rational: Mathematical Essays on Rational Human Behavior in a Social Setting.* New York: Wiley.
Simon, Herbert Alexander. 1947. *Administrative Behavior: A Study of Decision-Making Processes in Administrative Organization.* New York: Macmillan.
Simon, Karla W. 2010. "International Non-Governmental Organizations and Non-Profit Organizations." *International Lawyer* 44: 399–414.
Sims, Beth. 1992. *Workers of the World Undermined: American Labor's Role in U.S. Foreign Policy.* Boston: South End Press.
Singer, Peter. 1993. *Practical Ethics.* 2nd ed. Cambridge, UK: Cambridge University Press.
———. 2005. *Animal Liberation.* New York: Harper Perennial.
———. 2009. *The Life You Can Save.* New York: Random House.
Sinha, Mrinalini, Donna Guy, and Angela Woollacott, eds. 1999. *Feminisms and Internationalism.* Oxford, UK: Blackwell Publishers.
Sjoberg, Gideon. 1999. "Some Observations on Bureaucratic Capitalism: Knowledge about What and Why?" In *Sociology for the Twenty-First Century: Continuities and Cutting Edges*, edited by Janet Abu-Lughod, 43–64. Chicago: University of Chicago Press.
Sjoberg, Gideon., E. A. Gill, B. Littrell, and N. Williams. 1997. "The Reemergence of John Dewey and American Pragmatism." *Studies in Symbolic Interaction* 23: 73–92.
Sjoberg, Gideon., E. A. Gill, and J. E. Tan. 2003. "Social Organization." In *Handbook of Symbolic Interactionism*, edited by Larry T. Reynolds and Nancy J. Herman-Kinney, 411–432. New York: AltaMira Press.
Sjoberg, Gideon., E. A. Gill, N. Williams, and K. E. Kuhn. 1995. "Ethics, Human Rights and Sociological Inquiry: Genocide, Politicide and Other Issues of Organizational Power." *American Sociologist* 26: 8–19.

Sjoberg, Gideon., and T. R. Vaughan. 1993. "The Ethical Foundations of Sociology and the Necessity for a Human Rights Alternative." In *A Critique of Contemporary American Sociology*, edited by T. R. Vaughan, G. Sjoberg, and L. T. Reynolds, 114–159. Dix Hills, NY: General Hall.

Sjoberg, Gideon, Elizabeth A. Gill, and Leonard Cain. 2003. "Counter System Analysis and the Construction of Alternative Futures." *Sociological Theory* 21, no. 3: 214–235.

Sjoberg, Gideon, Elizabeth A. Gill, and Norma Williams. 2001. "A Sociology of Human Rights." *Social Problems* 48, no. 1: 11–47.

Sklar, Martin J. 1988. *The Corporate Reconstruction of American Capitalism, 1890–1916: The Market, the Law, and Politics*. New York: Cambridge University Press.

Skocpol, Theda. 1979. *States and Social Revolutions: A Comparative Analysis of France, Russia, and China*. Cambridge, UK: Cambridge University Press.

———. 1984. "Sociology's Historical Imagination." In *Vision and Method in Historical Sociology*, edited by Theda Skocpol. New York and Cambridge, UK: Cambridge University Press.

———. 1992. *Protecting Soldiers and Mothers: The Political Origins of Social Policy in the United States*. Cambridge, MA: Belknap Press.

Skrentny, John D. 2002. *The Minority Rights Revolution*. Cambridge, MA: Harvard University Press.

Slovic, Paul. 2000. *The Perception of Risk*. London: Routledge.

Smaje, Chris. 2000. *Natural Hierarchies: The Historical Sociology of Race and Caste*. Malden, MA: Blackwell.

Small, Mario Luis. 2009. *Unanticipated Gains: Origins of Network Inequality in Everyday Life*. New York: Oxford University Press.

Smith, Adam. 2002 [1759]. *The Theory of Moral Sentiments*, edited by Knud Haakonssen. New York: Cambridge University Press.

Smith, Christian. 2010. *What Is a Person?* Chicago: University of Chicago Press.

Smith, Dorothy E. 1987. *The Everyday World as Problematic: A Feminist Sociology*. Toronto: University of Toronto Press.

———. 1990. *Texts, Facts, and Femininity: Exploring the Relations of Ruling*. New York: Routledge.

———. 1999. *Writing the Social: Critique, Theory, and Investigations*. Toronto: University of Toronto Press.

Smith, Jackie. 1999. "Human Rights and the Global Economy: A Response to Meyer." *Human Rights Quarterly* 21, no. 1: 80–92.

———. 2004. "Exploring Connections between Global Integration and Political Mobilization." *Journal of World-Systems Research* 10, no. 1: 255–285.

———. 2005. "Response to Wallerstein: The Struggle for Global Society in a World System." *Social Forces* 83, no. 3: 1279–1285.

———. 2008. *Social Movements and Global Democracy*. Baltimore: Johns Hopkins University Press.

Smith, Jackie, Melissa Bolyard, and Anna Ippolito. 1999. "Human Rights and the Global Economy: A Response to Meyer." *Human Rights Quarterly* 21, no. 1: 207–219.

Smith, Jackie, and Hank Johnston, eds. 2002. *Globalization and Resistance: Transnational Dimensions of Social Movements*. Lanham, MD: Rowman & Littlefield.

Smith, Jackie, Marina Karides, Marc Becker, Christopher Chase Dunn, Dorval Brunelle, Donnatella Della Porta, Rosalba Icaza, Jeffrey Juris, Lorenzo Mosca, Ellen Reese, Jay Smith, and Rolando Vasquez. 2008. *The World Social Forums and the Challenges for Global Democracy*. Boulder, CO: Paradigm Publishers.

Smith, Jackie, Ron Pagnucco, and George A. López. 1998. "Globalizing Human Rights: The Work of Transnational Human Rights NGOs in the 1990s." *Human Rights Quarterly* 20, no. 2: 379–412.

Smith, Jackie, and Dawn Wiest. 2005. "The Uneven Geography of Global Civil Society: National and Global Influences on Transnational Association." *Social Forces* 84, no. 2: 621–652.

Smith, Linda Tuhiwai. 1999. *Decolonizing Methodologies: Research and Indigenous Peoples*. New York: Zed Books.

———. 2005. "On Tricky Ground: Researching the Native in an Age of Uncertainty." In *Handbook of Qualitative Research*, edited by Norman Denzin and Yvonna Lincoln, 18–108. Beverly Hills, CA: Sage Publications.

Smith, Philip. 2008. *Punishment and Culture*. Chicago: University of Chicago Press.

Smith, Robert. 2005. *Mexican New York: Transnational Lives of New Immigrants*. Berkeley: University of California Press.

Smith, Sylvia. 2005. "The $100 Laptop–Is It a Wind-Up?" CNN.com. http://edition.cnn.com/2005/WORLD/africa/12/01/laptop (accessed January 23, 2010).

Smith, Thomas Spence. 2004. "Where Sociability Comes From: Neurosociological Foundations of Social Interaction." In *The Dialogical Turn: New Roles for Sociology in the Postdisciplinary Age*, edited by Charles Camic and Hans Joas, 199–220. Lanham, MD: Rowman & Littlefield.

Smith, Tom W. 2009. "National Pride in Comparative Perspective." In *The International Social Survey Programme, 1984–2009: Charting the Globe*, edited by Max Haller, Roger Jowell, and Tim W. Smith, 197–221. New York: Routledge.

Smith-Doerr, Laurel. 2004. *Women's Work: Gender Equality vs. Hierarchy in the Life Sciences*. Boulder, CO: Lynne Rienner Publishers.
Snipp, C. Matthew. 2003. "Racial Measurement in the American Census: Past Practices and Implications for the Future." *Annual Review of Sociology* 29: 563–588.
Snow, David A. 2004. "Framing Processes, Ideology, and Discursive Fields." In *The Blackwell Companion to Social Movements*, edited by David A. Snow, Sarah A. Soule, and Hanspeter Kreisi, 380–412. Oxford: Blackwell.
Snow, David A., and Leon Anderson. 1987. "Identity Work among the Homeless: The Verbal Construction and Avowal of Personal Identities." *American Journal of Sociology* 92: 1336–1371.
Snow, David, E. Burke Rochford Jr., Steven K. Worden, and Robert D. Benford. 1986. "Frame Alignment Processes, Micro-Mobilization and Movement Participation." *American Sociological Review* 51: 464–481.
Snyder, Howard. 2011. "Arrest in the United States: 1980–2009." Bureau of Justice Statistics. http://bjs.ojp.usdoj.gov/content/pub/pdf/aus8009.pdf (accessed October 2011).
Snyder, Jack, and Leslie Vinjamuri. 2003/2004. "Trials and Errors: Principle and Pragmatism in Strategies of International Justice." *International Security* 28: 5–44.
Sobell, L. C., M. B. Sobell, D. M. Riley, F. Klajner, G. I. Leo, G. Pavan, and A. Cancill. 1986. "Effect of Television Programming and Advertising on Alcohol Consumption in Normal Drinkers." *Journal Studies of Alcohol and Drugs* 47: 333–340.
Sok, Chivy, and Kenneth Neubeck. Forthcoming. "Building U.S. Human Rights Culture from the Ground Up: International Human Rights Implementation at the Local Level." In *In Our Own Backyard: Human Rights, Injustice, and Resistance in the United States*, edited by Bill Armaline, Bandana Purkayastha, and Davita Silfen Glasberg, 231–243. Philadelphia: University of Pennsylvania Press.
Soley, Lawrence. 1999. *Leasing the Ivory Tower: The Corporate Takeover of Academia*. Boston: South End Press.
Sombart, Werner. 1913. *Krieg und Kapitalismus*. Munich: Duncker and Humblot.
Somers, Margaret R. 2008. *Genealogies of Citizenship: Markets, Statelessness, and the Right to Have Rights*. New York: Cambridge University Press.
Somers, Margaret R., and Christopher Roberts. 2008. "Towards a New Sociology of Rights: A Genealogy of 'Buried Bodies' of Citizenship and Human Rights." *Annual Review of Law and Social Science* 4: 385–425.
Soohoo, Cynthia, Catherine Albisa, and Martha F. Davis, eds. 2008. *Bringing Human Rights Home: Portraits of the Movement*. Vol. 3. Westport, CT: Praeger.
Sorenson, John. 2011. "Constructing Extremists, Rejecting Compassion: Ideological Attacks on Animal Advocacy from Right and Left." In *Critical Theory and Animal Liberation*, edited by John Sanbonmatsu, 219–238. Lanham, MD: Rowman & Littlefield.
Sørensen, Aage B. 1979. "A Model and a Metric for the Analysis of the Intragenerational Status Attainment Process." *American Journal of Sociology* 85: 361–84.
South African Human Rights Commission (SAHRC). 1998. *My Rights, Your Rights: Respect, Responsibilities and the SAHRC*. English ed. Pretoria: Government of South Africa.
Soysal, Yasemin. 1994. *Limits of Citizenship: Migrants and Postnational Membership in Europe*. Chicago: University of Chicago Press.
Speier, Matthew. 1973. *How to Observe Face-to-Face Communication: A Sociological Introduction*. Pacific Palisades, CA: Goodyear.
Spencer, Herbert. 1967. *Evolution of Society*. Chicago: University of Chicago Press.
Spirer, Herbert F. 1990. "Violations of Human Rights: How Many? The Statistical Problems of Measuring Such Infractions Are Tough, but Statistical Science Is Equal to It." *American Journal of Economics and Sociology* 49: 199–210.
Spring, Joel. 2000. *The Universal Right to Education*. Mahwah, NJ: Lawrence Erlbaum Associates.
———. 2007. *A New Paradigm for Global School Systems*. New York: Routledge.
Squires, Gregory, and Charis B. Kubrin. 2006. *Privileged Places: Race, Residence, and the Structure of Opportunity*. Boulder, CO: Lynne Rienner Publishers.
St. Jean, Peter K. B. 2007. *Pockets of Crime: Broken Windows, Collective Efficacy, and the Criminal Point of View*. Chicago: University of Chicago Press.
Stacey, Judith. 1988. "Can There Be a Feminist Ethnography?" *Women's Studies International Forum* 11: 21–27.
———. 1991. "Can There Be a Feminist Ethnography?" In *Women's Words*, edited by Sherna B. Gluck and Daphne Patai, 111–119. New York: Routledge.
Stack, Carol. 1974. *All Our Kin: Strategies for Survival in a Black Community*. New York: Harper and Row.
Stacy, Helen. 2009. *Human Rights in the 21st Century*. Stanford, CA: Stanford University Press.
Staggenborg, Suzanne. 1988. "The Consequences of Professionalization and Formalization in the Pro-Choice Movement." *American Sociological Review* 53, no. 4: 585–605.

Stammers, Neil. 1999. "Social Movements and the Social Construction of Human Rights." *Human Rights Quarterly* 21: 980-1008.
———. 2009. *Human Rights and Social Movements*. New York: Pluto Press.
Stamp Dawkins, Marian. 2006. "The Scientific Basis for Assessing Suffering of Animals." In *In Defense of Animals: The Second Wave*, edited by Peter Singer. Cambridge, MA: Blackwell Publishers.
Stanton, Timothy, Dwight Giles, and Nadine Cruz. 1999. *Service Learning: A Movement's Pioneers Reflect on Its Origins, Practice, and Future*. San Francisco, CA: Jossey-Bass.
Stark, Barbara. 1992-1993. "Economic Rights in the United States and International Law: Towards an Entirely New Strategy." *Hastings Law Journal* 44: 79-130.
Staudt, Kathleen. 1990. *Women, International Development, and Politics: The Bureaucratic Mire*. Philadelphia: Temple University Press.
———. 1997. "Gender Politics in Bureaucracy: Theoretical Issues in Comparative Perspective." In *Women, International Development, and Politics*, edited by Kathleen Staudt, 3-36. Philadelphia: Temple University Press.
Stearns, Peter N. 1994. *American Cool: Constructing a Twentieth-Century Emotional Style*. New York: New York University Press.
Stein, Dorothy. 1988. "Burning Widows, Burning Brides: The Perils of Daughterhood in India." *Pacific Affairs* 61: 465-485.
Steiner, Gary. 2010. *Anthropocentrism and Its Discontents: The Moral Status of Animals in the History of Western Philosophy*. Pittsburgh, PA: University of Pittsburgh Press.
Steiner, Henry J., Phillip Alston, and Ryan Goodman. 2008. *International Human Rights in Context: Law, Politics, Morals*. Oxford: Oxford University Press.
Steinmetz, George. 2007. *The Devil's Handwriting: Precoloniality and the German Colonial State in Qingdao, Samoa, and Southwest Africa*. Chicago: University of Chicago Press.
Steinmo, Sven, Kathleen Thelen, and Frank Longstreth, eds. 1992. *Structuring Politics: Historical Institutionalism in Comparative Analysis*. New York: Cambridge University Press.
Stephan, W. G., C. W. Stephan, and W. B. Gudykunst. 1999. "Anxiety in Intercultural Relations: A Comparison of Anxiety/Uncertainty Management Theory and Integrated Threat Theory." *International Journal of Intercultural Relations* 23: 613-628.
Stephens, Lowndes. 1979. "The Goebbels Touch." *Journal of Communication* 29: 2205-2206.
Stets, Jan E., and Emily K. Asencio. 2008. "Consistency and Enhancement Processes in Understanding Emotions." *Social Forces* 86: 1055-1078.
Stets, Jan E., and Jonathan H. Turner, eds. 2007. *Handbook of the Sociology of Emotions*. New York: Springer.
Stevens, Fred. 2001. "The Convergence and Divergence of Modern Health Care Systems." In *The Blackwell Companion to Medical Sociology*, edited by William Cockerham, 159-176. Malden, MA: Blackwell Publishing.
Stevenson, Betsey, and Justin Wolfers. 2007. "Marriage and Divorce: Changes and Their Driving Forces." *Journal of Economic Perspectives* 21, no. 2: 27-52.
Stinchcombe, Arthur L. 1997. "On the Virtues of the Old Institutionalism." *Annual Review of Sociology* 23: 1-18.
Stolleis, Michael. 2007. "Law and Lawyers Preparing the Holocaust." *Annual Review of Law and Social Science* 3: 213-232.
Stover, Eric. 2005. *The Witnesses: War Crimes and the Promise of Justice in The Hague*. Philadelphia: University of Pennsylvania Press.
Straus, Scott, and Robert Lyons. 2006. *Intimate Enemy: Images and Voices of the Rwandan Genocide*. Cambridge, MA: MIT Press.
Strauss, Anselm L. 1978. *Negotiations*. New York: Wiley.
———. 1993. *Continual Permutations of Action*. New York: Aldine De Gruyter.
Streeck, Wolfgang. 1992. *Social Institutions and Economic Performance: Studies of Industrial Relations in Advanced Capitalist Economies*. London: Sage Publications.
Streeter, Sonya, Jhamirah Howard, Rachel Licata, and Rachel Garfield. 2011. "The Uninsured, a Primer: Facts about Americans without Health Insurance." Kaiser Family Foundation. http://www.kff.org/uninsured/upload/7451.pdf (accessed July 19, 2012).
Strickland, D. E. 1983. "Advertising Exposure, Alcohol Consumption and Misuse of Alcohol." In *Economics and Alcohol: Consumption and Controls*, edited by M. Grant, M. Plant, and A. Williams, 201-222. New York: Gardner.
Strom, Elizabeth A., and John H. Mollenkopf, eds. 2006. *The Urban Politics Reader*. New York: Routledge.
Stryker, Sheldon. 1980. *Symbolic Interactionism: A Social Structural Version*. Menlo Park, CA: Benjamin Cummings.

Stryker, Sheldon, and Kevin D. Vryan. 2003. "The Symbolic Interactionist Frame." In *Handbook of Social Psychology*, edited by John DeLamater, 3-28. New York: Kluwer.
Stuart, Alan, and J. Keith Ord. 1987. *Kendall's Advanced Theory of Statistics*. Vol. 1: *Distribution Theory*. 5th ed. Originally by Sir Maurice Kendall. New York: Oxford University Press.
Stuart, Tristram. 2006. *The Bloodless Revolution: A Cultural History of Vegetarianism from 1600 to Modern Times*. New York: W. W. Norton and Co.
Stuhr, John J. 2010. *100 Years of Pragmatism: William James's Revolutionary Philosophy*. Bloomington: Indiana University Press.
Substance Abuse and Mental Health Services Administration (SAMHSA). 2010. *Results from the 2009 National Survey on Drug Use and Health*. SAMHSA. http://oas.samhsa.gov/NSDUH/2k9NSDUH/2k9Results .htm#7.3.1 (accessed January 1, 2011).
Sunder, Madhavi. 2003. "Piercing the Veil." *Yale Law Journal* 112: 1401-1472.
Sutter, Molly Hazel. 2006. "Mixed-Status Families and Broken Homes: The Clash between the U.S. Hardship Standard in Cancellation of Removal Proceedings and International Law." *Transnational Law and Contemporary Problems* 783: 1-28.
Swedberg, Richard. 2010. "The Structure of Confidence and the Collapse of Lehman Brothers." In *Markets on Trial: The Economic Sociology of the U.S. Financial Crisis*, edited by Michael Lounsbury and Paul M. Hirsch, 71-114. Research in the Sociology of Organizations 30A. London: Emerald Group Publishing.
Swidler, Anne. 1986. "Culture in Action: Symbols and Strategies." *American Sociological Review* 51: 273-286.
Switzer, J. V. 2003. *Disabled Rights: American Disability Policy and the Fight for Equality*. Washington, DC: Georgetown University Press.
Symington, Alison. 2004. "Intersectionality: A Tool for Gender and Economic Justice." Association for Women's Rights in Development. http://www.awid.org/content/download/48805/537521/file/intersectionality_en.pdf (accessed September 17, 2012).
Szell, G. 1994. "Technology, Production, Consumption and the Environment." *International Social Science Journal* 140: 213-225.
Tabak, Mehmet. 2003. "Marxian Considerations on Morality, Justice, and Rights." *Rethinking Marxism* 15, no. 4: 523-540.
Tajfel, H. 1970. "Experiments in Intergroup Discrimination." *Scientific American* 223: 96-102.
Takacs-Santa, A. 2004. "The Major Transitions in the History of Human Transformation of the Biosphere." *Human Ecology Review* 11, no. 1: 51-66.
Takagi, Dana. 1994. "Maiden Voyage: Excursion into Sexuality and Identity Politics in Asian America." *Amerasia Journal* 20, no. 1: 1-17.
Takeuchi, David T., Emily Walton, and ManChui Leung. 2010. "Race, Social Contexts and Health: Examining Geographic Spaces and Places." In *Handbook of Medical Sociology*, edited by Chloe Bird, Peter Conrad, Allen Fremont, and Stephan Timmermans, 92-105. 6th ed. Nashville, TN: Vanderbilt University Press.
Takeuti, N. 2010. Personal communication with J. M. Fritz. December 14.
Tarnas, Richard. 1991. *The Passion of the Western Mind: Understanding the Ideas that Have Shaped Our World View*. New York: Ballantine Books.
Tarrow, Sidney G. 1998. *Power in Movement: Social Movements and Contentious Politics*. New York and Cambridge, UK: Cambridge University Press.
———. 2005. *The New Transnational Activism*. New York: Cambridge University Press.
Tatum, Beverly Daniel. 2003. *"Why Are All the Black Kids Sitting Together in the Cafeteria?" and Other Conversations about Race*. New York: Basic Books.
Taylor, Frederick W. 1910. *The Principles of Scientific Management*. New York: Harper and Brothers.
Taylor, Greg. 2003. "Scientology in the German Courts." *Journal of Law and Religion* 19: 153-198.
Taylor, J. 1999. "The New Economics of Labour Migration and the Role of Remittances in the Migration Process." *International Migration* 37, no. 1: 63-68.
Tazreiter, Claudia. 2010. "Local to Global Activism: The Movement to Protect the Rights of Refugees and Asylum Seekers." *Social Movement Studies* 9, no. 2: 201-214.
Teitel, Ruti. 1997. "Human Rights Genealogy (Symposium: Human Rights on the Eve of the Next Century)." *Fordham Law Review* 66: 301-317.
———. 2000. *Transitional Justice*. Oxford: Oxford University Press.
TenHouten, Warren D. 2005. "Primary Emotions and Social Relations: A First Report." *Free Inquiry in Creative Sociology* 33, no. 2: 79-92.
Terl, Allan H. 2000. "An Essay on the History of Lesbian and Gay Rights in Florida." *Nova Law Review* 24 (spring): 793-853.

Thayer, Carlyle A. 2004. "Laos in 2003: Counterrevolution Fails to Ignite." *Asian Survey* 44, no. 1: 110-114.
Thayer-Bacon, Barbara. 2004. "An Exploration of Myles Horton's Democratic Praxis: Highlander Folk School." *Educational Foundation* 18, no. 2, 5-23.
Theil, Henri. 1967. *Economics and Information Theory*. Amsterdam: North-Holland.
Therborn, G. 1980. *The Ideology of Power and the Power of Ideology*. London: Verso.
Thomas, George. 2004. "Constructing World Civil Society through Contentions over Religious Rights." *Journal of Human Rights* 3: 239-251.
Thomas, George M. 1987. *Institutional Structure: Constituting State, Society, and the Individual*. Newbury Park, CA: Sage Publications.
———. 2001. "Religions in Global Civil Society." *Sociology of Religion* 62: 515-533.
Thomas, James. 2010. "The Racial Formation of Medieval Jews: A Challenge to the Field." *Ethnic and Racial Studies* 33: 1737-1755.
Thomas, James, and David Brunsma. 2008. "Bringing Down the House: Reparations, Universal Morality, and Social Justice." In *Globalization and America: Race, Human Rights, and Inequality*, edited by Angela Hattery, David G. Embrick, and Earl Smith, 65-81. Lanham, MD: Rowman & Littlefield.
Thomas, John, John W. Meyer, Francisco O. Ramirez, and John Boli. 1987. *Institutional Structure: Constituting State, Society, and the Individual*. Newbury Park, CA: Sage.
Thomas, Nigel, Brian K. Gran, and Karl Hansen. 2011. "An Independent Voice for Children's Rights in Europe? The Role of Independent Children's Rights Institutions in the EU." *International Journal of Children's Rights* 19, no. 3: 429-449.
Thomas, Robert J. 1994. *What Machines Can't Do: Politics and Technology in the Industrial Enterprise*. Berkeley: University of California Press.
Thomas, W. H. 2004. *What Are Old People For? How Elders Will Save the World*. Acton, MA: VanderWky and Burnham.
Thompson, E. P. 1963. *The Making of the English Working Class*. London: V. Gollancz.
———. 1978. *The Poverty of Theory*. London: Merlin Press.
Thompson, Silvanus P. 1946 [1910]. *Calculus Made Easy*. 3rd ed. New York: St. Martin's Press.
Thorne, B. 1993. *Gender Play: Boys and Girls in School*. Piscataway, NJ: Rutgers University Press.
Thorne, S., B. Paterson, S. Acorn, C. Canam, G. Joachim, and C. Jillings. 2002. "Chronic Illness Experience: Insights from a Metastudy." *Qualitative Health Research* 12, no. 4: 437-452.
Tiefer, Lenore. 2004. *Sex Is Not a Natural Act and Other Essays*. Boulder, CO: Westview Press.
Tilly, Charles. 1978. *From Mobilization to Revolution*. New York: McGraw-Hill Companies.
———. 1992. *Coercion, Capital and European States*. Oxford: Blackwell.
Timasheff, N. S. 1941. "Fundamental Problems of the Sociology of Law." *American Catholic Sociological Review* 2, no. 4: 233-248.
Timmermans, S. 2001. "Social Death as Self-Fulfilling Prophecy." In *Sociology of Health and Illness: Critical Perspectives*, edited by P. Conrad, 305-321. New York: Worth.
Tinkler, Penny. 1995. *Constructing Girlhood*. Oxfordshire, UK: Taylor and Francis.
Tisdall, E. K. M. 2008. "Is the Honeymoon Over? Children and Young People's Participation in Public Decision-Making." *International Journal of Children's Rights* 16, no. 3: 343-354.
Tocqueville, Alexis de. 1960 [1835]. *Democracy in America*. New York: Alfred A. Knopf.
Tolman, Deborah L. 1994. "Doing Desire: Adolescent Girls' Struggles for/with Sexuality." *Gender and Society* 8, no. 3: 324-342.
Tomasevski, Katerina. 1995. *Women and Human Rights*. London: Zed Books.
Toney, Jeffery H., H. Kaplowitz, R. Pu, F. Qi, and G. Chang. 2010. "Science and Human Rights: A Bridge towards Benefiting Humanity." *Human Rights Quarterly* 32, no. 4: 1008-1017.
Tonry, Michael H. 1995. *Malign Neglect–Race, Crime, and Punishment in America*. New York: Oxford University Press.
Torres, Bob. 2007. *Making a Killing: The Political Economy of Animal Rights*. Oakland, CA: AK Press.
Toulmin, Stephen. 1953. *The Philosophy of Science: An Introduction*. London: Hutchinson.
———. 1978. "Science, Philosophy of." In *The New Encyclopaedia Britannica, Macropaedia 16*: 375-393. 15th ed. Chicago: Britannica.
Touraine, Alain. 1981. *The Voice and the Eye*. Cambridge, UK: Cambridge University Press.
———. 1983. *Solidarity: The Analysis of a Social Movement, Poland 1980-1981*. Cambridge, UK: Cambridge University Press.
Townsend, Peter. 2006. "Policies for the Aged in the 21st Century: More 'Structured Dependency' or the Realisation of Human Rights?" *Aging and Society* 26: 161-179.
Traer, Robert. 1991. *Faith in Human Rights: Support in Religious Traditions for a Global Struggle*. Washington, DC: Georgetown University Press.

Trevino, Javier A. 1996. *The Sociology of Law: Classical and Contemporary Perspectives.* New York: St. Martin's Press.
——. 1998. "The Influence of C. Wright Mills on Students for a Democratic Society: An Interview with Bob Ross." *Humanity and Society* 22: 260-277.
Tripp, Aili, and Myra Marx Ferree, eds. 2006. *Global Feminism: Transnational Women's Activism, Organizing, and Human Rights.* New York: New York University Press.
Trucios-Haynes, Inid. 2001. "Why 'Race Matters': LatCrit Theory and Latina/o Racial Identity." *La Raza Law Journal* 12, no. 1: 1-42.
Tsutsui, Kiyoteru. 2004. "Global Civil Society and Ethnic Social Movements in the Contemporary World." *Sociological Forum* 19, no. 1: 63-87.
Tuan, Mia. 1999. *Forever Foreigners or Honorary Whites? The Asian Ethnic Experience Today.* New Brunswick, NJ: Rutgers University Press.
Tuchman, Gaye. 2011. *Wannabe U: Inside the Corporate University.* Chicago: University of Chicago Press.
Turk, Austin. 1969. *Criminality and Legal Order.* Chicago: Rand McNally.
——. 1982. *Political Criminology.* Thousand Oaks: Sage.
Turmel, André. 2008. *A Historical Sociology of Childhood.* New York: Cambridge University Press.
Turner, Bryan S. 1993. "Outline of the Theory of Human Rights." In *Citizenship and Social Theory*, edited by Bryan S. Turner, 162-190. London: Sage.
——. 1995. "Symposium: Human Rights and the Sociological Project (Introduction)." *Australian and New Zealand Journal of Sociology* 31: 1-8.
——. 1996. *Vulnerability and Human Rights: Essays on Human Rights.* University Park: Penn State University Press.
——. 2002. "The Problem of Cultural Relativism for the Sociology of Human Rights: Weber, Schmitt and Strauss." *Journal of Human Rights* 1, no. 4: 587-605.
——. 2006. "Global Sociology and the Nature of Rights." *Societies without Borders* 1: 41-52.
——. 2010. "The Problem of Cultural Relativism for the Sociology of Human Rights: Weber, Schmitt and Straus." *Journal of Human Rights* 1, no. 4: 587-605.
Turner, Jonathan H. 2007. *Human Emotions: A Sociological Theory.* New York: Routledge.
Turner, Jonathan H., and Alexandra Maryanski. 2005. *Incest: The Origin of the Taboo.* Boulder, CO: Paradigm Publishers.
——. 2008. *On the Origins of Societies by Natural Selection.* Boulder, CO: Paradigm Publishers.
Turner, Jonathan H., and Jan E. Stets. 2005. *The Sociology of Emotions.* Cambridge, UK: Cambridge University Press.
——. 2006. "Sociological Theories of Human Emotions." *Annual Review of Sociology* 32: 25-52.
Turner, R. J., B. Wheaton, and D. A. Lloyd. 1995. "The Epidemiology of Social Stress." *American Sociological Review* 60: 104-125.
Turner, Ralph. 1976. "The Real Self: From Institution to Impulse." *American Journal of Sociology* 81: 989-1016.
Turner, Ralph H., and Steven Gordon. 1981. "The Boundaries of the Self: The Relationship of Authenticity in the Self-Conception." In *Self-Concept: Advances in Theory and Research*, edited by Mervin D. Lynch, Ardyth A. Norem-Hebeisen, and Kenneth J. Gergen, 39-57. Cambridge, MA: Ballinger.
Turner, Stephanie S. 1999. "Intersex Identities: Locating New Intersections of Sex and Gender." *Gender and Society* 13, no. 4: 457-479.
Turner, Stephen. 1977. "Blau's Theory of Differentiation: Is It Explanatory?" *Sociological Quarterly* 18: 17-32.
——. 2007. "A Life in the First Half-Century of Sociology: Charles Ellwood and the Division of Sociology." In *Sociology in America: A History*, edited by Craig Calhoun, 115-154. Chicago: University of Chicago Press.
Udehn, L. 2001. *Methodological Individualism. Background, History, and Meaning.* London: Routledge.
Udry, J. Richard. 2000. "Biological Limits of Gender Construction." *American Sociological Review* 65, no. 3: 443-457.
Uhlenberg, Peter. 2009a. "Children in an Aging Society." *Journals of Gerontology, Series B: Psychological Sciences* 64B: 489-496.
——, ed. 2009b. *International Handbook of Population Aging.* Dordrecht, The Netherlands: Springer.
Uhlenberg, Peter, and Michelle Cheuk. 2010. "The Significance of Grandparents to Grandchildren: An International Perspective." In *Sage Handbook of Social Gerontology*, edited by D. Dannefer and C. Phillipson, 447-458. London: Sage.
Uhlenberg, Peter, and Jenny de Jong Gierveld. 2004. "Age-Segregation in Later Life: An Examination of Personal Networks." *Ageing and Society* 24: 5-28.
Underhill, Kristen, Paul Montgomery, and Don Operario. 2007. "Systematic Review of Abstinence-Only Programmes Aiming to Prevent HIV Infection in High-Income Countries." *British Medical Journal* 335: 248.

United Nations. 1948. "The Universal Declaration of Human Rights." United Nations. www.un.org/en/documents/udhr/index.shtml (accessed December 10, 2010).
———. 1991. "The Protection of Persons with Mental Illness and the Improvement of Mental Health Care." United Nations. http://www.un.org/documents/ga/res/46/a46r119.htm (accessed November 10, 2010).
———. 1992. *Rio Declaration on Environment and Development*. 31 ILM874. United Nations. www.un-documents.net/rio-dec.htm (accessed January 20, 2012).
———. 1993. "Vienna Declaration and Programme of Action." Office of the United Nations High Commissioner for Human Rights. http://www.unhchr.ch/huridocda/huridoca.nsf/(symbol)/a.conf. 157.23 .en (accessed July 20, 2012).
———. 1995. *UN Report of the Fourth World Conference on Women*. New York: United Nations.
———. 2000. "Gender and Racial Discrimination Report of the Expert Group Meeting." United Nations. http://www.un.org/womenwatch/daw/csw/genrac/report.htm (accessed January 11, 2012).
———. 2001. "Background Briefing on Intersectionality, Working Group on Women and Human Rights, 45th Session of the UN CSW." Center for Women's Global Leadership. http://www.cwgl.rutgers.edu/csw01/background.htm (accessed March 31, 2011).
———. 2002. "Johannesburg Declaration on Sustainable Development." United Nations. http://www.un.org/esa/sustdev/documents/WSSD_POI_PD/English/POI_PD.htm (accessed July 20, 2012).
———. 2007. "United Nations Declaration on the Rights of Indigenous Peoples." New York: Official Records of the General Assembly, Sixty-First Session, Supplement No. 53 (A/61/53), Pt. One, Ch. 2, Sect. A, and 107th Plenary Meeting, September 13.
———. 2008. "International Migrant Stock: The 2008 Revision." United Nations. http://esa.un.org/migration/index.asp?panel=1 (accessed October 12, 2010).
———. 2009. *15 Years of the United Nations Special Rapporteur on Violence against Women, Its Causes and Consequences*. Office of the High Commissioner for Human Rights. http://www2.ohchr.org/english/issues/women/rapporteur/docs/15YearReviewofVAWMandate.pdf (accessed January 11, 2012).
———. 2010. "Gender Dimensions of Agricultural and Rural Employment: Differentiated Pathways out of Poverty." UN Food and Agriculture Organization. http://www.fao.org/docrep/013/i1638e/i1638e00.htm (accessed January 21, 2011).
United Nations Development Program (UNDP). 1987. *Brundtland Report*. New York: UNDP.
United Nations Educational Scientific and Cultural Organization (UNESCO). 1990. "Meeting Basic Learning Needs: A Vision for the 1990s." UNESCO. http://www.unesco.org/en/efa/the-efa-movement/ jomtien-1990.
United Nations Food and Agriculture Organization (UNFAO). 2006. "Livestock's Long Shadow: Environmental Issues and Options." UNFAO. http://www.fao.org/docrep/010/a0701e/a0701e00.htm (accessed July 20, 2012).
———. 2010. *Gender Dimensions of Agricultural and Rural Employment: Differential Pathways out of Poverty*. Rome: UNFAO, International Fund for Agricultural Development, and International Labour Office.
United Nations High Commissioner for Refugees (UNHCR). 1966. "International Covenant on Economic, Social, and Cultural Rights." UNHCR. http://www2.ohchr.org/english/law/cescr.htm (accessed January 11, 2012).
———. 2010. "UNHCR Refugee Figures." UNHCR. http://www.unhcr.org/pages/49c3646c1d.html (accessed on January 11, 2012).
United Nations Human Development Reports. 2010. "The Real Wealth of Nations: Pathways to Human Development." UN Human Development Reports. http://hdr.undp.org/en/reports/global/hdr2010 (accessed July 20, 2012).
United Nations Human Rights Council. 2008. "Human Rights and Climate Change." UN Human Rights Council Resolution 7/23, March 28.
United Nations Office on Drugs and Crime (UNODC). 2010. *Drug Control, Crime and Prevention: A Human Rights Perspective*. International Centre on Human Rights and Drug Policy. http://www.humanrightsanddrugs.org/wp-content/uploads/2010/03/UNODC-Human-Rights-Conference-Paper. pdf (accessed January 1, 2011).
United States 111th Congress. 2009. *Afghan's Narco War: Breaking the Link between Drug Traffickers and Insurgents*. Government Printing Office. http://www.gpoaccess.gov/congress/index.html (accessed January 1, 2011).
United States Census Bureau. 2008. "U.S. Population Projections." US Census Bureau. http://www.census.gov/population/www/projections/summarytables.html (accessed January 29, 2012).
United States Department of Defense. 2003. *An Abrupt Climate Change Scenario and Its Implications for United States National Security*. Washington, DC: US Department of Defense.

United States Department of Health and Human Services. 2010. "Fact Sheet: Sex Trafficking." Administration for Children and Families. http://www.acf.hhs.gov/trafficking/about/fact_sex.html (accessed December 21, 2010).
United States Department of State. 2009. "2009 Human Rights Report: Singapore." US Department of State. http://www.state.gov/g/drl/rls/hrrpt/2009/eap/136008.htm (accessed October 1, 2011).
———. 2010a. "2010 Human Rights Report: Saudi Arabia." US Department of State. http://www.state.gov/documents/organization/160475.pdf (accessed October 1, 2012).
———. 2010b. "2010 Human Rights Report: China (Includes Tibet, Hong Kong, and Macau)." US Department of State. http://www.state.gov/g/drl/rls/hrrpt/2010/eap/154382.htm (accessed October 20, 2011).
United States Government Accountability Office (GAO). 2005. "Drug Offenders: Various Factors May Limit the Impacts of Federal Laws that Provide for Denial of Selected Benefits." GAO-05-238. GAO. http://www.gao.gov/new.items/d05238.pdf (accessed September 2011).
United States Human Rights Fund. 2010. *Perfecting Our Union: Human Rights Success Stories from across the United States*. New York: US Human Rights Fund.
United States Human Rights Network. 2011. http://www.ushrnetwork.org (accessed May 26, 2011).
United States National Institute of Standards and Technology (NIST). 2003. *Engineering Statistics Handbook*. NIST. http://www.itl.nist.gov/div898/handbook (accessed January 20, 2012).
University of Warwick, Sociology Department. n.d. "The Module in 10 Points." University of Warwick. http://www2.warwick.ac.uk/fac/soc/sociology/staff/emeritus/robertfine/home/teachingmaterial/humanrights/tenpoints (accessed January 1, 2011).
Unno, Mark T. 1999. "Review: Questions in the Making: A Review Essay on Zen Buddhist Ethics in the Context of Buddhist and Comparative Ethics." *Journal of Religious Ethics* 27, no. 3: 507–536.
Updegraff, K., A. Booth, and Shawna Thayer. 2006. "The Role of Family Relationship Quality and Testosterone Levels in Adolescents' Peer Experience: A Biosocial Analysis." *Family Psychology* 20: 21–29.
US Constitution Online. "U.S. Constitution—Amendment 1." 1791. US Constitution Online. http://www.usconstitution.net/xconst_Am1.html (accessed July 20, 2012).
Vaillancourt, Jean-Guy. 2010. "From Environmental Sociology to Global Ecosociology: The Dunlap-Buttel Debates." In *The International Handbook of Environmental Sociology*, edited by Michael R. Redclift and Graham Woodgate, 48–62. Northampton, MA: Edward Elgar Publishing.
Valentine, David. 2007. *Imagining Transgender: An Ethnography of a Category*. Durham, NC: Duke University Press.
Valenzuela, Angela. 1999. *Subtractive Schooling*. Albany: State University of New York.
Valliant, George E. 1983. *The Natural History of Alcoholism*. Cambridge, MA: Harvard University Press.
Van Aelst, Peter, and Stefaan Walgrave. 2002. "New Media, New Movements? The Role of the Internet in Shaping the 'Anti-Globalization' Movement." *Information, Communication, & Society* 5, no. 4: 465–493.
Van Bockstaele, J., M. Van Bockstaele, J. Malbos, M. Godard-Plasman, and N. Van Bockstaele. 2008. "Socioanalysis and Clinical Intervention." In *International Clinical Sociology*, edited by J. M. Fritz, 170–187. New York: Springer.
Van den Berghe, Pierre L. 1979. *Human Family Systems*. New York: Elsevier.
———. 1981. *The Ethnic Phenomenon*. New York: Elsevier.
Van der Kroef, Justus M. 1976. "Indonesia's Political Prisoners." *Pacific Affairs* 49, no. 4: 625–647.
Van Krieken, Robert. 1999. "The 'Stolen Generations': On the Removal of Australian Indigenous Children from Their Families and Its Implications for the Sociology of Childhood." *Childhood* 6, no. 3: 297–311.
Vanwesenbeeck, I. 1997. "The Context of Women's Power(lessness) in Heterosexual Interactions." In *New Sexual Agendas*, edited by L. Segal. New York: New York University Press.
Vaughan, Diane. 1999. "The Dark Side of Organizations: Mistake, Misconduct, and Disaster." *Annual Review of Sociology* 25: 271–305.
———. 2002. "Criminology and the Sociology of Organizations." *Crime, Law, and Social Change* 37: 117–136.
Vaughan, T. R., and G. Sjoberg. 1984. "The Individual and Bureaucracy: An Alternative Meadian Interpretation." *Journal of Applied Behavioral Science* 20: 57–69.
Vaughn, Michael G, Matt Delisi, Kevin M. Beaver, and John Paul Wright. 2009. "DAT1 and 5HTT Are Associated with Pathological Criminal Behavior in a Nationally Representative Sample of Youth." *Criminal Justice and Behavior* 36, no. 11: 1103–1114.
Vaughn, Ted R., Gideon Sjoberg, and Larry Reynolds, eds. 1993. *A Critique of Contemporary American Sociology*. Dix Hills, NY: General Hall.
Veblen, Thorstein. 1991. *The Theory of the Leisure Class*. Fairfield, CT: A. M. Kelley.
———. 1998. *The Nature of Peace*. New Brunswick, NJ: Transaction Publishers.

Vegans of Color. 2011. "Liberation Veganism." Vegans of Color. http://vegansofcolor.wordpress.com/tag/animal-rights (accessed March 28, 2011).
Velez, Veronica, Lindsay Perez Huber, Corina Benavides López, Ariana de la Luz, and Daniel G. Solorzano. 2008. "Battling for Human Rights and Social Justice: A Latina/o Critical Race Media Analysis of Latina/o Student Youth Activism in the Wake of 2006 Anti-Immigrant Sentiment." *Social Justice* 35, no. 1: 7-27.
Veltmeyer, Henry, and Mark Rushton. 2011. *The Cuban Revolution as Socialist Human Development.* Leiden, the Netherlands: Brill.
Venetis, Penny M. 2012. "Making Human Rights Treaty Law Actionable in the United States." *Alabama Law Review* 63, no. 1: 97-160.
Venkatesh, Sudhir Alladi. 2009. *Off the Books: The Underground Economy of the Urban Poor.* Cambridge, MA: Harvard University Press.
Verkutyten, Maykel, Jochem Thijs, and Hidde Bekhuis. 2010. "Intergroup Contact and Ingroup Reappraisal: Examining the Deprovincialization Thesis." *Social Psychology Quarterly* 73, no. 4: 358-379.
Vermeersch, Peter. 2003. "Ethnic Minority Identity and Movement Politics: The Case of the Roma in the Czech Republic and Slovakia." *Ethnic and Racial Studies* 26: 879-901.
Verrijn, Stuart, H. 2008. "The ICC in Trouble." *Journal of International Criminal Justice* 6: 409-417.
Vialles, Noelie. 1994. *Animal to Edible.* Translated by J. A. Underwood. Cambridge, UK: Cambridge University Press.
Vinck, Patrick, Phuong N. Pham, Laurel E. Fletcher, and Eric Stover. 2009. "Inequalities and Prospects: Ethnicity and Legal Status in the Construction Labor Force after Hurricane Katrina." *Organization and Environment* 22, no. 4: 470-478.
Virchow, R. 1848. *Die Medizinische Reform.* Berlin: Druck und Verlag von G. Reimer.
Viscusi, Kip W. 1998. "Constructive Cigarette Regulation." *Duke Law Journal* 47, no. 6: 1095-1131.
Volti, R. 1995. *Society and Technological Change.* New York: St. Martin's Press.
Voss, Kim. 1992. "Disposition Is Not Action: The Rise and Demise of the Knights of Labor." *Studies in American Political Development* 6: 272-321.
Wagner, David, and Joseph Berger. 1985. "Do Sociological Theories Grow?" *American Journal of Sociology* 90: 697-728.
Wagner, Jon. 1999a. "Beyond the Body in a Box: Visualizing Contexts of Children's Action." *Visual Sociology* 14: 143-160.
———. 1999b. "Visual Sociology and Seeing Kids' Worlds." *Visual Sociology* 14.
Waites, Matthew. 2009. "Critique of 'Sexual Orientation' and 'Gender Identity' in Human Rights Discourse: Global Queer Politics beyond the Yogyakarta Principles." *Contemporary Politics* 15, no. 1: 137-156.
Waitzkin, H. 1981. "The Social Origins of Illness: A Neglected History." *International Journal of Health Services* 11: 77-103.
Wakefield, Sara E. L., and J. Baxter. 2010. "Linking Health Inequality and Environmental Justice: Articulating a Precautionary Framework for Research and Action." *Environmental Justice* 3, no. 3: 95-102.
Walby, Sylvia. 2007. "Introduction: Theorizing the Gendering of the Knowledge Economy: Comparative Approaches." In *Gendering the Knowledge Economy: Comparative Perspectives,* edited by Heidi Gottfried, Karin Gottschall, Mari Osawa, and Sylvia Walby, 3-50. Houndsmill, UK: Palgrave.
———. 2009. *Globalization and Inequalities: Complexity and Contested Modernities.* Los Angeles and London: Sage.
Wales, Steven. 2002. "Remembering the Persecuted: An Analysis of the International Religious Freedom Act." *Houston Journal of International Law* 24: 579-648.
Wallace, John, Ryoko Yamaguchi, Jerald G. Bachman, Patrick M. O'Malley, John E. Schulenberg, and Lloyd D. Johnston. 2007. "Religiosity and Adolescent Substance Use: The Role of Individual and Contextual Influences." *Social Problems* 54, no. 2: 308-327.
Wallace, Michael, Beth A. Rubin, and Brian T. Smith. 1988. "American Labor Law: Its Impact on Working-Class Militancy, 1901-1980." *Social Science History* 12: 1-29.
Wallerstein, Immanuel. 1974. *The Modern World System I: Capitalist Agriculture and the Origins of the European World-Economy in the Sixteenth Century.* New York: Academic Press.
———. 1979. *The Capitalist World System.* Cambridge, UK: Cambridge University Press.
———. 1980. *The Modern World System II: Mercantilism and the Consolidation of the European World Economy, 1600-1750.* New York: Academic Press.
———. 1983. *Historical Capitalism.* London: Verso.
———. 1984. *The Politics of the World-Economy: The States, the Movements, and the Civilizations.* Cambridge, UK: Cambridge University Press.

———. 2002. "The Itinerary of World Systems Analysis: or, How to Resist Becoming a Theory." In *New Directions in Contemporary Sociological Theory*, edited by Joseph Berger and Morris Zelditch, 358–376. Lanham, MD: Rowman & Littlefield.
———. 2005a. "After Development and Globalization, What?" *Social Forces* 83, no. 3: 1263–1278.
———. 2005b. "Render unto Caesar? The Dilemmas of a Multicultural World." *Sociology of Religion* 66: 121–133.
Walsh, Catherine. 2010. "De-Coloniality, Decolonial Thinking and Doing in the Andes: A Conversation by Walther Mignolo with Catherine Walsh." *Reartikulacija* 10–13. http://www.reartikulacija.org/?p=1468 (accessed February 25, 2011).
Walters, Kerry S., and Lisa Portness, eds. 1999. *Ethical Vegetarianism: From Pythagoras to Peter Singer*. Albany: State University of New York Press.
Walters, Suzanna Danuta. 2001. "Take My Domestic Partner, Please: Gays and Marriage in the Era of the Visible." In *Queer Families, Queer Politics: Challenging Culture and the State*, edited by Mary Bernstein and Renate Reimann, 338–357. New York: Columbia University Press.
Waltz, Kenneth N. 1979. *Theory of International Politics*. New York: Random House.
Wang, Guang-zhen, and Vijayan K. Pillai. 2001. "Women's Reproductive Health: A Gender-Sensitive Human Rights Approach." *Acta Sociologica* 44, no. 3: 231–242.
Wardell, Mark L., and Stephen P. Turner, eds. 1986. *Sociological Theory in Transition*. Boston: Allen and Unwin.
Waring, Marilyn. 2003. "Counting for Something! Recognising Women's Contributions to the Global Economy through Alternative Accounting Systems." *Gender and Development* 11, no. 1: 35–43.
Warner, R. 1994. *Recovery from Schizophrenia*. Routledge: London.
Warner, Michael. 2000. *The Trouble with Normal: Sex, Politics and the Ethics of Queer Life*. Cambridge, MA: Harvard University Press.
Warner-Smith, Penny, Lois Bryson, and Julie Ellen Byles. 2004. "The Big Picture: The Health and Well-Being of Women in Three Generations in Rural and Remote Areas of Australia." *Health Sociology Review* 13, no. 1: 15–26.
Warren, John T. 2001. "Doing Whiteness: On the Performative Dimensions of Race in the Classroom." *Communication Education* 50, no. 2: 91–108.
Washington, DC, City Council. 2008. "Washington D.C. Human Rights City Resolution." American Friends Service Committee. December 10. http://afsc.org/resource/washington-dc-human-rights-city-resolution (accessed May 24, 2011).
Washington, Silvia H. 2010. "Birth of a Sustainable Nation: The Environmental Justice and Environmental Health Movements in the United States." *Environmental Justice* 3, no. 2: 55–60.
Waters, Malcolm. 1995. "Globalisation and the Social Construction of Human Rights." Symposium: "Human Rights and the Sociological Project." *Australian and New Zealand Journal of Sociology* 31: 29–36.
———. 1996. "Human Rights and the Universalization of Interests: Towards a Social Constructionist Approach." *Sociology* 30, no. 3: 593–600.
Watkins-Hayes, Celeste. 2009. "Two-Faced Racism: Whites in the Backstage and Frontstage (review)." *Social Forces* 87: 2183–2185.
Watson, D. R. 1981. "Conversational and Organisational Uses of Proper Names: An Aspect of Counselor-Client Interaction." In *Medical Work: Realities and Routines*, edited by Paul Atkinson and Christian Heath, 91–106. Farnborough, UK: Gower.
———. 1983. "The Presentation of Victim and Motive in Discourse: The Case of Police Interrogations and Interviews." *Victimology* 8: 31–52.
———. 1984. "Racial and Ethnic Relations." In *Applied Sociological Perspectives*, edited by R. J. Anderson and W. W. Sharrock, 43–65. London: George Allen and Unwin.
———. 1997. "Some General Reflections on 'Categorization' and 'Sequence' in the Analysis of Conversation." In *Culture in Action: Studies in Membership Categorization Analysis*, edited by Stephen Hester and Peter Eglin, 49–75. Washington, DC: International Institute for Ethnomethodology and Conversation Analysis and University Press of America.
Weber, Bruce. 2011. "Harold Garfinkel, a Common-Sense Sociologist, Dies at 93." *New York Times*. May 3.
Weber, Max. 1946. "Religious Rejections of the World and Their Direction." In *From Max Weber*, edited by H. H. Gerth and C. Wright Mills, 24–26. New York: Oxford University Press.
———. 1948a. "Class, Status, Party." In *Max Weber: Essays in Sociology*, edited by H. H. Gerth and C. Wright Mills, 180–195. Oxford: Oxford University Press.
———. 1948b. "Politics as a Vocation." In *Max Weber: Essays in Sociology*, edited by H. H. Gerth and C. Wright Mills, 77–128. New York: Oxford: Oxford University Press.
———. 1949. *The Methodology of the Social Sciences*. New York: The Free Press.

———. 1968 [1920]. *Economy and Society*. Translated by Guenther Roth and Claus Wittich. 3 vols. Berkeley: University of California Press.
———. 1978. *Economy and Society*, edited by Guenther Roth and Claus Wittich. Berkeley: University of California Press.
———. 2002. *The Protestant Ethic and the Spirit of Capitalism*. London: Penguin Books.
———. 2007 [1914]. "Basic Sociological Terms." In *Classical Sociological Theory*, edited by Craig Calhoun et al., 211-227. New York: Blackwell.
———. 2011. *The Protestant Ethic and the Spirit of Capitalism*. Rev. 1920 ed. USA: Intercultural Publishing.
Weeramantry, C. G., ed. 1993. *The Impact of Technology on Human Rights: Global Case Studies*. Tokyo: United Nations University Press.
Weglyn, Michi Nishiura. 1976. *Years of Infamy: The Untold Story of America's Concentration Camps*. Seattle: University of Washington Press.
Weibel-Orlando, Joan C. 1989. "Pass the Bottle, Bro!: A Comparison of Urban and Rural Indian Drinking Patterns." In *Alcohol Use among U.S. Ethnic Minorities*, edited by D. Spiegler, D. Tate, S. Aitken, and C. Christian, 269-289. Rockville, MD: National Institute on Alcohol Abuse and Alcoholism.
Weinstein, J. 2010. *Social Change*. 3rd ed. Lanham, MD: Rowman & Littlefield.
Weir, Margaret. 1992. *Politics and Jobs: The Boundaries of Employment Policy in the United States*. Princeton, NJ: Princeton University Press.
Weis, L., ed. 2008. *The Way Class Works: Readings on School, Family, and the Economy*. New York: Routledge.
Weissbrodt, David S., and Clay Collins. 2006. "The Human Rights of Stateless Persons." *Human Rights Quarterly* 28, no. 1: 245-276.
Weitz, Eric D. 2003. *A Century of Genocide: Utopias of Race and Nation*. Princeton, NJ: Princeton University Press.
———. 2008. "From the Vienna to the Paris System: International Politics and the Entangled Histories of Human Rights, Forced Deportations, and Civilizing Missions." *American Historical Review* 113, no. 5: 1313-1343.
Weitzer, Ronald, ed. 2000. *Sex for Sale: Prostitution, Pornography, and the Sex Industry*. New York: Routledge.
Wejnert, Barbara. 2005. "Diffusion, Development, and Democracy, 1800-1999." *American Sociological Review* 70: 53-81.
Wendt, Alexander. 1999. *Social Theory of International Politics*. Cambridge, UK: Cambridge University Press.
West, Nathaniel. 1841. "A Coppie of the Liberties of the Massachusetts Colonie in New England." In *American History Leaflets 25*, edited by Albert Bushnell Hart and Edward Channing. New York: A. Lovell and Co., 1896. http://www.lonang.com/exlibris/organic/1641-mbl.htm (accessed September 4, 2012).
Westra, Laura. 2011. *Globalization, Violence and World Governance*. Leiden, the Netherlands: Brill.
Whitbeck, Les B. 2009. *Mental Health and Emerging Adulthood among Homeless Young People*. New York: Psychology Press.
White, Geoffry D., ed. 2000. *Campus, Inc.: Corporate Power in the Ivory Tower*. New York: Prometheus Books.
White, Orion. 1974. "The Dialectical Organization: An Alternative to Bureaucracy." *Public Administration Review* 29, no. 1: 32-42.
Whitmeyer, Joseph M. 1997. "Endogamy as a Basis for Ethnic Behavior." *Sociological Theory* 15, no. 2: 162-178.
Whyte, William Foote. 1943. *Street Corner Society*. Chicago: University of Chicago Press.
Wieder, D. Lawrence. 1974. *Language and Social Reality: The Case of Telling the Convict Code*. The Hague: Mouton.
Wieviorka, Michael. 2005. "From Marx to Braudel and Wallerstein." *Contemporary Sociology* 34, no. 1: 1-7.
WILD for Human Rights. 2006. *Making Rights Real: A Workbook on the Local Implementation of Human Rights*. San Francisco: Women's Institute for Leadership Development for Human Rights.
Wilentz, Sean. 1984. "Against Exceptionalism: Class Consciousness and the American Labor Movement, 1790-1920." *International Labor and Working-Class History* 26: 1-24.
Wiley, Norbert. 1994. *The Semiotic Self*. Chicago: University of Chicago Press.
Wilkinson, Lindsey, and Jennifer Pearson. 2009. "School Culture and the Well-Being of Same-Sex-Attracted Youth." *Gender and Society* 23, no. 4: 542-568.
Wilkinson, Richard. 1992. "National Mortality Rates: The Impact of Inequality?" *American Journal of Public Health* 82: 1082-1084.
———. 1996. *Unhealthy Societies: The Afflictions of Inequality*. New York: Routledge.
Wilkinson, Richard, and Michael Marmot, eds. 2003. *Social Determinants of Health: The Solid Facts*. Geneva: World Health Organization.
William, Archbishop of Tyre. 1943. *A History of Deeds Done beyond the Sea*. Translated and annotated by Emily Atwater Babcock and A. C. Krey. New York: Columbia University Press.

Williams, B. 1994. "Patient Satisfaction—a Valid Concept?" *Social Science and Medicine* 38, no. 4: 509–516.
Williams, D. R., Y. Yu, J. S. Jackson, and N. B. Anderson. 1997. "Racial Differences in Physical and Mental Health: Socio-Economic Status, Stress and Discrimination." *Journal of Health Psychology* 2, no. 3: 335–351.
Williams, David R., and Michelle Sternthal. 2010. "Understanding Racial-Ethnic Disparities in Health: Sociological Contributions." *Journal of Health and Social Behavior* 51, no. 1: S15–S27.
Williams, William Appleman. 1962. *The Tragedy of American Diplomacy*. New York: Dell.
Williamson, Oliver E. 1985. *The Economic Institutions of Capitalism, Firms, Markets, Relational Contracting*. New York: The Free Press.
Willmott, Hugh, Todd Bridgman, and Mats Alvesson, eds. 2009. *The Oxford Handbook of Critical Management Studies*. New York: Oxford University Press.
Wilsnack, R. W., and R. Cheloha. 1987. "Women's Roles and Problem Drinking across the Lifespan." *Social Problems* 34: 231–248.
Wilson, Edward O. 1978. *On Human Nature*. Cambridge, MA: Harvard University Press.
Wilson, R. A. 1997. *Human Rights, Culture and Context: Anthropological Perspectives*. London: Pluto Press.
Wilson, William Julius. 1987. *The Truly Disadvantaged: The Inner City, the Underclass and Public Policy*. Chicago: University of Chicago Press.
———. 2009. *More Than Just Race: Being Black and Poor in the Inner City*. New York: W. W. Norton.
Winant, Howard. 2006. "Race and Racism: Towards a Global Future." *Ethnic and Racial Studies* 29, no. 5: 986–1003.
Winch, Peter. 2008. *The Idea of a Social Science and Its Relation to Philosophy*. 3rd ed. London: Routledge Classics.
Wines, Michael. 2011. "Deadly Violence Strikes Chinese City Racked by Ethnic Tensions." *New York Times*. July 31. http://www.nytimes.com/2011/08/01/world/asia/01china.html (accessed September 4, 2012).
Winter, Bronwyn. 2006. "Religion, Culture, and Women's Human Rights: Some General and Theoretical Considerations." *Women's Studies International Forum* 29, no. 4: 381–394.
Wirth, L. 1931a. "Clinical Sociology." *American Journal of Sociology* 37: 49–66.
———. 1931b. *Sociology: Vocations for Those Interested in It*. Vocational Guidance Series 1. Chicago: University of Chicago, Department of Special Collections. Louis Wirth Collection. Box LVI, Folder 6.
Wise, Steven. 2005. *Rattling the Cage: Toward Legal Rights for Animals*. New York: Perseus Press.
Wisner, Ben, Piers Blaikie, Terry Cannon, and Ian Davis. 2004. *At Risk: Natural Hazards, People's Vulnerability and Disasters*. New York: Routledge.
Witz, Ann. 2000. "Whose Body Matters? Feminist Sociology and the Corporeal Turn in Sociology and Feminism." *Body and Society* 6, no. 2: 1–24.
Wodak, Alex. 1998. "Health, HIV Infection, Human Rights, and Injecting Drug Use." *Health and Human Rights* 2, no. 4: 24–41.
Woddiwiss, A. 1998. *Globalisation, Human Rights, and Labour Law in Pacific Asia*. Cambridge, UK: Cambridge University Press.
———. 2003. *Making Human Rights Work Globally*. London: The Glass House Press.
———. 2005. *Human Rights*. London: Routledge.
Woehrle, Lynne M., Patrick G. Coy, and Gregory M. Maney. 2008. *Contesting Patriotism: Culture, Power and Strategy in the Peace Movement*. Lanham, MD: Rowman & Littlefield.
Wolf, Diane L., ed. 1996. *Feminist Dilemmas in Fieldwork*. Boulder, CO: Westview.
Wolf, Kurt. 1950. "Introduction." In *The Sociology of Georg Simmel*, edited and translated by Kurt H. Wolff, xvii–xiv. New York: The Free Press.
Women's Refugee Commission. 2011. *The Living Ain't Easy: Urban Refugees in Kampala*. New York: Women's Refugee Commission.
Wood, Charles. 1999. "Losing Control of America's Future: The Census, Birthright Citizenship, and Illegal Aliens." *Harvard Journal of Law and Public Policy* 22, no. 2: 465–522.
Woolford, Andrew. 2006. "Making Genocide Unthinkable: Three Guidelines for a Critical Criminology of Genocide." *Critical Criminology* 14: 87–106.
World Conference against Racism. 2001. "World Conference against Racism, Racial Discrimination, Xenophobia and Related Intolerance: Declaration." United Nations. http://www.un.org/durban review2009/pdf/DDPA_full_text.pdf (accessed July 20, 2012).
World Health Organization (WHO). 1948. *Constitution of the World Health Organization*. Geneva: WHO.
———. 2000. *Maternal Mortality in 2000: Estimates Developed by WHO, UNICEF, and UNFPA*. Relief Web. http://www.reliefweb.int/library/documents/2003/who-saf-22oct.pdf (accessed January 20, 2012).
———. 2001. *The World Health Report 2001: Mental Health: New Understanding, New Hope*. WHO. http://www.who.int/whr/2001/en (accessed July 20, 2012).

———. 2007. "Community Mental Health Services Will Lessen Social Exclusion, Says WHO." WHO. http:// www.who.int/mediacentre/news/notes/2007/np25/en/index.html (accessed January 20, 2012).
———. 2010. *Global Strategies for Women's and Children's Health*. New York: Partnership for Maternal, Newborn, and Child Health.
World People's Conference on Climate Change and the Rights of Mother Earth. 2010. "Draft Universal Declaration of the Rights of Mother Earth." Global Alliance for the Rights of Nature. http:// therightsofnature.org/wp-content/uploads/pdfs/FINAL-UNIVERSAL-DECLARATION-OF-THE-RIGHTS-OF-MOTHER-EARTH-APRIL-22-2010.pdf (accessed March 20 2011).
World Resources Institute's Earth Trends. 2008. World Resources Institute. http://earthtrends.wri.org/pdf_library/data_tables/food_water_2008.pdf (accessed January 22, 2011).
Wotipka, Christine Min, and Kiyoteru Tsutsui. 2008. "Global Human Rights and State Sovereignty: State Ratification of International Human Rights Treaties 1965–2001." *Sociological Forum* 23, no. 4: 724–754.
Wrench, John. 2011. "Data on Discrimination in EU Countries: Statistics, Research and the Drive for Comparability." *Ethnic and Racial Studies* 34: 1715–1730.
Wright, Eric R., and Brea L. Perry. 2010. "Medical Sociology and Health Services Research: Past Accomplishments and Future Policy Challenges." *Journal of Health and Social Behavior* 51: S107–S119.
Wright, James D. 2009. *Address Unknown: The Homeless in America*. Piscataway, NJ: Transaction Publishers.
Wright, Quincy. 1948. "Relationship between Different Categories of Human Rights." In *Human Rights: Comments and Interpretations*, edited by United Nations Educational Scientific and Cultural Organization (UNESCO). Paris: UNESCO.
Wronka, J. 1998. *Human Rights and Social Policy in the 21st Century*. Lanham, MD: University Press of America.
Yang, Alan S. 1998. *From Wrongs to Rights: Public Opinion on Gay and Lesbian American's Moves toward Equality*. Washington, DC: National Gay and Lesbian Task Force Policy Institute.
Yates, Michael D. 2009. *Why Unions Matter*. New York: Monthly Review Press.
Yeung, W. J., and D. Conley. 2008. "Black-White Achievement Gap and Family Wealth." *Child Development* 79: 303–324.
Yosso, T., M. Ceja, W. Smith, and D. Solorzano. 2009. "Critical Race Theory, Racial Microaggressions, and Campus Racial Climate for Latina/o Undergraduates." *Harvard Educational Review* 79: 659–690.
Young, Iris. 1990. *Justice and Politics of Difference*. Princeton, NJ: Princeton University Press.
Youngers, Coletta. 2005. "The Collateral Damage of the U.S. War on Drugs: Conclusions and Recommendations." In *Drugs and Democracy in Latin America*, edited by Eileen Rosin and Coletta Youngers. Boulder, CO: Lynne Rienner Publishers.
Youngers, Coletta, and Eileen Rosin. 2005. *Drugs and Democracy in Latin America: The Impact of U.S. Policy*. Boulder, CO: Lynne Rienner Publishers.
Yuker, H. E. 1994. "Variables that Influence Attitudes toward People with Disabilities: Conclusions from the Data." *Journal of Social Behavior and Personality* 9, no. 5: 3–22.
Yuval-Davis, N. 2006a. "Intersectionality and Feminist Politics." *European Journal of Women's Studies* 13, no. 3: 193–209.
———. 2006b. "Women, Citizenship and Difference." *Feminist Review* 57: 4–27.
Zajdow, Grazyna. 2005. "What Are We Scared Of? The Absence of Sociology in Current Debates about Drug Treatments and Policies." *Journal of Sociology* 41, no. 2: 185–199.
Zajdow, Grazyna, and Jo M. Lindsay. 2010. "Editorial: Sociology, Recreational Drugs and Alcohol." *Health Sociology Review* 19, no. 2: 146–150.
Zakaria, Fareed, and Kuan Yew Lee. 1994. "Culture Is Destiny: A Conversation with Lee Kuan Yew." *Foreign Affairs* 73, no. 2: 109–126.
Zald, Mayer N. 1992. "Looking Backward to Look Forward: Reflections on the Past and Future of the Resource Mobilization Research Program." In *Frontiers in Social Movement Theory*, edited by Aldon D. Morris and Carol McClurg Mueller, 326–348. New Haven, CT: Yale University Press.
Zeitlin, Irving M. 2000. *Ideology and the Development of Sociological Theory*. 7th ed. Englewood Cliffs, NJ: Prentice Hall.
———. 2009. "Education for Democracy in Peirce, James, Dewey and Mead: The North Central Sociological Association's Ruth and John Unseem Plenary Address." *Sociological Focus* 43, no. 4: 317–329.
Zellner, Robert, et al. 2008. "Brandeis in the Sixties." A panel presented at the annual meeting of the Association for Humanist Sociology, Boston, Massachusetts.
Zheng, Tiantian. 2010. *Sex Trafficking, Human Rights, and Social Justice*. New York: Routledge.
Zimmerman, Don H. 1970. "The Practicalities of Rule Use." In *Understanding Everyday Life: Toward the Reconstruction of Sociological Knowledge*, edited by Jack D. Douglas, 221–238. Chicago: Aldine.

Zinn, Maxine Baca, Lynn Weber Cannon, Elizabeth Higginbotham, and Bonnie Thornton Dill. 1986. "The Costs of Exclusionary Practices in Women's Studies." *Signs: Journal of Women in Culture and Society* 11: 290-303.
Zitzelsberger, Hilde. 2005. "(In)visibility: Accounts of Embodiment of Women in Physical Disabilities and Differences." *Disability and Society* 20, no. 4: 389-403.
Žižek, Slavoj. 2005. "Against Human Rights." *New Left Review* 34 (May-June): 115-131.
Zolberg, Aristide. 1986. "How Many Exceptionalisms?" In *Working-Class Formation: Nineteenth-Century Patterns in Western Europe and the United States*, edited by I. Katznelson and A. Zolberg, 397-455. Princeton, NJ: Princeton University Press.
Zou, M., and Zwart, T. 2011. "Rethinking Human Rights in China: Towards a Receptor Approach." In *Human Rights in the Asia-Pacific Region: Towards Institution Building*, edited by H. Nasu and B. Saul, 249-263. London: Routledge.
Zuberi, Tukufu, and Eduardo Bonilla-Silva. 2008. *White Logic, White Methods: Racism and Methodology.* Lanham, MD: Rowman & Littlefield.
Zukin, Sharon. 2011. *Naked City: The Death and Life of Authentic Urban Places.* New York: Oxford University Press.
Zuo, J., and Robert D. Benford. 1995. "Mobilization Processes and the 1989 Chinese Democracy Movement." *Sociological Quarterly* 36: 131-156.
Zweigenhaft, R., and G. Domhoff. 2006. *Diversity in the Power Elite.* Lanham, MD: Rowman & Littlefield.

About the Editors

David L. Brunsma is Professor of Sociology at Virginia Tech. His areas of research include sociologies of human rights and human rights sociologies, racial identity and racism, cognitive sociology and epistemologies, and multiraciality and whiteness. He is currently working on a major textbook about the social construction of difference. He is currently coeditor of *Societies without Borders: Human Rights and the Social Sciences* and section editor of the Race and Ethnicity section of *Sociology Compass*. He lives and loves with his family in Blacksburg, Virginia.

Keri E. Iyall Smith's research explores the intersections between human rights doctrine, the state, and indigenous peoples in the context of a globalizing society. She has published articles on hybridity and world society, human rights, indigenous peoples, and teaching sociology. She is author of *The State and Indigenous Movements* (2006), editor of *Sociology of Globalization* (2012), and coeditor of *Public Sociologies Reader* (with Judith R. Blau, 2006) and *Hybrid Identities: Theoretical and Empirical Examinations* (with Patricia Leavy, 2008). She is Assistant Professor of Sociology at Suffolk University in Boston, Massachusetts, where she teaches courses on globalization, sociological theory, Native Americans, and introductory sociology. She is a former vice president of Sociologists without Borders.

Brian K. Gran is a former lawyer whose sociological research focuses on human rights and institutions that support and hinder their enforcement, with a particular interest in whether law can intervene in private spheres. A cofounder of the ASA Human Rights Section, Gran is directing a project funded by the National Science Foundation (NSF) to develop an international Children's Rights Index. He serves on the Council of the Science and Human Rights Project of the American Association for the Advancement of Science. Gran was recently elected president of the ISA Thematic Group on Human Rights and Global Justice (TG03). For his research on independent children's rights institutions, he was a visiting fellow of the Fulbright grant to research and teach at the School of Law at Reykjavik University in Iceland.